Memory
Observed

"I apologise for the non-arrival of the guest speaker —— who I'm almost sure I invited!"

Memory Observed

Remembering in Natural Contexts

Selections and Commentary by

Ulric Neisser
Cornell University

⊞ W. H. Freeman and Company
San Francisco

Project Editor: Larry Olsen
Copy Editor: Julie Segedy
Designer: Nancy Warner
Production Coordinator: Sarah Segal
Illustration Coordinator: Cheryl Nufer
Artist: Patricia Goff
Compositor: Graphic Typesetting Service
Printer and Binder: The Maple-Vail Book Manufacturing Group
Cover Design: Sharon H. Smith

Library of Congress Cataloging in Publication Data
Main entry under title:

Memory observed: remembering in natural contexts.

(A Series of books in psychology)
Bibliography: p.
Includes index.
1. Memory.   2. Memory—Research—Field works.
I. Neisser, Ulric.   II. Series.
BF371.M455   153.1′2   81-15197
ISBN 0-7167-1371-3   AACR2
ISBN 0-7167-1372-1 (pbk.)

Printed in the United States of America

1 2 3 4 5 6 7 8 9   MP   0 8 9 8 7 6 5 4 3 2

*For Mark, and Eric, and Julie, and Philip,
and Toby, and Jenny, and Katherine,
and Joe.*

A Series of Books in Psychology

Editors: Richard C. Atkinson
Jonathan Freedman
Gardner Lindzey
Richard F. Thompson

Contents

Preface

Psychology has followed two routes in the study of memory. Travelers on the high road hope to find basic mental mechanisms that can be demonstrated in well-controlled experiments; those on the low road want to understand the specific manifestations of memory in ordinary human experience. *Memory Observed* is a kind of guidebook to the lower road. Like any guidebook, it acquaints the reader with the major landmarks, the significant and famous observations of memory that everyone should know. In addition, I hope it will be helpful to those travelers and explorers who are seeking remote areas and untrodden paths. The lower terrain has not been well mapped as yet, and much remains to be discovered.

The high road in the study of memory has been popular since Ebbinghaus opened it a century ago by memorizing long lists of nonsense syllables. He argued that the laws of association would be best revealed by the study of rote learning, using meaningless material that was indifferent to the vagaries of individual experience. His argument prevailed. The study of rote memory has had an established place in experimental psychology since Ebbinghaus' time, even during the long decades when behaviorism virtually outlawed the investigation of the human mind. When modern cognitive psychology began to appear, based on the new conceptions of information and coding that had emerged after World War II, memory was among its central concerns. Cognitiion includes (as I once put it) "all the processes by which the sensory input is transformed, reduced, elaborated, stored, recovered, and used." At least half of those hypothetical processes involve memory; hundreds of models of memory were soon proposed and tested in thousands of experiments. As I will argue at greater length in Selection 1, the upshot of so much effort has been disappointing. There is little sense of progress; genuinely important questions are rarely addressed; most research focuses on questions that are essentially methodological. It has taken me a long time to understand why.

At first, it seemed that we just had too many facts and not enough theory. There have been more memory experiments than anyone can count, enough to discourage even the most intrepid maker of systems. Yet without a theoretical framework all facts remain uncoordinated and uninteresting. Eventually, I realized that no theory can be expected to integrate an essentially arbitrary set of data. We have been accumulating the wrong *kind* of knowledge. Although we have found out a lot about performance in specific laboratory tasks, we do not know nearly enough about the phenomena that motivate the study of memory in the first place. Consequently, theories of memory are either so closely bound to particular experiments that they are uninteresting, or so vague that they are intellectually unsatisfying.

I believe that a similar state of affairs prevails in many areas of psychology. Perception, too, is studied mostly in laboratory settings that lack ecological validity (that is, settings that are not representative of the environment in which perception usually occurs). As a result, the prevailing theories of perception are inadequate in many ways, too numerous to list here. In 1976 I tried to present an alternative approach to perception in a book called *Cognition and Reality* (W. H. Freeman and Company), which stressed the need for a more ecological orientation throughout cognitive psychology.

Cognition and Reality had little to say about memory. By 1976 I had formed the opinion that there were too few facts in hand rather than too many: "We have almost no systematic knowledge about memory as it occurs in the course of everyday life." As it turns out, this assessment was overly pessimistic. Quite a few travelers have already taken the lower road. They include some distinguished company: Sigmund Freud and William Stern, Gregory Bateson and Alexander Luria, the United States Supreme Court and the Senate Watergate Investigating Committee. There are many others, whose names are less familiar but whose work is no less important. It is a privilege to present their observations in this book. Since the publication of *Cognition and Reality* I have often been asked to make suggestions for research. If the standard paradigms of cognitive psychology are inadequate, what is to be done? Here, at least, are some interesting things that have been done already.

I am grateful for all the help I have had in assembling *Memory Observed:* To the authors who wrote the selections and the publishers who have allowed me to reprint them; to my own publisher, who has put up with repeated delays and changes of plan; to the Psychology Department of the University of Pennsylvania, whose hospitality allowed me to spend a sabbatical putting things together; to all the students, undergraduate and graduate, who have helped me to think about memory in natural contexts. Students are far more generous with their professors than most people understand; they give time and energy, ideas and hypotheses, references and corrections, and endless valuable argument. Most of all, I am grateful to Arden Neisser, who has not only helped me to think about memories but given me so many that I cherish.

October 1981   Ulric Neisser

Part I
The Argument

In which the argument for the study of memory in natural settings is presented as strongly as possible, and other approaches are perhaps too casually dismissed.

1 Memory: What Are the Important Questions?

Ulric Neisser

These remarks were made at the 1978 conference on "Practical Aspects of Memory" that also inspired the frontispiece. They present what I hope is a straightforward argument. The orthodox psychology of memory has very little to show for a hundred years of effort, perhaps because it has always avoided the interesting issues. Just as the naturalistic, ethological study of animal behavior has proved to be more rewarding than traditional research on "learning," so a naturalistic study of memory may be more productive than its laboratory counterpart.

It is a distinct honor to open a conference on "Practical Aspects of Memory," and an unusual one. So far as I know, there has never been such a conference before. Perhaps it seems especially remarkable to me because I am an American, and therefore have relatively little experience of fruitful interchange between theoretical and applied psychology. British experimental psychologists have a long tradition of benefiting from that interchange, but we are less used to it in the United States. Unfortunately, the naturalistic tradition has been weaker in the study of memory than in many other areas, even in Britain. Nevertheless, it has not been entirely lacking: it was from Cambridge that Bartlett launched his quixotic challenge to the memory establishment of the 1920s and 1930s. He was convinced that his contemporaries under-

From M. M. Gruneberg, P. E. Morris, and R. N. Sykes (eds.), *Practical Aspects of Memory*. London: Academic Press, 1978. Copyright by Academic Press Inc. (London) Ltd. Reprinted by permission.

stood neither the purpose nor the nature of memory, and that standard laboratory procedures just obscure its real characteristics. His challenge went almost unheard for 40 years, from the publication of *Remembering* (1932) until this decade, but it is unheard no longer. There is suddenly a host of theorists talking about "schemata" (e.g., Rumelhart, 1975; Anderson, 1977) and a host of experimenters studying memory for stories (e.g., Bransford and Johnson, 1973; Mandler and Johnson, 1977). In my view this work is still somewhat deficient in ecological validity—hardly anyone memorizes one-page stories except in the course of psychological experiments—but it is still a great step forward. Perhaps, as someone once said of something else, the naturalistic study of memory is an idea whose time has come.

I am slightly embarrassed that I cannot remember the source of that particular expression, but not surprised. It is a frequent experience for me. I am often unable to recall the authors of phrases that I would like to quote, and have equal difficulty in remembering who told me things. These retrieval failures pose some interesting questions. Why do they occur? Do other people have less trouble recalling sources than I do? Is my difficulty in remembering the source of a written quotation related to other types of memory failure, or are they independent? In fact, how does one go about remembering sources, or arguments, or material appropriate to one's train of thought? What makes for skill in such activities?

These questions may not be the "important" ones that my title has promised, but they are interesting nevertheless. They involve real uses of memory in humanly understandable situations. It is therefore discouraging to find that nothing in the extensive literature of the psychology of memory sheds much light on them, so that anyone who wishes to study such problems must start from scratch. Unfortunately, this is not an isolated instance. It is an example of a principle that is nearly as valid in 1978 as it was in 1878: If *X* is an interesting or socially significant aspect of memory, then psychologists have hardly ever studied *X*.

Let me give another example of that principle, again drawn from my own immediate experience. In giving this address, I naturally hope that I will make some impression on you—that you will remember at least part of what I say. But what *do* people remember of speeches that they hear, or arguments made to them? Who remembers what, and why? The social psychologists have touched lightly on these issues in their examination of persuasion, but they have been interested in opinion change rather than in memory. Apart from their work, the effect of lectures on listeners has hardly been studied at all. A couple of recent exploratory experiments—one by Kintsch and Bates (1977) and the other by Keenan, MacWhinney and Mayhew (1977) [*see Selection 31*] suggest that such studies might yield intriguing results: listeners seem to remember the lecturer's irrelevant asides better than his text, for example.

This is part of a larger question. Most experimental psychologists of memory are also teachers. We earn our living by presenting information to students, often by lecturing, and at the end of the term we set examinations to see if they remember any of it. But what happens after that? Students attend universities partly because they hope to acquire knowledge that will be valuable to them afterwards; that is, they expect to remember some of it. We certainly share their hope. Despite the old saying that "Education is what is left over when you have forgotten what you learned" (which I also cannot reference properly), we would be dismayed if a kind of educational Korsakov amnesia regularly wiped out all trace of our teachings. How much, then, do students retain? This really *is* an important question. Higher education has become a central feature of Western culture, involving millions of people every year, and it depends heavily on the assumption that students remember something valuable from their educational experience. One might expect psychologists to leap at the opportunity to study a critical memory problem so close at hand, but they never do. It is difficult to find even a single study, ancient or modern, of what is retained from academic instruction. Given our expertise and the way we earn our livings, this omission can only be described as scandalous.

Other illustrations of the general principle are readily available. You need only tell any friend, not himself a psychologist, that you study memory. Given even a little encouragement, your friend will describe all kinds of interesting phenomena: the limitations of his memory for early childhood, his inability to remember appointments, his aunt who could recite poems from memory by the hour, the regrettable recent decline in his ability to recall people's names, how well he could find his way around his home town after a thirty years' absence, the differences between his memory and someone else's. Our research, of course, has virtually nothing to say about any of these topics.

Psychology's thundering silence on such questions might be excused if the study of memory had only just begun. One cannot do everything right away. The fact is, however, that we have been studying memory, and doing memory experiments, for nearly a hundred years. Research on the topic went on continuously even during the dreary decades of behaviorist domination, and has recently reached almost frenzied proportions. This research was not carried out by uneducated or incompetent people; some of the best minds in psychology have worked, and are presently working, in the area of memory. Why, then, have they not turned their attention to practical problems and natural settings?

The answer is not far to seek. Psychologists are not interested in such questions primarily because they believe they are doing something more important. They are working toward a general theory of memory, a scientific understanding of its underlying mechanisms, more fundamental and far-reaching than any research on worldly questions could possibly be. They can claim that their work has already established broad generalizations and led to new discoveries; it is even now converging on specific and powerful theories. If these claims were valid, they might justify neglecting problems that seem more obvious and interesting to our nonpsychologist friends. Therefore I will examine each of them briefly: the established principles, the new discoveries, and the theories themselves. As you may already suspect, the results of my survey will not be encouraging.

Let us take the empirical generalizations first. No one could deny that many of them are solid and well-established; so solid that occasional exceptions may be intriguing but cannot undermine their validity. Consider, for example, mnemonic interference and its dependence on similarity, the superiority of meaningful material (stories) over meaningless material (lists), the positive effect of increasing study time, or the savings that appear when once-familiar material is relearned. Such enduring principles comfort those of us who teach courses in memory, because they provide a refuge from the undecided quarrels of the theoreticians. Besides, they are true. Unfortunately, they rarely make much impression on our students, perhaps because they are so unsurprising. Students know them long before they hear our lectures. This has been made embarrassingly obvious by the results of Kreutzer, Leonard, and Flavell's (1975) interview study of children's knowledge about memory. Every one of the generalizations I have mentioned is familiar to the average middle-class third-grader in America from his own experience! Indeed, most of them are known to kindergarteners. If the psychology of memory must rest its case on accomplishments like these, it has little to boast of.

In teaching these familiar generalizations, of course, we do not confine ourselves to simply stating the naked facts. We emphasize method as well as content: appropriate experimental conditions, suitable control groups, well-defined terms, limiting cases. Most of all we emphasize theoretical explanations, of which there are never less than two for any phenomenon. In this way we always have a good deal to talk about, and there are many fine points by which the better students can be separated from the poorer ones. It is doubtful, however, whether the experimental details add anything to the power of the principles themselves. The opposite is more often the case. When a particular experimental result seems to contradict an established principle, a dozen psychologists leap into the breach to restore it. A case in point occurred when Tulving (1966) apparently showed that prior study of a list of words does not improve performance if that list appears later as part of a longer one. Tulving's finding seemed to undermine one of the commonplace principles, but it was an empty threat. The flaws in the experiment were soon revealed (e.g., Novinski, 1969; Slamecka, Moore, and Carey, 1972) and the status quo restored. The only long-run effect of the controversy was to provide another theoretical complication that students can be required to master.

Let me leave the familiar generalizations now and turn to the genuine discoveries. There certainly have been some, although perhaps no list of them could command universal agreement. One important cluster of discoveries concerns the various kinds of immediate and short-term memories. We *do* know more about these now than third-graders, and for that matter more than William James or Ebbinghaus did. Although we are not yet entirely clear about the details of the iconic and posticonic mechanisms in vision, for example, a good deal of progress has been made. Similarly, we have begun to unravel the tangle of echoic stores, articulatory loops, and working memories that are related to hearing and to speech. This is an important area, and I would not deny that the work has added to our understanding of cognition. Nevertheless, it stretches a point to call such mechanisms "memories." They fit the formal definition, but what most people mean by "memory" is quite different. It is disconcerting to find that contemporary textbooks of memory devote a quarter or a third of their pages to "memories" that last less than a minute. Shouldn't memory have something to do with the past?

If the work on short-term memory seems to be leading to significant progress, other discoveries have fared less well. A particularly discouraging example is Sternberg's (1966) discovery that what may be called "memory search time" increases linearly with the number of alternatives that must be searched, at least in many situations. This phenomenon seemed important when it was first reported, but by now it has almost become a bore. It has been so thoroughly investigated and described that everything is known except what it means. We have found out too much about it, and yet not enough. Psychology seems to exploit its experimental effects somewhat in the way that the mass media exploit public figures. It is as difficult for a phenomenon to remain interesting as for a statesman to remain impressive and admirable, given the relentless scrutiny of television and the press. In that case, too, the details with which we are bombarded never add up to a genuine understanding of the subject himself. Instead, we are presented with a continuous stream of reactions, elaborations, and details that ends by putting us to sleep. The linear search function has suffered a similar fate. It may even be at a greater disadvantage than the politicians, whose power over us makes them intrinsically interesting. We return to the television set again and again in the faint hope of understanding the people whose decisions are significant for us. Once we have become disenchanted with Sternberg's linear function, however, why should we ever go back to it?

Another important discovery on my short list is the possibility of deliberately rotating mental images, established by Roger Shepard and his colleagues (Shepard and Metzler, 1971; Cooper and Shepard, 1973, etc.) It has not yet been overexploited, and there are tantalizing promises of more discoveries to come. Recent work by Lynn Cooper (1976), for example, suggests that there may be fundamental individual differences in how people make the visual comparisons that such experiments require. Unfortunately, little work is being done to follow up her finding. Instead, everyone's attention is riveted on much weightier theoretical issues. Does the existence of mental rotation force us to assume that there are "analogue" representations in memory, or can the phenomenon be reconciled with the hypothesis that all mental structures are "propositional"? This is just the sort of question that psychologists love—the kind that has kept us busy for a hundred years. After an overall theory of forgetting or storage or remembering is established, the effort to bring every new experimental result under its umbrella can occupy an army of researchers for a decade at a time. Has it been an effective way to study memory? Let's look at the record.

Before the current crop of theories—EPAM, HAM, ACT, ELINOR, and their highly capitalized competitors—there were others. For example, there was the interference theory of forgetting (McGeoch, 1942; Postman and Underwood, 1973). Interference theorists believed (some still believe) that all forgetting is due to interference from irrelevant associations, and have occasionally tried to demonstrate it directly. More often, they have tried to settle questions about the nature and origin of the interference: response competition, unlearning, intraexperimental interference, extraexperimental interference, and so on. Like almost all theorists, they took certain assumptions for granted (motives as drives, spontaneous recovery of extinction over time) while they treated others as taboo (repression, decay of memories). Now that their approach has gone out of fashion, we can see that this selection of assumptions was questionable. Why should we take some motivational effects as fundamental and treat others as epiphenomena, or accept time as an independent variable for spontaneous recovery but not for spontaneous decay? That particular pattern of assumptions appeared because interference theory was an offshoot of a more general stimulus–response psychology, or "learning theory," of whose decline and fall I shall have more to say shortly. With learning theory out of fashion, the experiments of the interference theorists seem like empty exercises to most of us. Were they ever anything else?

To me, the very notion of uncovering the "cause of forgetting" seems rather strange. It is a little like trying to establish the cause of juvenile delinquency or crime. Such studies are no longer popular, because both "crime" and "cause" turned out to be much richer notions than had been supposed. There are white-collar crimes and violent crimes, premediated crimes and crimes of passion, crimes committed by the poor and by the rich, undiscovered crimes and crimes leading to conviction, crimes that are part of an accepted cultural pattern and crimes committed by lonely and desperate individuals. There are causes of crime like racism and capitalism, like ignorance and folly, like opportunity and lack of opportunity, like an impoverished childhood or a spoiled one, like inadequate law enforcement or the enactment of absurd laws, like criminal organizations, iike lust and greed and the other five sins but also like the demands of conscience and the clear-eyed perception of all the alternatives. Most of all, there is the complexly intertwined history of a particular individual who encounters particular situations. How, then, can one hope to discover the cause of crime?

Forgetting is an equally incoherent notion. Perhaps you fail to retrieve a piece of information that, by some standard, should have been available: you can't think of my name. At the same time, though, there is a lot that you *are* thinking of. What you do and what you think in every human situation has many causes at many levels, ranging from social convention to unconscious drive. What you do *not* do (i.e., think of my name) is an aspect of what you are doing, and has just as many causes. A great deal is going on. To point this out is not to argue that forgetting is due only to interference and not to decay. The matter is equally complex if the necessary information has decayed simply because you and I were introduced too long ago. Even then, its nonexistence would be a cause of remembering just as much as of forgetting—of what you do as well as of what you don't do. What is needed to understand such failures is a detailed examination of what actually happens in them, rather than the theoretical manipulation of abstract and a priori concepts. But I am getting ahead of my story.

Today the interference theory of forgetting has few supporters. It has been replaced by new theories, mostly models of information storage and retrieval systems with various subdivisions and properties. Before considering their importance and probable fate, I would like to review another part of the history of psychology. It offers an analogy that can teach us a great deal, and perhaps help us to avoid some unnecessary labor. As someone (whom I again cannot remember) once put it, those who do not study history are condemned to repeat it. The history I have in mind is that of learning theory and behaviorism.

Not long ago, learning theory dominated almost the whole of experimental psychology (at least in America). It set the problems, prescribed the methods, defined the range of permissible hypotheses, and seemed generalizable to every aspect of life. Its intellectual leaders wrote books with titles like *Principles of Behavior* and *The Behavior of Organisms*, and their broad claims were backed up by hundreds of experiments. To be sure, the experimental subjects were almost always white rats; a few skeptics wondered whether it was quite safe to generalize from "animals" to humans, but hardly anyone doubted that at least animal behavior was being investigated in a scientifically fruitful way. The most influential philosophers of the time produced accounts of scientific method—hypothesis testing, manipulation of variables, and the like—that justified the learning theorists at every step. There was dispute about whether Hull, Spence, Skinner, or (as an outside possibility) Tolman was closest to ultimate truth, but not much about the merit of their common enterprise.

Today, learning theory has been almost completely swept away. Not entirely, perhaps: with the mainland of animal behavior lost to their foes, a behaviorist remnant is holding out on well-defended islands like "behavior modification" or "behavior therapy." They still sound confident, but they are watching the straits with an anxious eye. There are even a few stalwarts fighting rearguard actions in the rat laboratories, putting out research reports that the triumphant majority don't bother to read. Nevertheless, the battle is essentially over, and it was surprisingly brief. What happened?

The fundamental blow was struck by a small group of scientists who called themselves "ethologists," not psychologists, and who were not concerned with learning theory at all. They wanted to know how animals really behaved in natural environments. They were not so much interested in hypotheses as in the animals themselves. Wasps, herring gulls, ducklings, and jackdaws are a curious base on which to build a scientific revolution, but one occurred. The work of the ethologists showed that the concepts and methods of learning theory were simply irrelevant to the understanding of natural behavior. Every species seems to have a different set of learning abilities, and to respond to different sorts of variables. Even in a single species or a single organism, patterns of behavior vary drastically with changes in the gross environment, with fluctuations in hormone levels, with stages of maturation. Given these facts, notions like "conditioning," "reinforcement," "extinction," and "generalization" require constant reinterpretation if they are to survive at all. The very distinction between what is learned and what is innate has become uncertain. Even the laboratory rat has turned on his old friends (rats are apparently treacherous after all) by exhibiting a kind of learning that none of the old models could accommodate: a food aversion acquired on a single trial with a reinforcement delay of many hours.

This new wave of research has not resulted in universal agreement on theoretical issues. The disputes among "behavioral biologists," as these investigators are now often called, are just as vigorous as the arguments between learning theorists once were. Many of them will surely seem just as pointless to the eye of the historian. But whatever the ultimate fate of the theories may be, the observations of animal behavior that are now being made can never become irrelevant or uninteresting. We are finding out what really happens in the world around us, and that will be worth knowing in any imaginable future.

I have dwelt on this bit of psychological history at some length because I believe it has a clear application to the subject at hand. Theories of memory are invariably based on the performance of experimental subjects in specialized laboratory tasks. So, too, were the learning theories of the 1930s and 1940s. The tasks themselves are ingeniously designed to shed light on the experimenter's hypothesis, or to decide among competing theories. So, too, were the procedures of the behaviorists. The most widely acclaimed memory theories are those which seem most far-reaching and which explain many experimental results on the basis of relatively few assumptions. This, too, characterized the glory days of stimulus–response psychology. A plausible and explicit set of methodological assumptions justifies current research practices. The same thing was true in the case of learning theory, although the old reliance on the hypothetico-deductive method has been replaced by a new attachment to computer simulation. Finally, modern theories of memory have as little relevance to everyday memory as learning theory had to what is usually called "learning." The sentences and brief "stories" that are popular in research laboratories today are an improvement on the nonsense syllable, but they are far from representative of what ordinary people remember and forget.

In short, the results of a hundred years of the psychological study of memory are somewhat discouraging. We have established firm empirical generalizations, but most of them are so obvious that every ten-year-old knows them anyway. We have made discoveries, but they are only marginally about memory; in many cases we don't know what to do with them, and wear them out with endless experimental variations. We have an intellectually impressive group of theories, but history offers little confidence that they will provide any meaningful insight into natural behavior. Of course, I could be wrong: perhaps this is the exceptional case where the lessons of history do not apply, and the new theories will stand the test of time better than the old ones did. Let me be frank: I have not pinpointed any fatal flaw in Hunt's distributed memory model (Hunt, 1971), Tulving's conception of encoding specificity (Tulving, 1974), Anderson's ACT (1976), or the others. I cannot prove that they are misguided. But because they say so little about the everyday uses of memory, they seem ripe for the same fate that overtook learning theory not long ago.

The psychologists who have spent a century studying esoteric forms of memory in the laboratory are not really uninterested in its more ordinary manifestations, and have always hoped that their work would have wide applicability sooner or later. Their preference for artificial tasks has a rational basis: one can control variables and manipulate conditions more easily in the lab than in natural settings. Why not work under the best possible conditions? Memory is memory, or so it would seem. This methodological assumption resembles the assumptions made by the learning theorists in their study of "learning." Unfortunately, it turned out that "learning" in general does not exist: wasps and songbirds and rats integrate past experiences into their lives in very different ways. I think that "memory" in general does not exist either. It is a concept left over from a medieval psychology that partitioned the mind into independent faculties: "thought" and "will" and "emotion" and many others, with "memory" among them. Let's give it up, and begin to ask our questions in different ways. Those questions need not be uninformed by theory, or by a vision of human nature, but perhaps they can be more closely driven by the characteristics of ordinary human experience.

What we want to know, I think, is how people use their own past experiences in meeting the present and the future. We would like to understand how this happens under natural conditions: the circumstances in which it occurs, the forms it takes, the variables on which it depends, the differences between individuals in their uses of the past. "Natural conditions" does not mean in the jungle or on the desert, unless that happens to be where our subjects live. It means in school and at home, on the job and in the course of thought, as carefree children and as reflective old men and women. Because changes in the social and cultural environment can change the uses of the past, we will have to study many settings. The psychological laboratory is the easiest of these settings in which to work, but it is also among the least interesting; we ourselves are the only people who spend much time there voluntarily.

The task before us is much harder than that which confronted the ethologists. They had several great advantages. For one thing, it is easier to observe animals than people. Animals don't mind it as much (if you are quiet) and are not so aware of what you are up to. Their habitats are more limited, in many cases, and their behaviors more stereotyped. Moreover, the time-dependence of their behavior is much shorter: you rarely have to consider events of twenty years ago to understand what an animal is doing today. They do not have language to help them control the application of the past to the present, and seem to spend more of their time in action as opposed to thought.

One difference between our task and that of the ethologists deserves special mention. They began with a ready-made categorization of their subject matter, whereas we have none. It is obvious that there are many different kinds of animals—species—which can be studied separately. In setting out to do a field study of animal behavior, one usually need not worry about how to distinguish the robins from the herring gulls. In studying memory, however, we do not know how to separate different kinds of cases. Indeed, we cannot even be sure whether any natural lines of demarcation exist. This is a genuinely important question, and one of the first things we should be trying to find out. Are there functionally different types of memory in everyday life? If so, what are they?

Although I am far from sure how to classify the phenomena of memory, I must put them in some kind of order to discuss them at all. Science cannot proceed without some way of defining things so we can set out to study them. The organization I will use is based on the functions of memory. What do we use the past *for*? Happily, when the question is put in this way, it turns out that the sum total of relevant psychological work is not zero after all. There has been some valuable research and thinking about the natural uses of memory, usually by individuals outside the mainstream of contemporary theory. These beginnings offer promising leads for further work; I will mention some of them below.

First of all, everyone uses the past to define themselves. Who am I? I have a name, a family, a home, a job. I know a great deal about myself: what I have done, how I have felt, where I have been, whom I have known, how I have been treated. My past defines me, together with my present and the future that the past leads me to expect. What would I be without it? Much of that formative past is now tacit rather than explicit knowledge: I do not dwell on it, and I cannot recall it as such. The specifics are beyond recall, although their resultant is here in person. Some things, however, I can remember very explicitly when I choose. I think back on my childhood, or my youth, or on something that happened this morning. Typically I do this alone, silently, without telling anybody. I often do it deliberately and voluntarily, but memories may also come unbidden—"involuntary memories," as Salaman (1970) [*see Selection 5*] calls them—either in waking life or in sleep. All these are cases where the past becomes present to me, and to me alone.

Many questions suggest themselves about such personal evocations. Some were asked long ago by Freud and the psychoanalysts. Why do just these memories come, and not others? When are they trustworthy, and when fabricated? Why do I have so few from my very early childhood? Do some people have more of them than others, and if so why? What function do they serve? How does the nature and incidence of personal recollection vary with age, culture, sex, and situation? What happens when whole sections of the past become inaccessible, as in functional amnesias?

Work has been done on some of these questions, but not much. Freud (1905) drew attention to the phenomenon of infantile amnesia and tried to explain it by repression; Schachtel (1947) [*see Selection 18*] later proposed a cognitive account which seems more plausible (cf. Neisser, 1962). Freud also wrote two papers on early memories (1899, 1917) [*see Selection 6*], a topic which has been studied sporadically over the years by many psychologists (Dudycha and Dudycha, 1941) recently including Douglas Herrmann and me. Our questionnaire study (Herrmann and Neisser, 1978) suggests that women college students may have slightly better memory of childhood experiences than men do. Others have noticed the same sex difference in early memories; I wish I understood it. We still know very little about these questions, and what we do know mostly concerns deliberate, voluntary remembering. Spontaneous recall may be quite a different matter. Esther Salaman's fascinating autobiographical book *A Collection of Moments* (1970) [*see Selection 5*], which describes many images of early childhood that came to her unbidden and unexpected, may be a useful source of hypotheses about spontaneous memory.

One frequently recalls past experiences in search of some sort of self-improvement. Where did I go wrong? Could I have done things differently? What were my alternatives? How did all this start? These questions can be asked privately or with a listener. "Going public," even to a single individual, makes a difference. Both private and shared recollection can have profound consequences for that sense of self which is so dependent on what one remembers. Psychoanalysis and psychotherapy are obvious examples of this use of the past, but they are by no means the only ones. Something similar probably happens in the Catholic confessional, of which I know very little. Some Communist countries have institutionalized confession as a way of strengthening social unity and reforming individual behavior. To be sure, those who confess in political settings must be quite careful about what they say. Is that selectivity exhibited only in their public statements, or does it extend to what they remember privately?According to recent experimental evidence, people's memory of their own prior attitudes can change dramatically when the attitudes themselves have shifted (Goethals and Reckman, 1973) [*see Selection 17*].

There are other occasions when one's personal memories achieve a kind of public importance. A familiar example occurs in legal testimony, where an exact account of the past can be critical in determining a defendant's future. Psychologists have been interested in this issue for many years. At the beginning of the century William Stern published several volumes of a scholarly journal devoted exclusively to the psychology of testimony (*Beiträge zur Psychologie der Aussage*) [*see Selection 9*] and Münsterburg wrote a widely cited book about it called *On the Witness Stand* (1909). Unfortunately, this early work produced few insights except that the testimony of eyewitnesses is often inaccurate. A series of ingenious experiments by Elizabeth Loftus (e.g., Loftus and Palmer, 1974 [*see Selection 10*]; Loftus, 1975) has revived interest in the problem, and begun to define the kinds of distortions that can occur as well as their sources.

One does not remember only events that one has personally experienced, but also those known at secondhand—things that have happened to other people. We learn from the experiences of our friends and acquaintances, and also from historical figures whose lives are somehow relevant to our own. In a literate society, we do not often think of history as something remembered; it is usually something written down. In many parts of the world, however, history has long been the responsibility of memory specialists, or oral historians, whose knowledge of ancient deeds and agreements exerts a controlling influence on contemporary events. D'Azevedo (1962) [*see Selection 25*] has described the role of oral historians among one African tribe, the Gola; it seems clear that this cultural practice is widespread in Africa and elsewhere. The history that is passed on through generations in this way is surprisingly accurate. The historians do not learn it by rote, but in an integrated and intelligent way. Whether this requires special gifts and special training, or whether anyone could remember any amount of oral history if it were appropriate to do so, is an open question.

In general, the relation between literacy and memory is poorly understood. It is one of those issues where every possible position can be and has been plausibly argued. Perhaps unschooled individuals from traditional societies have particularly *good* memories, because they must rely on those memories so heavily where nothing can be written down (Riesman, 1956). Perhaps, however, they have relatively *poor* memories because they lack the general mnemonic skills and strategies that come with literacy and schooling (Scribner and Cole, 1973). Certainly they perform badly in standard psychological memory experiments (Cole, Gay, Glick, and Sharp, 1971). Or maybe they are just like us: good at remembering what interests them. That is what Bartlett (1932) thought, though he could not resist endowing nonliterate Africans with a special facility for low-level "rote recapitulation" as well. In my own view, [*see Selection 23*] it may be a mistake to treat culture and literacy as overriding variables: individual differences and individual experience are more important. If the experimental task is remembering oral stories, then experience in listening to stories will make a big difference. That is probably why E. F. Dube (1977) [*see Selection 27*] recently found that both schooled and unschooled young people from Botswana were far better at story recall than American school children of the same age. However, he also found enormous individual differences correlated with estimates of the subjects' intelligence, made by tribal elders for the nonliterate children and on the basis of school grades for the others. The best of the unschooled subjects exhibited remarkably high levels of recall.

Memory is also involved in many activities of daily life. We make a plan and have to remember to carry it out, put something down and have to recall where it is, are given directions and must remember them if we are to reach our destination, encounter a prior acquaintance and want to pick up the relationship where it left off. Our access to the past is probably better when remembering is embedded in these natural activities than when it occurs in isolation. At least this is true for young children, as Istomina (1975) [*see Selection 35*] has shown in an elegant series of experiments. Different individuals are unequally skilled in different kinds of everyday memory, according to questionnaire data that Herrmann and I have recently collected (Herrmann and Neisser, 1979). But we still know almost nothing about these practical uses of memory, important as they are.

In most instances of daily remembering, it is meanings and not surface details that we must recall. Just as the oral historian remembers what happened instead of memorizing some formula of words that describes it, so too we recall the substance of what we heard or read rather than its verbatim form. This is now generally acknowledged, even in laboratory research. The new wave of enthusiasm for Bartlett's ideas and for the use of stories as memory materials has led us to devalue the study of rote remorization almost completely. This is entirely appropriate, if "rote memory" means the learning of arbitrary lists of words or syllables for experimental purposes. The fact is, however, that many cultural institutions depend heavily on exact and literal recall. When we speak of remembering a song or a poem, for example, we do not mean that we have the gist of it but that we know the words.

Rubin (1977) [*see Selection 29*] has recently shown that literal memory for the National Anthem, the Lord's Prayer, and similar texts is widespread among Americans. Verbatim memory is even more important in other societies, I think; some memorize the Koran where others study the Bible and still others learn long speeches from Shakespeare. This happens whenever it is the text itself, and not just its meaning, that is important. A text can be important for many reasons: patriotic, religious, esthetic, or personal. For singers and actors, the reason can even be professional. Whatever the reason, people's ability to recite appropriate texts verbatim at appropriate times ought to be deeply interesting to the psychology of memory. The fact that we have not studied it is another particularly striking example of my original proposition: If X is an interesting memory phenomenon, psychologists avoid it like the plague. Hundreds of experimentalists have spent their lives working on rote memory, without ever examining the rote memorization that goes on around them every day.

The last use of the past that I will discuss concerns intellectual activity itself. Although I have little talent for recalling the sources of quotations, I am not too bad at remembering experiments; if it were otherwise, I could not have prepared this address. However, this ability certainly does not make me unique. Everybody who is skilled at anything necessarily has a good memory for whatever information that activity demands. Physicists can remember what they need to know to do physics, and fishermen what they need for fishing; musicians remember music, art critics recall paintings, historians know history. Every person is a prodigy to his neighbors, remembering so much that other people do not know. We should be careful in what we say about memory in general until we know more about these many memories in particular.

These are some of the important questions, and we must seek the answers as best we can. Our search need not be entirely haphazard; I am not recommending an aimless accumulation of ecological minutiae. We will surely be guided by our general conceptions of human nature and human social life, as well as by more particular hypotheses about the phenomena we study. Without such conceptions and hypotheses, we can make little progress. The challenge will be to shift from testing hypotheses for their own sake to using them as tools for the exploration of reality.

It is a challenge that will not be easy to meet. The realistic study of memory is much harder than the work we have been accustomed to—so much harder that one can easily forgive those who have been reluctant to undertake it. After all, we bear no malice toward that legendary drunk who kept looking for his money under the streetlamp although he had dropped it ten yards away in the dark. As he correctly pointed out, the light was better where he was looking. But what we want to find *is* in the dark, out there where real people make use of their pasts in complicated ways. If we are to find it, we must look there. The convening of this conference may suggest that we are finally heading in that direction.

REFERENCES

Anderson, J. R. *Language, Memory, and Thought*. Hillsdale, N.J.: Lawrence Erlbaum, 1976.

Anderson, R. C. The notion of schemata and the educational enterprise. In R. C. Anderson, R. T. Spiro, and W. E. Montague (eds), *Schooling and the Acquisition of Knowledge*. Hillsdale, N.J.: Lawrence Erlbaum, 1977.

Bartlett, F. C. *Remembering*. Cambridge: Cambridge University Press, 1932.

Bransford, J. D., and Johnson, M. K. Consideration of some problems of comprehension. In W. G. Chase (ed), *Visual Information Processing*. New York: Academic Press, 1973.

Cole, M., Gay, J., Glick, J. A., and Sharp, D. W. *The Cultural Context of Learning and Thinking*. New York: Basic Books, 1971.

Cooper, L. A. Individual differences in visual comparison processes. *Perception and Psychophysics; 1976, 19*, 433–444.

Cooper, L. A., and Shepard, R. N. Chronometric studies of the rotation of mental images. In W. G. Chase (ed), *Visual Information Processing*. New York: Academic Press, 1973.

D'Azevedo, W. L. Uses of the past in Gola discourse. *Journal of African History*, 1962, *3*, 11–34.

Dube, E. F. *A Cross-Cultural Study of the Relationship Between "Intelligence" Level and Story Recall*. Doctoral Dissertation, Cornell University, Ithaca, N.Y., 1977.

Dudycha, G., and Dudycha, M. Childhood memories: A review of the literature. *Psychological Bulletin*, 1941, *38*, 668–682.

Freud, S. Three contributions to the theory of sex. In A. A. Brill (ed), *The Basic Writings of Sigmund Freud*. New York: Random House, 1905; republished 1938.

Freud, S. Screen memories. In J. Strachey (ed.), *Collected Papers of Sigmund Freud* (Vol. 5). London: Hogarth Press, 1899; republished 1956.

Freud, S. Eine Kindheitserinnerung aus 'Dichtung und Wahrheit'. *Imago*, 1917, *5*.

Goethals, G. R., and Reckman, R. F. The perception of consistency in attitudes. *Journal of Experimental Social Psychology*, 1973, *9*, 491–501.

Herrmann, D. J., and Neisser, U. An inventory of everyday memory experiences. In M. M. Gruneberg, P. E. Morris, and R. N. Sykes (eds.), *Practical Aspects of Memory*. London: Academic Press, 1978.

Hunt, E. What kind of a computer is man? *Cognitive Psychology*, 1971, *2*, 57–98.

Istomina, Z. M. The development of voluntary memory in preschool-age children. *Soviet Psychology*, 1975, *13*, 5–64.

Keenan, J. M., MacWhinney, B., and Mayhew, D. Pragmatics in memory: A study of natural conversation. *Journal of Verbal Learning and Verbal Behavior*, 1977, *16*, 549–560.

Kintsch, W., and Bates, E. Recognition memory for statements from a classroom lecture. *Journal of Experimental Psychology: Human Learning and Memory*, 1977, *3*, 150–159.

Kreutzer, M. A., Leonard, C., and Flavell, J. H. An interview study of children's knowledge about memory. *Monographs of the Society for Research in Child Development*, 1975, *40*, Serial No. 159.

Loftus, E. G. Leading questions and the eye-witness report. *Cognitive Psychology*, 1975, *7*, 560–572.

Loftus, E. G., and Palmer, J. C. Reconstruction of automobile destruction: An example of the interaction between language and memory. *Journal of Verbal Learning and Verbal Behavior*, 1974, *13*, 585–589.

Mandler, J. M., and Johnson, N. S. Remembrance of things parsed: Story structure and recall. *Cognitive Psychology*, 1977, *9*, 111–151.

McGeoch, J. A. *The Psychology of Human Learning*. New York: Longmans, Green, 1942.

Munsterburg, H. *On the Witness Stand*. New York: Doubleday, 1909.

Neisser, U. Cultural and cognitive discontinuity. In T. E. Gladwin and W. Sturtevant (eds), *Anthropology and Human Behavior*. Washington, D.C.: Anthropological Society of Washington, D.C., 1962.

Neisser, U., and Hupcey, J. A Sherlockian experiment. *Cognition*, 1974, *3*, 307–311.

Novinski, L. S. Part–whole and whole–part free recall learning. *Journal of Verbal Learning and Verbal Behavior*, 1969, *8*, 152–154.

Postman, L., and Underwood, B. J. Critical issues in interference theory. *Memory and Cognition*, 1973, *1*, 19–40.

Riesman, D. *The Oral Tradition, the Written Word, the Screen Image*. Yellow Springs, Ohio: Antioch Press, 1956.

Rubin, D. C. Very long-term memory for prose and verse. *Journal of Verbal Learning and Verbal Behavior*, 1977, *16*, 611–622.

Rumelhart, D. E. Notes on a schema for stories. In D. G. Bobrow and A. Collins (eds.), *Representation and Understanding*. New York: Academic Press, 1975.

Salaman, E. *A Collection of Moments*. London: Longman Group, 1970.

Schachtel, E. G. On memory and childhood amnesia. *Psychiatry*, 1947, *10*, 1–26.

Scribner, S., and Cole, M. Cognitive consequences of formal and informal education. *Science*, 1973, *182*, 553–559.

Shepard, R. N., and Metzler, J. Mental rotation of three-dimensional objects. *Science*, 1971, *171*, 701–703.

Slamecka, N. J., Moore, T., and Carey, S. Part-to-whole transfer and its relation to organization theory. *Journal of Verbal Learning and Verbal Behavior*, 1972, *11*, 73–82.

Sternberg, S. High-speed scanning in human memory. *Science*, 1966, *153*, 652–654.

Tulving, E. Subjective organization and effects of repetition in multi-trial free-recall learning. *Journal of Verbal Learning and Verbal Behavior*, 1966, *5*, 193–197.

Tulving, E. Recall and recognition of semantically encoded words. *Journal of Experimental Psychology*, 1974, *102*, 778–787.

Part II Remembering

In which some vivid and long-lasting memories are described and analyzed. It appears that we remember even unimportant aspects of important events—or at least believe that we do; conversely, we may remember unimportant events because of their hidden importance. Data from Linton's diary study show, however, that neither "event" nor "importance" is a simple concept.

2 Flashbulb Memories

Roger Brown and James Kulik

Almost everyone, except those who are too young, remembers how they heard the news that President Kennedy had been shot. Brown and Kulik elicited reports of such "flashbulb memories" by asking eighty subjects if they recalled hearing the news of nine noteworthy events (assassinations, etc.), and of a single self-selected personally relevant event as well. "Flashbulbs" were more likely for events that subjects rated as more "consequential," and differences between black and white subjects in the consequentiality of certain events were reflected in different likelihoods for certain flashbulbs. Reports of rehearsals were also obtained.

The phenomenon is a robust one: Yarmey and Bull (1978) found that Canadians recall John Kennedy's assassination in much the same way, and Colegrove's subjects (Selection 3) had equally vivid memories of the day they heard about Lincoln. Why are these memories so durable? Brown and Kulik suggest a physiological hypothesis; I offer a different interpretation in Selection 4.

"Hardly a man is now alive" who cannot recall the circumstances in which he first heard that John Kennedy had been shot in Dallas. Not just the *fact* that John Kennedy was shot and died; we remember that too, of course, but we really do not need to since it is recorded in countless places and in many forms. It is not the memory of the tragic news that invites inquiry, but the memory of one's own circumstances on first hearing the news. There is no obvious utility in such memories.

The second author recalls: "I was seated in a sixth-grade music

From *Cognition*, 1977, *5*, 73–99. Reprinted by permission.

class, and over the intercom I was told that the president had been shot. At first, everyone just looked at each other. Then the class started yelling, and the music teacher tried to calm everyone down. About ten minutes later I heard over the intercom that Kennedy had died and that everyone should return to their homeroom. I remember that when I got to my homeroom my teacher was crying and everyone was standing in a state of shock. They told us to go home."

The first author recalls: "I was on the telephone with Miss Johnson, the Dean's secretary, about some departmental business. Suddenly, she broke in with: 'Excuse me a moment; everyone is excited about something. What? Mr. Kennedy has been shot!' We hung up, I opened my door to hear further news as it came in, and then resumed my work on some forgotten business that 'had to be finished' that day."

Ten years after the assassination, the always-enterprising *Esquire* magazine (1973) asked a number of famous people a question similar to ours: "Where were you?" Julia Child was in the kitchen eating soupe de poisson. Billy Graham was on the golf course, but he felt a presentiment of tragedy. Philip Berrigan was driving to a rally; Julian Bond was in a restaurant; Tony Randall was in the bathtub. The subtitle of the 1973 *Esquire* article could, we are sure, be used again today: "Nobody Forgets."

Probably everyone who has read until this point is primed with an account of his own, which he would rather like to tell, perhaps because there is something strange about this recall. John Kennedy was shot thirteen years ago. What else can one remember from 1963? Almost everyone testifies that his recall of his circumstances is not an inference from a regular routine. It was a primary, "live" quality that is almost perceptual. Indeed, it is very like a photograph that indiscriminately preserves the scene in which each of us found himself when the flashbulb was fired. But why should the human species have such a flashbulb potentiality? Where is the use in carrying certain scenes in permanent store?

"Flashbulb memory" (FB) is a good name for the phenomenon inasmuch as it suggest surprise, an indiscriminate illumination, and brevity. But the name is inappropriate in one respect that had better be brought forward at once. An actual photograph, taken by flashbulb, preserves everything within its scope; it is *altogether* indiscriminate. Our flashbulb memories are not. The second author's crying teacher had a hairdo and a dress that are missing from his memory. The first author faced a desk with many objects on it, and some kind of weather was visible through the window, but none of this is in his memory picture. In short, a flashbulb memory is only somewhat indiscriminate and is very far from complete. In these respects, it is unlike a photograph.

Is it only the news of John Kennedy's assassination that has ever set off the flashbulb registration of each person's circumstances on

first hearing the news? Anticipating our data, it seems to have precip-
itated the effect in greater strength, and for a larger number of persons,
than any other event of recent history. However, it is not the only event
that has fired flashbulbs. There are, in the first place, other events in
our recent national history that have had this effect for some: the
assassinations of Robert Kennedy and of Martin Luther King and the
attempted assassinations of George Wallace and Gerald Ford, as well
as the startling Chappaquiddick episode involving Ted Kennedy.

But unexpected events that involve nationally prominent persons
simply constitute a class of events for which one may reasonably hope
to uncover a good number of flashbulb memories. There are also the
sundry private shocks in each person's life. Some of our older informants had, prior to 1963, been jolted by midnight phone calls bringing
the sad news of the unexpected death of a parent. And slightly younger
subjects heard, out of the blue, that a friend had been killed in an
accident or by an overdose of heroin. Such personal jolts also cause
flashbulb memories; that is, memories not just of the crucial event, but
of the circumstances in which one first learned of them. What chiefly
differentiates them from presidential assassinations and the like is the
absence of a very large population of like-minded people. Only a few
feel the shock of a family death or are interested in how you felt when
you heard. There is, therefore, no named central event that one can
use to retrieve possible flashbulb memories. The best one can do is to
ask each informant to search his memory for events of this order.

We began with a familiar phenomenon which, however, does not
follow from such well-established determinants of memory as primacy
or recency or repetition, even though the data one can collect are a
variety of verbal free recall. We had definite intuitions about the variables that might be important and also a large quantity of general
curiosity which guided us in the construction of a very long and difficult questionnaire. When about half the data had been collected, we
came upon a neurophysiological theory that paralleled our intuitions
in its own terms and we decided to bring out the parallels in our
exposition. The theory is Robert B. Livingston's (1967a,b), and it is called
by the evocative name: "Now Print!"[1]

---

[1]Some friends, among physiological psychologists, have advised us that the "Now Print!"
theory is, as we had guessed, entirely speculative. Furthermore, and this we did not
know, it has inspired little or no direct psychophysiological research. There is apparently
no clear reason why the theory could not be correct, but it has not had heuristic value
in psychophysiology and so there is really nothing clearly pro or con. We were sorry to
learn that the "Now Print!" theory has been of such slight consequence in physiological
psychology and, of course, we could not very well provide any direct evidence as to its
truth value with a paper-and-pencil study. In actual fact, as you will see, all of our own
measures and concepts are behavioral, and our theory is completely independent of
Livingston's. Nevertheless, at the considerable risk of seeming naive or willful, we have
elected to build Livingston's theory into our exposition because his speculations did
interest us and we see no harm in stretching an arm (or is it a neck?) in the direction of
ultimate synthesis.

The steps are postulated to occur as follows: (1) Reticular recognition of novelty; (2) Limbic discrimination of biological meaning for that individual at that moment; (3) Limbic discharge into the reticular formation; (4) A diffusely projecting reticular formation discharge distributed throughout both hemispheres, a discharge conceived to be a 'Now print!' order for memory; and finally (5) All recent brain events, all recent conduction activities will be 'printed' . . . (1967b, p. 576).

Without the neurology one may say: First comes the recognition of high novelty or unexpectedness; then comes a test for biological meaning for the individual; if this second test is met, there follows the permanent registration not only of the significant novelty, but of all recent brain events. What confirmed our interest in this theory was Livingston's first application of it: "I suggest that almost all of you will remember exactly where you were on November 22, 1963, when you heard the news that President Kennedy had been assassinated. You can probably tell us where you were, with whom, and very likely whether you were sitting, standing, or walking—almost which foot was forward when your awareness became manifest" (1967b, p. 576).

METHOD

We had two major intuitions about the determinant of FBs when we designed our study and before we knew of their neurological parallels in Livingston's theory. Perhaps the most obvious property of President Kennedy's assassination was its extreme unexpectedness; in most of our lives no other major political figure had been assassinated. And, in selecting events to use in prospecting for FBs, we generalized this property and so chose ten very unexpected or novel events, among which assassinations loom large. As a consequence, one can reasonably say that for all the events we chose, the first operation in Livingston's theory was satisfied: the registration of novelty. However, we know that the level of novelty varied a good deal, and there is some reason to suppose that the only full-fledged FB effects we obtained were for John Kennedy and for the personal shock described by each person.

The second intuition we luckily had was that, among national events like assassinations, there might well be a difference between white Americans and black Americans, in the public figures who set off FBs.[2] How many white Americans, for instance, could say just where

---

[2] Nowadays, it is perhaps the case that any study comparing black Americans and white Americans on any sort of cognitive task risks suspicion of seeking tendentious or even downright invidious comparisons. Nothing of the sort is true in the present study. We

they were and what they were doing when they first head that Martin Luther King had been shot? Not many, we suspected, but probably quite a few black Americans would be able to do so. What should account for a difference of this kind if it were, indeed, attained? We guessed that what would matter would be the comparative *consequentiality* for the black and white individual of each national event. And so we composed a five-point scale for the rating of consequentiality which, as we shall see, we defined in a way that makes it a plausible parallel to Livingston's "biological significance."

Our behavioral data were more fine-grained than the parallel concepts in Livingston's theory. By eliciting spontaneous accounts of whatever length and by conceiving of consequentiality as a five-point scale, we obtained data clearly important to the further development of a behavioral theory. Livingston does not attempt to account for the length or elaborateness of the memory, but our data presented us with wide variation in this respect, and we thought it possible that the rated degree of consequentiality (interpreted as biological significance) would be one of the determinants.

Subjects

Forty white Americans and forty black Americans filled out our questionnaire. The age range was 20–54 for whites with a median age of 27; for blacks the range was 20–60 with a median of 25. We had to tolerate these small differences of age distribution because the length of the questionnaire made it somewhat difficult to recruit enough informants. We used several means to attract informants, including newspaper advertisements and posters in Harvard University buildings. Our collection of informants cannot be considered a random sample of any definable population. We, ourselves, think that the population for which the major results, in abstract form, hold true, may be the human species.

---

worked with black Americans and white Americans, only because there have been a number of assassinations in America in recent years which might reasonably be expected to differ in importance or emotional significance for these two demographic populations. We would expect the same kinds of differences for any two groups, such as two ethnic minorities, two professions, the two sexes or, for that matter, two individuals, providing there were highly publicized and surprising events known to both, but differing in significance. In fact, however, only recent assassinations in America and their effects on blacks and whites meet the requisite criteria and exist in some substantial number of instances for large populations. As we shall see, when the data are reported, our black subjects and our white subjects followed the same principles of human memory, and there is nothing at all suggestive of, or relevant to, differences in any intellectual capacity.

The Questionnaire

The heart of the questionnaire is the set of persons set down in Table 2-1. We used a little over two pages to describe the exact nature of the flashbulb effect—a vivid recall of the circumstances in which one first learned of some important event. Since almost everyone had such recall in connection with the assassination of John Kennedy, it was possible to illustrate the mental state we hoped to evoke with the two examples provided by the memories of the authors. All informants but two (whom we have excluded from the analysis) correctly understood what we meant. The two who misunderstood reported various facts about the events as they have been described in the press, rather than their personal circumstances on hearing the news. Essentially, the questionnaire was composed by using each of the person–event pairs of Table 2-1 to form the nucleus of a set of similar inquiries. We will describe here only those that are directly relevant to the argument we want to make.

Initial Free Accounts

In the case of each person–event listed in Table 2-1 informants were first asked: "Do you recall the circumstances in which you first heard that . . . ?" In the event that he did not, the informant checked "no" and was directed to turn four pages or so to the next person–event. Whenever he checked "yes," he was asked to write a free recall of the circumstances in any form or order and at any length he liked.

The first set of inquiries offered three possible criteria of a flashbulb effect: (a) the subject's simple response "yes" or "no"; (b) some number of words that we might arbitrarily require for an account to be considered a genuine flashbulb; (c) a content coding of the circumstances reported in terms of such prevalent categories as "Place," "Ongoing Event," "Informant," and so on. Of course, these potential criteria were all closely intercorrelated. However, in spite of that fact, there were reasons to prefer one possible criterion over another.

Simple reliance on the informant's "yes" and "no" would only dichotomize responses into those that are flashbulbs and those that are not, whereas many things indicated that the division was not so absolute and, more importantly, that within the accounts themselves there was much to interest us. Adding up the number of words (or any other objective index of length of account) would enable us to represent the fact that flashbulbs varied in degree, but did not represent variations as well as constancies evident to us in the content of the reports. It is possible reliably to report our conclusions about content,

TABLE 2-1
Chronological order of events used to search for flashbulb memories

Name	Race	Event	Date	Place
1. Medgar Evers	Black	Shot to death	June 12, 1963	Mississippi
2. John F. Kennedy	White	Shot to death	Nov. 22, 1963	Dallas
3. Malcolm X	Black	Shot to death	Feb. 21, 1965	Harlem
4. Martin Luther King	Black	Shot to death	April 1, 1968	Memphis
5. Robert F. Kennedy	White	Shot to death	June 6, 1968	Los Angeles
6. Ted Kennedy	White	Drowning involvement	July 19, 1969	Chappaquiddick
7. George Wallace	White	Shot, but not killed	May 15, 1972	Laurel, Md.
8. Gerald Ford	White	Failed attempt at assassination	Sept. 5, 1975	San Francisco
9. Gen. Francisco Franco	White	Died of natural causes	Nov. 20, 1975	Madrid

10. A personal, unexpected shock, such as death of a friend or relative, serious accident, diagnosis of a deadly disease, etc.

using content analysis, but these conclusions cannot be proved to be necessary emanations of the data. Still, they are too suggestive and, in our eyes, obvious to go unreported.

The first author read 20 FB accounts of the assassinations of President John Kennedy, and to him it seemed that there were only six classes of information reported in 50 percent or more of the accounts. An informant was most likely to report the "Place" in which he learned of the assassination, the "Ongoing Event" that was interrupted by the news, the "Informant" who brought him the news, "Affect in Others" upon hearing the news, as well as "Own Affect," and finally some immediate "Aftermath" for himself on hearing the news. Sampling the flashbulb accounts for all nine historical events, it appeared that the six categories listed were a kind of "canonical" form for the historical FB memory in the sense that they were more likely to be recalled than any other content though, of course, no informant always used all six.

It is important to bear in mind that the canonical categories listed are abstractions. Each informant's "Place" of hearing the news and "Ongoing Activity" and so on, was, of course, unique. The variation is dramatic: ". . . conversation with a classmate at Shaw University in North Carolina"; ". . . engaging in a game of softball"; ". . . talking to a woman friend on the telephone"; ". . . working for a market research organization"; ". . . I was having dinner in a French restaurant"; etc. For an instant, the entire nation and perhaps much of the world stopped still to have its picture taken.

In addition to the variation within each canonical category, there was, in many records, a sentence or so that fit none of the abstract categories, but was as idiosyncratic on the abstract level as on the concrete: "The weather was cloudy and gray"; "She said, 'Oh, God! I knew they would kill him' "; ". . . We all had on our little blue uniforms"; ". . . I was carrying a carton of Viceroy cigarettes which I dropped . . . ." Responses like these fell outside the canonical categories and also were so unlike one another as to resist grouping in some new category. Is it possible that so endlessly diverse a collage satisfies one law? Both facts about the content are important: the existence of six abstract canonical categories into which most of the, always unique, content could be easily and naturally placed; the existence in some accounts, but not all, of completely idiosyncratic content that the first author could not subsume under any recurrent categories.

[*Methodological details omitted.*]

. . .

A "yes" answer to our initial question and a canonical content score of 1 or more defined the flashbulb (FB) effect in this study. Of course, the higher the content score, the more elaborated the account. However, since the coding is ultimately not an "objective" feature of the data, we shall also sometimes cite number of words, an objective index of the degree of elaboration.

Consequentiality

For each of the ten persons referred to in Table 2-1, there was a 5-point Consequentiality Scale, labeled "Little or no consequentiality for me" at 1 and "Very high consequentiality for me" at 5. The scale came at the end of the questionnaire to minimize the likelihood of disclosing the point of the inquiry.

We spilled a lot of ink in our questionnaire trying precisely to define consequentiality and beseeching our informants to keep the exact sense always in mind, answering as painstakingly as possible. To quote our own efforts at defining the concept: "In order to rate the consequentiality in your life of the death of someone, let us say President John F. Kennedy, you must try to imagine the things that might have gone differently had President Kennedy lived." We pointed out that not only world figures had consequentiality for oneself, but also, obviously, relatives, friends, admired persons, and others could be very consequential. To quote again: "Probably the best single question to ask yourself in rating consequentiality is, "What consequences for my life, both direct and indirect, has this event had?" While no one could possibly tote up all the consequences for himself of any particular event, the judgment proved to be one informants could make and, in the data, there are several indications that they followed our directions. It is certain that they did not simply report attitudes or historical prominence.

Rehearsal

For the purposes of this paper, it remains only to describe several items included in the set of questions asked concerning each figure in Table 2-1. To investigate the role of rehearsal as a determinant of flashbulb memories, we asked each informant to indicate, if he gave a flashbulb account at all, how often he had related that account:

> "... never told anyone."
> "... gave the same account roughly 1–5 times."

"... gave the same account roughly 6–10 times."
"... gave the same account more than 10 times."

[*Some speculative discussion omitted here.*]

. . .

We propose that higher consequentiality of an event for an individual works both to make more elaborate flashbulb memories and also to compel more frequent rehearsal of that which is all or part of the FB memory. An event which has great consequentiality for an individual is more likely both to be "on the mind" of the person (covert rehearsal) and to be worked into conversation (overt rehearsal). However, we doubt that this rehearsal of the memory is a simple reproduction of the brain events constituting the memory, but think it must also be a constructive process, especially when it is an overt account. Probably, the rehearsal process, set off by high consequentiality, draws its content from the unchanging FB memory, but, in rehearsal, a verbal narrative is likely to be created.

We propose that rehearsals build up associative strength between the verbal narrative created and the (retrieval) cues used in the various settings. It seems likely that the sort of cue that elicited overt rehearsals in our subjects in the past would have been similar to our cue in the present study. A typical cue in our experience has not been "Do you remember the facts of John Kennedy's assassination?" but rather one more along the lines of "Do you remember what you were doing when you heard that John Kennedy had been assassinated?" If such is the case for our informants, we might expect informants who report more frequent rehearsals to have easier access to their verbal accounts by virtue of having relatively greater associations between cue and verbal narrative. In addition, the fact that qualitatively different cues are also likely to have been used would build additional associations between those cases and different aspects of the FB memory. Subjects who have rehearsed their accounts should thus be more likely to give more extensive verbal accounts in the present scheme. It is our assumption then that the FB memory is always there, unchanging as the slumbering Rhinegold, and serving by means of rehearsal to generate some variety of accounts.

Of course, rehearsal need not be either overt or verbal. Bellugi, Klima, and Siple (1975) have given evidence that, in the deaf, rehearsal is manual, at least as reflected on the periphery. But that is still a semantic sort of rehearsal. We believe, with Norman, that: "When the items to be rehearsed are not words but are actions, sounds, visual scenes, tastes, or smells, then the rehearsal tends to mimic the properties of these sensory modalities. Almost nothing is known about rehearsal for nonverbal items, but almost everyone has experienced it" (1976, p. 101). Certainly we have, since we started to attend to the process. Following a sudden consequential automobile accident, one of us finds his covert rehearsal of the circumstances as uncontrollable as the tongue that seeks an aching tooth. Of course, one of the principal things we should like to know about nonverbal rehearsal is whether it tends to build into narrative accounts. Our introspection suggests that it somehow operates on the materials from the FB memory so that a narrative is promptly produced when an audience exists that cares about the story.

Our abstract speculation may be made clear with an example. The shooting of President Kennedy was, we know, much the most surprising of all our historical events. It "bowled over" just about everybody. The rated consequentiality of the event was, for whites, also highest in the historical list and only slightly edged out by the category of "Personal Shocks." For blacks, Kennedy was also rated very high on consequentiality. On the evidence, John Kennedy rated as a member of almost everyone's immediate family. In these circumstances, we expect Livingston's "Now Print!" mechanism to operate and to record permanently all immediately previous and contemporaneous brain events above some level of organization. We further believe that this inaccessible memory will be more elaborated (in canonical content forms or words) than any other historical memory in spite of the fact that it occurred thirteen years ago before all assassinations but that of Medgar Evers. It was so, for blacks as well as whites.

Of course, the memory is not directly accessible and what we have, in fact, is 79 FB accounts, similar in their references to "Place," "Ongoing Event," and the other canonical categories but, in some irrelevant detail, always unique. These accounts are by far the most elaborated in content or in words of any historical event; in content they are slightly less so than the "Personal Shocks." How should it happen that the accounts reflect the high degree of elaboration we attribute to the memories? We have data on overt rehearsals though not on covert. Overt rehearsal would be expected to be especially frequent relative to covert in just this case because there existed a national, indeed an international, highly interested audience. The overt rehearsals reported were far higher than those for any other event; 73 percent of whites and 90 percent of blacks reported telling their personal tales more than once and generally between 1–5 or 5–10 times. Those who did not report overt rehearsals, but nevertheless gave FB accounts, must either be assumed to have forgotten past rehearsals and/or to have rehearsed covertly. It is of some importance that no one reported an overt rehearsal within the past year. In short, we propose that frequent rehearsals, covert and overt, made accessible elaborate FB accounts because of the high consequentiality posited to produce both an elaborate memory and many rehearsals.

· · ·

RESULTS

Race Membership and Frequency of FB Memories

Our advance prediction was that the 40 black informants would be most likely to register biological significance in the case of those national leaders who were most involved with American civil rights, whether the leader be black or white, a friend or an enemy of the black minority. Our intuitive guess was that three such leaders in our set were black and were clear champions of the civil rights of black Americans: Medgar Evers, Malcolm X, and Martin Luther King. These men could truly be said to have attempted to advance the position of American blacks in a way that was ultimately biological since their immediate concerns with education, employment opportunities, and income must ultimately translate into improved opportunities for blacks to survive and contribute to the American gene pool. The fourth leader closely identified with civil rights is former Governor George Wallace, a white man. Whatever George Wallace may have intended his rhetoric to suggest, it was clear to our black informants that he was an enemy (they rated their attitude to him as "extremely unfavorable"). Wallace seemed interested in preserving the disadvantage of the black minority. The other national leaders—Franco, Ford, and the Kennedys—seemed to us not so strongly concerned with civil rights.

In Table 2-2 we have the absolute frequencies of FB memories (really, of course, FB accounts) for each racial group and the nine political leaders. It is possible to use frequencies rather than percentages because the numbers were the same for both groups. Perhaps the easiest way to absorb the information in this table is to look first at the four leaders we have identified as strongly concerned with civil rights and so most likely to elicit FB memories from blacks. For Malcolm X and Martin Luther King, the difference in frequency of FBs is in the predicted direction (blacks greater than whites) and is very highly significant. For Wallace, the difference is again as predicted (nearly twice as many FBs for blacks as for whites), but the significance level is lower.

TABLE 2-2
Numbers of white and black subjects reporting flashbulb memories for various events

Event	FB Whites ($N = 40$)	FB Blacks ($N = 40$)
*1. Medgar Evers	0	5
2. John F. Kennedy	39	40
***3. Malcolm X	1	14
***4. Martin Luther King	13	30
5. Robert F. Kennedy	25	20
6. Ted Kennedy	13	10
**7. George Wallace	11	20
8. Gerald Ford	23	16
9. Gen. Francisco Franco	17	13
10. A personal, unexpected shock	37	32 (36)[a]

By chi square analysis:

***$p < 0.001$

**p between 0.05 and 0.02

*p with Yates's correction between 0.10 and 0.05

[a]Four informants said they had a FB memory for a personal shock but that it was too personal to relate, and so these four did not fully satisfy the definition for a FB account which includes at least one canonical content category.

For Medgar Evers, only five informants of all 80 had a FB memory, but all five were blacks, and so the difference approaches significance.

After the fact, it is clear why the Evers' FBs were so few. Medgar Evers was assassinated in June of 1963; 24 of our informants were, in 1976, between 20 and 24 years of age and so, in 1963, would have been between 7 and 11 years old. John Kennedy was also assassinated in 1963, and yet all but one of the full 80 informants, including the youngest, had FB memories of that event. Reading the accounts of their circumstances when they heard the news, it is clear that some, especially the youngest, knew nothing, or next to nothing, of President Kennedy. Had the news (inconceivably) been reported as no more than a routine newspaper headline, the early school-age informants would not have registered surprise, nor probably would they have experienced the event as a consequential one.

In fact, however, they did, most of them, experience surprise and consequentiality. But they experienced them in the microcosms of their own lives, usually in school, where the regularities of life were disturbed by reflection from the events in Dallas. Principals made unscheduled announcements over public address systems, teachers or parents burst into tears, and school was dismissed for the day. Events unthinkably surprising and consequential when you are 7 years old. But for Medgar Evers, not a very famous figure, no schools were closed, no announcements were made by principals, some tears were shed but not so many, with blacks still predominantly resigned to injustice.

Looking next, in Table 2-2, at the leaders thought not to be deeply involved in civil rights—John Kennedy, Robert Kennedy, Ted Kennedy, Gerald Ford and General Franco—we find, as predicted, no significant differences between the groups. The tenth event, a personal unexpected shock, was, of course, entirely different for each informant. The very high levels of personal FBs, almost identical for blacks and whites, simply mean that almost everyone could find in his memory an event answering to our abstract description.

In Table 2-3 we have arrayed the mean consequentiality scores assigned each event by the total groups of blacks and whites. Let us look first at what does not take us by surprise. The mean consequentiality scores for the civil rights leaders—Medgar Evers, Malcolm X, and Martin Luther King—are all very significant and, as anticipated, their consequentiality is greater for blacks. George Wallace's consequentiality is also greater for blacks, but at a borderline level of significance. The simplest way, then, to read Table 2-3 is to say that it provides independent validation of our obvious-enough notion that just these men had greater biological significance or consequentiality for blacks than for whites. Since the notions are obvious, one may also say that the results provide a degree of validation for the consquentiality scale. There is firmer validation in the fact that whites gave a higher consequentiality score to their personal shocks than to any events on the national level, and blacks rated only the consequentiality of the death of Martin Luther King above their personal shocks.
[*Some data summaries omitted here.*]

. . .

As can be seen in Table 2-4, the *rho* between consequentiality and overt rehearsals for whites is so high (0.886) that even with only 6 subjects, it is significant. The value for blacks is positive and moderately high, but with an *N* of 7 not significant. If a *post hoc* suggestion is not out of order, we have a notion why the value was as low as this. Blacks may have felt a kind of racial obligation to rank Martin Luther King and Malcolm X above any white man; the word "consequentiality" has, after all, some semantic overlap with importance. But with respect to rehearsals, blacks give their highest value to John Kennedy (90 percent > 0 rehearsals) even as did whites. It is difficult to imagine any participant in the American culture at that time doing otherwise.

We have suggested that the kind of cue most frequently eliciting overt rehearsals in the past would probably be similar to the cues by

TABLE 2-3
Mean consequentiality scores for all subjects in two groups

	Whites (N = 40)	Blacks (N = 40)	Significance level of difference by student's t
1. Medgar Evers	1.39[a]	3.00[b]	p < 0.001
2. John F. Kennedy	3.39	3.81	p < 0.10
3. Malcolm X	1.49[c]	3.40	p < 0.001
4. Martin Luther King	2.88	4.34	p < 0.001
5. Robert F. Kennedy	3.08	3.56	p < 0.10
6. Ted Kennedy	2.07	2.16	
7. George Wallace	1.75	2.23	p < 0.10
8. Gerald Ford	1.88	1.63	
9. Gen. Francisco Franco	1.55	1.29	
10. A personal, unexpected shock	3.68[c]	4.22[d]	

[a]Four informants failed to complete this item.
[b]One informant failed to complete this item.
[c]Three informants failed to complete this item
[d]Seven informants failed to complete this item.

TABLE 2-4
Spearman rank correlation coefficients for certain pairs of variables

	Whites	Exact p	Blacks	Exact p
Consequentiality; Overt rehearsals > 0	0.886 (N = 6)	0.017	0.536 (N = 7)	0.118
Consequentiality; Content categories	0.786 (N = 8)	0.014	0.883 (N = 9)	0.0015
Consequentiality; Length in words	0.810 (N = 8)	0.011	0.883 (N = 9)	0.0015
Overt rehearsals > 0; Content categories	0.771 (N = 6)	0.051	0.893 (N = 7)	0.0062
Overt rehearsals > 0; Length in words	0.771 (N = 6)	0.051	0.893 (N = 7)	0.0062
Content categories; Length in words	0.786 (N = 8)	0.014	0.933 (N = 9)	0.00037

which we attempted to retrieve FB memories. We have also suggested that consequentiality should vary directly with the elaboration of a neurological memory and that rehearsals, while drawing on the materials of the memory, would also have a constructive role in building up verbal narratives from the memories. It follows that the consequentiality value of an event ought to be positively related to the degree of elaboration and length in words of a retrieved account by virtue of the mediating rehearsal process. We have then a whole set of predictions.

Consequentiality should be positively correlated with the elaboration of an account in canonical categories. It is (*rhos* are 0.786 and 0.883). Consequentiality should be positively correlated with account length in words. It is (*rhos* are 0.810 and 0.883). Rehearsals, as the mediating variable between FB memories and FB accounts, should be related to both the content elaboration and word length values of accounts; *rhos* are, respectively, 0.771 and 0.771 for whites and 0.893 and 0.893 for blacks.

Finally, of course, some positive correlation between content measures of elaboration and word counts of length is to be expected, but obtained values as high as 0.786 and 0.933 are hardly an a priori necessity. The content coding into six categories for historical events and nine for personal shocks is to be compared with a range in word counts from 6 to 343. If the so-called canonical categories were not close to the essence of the degree of elaboration in the neurological memories, we might find that long accounts did not necessarily include most or all of the canon but were often exhausted on irrelevant matters such as the weather, one's clothing, one's most recent meal, one's favorite novel, or what have you, with the canon omitted. At the same time, the canon is so small that, in principle, very few words could cover the lot. The suggestion is that "Place," "Ongoing Activity," "Informant" and so on are, in fact, the uniform terms in which the event was experienced, that they well represent the regnant brain processes at the time of the event.

DISCUSSION

[Part of Brown and Kulik's discussion is omitted.]

. . .

The "Now Print!" neurobiological mechanism surely did not evolve in the human species in historical time, that is, in the few thousand years since writing was invented or the few hundred since printing was invented. The mechanism surely evolved much earlier in the (roughly) 1 million years since our species appeared. At the time when the mechanism evolved, there was no actual printing; there was only the human memory. What surely had to be printed neurologically and put in permanent store was not the circumstances of an unexpected and biologically significant event, but the event itself. To survive and leave progeny, the individual human had to keep his expectations of significant events up to date and close to reality. A marked departure from the ordinary in a consequential domain would leave him unprepared to respond adequately and endanger his survival. The "Now Print!" mechanism must have evolved because of the selection value of permanently retaining biologically crucial but unexpected events. It seems to be an irony of evolution that it is just the central newsworthy events that no longer need to be retained because cultural devices have taken over the job. And today the automatic recording of the circumstances, concomitant to the main event, is what captures our interest and calls for explanation.

But the explanation has not been given. Certainly the surprising and consequential had to be permanently remembered, but why should man ever have developed a mechanism for storing his concomitant circumstances? When—ever—would such memories have had survival value?

Suppose we imagine a state of life for primitive man. We are not now at a time when presidential assassinations are the critical events to evoke. They would be something more like the appearance in one's territory of a new dangerous carnivore or the sight of a serious injury to a dominant male of the same species or the moving on, of a troop of baboons, to a new and remote range. These things have to be stored in memory promptly and enduringly and are most closely similar to the "Person" and "Event" categories which in our "Personal Shock" cases were never, literally never, omitted from the account. What might the concomitant circumstances have been like, and would there have been any reason to remember them?

Place, after all, is important almost always. Where was the primitive man when he saw the new carnivore or the baboon troop on the march? The significance of the main event is, in great degree, defined by its locus. Nothing is always to be feared or always to be welcomed. It depends. In part on place. What about ongoing activity? Well, perhaps it is the nature of that activity that has attracted an animal or enraged him or allowed him to draw near without being noticed. Affect in others may well be a clue from more experienced conspecifics of the character of an intruder or the quality of some prey or some sheltering space. So it is not really difficult to conceive of reasons for permanently remembering the circumstances in which something novel and consequential occurred. But we have not yet quite unraveled the mystery of these memories.

The canonical category called "Informant" was the category most often specified in FB accounts and, in that fact, we find the reason why these enduring memories for personal circumstances struck us as mysterious in the first place. All of the ten events we used to search for FB memories were events like John Kennedy's assassination, in which there was a sharp separation between the time and place of the significant event and the circumstances in which each of many millions first heard of that event. An informant was essential for all who were not on the scene, and that informant was usually radio or tele-vision. Primitive man, lacking such instruments of telecommunication, would not so regularly register an informant. Sometimes, of course, he would, at least for separations of moderate length since spoken and gestural language may be as old as the species.

But what if there were no informant, then or now, no separation between the event and the circumstances in which one learned of it? You are in a startling and serious automobile accident, or you narrowly miss being struck by lightning. There is novelty and biological signifi-cance, and also a FB memory. But what now are the preceding and concomitant circumstances? Still, perhaps, place and maybe time and ongoing activity and affect with only informant missing. But what a difference it makes! The place of an automobile accident, the ongoing activity, the affect are no longer circumstances attendant upon hearing the news. In a way, they are the news, at least parts of it or dimensions of it. The precise intersection, the make of the car, the signal unob-served all together define the event. And so it makes sense that all of these brain patterns should have to be permanently stored and that a "Now Print!" mechanism for doing it would have evolved. What is relatively new is telecommunication which makes an informant a necessity and creates the sharp separation between news and circum-stances of hearing the news, and that is what first made us think we were on the trail of a mystery. Probably the same "Now Print!" mech-anism accounts both for the enduring significant memories in which one has played the role of protagonist and those in which one has only been a member of an interested audience of millions.

REFERENCES

Bellugi, U., Klima, E. S., and Siple, P. Remembering in signs. *Cognition*, 1975, *3*, 93–125.

Berendt, J. Where were you? *Esquire*, November, 1973.

Livingston, R. B. Brain circuitry relating to complex behavior. In G. C. Quarton, T. Melnechuck, and F. O. Schmitt (eds.), *The Neurosciences: A Study Program*. New York: Rockefeller University Press, 1967a, 499–514.

Livingston, R. B. Reinforcement. In G. C. Quarton, T. Melnechuck, and F. O. Schmitt (eds.), *The Neurosciences: A Study Program*. New York: Rocke-feller University Press, 1967b, 568–576.

Norman, D. A. *Memory and Attention*, 2nd ed. New York: Wiley, 1976.

ADDITIONAL REFERENCES

Yarmen, A. D., and Bull, M. P. Where were you when President Kennedy was assassinated? *Bulletin of the Psychonomic Society*, 1978, *11*, 133–135.

3 The Day They Heard About Lincoln

F. W. Colegrove

*Whatever the correct explanation of "flashbulb
memories" may be, the phenomenon is at least a
robust one. Kennedy, King, and Evers were not the
first American political leaders to be assassinated,
and Brown and Kulik were not the first psychologists
to ask Americans to recall how they heard such news.
Colegrove's nineteenth-century report shows that the
apparent vividness of such memories is not a product
of modern sensibilities or modern media of
communication.*

. . . A well-known pedagogical principle is that vivid impressions are
easily recalled. With frequency, recency, and emotional congruity, vividness plays an important role in association. In order to test the abiding character of a vivid experience, 179 middle-aged and aged people
were asked in personal interviews the following question: "Do you
recall where you were when you heard that Lincoln was shot?" An
affirmative answer required the exact location, an example of which is
the following reply: "My father and I were on the road to A—in the
State of Maine to purchase the 'fixings' needed for my graduation.
When we were driving down a steep hill into the city we felt that
something was wrong. Everybody looked so sad, and there was such
terrible excitement that my father stopped his horse, and leaning from
the carriage called: 'What is it, my friends? What has happened?'

From F. W. Colegrove, Individual memories, *American Journal of Psychology*,
1899, *10*, 228–255.

'Haven't you heard?' was the reply—'Lincoln has been assassinated.' The lines fell from my father's limp hands, and with tears streaming from his eyes he sat as one bereft of motion. We were far from home, and much must be done, so he rallied after a time, and we finished our work as well as our heavy hearts would allow."

Not all the replies were so vivid as this one, but only those were accounted as affirmative which contained facts as to time of day, exact location, and who told them.

> J.P., age 76: I was standing by the stove getting dinner; my husband came in and told me.
> M.B., age 79: I was setting out a rose bush by the door. My husband came in the yard and told me. It was about 11 o'clock A.M.
> H.R., age 73: We were eating dinner. No one ate much after we heard of it.
> J.T., age 73: I was fixing fence, can go within a rod of the place where I stood. Mr. W. came along and told me. It was 9 or 10 o'clock in the morning.
> L.B., age 84: It was in the forenoon; we were at work on the road by K.'s mills; a man driving past told us.

Of the 179 persons interviewed, 127 replied in the affirmative, and were able to give full particulars; 52 replied in the negative. A few who gave a negative reply recalled where they were when they heard of Garfield's death. Inasmuch as 33 years have elapsed since Lincoln's death, the number who made an affirmative reply must be considered large, and bears testimony to the abiding character of vivid experiences.

4 Snapshots or Benchmarks?

Ulric Neisser

A "flashbulb memory" is a subjectively compelling recollection of an occasion when we heard an important piece of news. There is an impressive consistency to the organization of such memories: Cole-grove's account of how his subjects remembered hearing about Lincoln is strikingly similar to what Brown and Kulik's subjects say when they recall getting the news about John F. Kennedy. Yet although the phenomenon itself is clear enough, its interpretation is not. At least, it seems to me that the interpretation offered by Brown and Kulik should not go unchallenged.

Why is any interpretation necessary at all? At first glance, flash-bulb memories appear to be obvious illustrations of a commonsense principle: people remember what is important. The problem arises only when we realize (with Brown and Kulik) that the actual content of flashbulb memories does not meet that criterion. The fact of John F. Kennedy's death may be important, but what difference does it make who told *me* about it, or where *I* was when I heard the news? None, really. Why, then, do I seem to remember such things? Brown and Kulik think that a special "Now Print" mechanism in my brain is triggered whenever I believe that an important or "consequential" event is taking place. Supposedly this mechanism "prints" the whole event—including many though not all unimportant details—into a permanent record for later recall. This hypothesis implies (a) that flashbulb memories are accurate; (b) that the process by which the memory is created occurs at the time of the event itself; (c) that surprise, emotionality, and similar reactions are closely correlated with the "consequentiality" of an event, and that higher levels of surprise and emotionality lead to good memory; and (d) that the similarities among different flashbulb memories reflect the common characteristics of an underlying neural mechanism. All these implications deserve careful scrutiny.

THE ACCURACY OF FLASHBULB
MEMORIES

Brown and Kulik never doubt their informants. They take it for granted that a carton of Viceroy cigarettes *was* dropped, that there *was* a game of softball, that Kulik *was* in his sixth-grade music class, that Berrigan *was* on his way to a rally. They are no more skeptical than Livingston, whom they quote approvingly: "You can probably tell us where you were, with whom, and very likely whether you were sitting, standing, or walking—almost which foot was forward when your awareness became manifest" (1967, p. 576). I find such unquestioning acceptance remarkable: If someone offered to tell me which of his feet had been "forward" at a specific moment in 1963, I would assume he had only a 50-percent chance of being right. Unfotunately, there is ample precedent for this kind of credulity about memory. When hypnotized subjects are "age-regressed," for example, their vivid descriptions of long-past events are often taken at face value even by well-trained scientists. This is a mistake: Careful studies of hypnotic age regression demonstrate that it produces much confabulation and little or no hypermnesia (O'Connell, Shor, and Orne, 1970). In a similar vein, Penfield's (e.g., 1952) accounts of the "recollections" triggered by electrical stimulation of the brains of certain patients are often accepted uncritically even though none of the alleged recollections has ever been verified. (For additional discussion of this issue see Neisser, 1967; Loftus and Loftus, 1980.) By virtue of their vividness and detail, flashbulb memories seem to elicit the same unhesitating assent.

They shouldn't. The psychology of testimony—see Part III of this book—teaches over and over again that vivid recollection and accurate testimony may be wrong. Indeed, there is at least one documented example of complete fabrication in a flashbulb. Marigold Linton, whose work we shall consider shortly (Selection 8), began her study of memory as Brown and Kulik did: she asked people what they were doing when John Kennedy was assassinated. She abandoned the method abruptly when one of her subjects replied as follows (1975, pp. 386–387):

> When I'm reminded of that date, particularly by you, I remember that you were the one who told me about the assassination, or at least that's the way I remember it.... I believe that you, I *know* that you came down and told me about what you ... had heard on the news. I don't know what time it was. Because down in the hole in F_____ Hall one tended to lose track of time.... I had been working for some extended period of time and I was very much concentrating on what I was doing when I was interrupted by you having heard something about it. You said, I'm sure it was you who said, "The President has been assassinated, or shot—

shot." And I probably looked up and said, "What?" and you said, "Kennedy, he's been shot." And I said "What do you mean? Where?" and you said you didn't know. . . .

This recollection is incorrect. Linton has no memory of such an exchange. More significantly, she writes that " . . . Examination of a variety of documentable external events demonstrates that the two of us could not then have been at the same place" (p. 387).

I can supply another counterexample from my own experience. For many years I have remembered how I heard the news of the Japanese attack on Pearl Harbor, which occurred on the day before my thirteenth birthday. I recall sitting in the living room of our house—we only lived in that house for one year, but I remember it well—listening to a baseball game on the radio. The game was interrupted by an announcement of the attack, and I rushed upstairs to tell my mother. This memory has been so clear for so long that I never confronted its inherent absurdity until last year: no one broadcasts baseball games in December! (It can't have been a football game either: professional football barely existed in 1941, and the college season ended by Thanksgiving.) Apparently flashbulbs can be just as wrong as other kinds of memories; they are not produced by a special quasi-photographic mechanism.

WHEN ARE FLASHBULBS ESTABLISHED?

The metaphor of a "flashbulb" suggests that the peculiar strength of these memories is established at the moment of the event itself. Brown and Kulik attribute their creation to the hypothesized special "Now Print" mechanism, while Colegrove gives credit to the more familiar principle that " . . . vivid impressions are easily recalled." I believe, however, that memories become flashbulbs primarily through the significance that is attached to them *afterwards*: later that day, the next day, and in subsequent months and years. What requires explanation, after all, is not the immediate survival of the memory—we can all give good accounts of what happened earlier today—but its long endurance. Moments like these are sure to be pondered, discussed, and redescribed on subsequent occasions: why shouldn't we suppose that their persistence is due to the frequent reconsideration they receive? Brown and Kulik treat rehearsals as mere products of the flashbulb memory, itself "as unchanging as the slumbering Rhinegold," but they may play a more essential role.

If flashbulbs are created after the fact, we can easily understand that they may be inaccurate. A long tradition in psychology teaches us that memories can be altered. The names of Freud and Bartlett come to mind immediately in this context; many later selections in this book make the same point. It also explains how we can have flashbulbs for events whose "consequentiality" was established only later. One informant has told me that she remembers how she heard the news about Kennedy even though she did not believe it at the time; only afterward did she find out that it was true.

"CONSEQUENTIALITY"

It is somewhat surprising that Brown and Kulik asked their subjects to rate the flashbulbed events by their effects: "What consequences for my life, both direct and indirect, has this event had?" Such a question accepts—or asks subjects to accept—the "great man" theory of history. To believe that my life would be different today if one or another of these assassinations had not occurred is to believe that particular political leaders, rather than cultural or economic forces, determine our destinies. Surely this cannot be casually taken for granted. (Moreover, such a criterion contradicts the "Now Print" idea: often, we do not evaluate the significance of an event "now" but only later.) My guess is that the subjects in Brown and Kulik's study were wise enough not to take their instructions too literally; that their ratings were probably based less on "consequences" than on another criterion of importance to be considered below.

Whatever its significance for the subsequent course of events, the first Kennedy assassination was certainly *unexpected*; it took everyone by surprise. Is surprisingness essential for flashbulb formation? Livingston's theory begins with the recognition of novelty, but I doubt that it can be crucial. Long-expected events may also give rise to flashbulbs. The death of General Franco, for example, had been anticipated for weeks in the press. I can offer another relevant case from my own experience. One of my most vivid memories is of a political event that had been eagerly awaited in many quarters: President Nixon's resignation. I vividly recall the circumstances and the company in which I watched the resignation speech, but my memory includes no element of surprise. To be sure it was an emotional occasion, as are many such moments. But emotionality itself is also a poor candidate for the defining characteristic of flashbulbs: the study of testimony does not indicate that emotional experiences are especially well remembered. High levels of arousal are often said to narrow the focus of attention as they energize ongoing activity; it is unlikely that they also promote detailed recall of circumstances.

THE STRUCTURE OF THE MEMORIES

Brown and Kulik are right, I think, to stress the similarities of structure of the many flashbulb memories they collected. Place, ongoing activity, informant, aftermath, one's own affect and that of others: these are important aspects of the memories, and they appear again and again. Nevertheless it may be a mistake to attribute them to "the uniform terms in which the event was experienced," or to "the regnant brain processes at the time." They seem more like narrative conventions to me. News reporters and novelists, mythmakers and autobiographers have a fairly coherent idea of how events should be described, of what readers and listeners want to know. Everyone in our culture is at least roughly aware of these conventions. In effect, we have *schemata* for the arrival of important news as we have for other kinds of social trans-actions, and we apply these schemata when we try to remember how we heard about President Kennedy's assassination. Traditional advice to newspaper reporters is to include *who*, *what*, *when*, *where*, and *why* in their stories, preferably with a little *human interest* thrown in. *When* and *why* are self-evident for the flashbulbs that an experimenter asks about; *who, what, where* and *human interest* remain, and generate the canonical categories of recall.

In my view, the notion of narrative structure does more than explain the canonical form of flashbulb memories; it accounts for their very existence. The flashbulb recalls an occasion when two narratives that we ordinarily keep separate—the course of history and the course of our own life—were momentarily put into alignment. All of us have a rough narrative conception of public affairs: Time runs on, events unfold, and occasionally there are "historic moments." History has to have such moments, because otherwise it wouldn't be much of a story. The death of a prominent person—or the resignation of a president—is a good place to end a chapter or to highlight a theme. This means that judgments of "importance" are a kind of *metacognition*. They are not so much judgments of the event itself as of how it has been or will be used by the media, by historians, and by ordinary people thinking about their experiences. How dramatic was the event, how central, how "big"? This, I think, is what Brown and Kulik's subjects called its "consequentiality."

In addition to the narrative of public events that we all keep to some extent, everyone elaborates another and more detailed story as well: his own. Our lives are laid out behind us in a richly structured way, full of landmarks and stages and critical moments. I break a leg, I move to a new city, I have a spectacular vacation, I get married—the list stretches distantly into the past and hopefully into the future. (I think it is because young children do not have such a conception of themselves in time that no one has coherent memories of his early childhood; see Selection 18 for Schachtel's exposition of a similar view.) But this otherwise absorbing story has one disadvantage: it bears little relation to the historical period in which I have actually lived. All those important public events, and where was I? Well, I can tell you *just* where I was: I got the news of President Kennedy's assassination as I. . . .

My suggestion is that we remember the details of a flashbulb occasion because those details are the links between our own histories and "History." We are aware of this link at the time and aware that others are forging similar links. We discuss "how we heard the news" with our friends and listen eagerly to how *they* heard. We rehearse the occasion often in our minds and our conversations, seeking some meaning in it. Indeed, in a good novel there *would* be some meaning to such a sudden eruption of the public into the private; something later in the story would hinge on it. In real life there may be no such meaning, but we cannot help seeking it. The more we seek it, the more compelling our memory of the moment becomes. That memory may be accurate—frequent rehearsal and discussion probably contribute to accuracy—but it need not be. Its purpose is served equally well whether or not the details are correct. It is the very existence of the memory that matters, not its contents. The term "flashbulb" is really misleading: such memories are not so much momentary snapshots as enduring benchmarks. They are the places where we line up our own lives with the course of history itself and say "I was there."

REFERENCES

Linton, M. Memory for real-world events. In D. A. Norman and D. E. Rumelhart (eds.), *Explorations in Cognition*. San Francisco: W. H. Freeman and Company, 1975.

Livingston, R. B. Reinforcement. In G. C. Quarton, T. Menelchuk, and F. O. Schmitt (eds.), *The Neurosciences: A Study Program*. New York: Rockefeller University Press, 1967.

Loftus, E. F., and Loftus, G. R. On the permanence of stored information in the human brain. *American Psychologist*, 1980, *35*, 409–420.

Neisser, U. *Cognitive Psychology*. New York: Appleton-Century-Crofts, 1967.

O'Connell, D. N., Shor, R. E., and Orne, M. T. Hypnotic age regression: An empirical and methodological analysis. *Journal of Abnormal Psychology*, 1970, *76* (Monograph Supplement No. 3), 1–32.

Penfield, W. Memory mechanisms. *AMA Archives of Neurology and Psychiatry*, 1952, *67*, 178–191.

5 A Collection of Moments

Esther Salaman

In this selection Esther Salaman, a Russian novelist, describes a kind of memory that psychologists have almost completely ignored. "Involuntary memories" are those that come "unexpectedly, suddenly, and bring back a past moment accompanied by strong emotions, so that a 'then' becomes a 'now'." She presents us with many beautiful examples, from her own experience as well as from others' autobiographies; she tries to analyze the conditions that give rise to such memories, the degree to which they are reliable, and their relationship to more conscious and deliberate kinds of remembering.

Writing about memories, towards the end of his life, Dostoyevsky says that a man could not go on living without them, especially the sacred and precious memories of childhood. "Some people appear not to think of their memories of childhood, but all the same preserve such memories unconsciously. They may be grave, bitter, but the suffering we have lived through may turn in the end into sacred things for the soul."

This is an obvious truth, recognizable by anyone who has recollected childhood, and it makes the lack of knowledge of the nature of memories quite unbelievable. There is widespread and dense ignorance. How, for instance, is it possible for serious students of Proust to

From E. Salaman, *A Collection of Moments: A Study of Involuntary Memories*. London: Longman, 1970. Reprinted by permission of the author.

describe his involuntary memories as a discovery, a revelation, a miracle, when so many others have had these experiences? Harriet Martineau, De Quincey, Aksakov, Rousseau, Edwin Muir, Dostoyevsky, to mention but a few. Why, there can be hardly a person who has fully recollected his childhood who has not experienced involuntary memories!

Subjectively the feeling is miraculous, miraculous as a moment of love, the first sight of a newborn healthy baby to a mother, the sudden light of understanding of your idea in another person's eyes, or a moment of recognition of beauty in a work of art or a scientific theory.

Where would you expect a knowledge about memories in general, and of this particular phenomenon, involuntary memories? Among poets, novelists, autobiographers: all those to whom memories are their quarry. Years ago, while I was a student of physics and mathematics, walking occasionally into a lecture on psychology I had the impression that writers knew things about memories and their relation to the creative process of which the psychologists knew next to nothing. The distinguished psychoanalyst Anton Ehrenzweig writes: "Psychoanalysis knows as yet little about the lower levels of perception that become activated during creative work. So far it has been concerned with the content of the unconscious and its fantastic symbolism. The study of creative work requires more" (*Nature*, 16 June 1962).

Why so little of what writers knew about memories was available to others I realized only after writing some autobiographical novels. I made extensive use of memories, but like other writers, I used them as a means to an end, and made only passing observations about their general nature.

For many years my experience of involuntary memories was unpredictable, sporadic, and elusive. Only in maturity, when a large number came back within a comparatively short period of time, did a pattern of their general nature begin to appear. But I was then too preoccupied by the submerged ship of childhood, adolescence, and early youth, which was rising to the surface, to concentrate on the nature of memories as an end in itself. It was not till some years later that I began to decipher my own observations about memories, and to understand other writers' passing remarks. It was then that I became certain that one can gather much knowledge about the nature of memories from writers.

I shall deal with many aspects of involuntary memories, and try to make it clear how they differ from the conscious memories which are available to us. A number of conclusions are confirmed by psychoanalysis. I. M. L. Hunter, professor of psychology at Keele University, who has done important work on the nature of memory, read an early version of the book, and by his appreciation and comments did me great service. Commenting on my involuntary memories he said: "These remarkably fresh memories concern somewhat traumatic experiences which are, therefore, important to the person but have now lost their trauma for the current way of life.... Psychoanalytic thought holds a similar notion of repressed memories once they are 'allowed to appear'." This was new to me. He went on: "In all honesty I have never been impressed by this notion as a generality but have always tended to think of the phenomena the other way round, i.e., the person is now able to construct remembering which formerly he was not interested in constructing. But perhaps these seemingly opposed views are merely matters of taste rather than fact."

I found this comment most stimulating. The two views are not opposed. The memories which came back involuntarily in maturity (I was in my early fifties), when I was writing about childhood, adolescence, and youth, added many new memories of moments to my old conscious memories. It was then that their traumatic origin became apparent, though by that time the fear, shame, and guilt had faded. But if I had not had the urge to write a book they would not have come back, certainly not in such large numbers. The autobiographer is not trying to get rid of a neurosis, is not even in pursuit of self-knowledge, as Stendhal believed he was—self-knowledge is a by-product: his primary purpose is the same as that of the artist.

Why are so many autobiographies of childhood written late in life? De Quincey and Aksakov both found that childhood was dead to them in their middle age. De Quincey believed that there was no such thing as forgetting, but that our memories, or as he calls them "the secret inscriptions," are "waiting to be revealed when the obscuring daylight shall have withdrawn." Proust expressed the same idea, using a different image. Marcel says that the echo of his tears, in his traumatic memory of demanding his mother's kiss, never ceased, but was not audible until life grew quiet, like those convent bells which are drowned in the noise of daytime, and sound out again in the silence of the evening.

· · ·

A vast amount of information is stowed away in our brain; that much we know for certain. There is a great variety in the faculty of memory: verbal, musical, mathematical, sculptural, a memory for chess configurations, for faces, names, habits, customs, and so on. Very often a person excels in one and not in the others. From observation alone we can tell that children of very similar IQ have very different kinds of memory. The memory for experiences is as common as any of the other kinds, but varies from person to person. Let anyone confine himself to a particular period, preferably to one before he settled down, in youth, adolescence, or childhood, and he will find a number of memories available to him. If he concentrates he will find that many more come back, and even make him wonder how he could have forgotten them.

There is another kind of memory of experience, which comes unexpectedly, suddenly, and brings back a past moment accompanied by strong emotions, so that a "then" becomes a "now." Proust was not the first to describe such memories. Some have called such memories "spontaneous," others, "revived"; they have also been called "unconscious" or "involuntary." Of all these names, none of which is perfect, I choose "involuntary." I believe that the experience of involuntary memories is not uncommon, and hope to make it clear why many people are not aware of having experienced them. But to begin with, here are a few typical examples.

The first is from Chateaubriand's *Memoires d'Outre-Tombe*. Walking alone in the evening, "I was drawn from my reflections by the warbling of a thrush perched upon the highest branch of a birch tree. At that instant the magical sound brought my paternal estate before my eyes; I forgot the catastrophes of which I had been a witness and, transported suddenly into the past, I saw again that country where I had so often heard the thrush sing."

There are a number of distinct features in this involuntary memory. He is walking alone in a disturbed state of mind; he suddenly hears a thrush, and it is "magical" to him; but the magic is not in the immediate impression but in his memory. Immediately it brings back his home, the country where he had often heard a thrush sing, and he forgets the painful present and lives in the past. Many involuntary memories have a similar pattern. Proust quotes this memory of Chateaubriand's in *A la Recherche du Temps Perdu*; Marcel says that he was reassured to discover that his involuntary memories were "fundamentally analogous to experiences of other writers." But we cannot take Marcel's experiences at face value: they are not always Marcel Proust's. Proust used involuntary memories for a purpose: to make his ingenious plot. So I will take an example of a real memory of Proust's, analogous to Chateaubriand's, from *Jean Santeuil*, an autobiographical novel, which Proust abandoned and never revised. Jean (who, by the way, sometimes becomes "I") had started out on his way to the Lake of Geneva in a low mood, but when the sight of it suddenly brought him back the memory of Begmeil his disappointment vanished. He had often made an effort to bring back his memories of Brittany, but they seemed dead. Now, "In a flash that life in Brittany, which he had thought useless and unusable, appeared before his eyes in all its charm and beauty, and his heart swelled within him as he thought of his walks at Begmeil when the sun was setting and the sea stretched out before him." The analogy to Chateaubriand's experience is pretty close. Proust had also set out in a depressed state of mind, and the sight of the lake was "magical" to him because it brought back a memory of the sea at Begmeil.

Another example is De Quincey's memory of Altrincham Market Place. It comes in the revised version of the *Confessions of an English Opium-Eater*. When De Quincey was seventeen he ran away from school. He set out that morning on foot for Altrincham in a disturbed state of mind and full of misgivings. It was a heavenly early morning in July, and when he reached the town a memory of just such a dazzling morning when he had stayed at Altrincham with his nurse when he was three years old came back to him. He had waked early and woken up the nurse, and when she lifted him in her arms and threw open the window, he saw the gayest scene he had ever seen: the market-place at Altrincham at eight o'clock in the morning. It was market day: "fruit, such as can be had in July, and flowers were scattered about in profusion: even the stalls of the butchers, from their brilliant cleanliness, appeared attractive: and the bonny young women of Altrincham were tripping about in caps and aprons coquetishly disposed. . . ."

Just as to Chateaubriand there was magic in the song of a thrush, to Proust in the sight of the Lake of Geneva, so there was to De Quincey in the sight of the marketplace at that early hour; and in every case it is made clear that it was not the impression itself which took them out of their despondency but a memory of a similar impression. De Quincey becomes the child of three: "perhaps the window of my bedroom was still open, only my nurse and I were not looking out: for alas! on recollection, fourteen years had passed since then." He was refreshed by the walk and the memory, and after a rest and breakfast "all my gloom and despondency were already retiring to the rear." Such a memory, as Proust said, overthrows the order of time and makes one live in another period. Had more people recognized these experiences there would not have been so much nonsense talked about Proust's involuntary memories in *A la Recherche du Temps Perdu*. Why did they not? What Chateaubriand, Proust, and De Quincey had in common was a long experience of recapturing memories.

To show how elusive involuntary memories are, I will go for further examples to my own experience of them in youth, when they were comparatively frequent. They puzzled me then, but later they afforded me material to work on. I left Russia in 1920, and a couple of years later, when I was a student in Berlin, I began to suffer homesickness:

to be exact I was visited by it. But there was no longer any home in Russia: my father had died of typhus and the rest of the family had left the country.

I had known homesickness as a child. I remember it coming over me at twilight when I was staying with an aunt. The house was very quiet. I felt that I was in a mist—she never lit the lamps until it was quite dark—the sunlit hours had vanished as if they had never existed, and the *now* felt endless in memory. I pined for home, as if stretching out towards it.

My new homesickness, in Berlin, did not resemble the old one in the least: it did not come at twilight, or at any definite time; I did not pine: on the contrary it was as if something came to me, bringing a sense of mystery, magic, and loss. For years I did not know how to describe this kind of homesickness.

The next thing I noticed (there seems an infinity of time between the two observations, as there must seem to the baby between rolling over and crawling) was that my homesickness did not come when I might well have expected it: sitting with Russians round the samovar, reminiscing nostalgically about lilac and syringa, school outings in May and wild strawberries and cream, teachers of literature and essays on Turgenev's women, or moved to tears by a line in a Russian song. Such purposeful journeys in chosen company were not at all like my unpredictable, sudden homesickness, my feelings of something precious in the past, reassuring by its mere existence, a fleeting joy, not to be held even for a moment in the mind. It was then that I used to say, being still in my early twenties, that I would give ten years of my life to revisit Russia. In time it dawned on me that some of the Russian emigres I met, whose childhood had been a paradise, did not seem to know my kind of homesickness. So why did I, whose childhood had been full of darkness as well as light, have these intimations of a paradise lost?

I never knew when this homesickness would come or why, nor what started it, and though it was usually gone before my conscious mind seized anything, I sometimes caught an aspect of a street, the hour of the day, a colour, a face: unmistakable fragments of Russian memories. One day I was walking in the Tiergarten when my homesickness touched me: at once I found myself turning my head in the direction it seemed to have come from. That the magic feeling was in a memory of Russia I was certain from the start, but the memory itself eluded me. It did not occur to me that I may have turned towards a sound or a scent similar to one in which the memory was preserved. In fact, I remember thinking that I had turned east, in the direction of Russia.

Another time was when I was coming out of the University, one fine afternoon in summer, in a troubled mood. All my friends had arranged to start their work for the Ph.D. degree, and that afternoon they had asked my why I was so dilatory about it. I had said without thinking: "If I stay another three years I shall never leave Germany. I'll become a German." A friend had comforted me, laughing affectionately: "You'll never become a German." But a mood of anxiety had persisted through the next lecture. As I reached the gateway on to the Unter-den-Linden, I halted. I looked up, and saw a small white cloud slightly to my right: at once I was transported home, to the street in which we lived, on just such a summer afternoon, but with a sky unmistakably stretching over my native town. In memory I am still standing in the gateway aware of the statues of the brothers Humboldt on either side.

To sum up my experiences of involuntary memories in Berlin: they always came suddenly, they brought me great joy, and more often than not I lived in the "then" and forgot the "now." In *Contre Sainte-Beuve*, where Proust described his real experience of involuntary memories, he says that it happens that we come upon an object and a lost sensation thrills in us, but we cannot give it a name. Still more elusive was an element of fear and it was years before I found this confirmed in Proust's experience recorded in *Jean Santeuil*.

So elusive are these experiences of involuntary memories that Aksakov goes so far as to say that when involuntary memories came back to him in childhood the moment was "imperceptible to consciousness."

Often one notices nothing more than a change of mood. If I had not been the kind of person who is drawn to his memories like a musical person to sounds, and had not re-created many of them in words, nothing more than fragments would have been left of my experience of involuntary memories in youth. One thing I remember clearly: saying to myself that they helped me to live; yes, they sustained me and gave me courage, which I needed in the utter insecurity in which I, like so many emigres and refugees, found myself.

It was years before I realized that my homesickness in Berlin had been for the past, that people who have never left their country have similar experiences: we are all exiles from our past. It was then that I was surprised, indeed amazed, that my involuntary memories in Berlin had not reminded me of similar experiences which I had had before I left home: memories of a pale blue figured-velvet outfit, a little yellow magic stick, colors changing in the neck of a drake, for these and other fragments had brought me indescribable joys when I was still a schoolgirl.

Looking back I can see now what made confusion worse confounded. As well as being unpredictable, elusive, and desultory, my involuntary memories did not always bring me joy: some brought only great distress. Some had the glory and freshness of a dream, but others were nightmares. I had a memory of my sister who died before she was four of diptheria. I was nine years old, the eldest, and she the fourth. I had memories of her, playing with Father, unafraid of him, and delighting me as she did him. But the memory of her dying, which came back to me while I was still a child suddenly and unexpectedly, did something terrible to me. I am standing in the doorway, she is lying on her back on the bed, and her face in agony is in a pool of morning sunlight coming from the window opposite. My father on one side, my mother on the other, are desperately trying to help her. Death was not new to me: my grandfather died in our house not many months earlier, neighbors' children had died. I cannot separate the components in my unmitigated horror when this memory suddenly hit me, and I know for certain it happened more than once, but I do remember trying to shake off the memory as one tries to wake from a nightmare.

. . .

As examples of this process of piecemeal transference of material from the unconscious into the conscious mind, I choose now three memories from childhood rather than adolescence or youth, because the former are of first experiences, while the latter have too many antecedents. I have a memory of being bitten by a dog when I was three. I have always remembered this: I am standing outside the closed front door when I suddenly see a big dog bounding towards me, his broken rope trailing on his left; there is no snow or mud, the season is late spring. There is a lull in the traffic—no cabs going to and from the station, no peasants yet going home from the market—it is a middle-of-the-day hour. Another moment which I have always remembered holds the noise of people rushing towards me and lifting me from the ground—a vague moment. But the moment which came back after fifty years was this: the dog has knocked me over, and I am actually turning my head away and burying my face in the earth while the dog is searching between my petticoats and the long black stockings on my left leg for bare flesh to dig his teeth into. It is like a picture in slow motion. Today I am writing only a memory of a memory, but at the time it came back I was actually that child of three; the "then" was "now," and time stood still. The pain I have never remembered. The new moment was a panel which fitted between the other two which had always been in my conscious mind. Harriet Martineau describes very similar experiences in her *Autobiography*: moments came back to her involuntarily after fifty years, and she says: "I know nothing more strange than this power to reenter, as it were, into the narrow mind of an infant, so as to compare it with that of maturity."

The next is a far more complex memory, not of the shock of fear caused by an outside agent, but the shock of bewilderment and doubt, caused by those giants of one's childhood, parents, infinitely complicated by one's own fear and shame. Ever since I can remember, a sporadic involuntary memory used to bring me back my Kiev cousin's pale-blue figured-velvet coat, bonnet, and muff—all of the same material, and my feelings in memory for this celestial outfit were "monstrous," to use Harriet Martineau's word. In that memory the child is held by a woman whose face I do not see. I often heard as a child about this visit of my uncle and aunt from Kiev, a great event, and that they brought their daugher who was not yet two. I was some months older. As a grown-up person, on more than one occasion I have gone into a shop to buy myself a piece of that color, but somehow no shade seemed quite right. Only in the sky have I seen for a moment that exact blue. The memory of the child's blue outfit remained for years a fragment, until once, at a time I cannot fix, an involuntary memory brought me back further moments: I am in bed and it is night; there is a light in the room, but I cannot tell whether it is a candle or a lamp. At the foot of my bed are two women and my uncle, and one of the women is holding my cousin on her left arm, dressed in that heavenly outfit. My desire for it is monstrous, and I cry. I cannot remember my feelings towards my cousin. My uncle says: "It is very cold traveling at night; she can't go without it. But I'll send you an outfit exactly like it from Kiev."

Towards the end of re-creating childhood, fifty-three years after the event, a new moment in the drama came back. I turn my head to the left: for the first time I see Father, and hear him say to Uncle, "Don't take any notice of her" in a tone of impatience, ashamed of me. Immediately I see that I am not merely crying, but making a scene, that Mother is bending over me, on my right, trying to pacify me. Her face I see only vaguely, but Father's is wonderfully clear, or rather was when it came and I immediately wrote down what I had seen. Not only his face, but his figure, as he takes a step towards the foot of the bed where Uncle is standing, and apologizes. He looks very tall: he was, in fact, inches taller than my uncle—to me a giant. For a moment I was that child again, and my father's look, both distinctly different from the way he looked in all other memories and at the same time an unmistakable portrait, fitted perfectly into the gallery of my portraits of him. Moreover, the pattern of his character which emerged from my memories often surprised me and yet was so coherent that I would have had to have been a very great writer to create it. Think of Harriet Martineau, or Aksakov, as they emerge from their real memories, and remember that they invented nothing!

One more example from the age of nine. While trying to write about a teacher who had a great influence on me, I dwelt on a painful memory of her calling me a chatterbox. I rationalized it thus: the memory makes me miserable because I annoyed my teacher, and also, being sensitive to words, I was upset by the harsh, ugly Russian word for chatterbox—*treshchotka*. I carried that painful word in my conscious mind for years. Once, still in Russia, an involuntary memory brought me back the exact place where I was sitting in the classroom when it happened, and with it my bewilderment. Since we changed classrooms each year, I could tell that I was in my first year, and that I was nine. Now this is what happened some forty-five years later. Another involuntary memory brought me back the moment immediately after I had heard the word "chatterbox": I am looking round, wondering whom it is meant for. I hear the teacher say: "I mean you, Polianovskaya," and I see the grey-haired woman with the clever penetrating green eyes turned sternly on me. But I was not aware that I had been talking! Now another panel was revealed: As soon as the bell had rung for break, I had turned with a feeling of relief to the girl on my right. The teacher must have told us to be quiet for another moment; the noise must have subsided, while I continued to talk. But how did it all happen without my knowing? I had neither heard her command, nor known that I had been talking. Now I knew why I looked so bewildered in the original involuntary memory. I recaptured, with complete certainty, myself not at ease, afraid inside, the room too long, the ceiling too far away. These panels fitted perfectly into the picture of the conscious memory, and they account for the fact that I had never had a feeling of shame or guilt about this incident, feelings familiar enough to me, nor had ever felt resentment against the teacher.

Compare this enlarged picture with the old available conscious memory: a child is miserable because it has been called a chatterbox. Write a childhood with your conscious memories only, and you will be rationalizing and inventing sentiments. The specific, individual child will elude you. This is what I had done years earlier. How hopeless that effort had been. Like collecting flotsam which had risen to the surface while the sunken ship remains submerged.

In my memories, as these examples show, I see, feel, react, but I use no words. Other people do: Father says: "Don't take any notice of her!"; the teacher scolds: "Chatterbox!" Often it is the words of other people which give the memory a name, like a label on a picture, making it easy to pick out of the stack. So I have a memory called "The Little Magic Stick," another "Mad Dog"; one is called "The Revolutionaries": all of them words or exclamations of other people. If I do remember my own words they are usually linked to another person's. Later, sometimes, when listening to or reading a story, I was reminded by some expression, such as "rooted to the spot," or "I wish I could sink through the ground" of feelings I had had in early childhood, at some particular moment, but had not expressed. De Quincey says, in a footnote in *Suspiria de Profundis*: "I 'felt.'—The reader must not forget, in reading this and other passages, that, though a child's feelings are spoken of, it is not the child who speaks. I decipher what the child felt in cipher ... a man must be grossly unobservant who is not aware of what I am here noticing, not as a peculiarity of this child or that, but as a necessity of all children." This was written when De Quincey was sixty and re-creating his memories of before he was seven.

How did my memories which came back involuntarily in such numbers in maturity differ from the earlier sporadic memories? In the latter I sometimes observed a link between a present and past sensation, as some of the others did, Chateaubriand, De Quincey, Proust. But the memories which came back in maturity came mostly while I was sitting in my study, blind and deaf to sensations. Proust, shut up in a cork-lined room, did not need a present sensation linked to a past one to bring him back a memory.

The involuntary memories in maturity were much more easily observed: a considerable number came back in a comparatively short time—just over a year. In many cases the new memory enlarged an existing conscious memory. With the memory of Father and his disapproval, my making a scene came back, and also Mother on my right trying to pacify me; with the teacher's words "I mean you, Polianovskaya," and my bewilderment, came the earlier moment when I had turned to the girl on my right, as soon as the bell rang, and had begun chattering. Childhood did not spring out of *one* involuntary memory, as Marcel claims that Combray sprang from one sensation, the taste of the *madeleine*, which brought a memory of childhood. But with each new memory an area was lit up, as actually happened to Proust in real life. (See the Prologue to *Contre Sainte-Beuve*.) An involuntary memory has this in common with the solution of an artistic, mathematical, or any other problem: it is a swift and usually unexpected contribution of the unconscious mind, while the conscious mind is taking infinite pains, yet almost immediately one recognizes its validity, and claims it as one's own.

Many of the memories which, earlier in life, had brought me guilt, shame, fear, no longer distressed me. Whenever a picture became enlarged it showed how errors and excuses had crept in. It was fascinating to find how the mind inserted a lie, concerning sometimes another person, sometimes oneself, without interfering with the physical details of the picture: ingenious rationalisations were put in the place of suppressed moments. When many new moments came back, memories were cleaned up; general explanations, rationalizations, excuses were replaced by the direct, specific reactions to the original complex experience of the individual child. But it was beyond me to clean up all my memories. In some cases I recovered fully a number of memories of an experience till only one moment was missing, the linch-pin. I could tell where it belonged, but could not recover it. I could think of explanations, but I now knew how spurious they could be. The same applies to some of the fears which I could name but failed to recover. For instance, there was fear in my memory of my baby sister on her death-bed. When that memory came back, there was something more in that fear than the shock of the moment of entering the room, seeing her in agony on the pillow in sunlight, and the despairing parents. It was a fear of death, but as it were on a wavelength at the borderline of what is an inaudible tone.

The experience of recovering so many early moments after more than half a lifetime, memories of before the age of seven, is not at all unique. Harriet Martineau recovered such memories after fifty years, Edwin Muir after more than sixty; a study of Aksakov shows that while writing his memories of boyhood in his sixties, some of his all-important early memories were still buried.

. . .

Our past is preserved in a variety of memories of very different nature. Take a person who has an urge to write about his past, for whatever reasons. He begins, let us say, with school and, endowed with a gift for selection, an eye for detail, and a love of words, he succeeds in giving us a picture of the background, the habits and customs of his schooldays. If he tells us they were very happy days, or unhappy, we take it on trust, but we cannot participate in his feelings. What he gives us is a summary of feelings, which very likely would add up differently ten years later. But no writer would be content with a description of the background; he would give us the impact on him of this or that boy, of a teacher, some impressions of his first day at school. Once he had succeeded in recapturing a particular moment, fixed in sensations, time, and space, he would hardly have to dwell on his feelings: they are inherent in the experience of the moment. The kind of autobiographers I have in mind need never have written fiction. Harriet Martineau never did, nor Aksakov, nor William Hutton; all recaptured many memories of moments, and transfused their feelings into us. In every case a pattern emerges, so that we end by knowing them intimately.

I stumbled by chance on the recognition of the different nature of memory of the background and memories of particular moments. It happened when I was working on early memories of before I was seven. In some of them I see only the objects and the little space where

I and the main actors are, as if a shaft of light illumines the center of the stage while all around there is complete darkness. For example, I am woken up one morning, and I see my bed by the wall, and a person whom I know bending over me, but not the rest of the room, not even the foot of the bed. We left that house when I was eight, and though I have a considerable number of memories fixed in this or that spot I have never been able to reconstruct the interior of the house.

One day, while working on some early memories, and living in one of the 1905 Revolution when I was five, I was terribly taken aback. I was looking out of the window, with my eyes on two women running past, just underneath, each frightened in her own way. They had neither hats nor kerchiefs and their hair was bobbed. "The Revolutionaries," Mother said, close behind me: I turned my head to her. To my amazement I realized that the room I was looking at was the sitting-room of the house to which we moved when I was thirteen! I looked again at my other early memories and now realized that I was using the background of the later house. Let me say straight away that this house, unlike the houses where we lived between 1908 and 1913, was on the same side of the road as the first house, not far from it, and not unlike it to look at. The parlor in both houses had two windows which looked out on the street.

I had a number of memories of events in the early house. In some the table in the center of the parlor figured, in others the stove, and in yet another the door in the wall opposite to the windows. I have a memory of the door being open and my standing and looking in amazement at the enormous red sun, low down, behind the trees. I have vivid memories of my paternal grandmother lying on the sofa which stood against the right wall when she had sprained her ankle. It is easy to date this, since she died before I was six. But what stood against the opposite wall? I could not see that wall at all; and then one day I discovered that it had a door in it.

Of the many early memories which came back to me towards the end of working on childhood, one was of my maternal grandmother, standing between the foot of the bed and the shuttered window, dressing in the faint light which came through the chinks round the shutters. I discover that her hair is brown (it was usually hidden in daytime under a kerchief, and at night under a cap); she is not as composed as I knew her, and what greatly amuses and surprises me is that she is trying to be very quiet, not realizing that I am watching her. I have not another memory of being in that room, where I know I slept with her when I was little. In my memory she turns to the right and I see the door which leads into the parlor. It is my first and only memory of that door. I try in imagination to go through the door into the parlor, but I cannot. What I see is the parlor of the 1913 house, but in that house the door did not exist, nor was there a bedroom on that side, for the parlor adjoined our neighbor's house, and a sofa stood along that wall. But in the first house, according to my memories, the sofa stood against the opposite wall, and indeed it could not have stood by the left wall for there was a door there.

Every early memory was an island without a background; the intrinsic objects in such a memory seemed not merely indispensable but immovable, and invariably precious. It struck me that such a memory was like a scene in a play which one can move as a whole, from one theater to another, from one period to another, changing the scenery. But I did not change the position of objects within my island memories: I did not move furniture about, and I did not duplicate objects. If we had not left the first house when I was eight but had stayed there a few more years, and I had acquired a knowledge of the backgound and had used it for my island memories, I should never have known that they were originally without a background.

. . .

The reader may object that we have innumerable fragment-memories: of faces, objects, names, lines of poetry, numbers. I have, for instance, a very poor verbal memory, but a good one for numbers: good enough to carry the telephone numbers of relations and friends in my head. Usually, once a number is no longer in use I forget it. But I remember thinking that I could never forget some numbers, for instance the telephone number of where I lived as a student. I found later that I had forgotten all except the first figure; two other figurers came back to me, but never the fourth or the order of the four. Scientists may one day produce a valid hypothesis for the persistence of such fragments, but it is safe, for the time being, to think that some are preserved by accident, even by some mechanical trick. When I concentrate on stories and poems which I read before I left school I find, again, a large number of fragments floating in my memory. In some cases I remember only the first line of a poem; I remember the name of a writer widely read at that time, and even how many of his novels I read, but not one incident, character, or even title. None of these fragments have ever come back to me involuntarily, never brought emotions, and nothing new was ever added to them. But, in contrast, the fragment memory of reading *Uncle Tom's Cabin* did come back involuntarily, and though it was not enlarged it brought me deep emotion: I am the child of nine or ten, I hold the large precious book in my hands, closed, the cover of the book has a patch of bright red in the lower right corner, and my feeling, caught in the net of sensations, is of amazement at what a book can contain.

To summarize the argument so far: I have shown that memories of events are easily distinguishable from memories of the background; that only memories of events come back involuntarily, bring with them strong emotions, and give a sensation of living in a past moment; that memories of events are of two kinds: whole memories, which always contain a disturbance or a shock, and fragment memories which do not; that because both of these bring back emotions of the same kind and intensity, and both give us the feeling of living in the past, they are probably basically similar, and therefore that the fragments were originally associated with a shock or disturbance which has been lost. I also pointed out that we all carry innumerable other floating fragment-memories—of faces, names, numbers—which are easily distinguishable from the kind of "precious fragments" I have been considering by the fact that they carry no strong emotions, do not give the feeling of living in the past, and never come back involuntarily.

6 An Early Memory from Goethe's Autobiography

Sigmund Freud

Why are a few, often apparently trivial memories of childhood preserved while so many others are lost? Freud, the thoroughgoing determinist, insisted that there must be a reason in every case. Memories that seem insignificant actually stand in some symbolic or associative or concealing relation to deeper, more important ideas. Often, he thought, the relationship can be uncovered by psychoanalysis. This idea, which was also emphasized by Alfred Adler, is discussed in several of Freud's papers; the one reprinted here seems to me especially impressive. It is a tour de force, *in which he explains an early memory of Johann Wolfgang Goethe, Germany's greatest poet. Does that seem an impossible undertaking? Read on.*

"When we try to remember what happened to us in early childhood, we often confuse what others have told us with our own directly perceived experiences." The poet Goethe makes this remark near the beginning of his account of his own life, an account which he began to write when he was 60 years old. It is preceded only by a brief descrip-

From S. Freud, Eine Kindheitserinnerung aus 'Dichtung and Wahrheit', *Imago*, 1917, *5*; translation by Ulric Neisser. The Hubback translation in Vol. 4 of Freud's *Collected Papers* (Basic Books, 1959) is entitled "A childhood recollection from 'Dichtung und Wahrheit'."

tion of his birth "... on August 28, 1749, at noon as the clock struck twelve." A favorable constellation of the stars may have been responsible for his survival: he was almost given up for dead at birth, and strenuous efforts were required before he saw the light of day. After the remark about memory, there is a brief description of the house he grew up in, and especially of an enclosed area that opened on to the street, which the children—he and his younger sister—liked best. But then Goethe really describes only a single event that can be assigned to his "earliest childhood" (before the age of four?), an event of which he seemed to have retained a personal memory. His account of this episode is as follows:

> Across the street lived the three brothers von Ochsenstein, sons of the late Village Mayor. They grew fond of me, and busied themselves with me and teased me in many ways.
> My family loved to tell all sorts of stories about the mischievous tricks to which those otherwise solemn and lonely men encouraged me. I will recount only one of these pranks here. There had been a pottery sale; not only had the kitchen been supplied for some time to come, but miniature crockery of the same sort had been bought for us children to play with. One fine afternoon, when there was nothing doing in the house, I played with my dishes and pots in the rooms (mentioned above) that fronted on the street. Since this didn't come to much, I tossed a piece of crockery out into the street and was delighted by its cheerful crash. The brothers saw how much this amused me, so that I clapped my hands with delight, and called out "another!" I did not hesitate to fling the next pot, and—encouraged by repeated shouts of "another"— a whole assortment of little dishes, saucepans, and jugs onto the pavement. My neighbors continued to signal their approval, and I was more than glad to amuse them. My supplies ran out, but they continued to shout "another!" I hurried straight to the kitchen and fetched the earthenware plates, which of course made an even jollier show as they broke. So I ran back and forth with one plate after another, as I could get them down from the shelf, and when the brothers still claimed to be unsatisfied I hurled every bit of crockery within my reach to ruin in the same way. Only later did someone appear to thwart me and put a stop to it. The damage was done, and in return for all that broken crockery there was at least a wonderful story, which amused the rogues who had been its prime movers till the end of their days.

In preanalytic times this passage would not have been disturbing and could be read without hesitation, but now the analytic conscience has come to life. We have formed definite opinions and have definite expectations about early childhood memories, and would like to suppose that they apply quite generally. It is not a meaningless or insignificant matter when some one particular of a child's life escapes the general forgetting of childhood. On the contrary, one must suppose that what has been retained in memory is also what was most significant for that period of life: either it already had great importance at the time or else it acquired that importance through the effect of later experiences.

It is true that the great significance of such childhood memories is rarely obvious. Most of them appear unimportant or even trivial, and at first it seemed incomprehensible that just these could defy the amnesia of childhood. The individual who had preserved them through long years as his own personal memories could no more do them justice than the stranger to whom he related them. Recognition of their significance required a certain amount of interpretive work— work that either showed how their contents should be replaced by something else, or demonstrated their connection to other unmistakably important experiences for which they had substituted as so-called "screen memories."

Whenever one works through a life history psychoanalytically, one always succeeds in clarifying the meaning of the earliest recollections in this way. As a rule it turns out that the very memory to which the analysand gives primacy, which he tells first as he begins his life story, is the most important and holds the key to the secret chambers of his mental life. But in the case of the little incident related by Goethe, we do not have enough to work with. The ways and means that we use to reach interpretations with our own patients are naturally unavailable here, and it does not seem possible to link the incident itself in any clear way with important experiences of his later life. A prank that damaged some household goods, carried out under the influence of outsiders, is surely not a suitable vignette to stand for everything Goethe tells us about his rich life experience. The impression of complete innocence and irrelevance seems to be confirmed for this childhood memory, which may thus teach us not to push the claims of psychoanalysis too far or to apply them on inappropriate occasions.

I had long since put this small problem out of my mind when chance brought me a patient who presented a similar childhood memory, but in a more comprehensible context. The patient was a highly cultured and intelligent man, twenty-seven years old, whose whole life was consumed by a conflict with his mother that reached into nearly every aspect of his existence, severely impairing the development of his capacity to love and to lead an independent life. The conflict went far back into his childhood, apparently to his fourth year. Before that time he had been a weak and always sickly child, but his memory had turned that difficult time into a paradise because he then possessed the unrestricted affection of his mother, not divided with anyone else. When he was not yet four his brother was born, a brother who is still living today. In reacting to this intrusion, he transformed himself in a headstrong and unmanageable lad who constantly provoked his mother's strictness. He never again got on the right track.

When he became my patient—not least because his bigoted mother detested psychoanalysis—he had long since forgotten his jealousy of his brother, a jealousy which in its time had even led him to try to kill the baby in its cradle. He now treated his younger brother with great respect. Nevertheless certain apparently unmotivated actions, in which he suddenly caused severe injury to animals that he otherwise loved—his hunting dog, and birds that he had carefully tended—were probably best understood as echoes of the hostile impulse once directed against his little brother.

This patient reported that on one occasion, around the time when he tried to kill his hated brother, he had thrown all the crockery he could reach out of the window of his house into the street. The very same thing that Goethe describes in his personal recollections! It is worth noting that my patient was a foreigner who had not had a German education; he had never read Goethe's autobiography.

This piece of information necessarily suggested to me that Goethe's childhood recollection might be interpreted in the way that my patient's story had made irresistible. But could the conditions necessary to support this interpretation be found in the poet's childhood? Goethe himself lays the responsibility for his childhood prank on the urgings of the von Ochsenteins, but his account actually indicates that his neighbors had only cheered him on to continue his own activity. He had begun quite spontaneously. When he gives "Since this (his playing) didn't come to much" as his reason for beginning, we can safely conclude that he was unaware of the real motive of his action at the time he wrote the autobiography, and probably for many years before.

It is known that Johann Wolfgang Goethe and his sister Cornelia were the oldest survivors of a larger set of rather sickly children. Dr. Hanns Sachs has been kind enough to provide me with the dates pertaining to those of Goethe's siblings who died young:

a. Hermann Jakob, christened on Monday, November 27, 1752, reached the age of six years and six weeks; buried on January 13, 1759.

b. Katharina Elisabetha, christened on Monday, September 9, 1754; buried on Thursday, December 22, 1755 (one year and four months old).

c. Johanna Maria, christened on Tuesday, March 29, 1757; buried on Saturday, August 11, 1759 (two years and four months old).

This was certainly the very charming and pretty young girl described by her brother.

d. Georg Adolph, christened on Sunday, June 15, 1760; buried, eight months old, on Wednesday, February 18, 1761.

Goethe's closest sister, Cornelia Friederica Christiana, was born on December 7, 1750, when he was one-and-a-quarter years old. The very small difference in their ages virtually excludes her as an object of jealousy. It is known that when children's emotional life is awakened, they never react so strongly against the siblings who are already there; they rather direct their antipathy toward the new arrivals. Then, too, it would be impossible to reconcile the scene we are trying to interpret with Goethe's tender age at the time of (and just after) Cornelia's birth.

Goethe was three-and-a-quarter years old when his first brother, Hermann Jakob, was born. About two years later, when he was about five, his second sister arrived. Both ages must be considered in trying to date the crockery-smashing incident. The first may be more likely; it also corresponds more closely with the case of my patient, who was about three-and-three-quarters when his brother was born.

It is worth noting that brother Hermann Jakob, to whom this attempt at interpretation seems to lead, was not such a fleeting guest in Goethe's nursery as the later siblings. Surprisingly, there is not a single word about him in his elder brother's life story.[1] He attained more than six years of age, and when he died Johann Wolfgang was nearly ten years old. Dr. Ed. Hitschmann, who was kind enough to make his notes on this matter available to me, has expressed this opinion:

> Young Goethe was also not unhappy at a younger brother's death. At least his mother gave the following account, reported by Bettina Brentano: "It seemed strange to his mother that he shed no tears at the death of his brother Jakob, who was his playmate; indeed, he seemed somewhat irritated at the lamentations of his parents and sisters. When the mother later asked the obstinate boy if he hadn't loved his brother, he ran to his room and brought out a pile of papers from under his bed. They were covered with lessons and stories, and he told her that he had done all this to teach it to his brother." Thus it seems that the older

---

[1] *[Freud added the following footnote to the article when it was republished in 1924.]* I will use this opportunity to retract an incorrect statement that never should have occurred. Later on in the first volume, the younger brother *is* mentioned and described. This is done in the course of Goethe's recollections of the burdensome illness of childhood, which afflicted his brother "not a little." "He was of a delicate constitution, quiet and self-willed; we never had a real relationship with one another. Also he did not really survive the years of childhood." *[Apparently Freud himself made a Freudian slip in his eagerness to establish what he thought was a Freudian slip on Goethe's part.]*

brother had at least enjoyed playing father to the younger, showing off his own superiority.

We can conclude that the throwing out of the crockery was a symbolic, or more precisely a magical act. By this act the child (Goethe as well as my patient) gives vigorous expression to his wish that the disturbing intruder be eliminated. We do not need to deny the delight that the child takes in the crashing objects. The fact that an action is pleasurable in itself does not prevent—indeed, it invites—repetition in the service of other motives. But we do not believe that delight in jingling and smashing could have assured these childish pranks a permanent place in the memories of grown men. We do not even hesitate to introduce an additional complication into our account of the motivation for this act. The child who breaks the crockery knows perfectly well that he is being naughty, and that the adults will scold him for it. If this knowledge does not restrain him, he probably has some grudge against his parents; he wants to show how bad he is.

Taking delight in breaking and in broken things would also be possible if the child just threw the fragile objects on the floor. On this basis, throwing them out the window into the street would remain unexplained. But "out" seems to be an essential component of the magical act, which stems from its hidden meaning. The new baby is to be removed through the window, perhaps because it came through the window in the first place. The whole affair would then be equivalent to what we are told was the response of one child when he was informed that the stork had brought him a little sister. "Let him take her away again" was his suggestion.

However, we are fully aware how dubious it is—apart from any internal uncertainties—to base the interpretation of a childhood event on a single analogy. For this reason I withheld my interpretation of the little scene from Goethe's autobiography for many years. Then one day I had a patient who began his analysis with the following sentences, which I reproduce verbatim:

> I am the oldest of eight or nine brothers and sisters.[2] One of my first memories is of my father sitting on his bed in his nightclothes, laughingly telling me that I had acquired a brother. I was then three-and-three-quarters years old; that is the difference in age between me and my closest brother. Then I know that shortly afterwards (or was it the year before?)[3] I threw various objects—brushes, or maybe just one brush, and

---

[2] A striking momentary lapse. Unquestionably it was already produced by the wish to get rid of the brother. (cf. Ferenczi, On the formation of transient symptoms during analysis, *Zentralblatt für Psychoanalyse*, 1912, 2.)

[3] This expression of doubt, attached to the most essential part of the patient's statement, is a form of resistance. The patient himself retracted it shortly thereafter.

shoes and other things—out the window into the street. I also have a still earlier memory. When I was two years old I spent the night with my parents in a hotel room in Linz when we were traveling to Salzkammergut. I was so restless during the night and cried so much that my father had to hit me.

In the face of this testimony I had to abandon all doubt. When a patient in the analytic setting produces two ideas one after the other, almost in a single breath, we must interpret their proximity as a causal connection. So it was as if the patient had said "Because I learned that I had acquired a brother, I threw those things into the street soon thereafter." The throwing out of the brushes, shoes, etc. is recognizable as a reaction to the birth of the brother. It is also helpful that this time the thrown objects were not crockery but other things, probably just those that happened to be within reach. In this way the throwing out itself is revealed as the essential element of the action. The delight in jingling and breaking, and the nature of the objects on which the "execution is carried out" are revealed as variable and inessential.

Naturally the principle of relatedness must also be valid for the patient's third memory, which was placed at the end of the sequence although it is actually the earliest. It is easily applied. We understand that the two-year-old child was restless because he couldn't stand his father and mother being together in bed. On the journey it was probably impossible to prevent the child from witnessing this intimacy. Of the feelings that were aroused in the tiny jealous child at that time, a bitterness against women remained as a continuing source of disturbance in the development of his later life.

After these two experiences, I suggested to a meeting of the Psychoanalytic Society that behavior of this sort in young children might not be so rare. In response, Dr. von Hug-Hellmuth has made two further observations available to me. Here are her reports:

I

At about three-and-a-half years, little Erich "very suddenly" acquired the habit of throwing everything that didn't suit him out the window. But he also did it to things that weren't in his way and had nothing to do with him. On his father's birthday, when he was three years, four-and-a-half-months old, he hauled a heavy rolling pin from the kitchen into another room and flung it out of a window of the third-floor apartment onto the street. A few days later the mortar-pestle went the same way, followed by a pair of his father's heavy mountaineering boots that he first had to take out of their storage box.[4]

At that time his mother had a miscarriage; she had been seven or eight months pregnant. After that the little boy "seemed to have been

---

[4]He always chose heavy objects.

transformed, he was so good and so quietly gentle." In the fifth or sixth month he had repeatedly said to his mother, "Mommy, I'm going to jump on your stomach," or "Mommy, I'll squash your stomach flat." In October, a few days before the miscarriage, he said, "If I really have to have a brother, let it at least not be till after Christmas."

II

A young woman of nineteen spontaneously offered the following as her earliest recollection:

I see myself sitting under the table in the dining room, ready to creep out, feeling terribly disobedient. On the table is my coffee-mug—I can see the pattern of the porcelain clearly, even now—which I had just been going to throw out the window when my grandmother happened to come into the room.

The fact was that nobody had been concerning themselves with me, and as a result a "skin" had formed on the coffee—which I always found loathsome and still do.

My brother, who is two-and-a-half years younger than I am, was born that day; that was why nobody had time for me.

They still talk about how unbearable I was that day. Around noon I threw my father's favorite glass off the table; I soiled my dress several times; I was in the foulest possible mood all day long. I also smashed one of my bathtub toys in my rage.

It is hardly necessary to comment on these two cases. They confirm, without any additional analysis, that the child's bitterness about the expected or actual appearance of a competitor expresses itself in the act of throwing things out the window as well as by other naughty and destructive deeds. The "heavy objects" in the first case probably symbolize the mother herself, at whom the child's anger is directed so long as the new baby has not yet actually appeared. The three-and-a-half-year old boy knows that his mother is pregnant, and is quite sure that she is sheltering the baby in her body. This is reminiscent of "Little Hans"[5] and his particular fear of heavily loaded wagons.[6] In the second case it is noteworthy that the child was so young, only two-and-a-half years old.

---

[5] Freud, S. Analysis of a phobia in a five-year-old child. In *Collected Papers, Vol. 3.* New York: Basic Books, 1959.

[6] Some time ago, a woman of more than fifty years brought me a further confirmation of this symbol of pregnancy. She had often been told that as a little child, so young that she could barely talk, she used to drag her father over to the window excitedly whenever a heavily laden furniture van passed on the street. By using her memories of the house she lived in, it was possible to establish that she must have been younger than two-and-three-quarters at the time. Her closest younger brother was born about that time, and they moved to a new home to accommodate the increased size of the family. At about the same period she often had an anxious sensation, just before she fell asleep, that something unnaturally large was coming toward her; simultaneously "her hands seemed to swell up so fat."

If we now return to Goethe's early memory, and put what we think we have learned from the cases of these other children in its place, we find a perfectly comprehensible connection that would otherwise have remained undiscovered. It runs as follows: "I was a child of fortune; fate kept me alive although I had been given up for dead when I came into the world. The same fate got rid of my brother, so that I did not have to share my mother's love with him." From there the train of his thoughts goes on to another person who died in that early period of his life: his grandmother, who lived like a quiet and friendly ghost in another room of his home.

As I have already said elsewhere, he who has been the unquestioned darling of his mother will keep that feeling of victory, that certainty of success, for the rest of his life. It is a feeling that not infrequently brings real success in its wake. And a remark like "My strength is rooted in my relationship with my mother" would have been an entirely appropriate way for Goethe to begin the story of his life.

7   Childhood Memories

Samuel Waldvogel

*This is the classical questionnaire study of early
childhood recollections. There have been many
others—see Dudycha and Dudycha (1941) for a review
of the literature—but Waldvogel's questionnaire is
probably the largest. The present brief excerpt from
his monograph includes only the basic age data and
some observations on sex differences.*

. . . This investigation was designed to study individual differences
among college students in their ability to recall childhood experiences.
Differences in both the frequency and affective character of memories
from the first eight years of life were studied. Further, an attempt was
made to relate these differences to various psychological traits—both
intellective and nonintellective.

The subjects, numbering 48 males and 76 females, recorded their
memories [in writing] during two recall periods lasting 85 minutes
each and separated by an interval ranging from 35 to 40 days. The
second recall period, which was not announced in advance, was used
as a check on the first, and the instructions for both periods were
identical.

While wide variations in the number of memories were noted
among the subjects, it was found that the averages for males and
females were remarkably similar, indicating very little, if any, sex differences in this respect. In order to determine individual consistency,
the number of memories of each subject for the first recall period was
correlated with the number of each for the second period. The coefficients were found to be .70 for the males and .76 for the females. It
was felt that these coefficients were sufficiently high to warrant the
conclusion that individual differences in the ability to recall childhood

From S. Waldvogel, The frequency and affective character of childhood memories, *Psychological Monographs*, 1948, 62, Whole No. 291.

events are not of a purely haphazard nature, some persons being able to recall consistently more of their childhood experiences than others.

A comparison of the memories for each of the two periods showed that an average of almost 50 percent of those recorded during the second period had not been recorded previously. Hence a total recall score was obtained by adding the new memories of the second period to the total of the first period. When this was done the average combined total was roughly 51 memories for males and 53 memories for females.

. . .

AGE OF RECALLED EXPERIENCES

The subjects were asked to approximate the age—to the nearest year at which each incident occurred. Behind this instruction was the recognition that only a rough approximation could be hoped for, but it was felt that even an approximate age for each experience might indicate significant age trends. The actual results—their tenuous nature granted—was quite revealing in this respect. The total and average number of memories appearing at each age, are included in Table 7-1. Since these data were derived from the combined recall scores, every unique memory recorded during both recall periods is represented. For those memories that were repeated, the age assigned them at the first recall was entered in the compilation of results.

The most notable feature of this table is the steady progression upward with age. Relatively few experiences are recalled before the third year. This is consistent with the investigations of the first child-

TABLE 7-1
Total and average number of memories recorded for each age

Age	Male		Female	
	Total	Average	Total	Average
Below 1	0	0	1	0.01
1–2	3	0.06	12	0.16
2–3	24	0.50	63	0.83
3–4	88	1.83	264	3.47
4–5	318	6.63	526	6.92
5–6	557	11.60	848	11.16
6–7	689	14.35	1051	13.83
7–8	776	16.17	1267	16.67

hood recollection, which are in agreement in placing the average age of first recall between the third and fourth year. Further, these studies indicate that the average age of first recall for females is slightly lower than for males, which is also in conformity with other results.[1] This conformity may be regarded as support for the reliability of the above data. A further check on reliability was made by determining the extent of correspondence between the ages given at the first recall and the ages given at the second recall for those memories that were repeated. This was accomplished by calculating the coefficient of contingency, or C, for the two series of ages. For males C, was .79 and for females C was .73. These coefficients indicate an appreciable degree of consistency from one report to the next. The age assigned to a memory is not, then, merely a chance matter. In this case consistency does not necessarily establish the authenticity of the ages. It is quite possible that the subjects were consistently wrong in reporting ages, but it is also conceivable that they were consistently correct. At any rate consistency is a *sine qua non*. Had there been no consistency from one report to the next, the age data would have been valueless.

. . .

When the memories were plotted according to the age of their origin, it was found that there was an increment from year to year which took the form of an ogive and seemed to parallel the growth of language and memory during childhood. This suggested, first, that memory for childhood events might be related to the level of mental development at the time of their occurrence; and, second, that factors besides repression determine the extent and content of childhood recollections. Indeed the relatively large number of memories from the early years (elicited under far from ideal conditions) and their gradual increase with age stand in apparent contradiction to the Freudian doctrines of infantile amnesia.

When the memories were studied in terms of their affect, it was found that the emotions which the subjects recalled as having pre-

---

[1]Dudycha and Dudycha (1933), who carefully authenticated the age of their subjects' first recollection, found that the average age was 3.67 for adolescent males and 3.50 for adolescent females. This corresponds quite closely to the results of other investigations, especially Gordon (1928), who obtained average ages of 3.64 for males and 3.40 for females.

In the present experiment the available data do not permit the computation of a precise average because the subjects were asked to indicate age only to the nearest year; and further they were not instructed to indicate which of their recollections was the first. Nevertheless a rough measure of average age of first recall was computed by averaging the ages at which memories first appeared for each subject, on the assumption that the memories were fairly evenly distributed for each year. This method yielded average ages of 3.64 for the males and 3.23 for the females, which parallel the preceding results quite strikingly.

vailed at the time of the original experiences were numerous and varied. Most commonly experienced was joy, which constituted about 30 percent of the total. Next in frequency was fear, about 15 percent, followed by pleasure, anger, grief, and excitement, all between 5 and 10 percent. Only very slight differences were noted between male and female subjects. The great variety and intensity of emotion accompanying these early experiences challenges the contention that childhood memories are for the most part banal screen memories.

Recall of pleasant events was more frequent than unpleasant or neutral events. In round numbers, pleasant memories constituted about 50 percent of the total, unpleasant memories about 30 percent, and neutral memories about 20 percent. While pleasant memories predominated with most subjects, some reversed this trend; and it was suggested that the terms, memory-optimist and memory-pessimist, used by other investigators, might also apply in this instance. The ratio of the number of unpleasant memories to the total number of memories (U/T) was used as an index of the degree of optimism–pessimism That this trait was reasonably consistent was demonstrated by correlating the U/T ratios of the first and second recall periods. The coefficients obtained were .64 for the males and .57 for the females. It is also interesting to note that while there was a gradual increase of the number of experiences recalled with age, the relative incidence of pleasant, unpleasant, and neutral memories remained quite constant from year to year.

Individual differences in the frequency of recall and the degree of optimism–pessimism were both studied in relation to the following traits: general intelligence, memory, emotional stability, ascendance-submission, and radicalism-conservatism. The results of these comparisons were essentially inconclusive. However, it was felt that the lack of observed relationship between psychological traits and childhood memory could easily have been due to the limitations of the measuring devices employed, and were not necessarily indicative of the absence of such a relationship.

. . .

REFERENCES

Dudycha, G. J. and Dudycha, M. M. Some factors and characteristics of childhood memories. *Child Development*, 1933, *4*, 265–278.

Dudycha, G. J. and Dudycha, M. M. Childhood memories: A review of the literature. *Psychological Bulletin*, 1941, *38*, 668–682.

Gordon, K. A study of early memories. *Journal of Delinquency*, 1928, *12*, 129–132.

8 Transformations of Memory in Everyday Life

Marigold Linton

In 1972, Marigold Linton undertook a singular memory experiment. Like Hermann von Ebbinghaus, who had founded the classical psychology of memory about a century earlier, she was her own subject. Every day she recorded at least two events from her own life; every month she tested her ability to remember, order, and date a sample of the events she had previously recorded. Linton has presented the basic results of the study elsewhere; here she reflects on some of its implications. How can we understand the effects of "emotionality" and "importance" on memory? What are the long-run consequences of repetition? What kinds of events will be remembered best? The answers are often surprising. Particularly intriguing is Linton's very un-Ebbinghausian forgetting curve: it is linear with a slope of 5 percent a year. How can we reconcile such a pattern of forgetting with the existence of memories more than twenty years old? Linton's own explanation, based on the diminishing effectiveness of the original retrieval cues, suggests that a different forgetting function might be observed with other forms of cueing. Perhaps she is right; perhaps, on the other hand, most of our oldest memories are the product of repeated rehearsal and reconstruction. So far, these are the only systematic data we have.

This article was written especially for the present volume.

Some years ago, my curiosity about how memory functions in a naturalistic setting led me to an investigation of my own memory. During the course of this six-year study I developed event items based on my own experiences, and later attempted to reconstruct the probable dates of the events' occurrences. (Dating may seem a rather restricted, perhaps even uninteresting behavior, but its quantifiability continues to appeal to me.) Performing a prolonged study on personal life events has, I believe, provided me with a unique perspective on memory functioning; perhaps some of these insights as well as a description of the unforeseen difficulties I encountered in conducting this research may be informative to others. I begin by briefly describing the study (more detailed presentations appear in Linton 1975, 1978) and then focus on issues that may be loosely labeled (1) episodic/semantic transformations in memory, and (2) emotion/memory interactions.

A LITTLE ABOUT THE STUDY

The stimuli for this long-term study were brief descriptions of events from my life written each day throughout the study's six-year duration. At first it seemed there might be a set of simple heuristics for describing events, but rather shortly I abandoned the search for simple regularities. So wide a range of content and presentation styles may be employed to specify events that the elements necessary or sufficient to describe "an event" have continued to elude me. To avoid unnecessary narrowness in my event pool I accepted all brief unique descriptions. (No description exceeded 180 letters, and when it was written, every item was discriminable from all other events then accessible in memory.) These criteria were dictated by my major dependent variables: dating accuracy (only unique items can be uniquely dated) and response speed (reading times must be brief/uniform enough not to differentially contribute to memory-search response times). Each newly written item was rated for salience on a number of dimensions. I return to emotionality ratings in a later section.

Memory tests proceeded as follows: Once a month items were drawn semirandomly from the accumulated event pool. After reading a pair of randomly paired event descriptions, I estimated their chronological order and attempted to reconstruct each item's date. Next I briefly classified my memory search (for example, I might "count backwards" through a series of similar events, as school quarters, Psychonomic Society meetings, and the like) and reevaluated each item's salience. After six years the experiment had reached imposing dimensions. I had written more than 5,500 items (a minimum of two times each day) and tested (or retested) 11,000 items (about 150 items each month). Item generation required only a few minutes each day but the monthly test was extremely laborious, lasting 6–12 hours. The time required for individual memory searches varied widely from month to month as well as from item to item in the course of a single day.

MEMORY: SOME CONCEPTUAL ISSUES

The study of autobiographical memory is complicated by the modifications and changes that any newly encoded information undergoes as the result of interactions with information already in memory and through reinterpretations of existing data forced by the acquisition of subsequent knowledge. I'm speaking therefore, not only of the role that semantic memory plays in interpreting new information, but also of progressive changes in interpretation and evaluation that occur as the target information interacts with relevant information, either existing or acquired later, in the knowledge base. In our personal history, as in political or cultural histories, the importance of a singular event may be interpreted in a variety of ways, from differing historical perspectives, and may be reinterpreted repeatedly as its role in different contexts emerges. And in personal, as in many other histories, first or early events in sequences receive royal treatment, with better encoding and associated recall.

Transformation from Episodic to Semantic Memory

The issues to be raised are probably best understood if I first present my conclusion concerning the acquisition of episodic and semantic memories. Figure 8-1, which depicts this conclusion, may be summarized: "Number of trials (or experiences) has contrastive effects on episodic and semantic memories. Increased experience with any particular event class increases semantic (or general) knowledge about the event and its context. Increased experience with similar events, however, makes specific episodic knowledge increasingly confusible, and ultimately episodes cannot be distinguished." Examples of this pervasive phenomenon abound in both the laboratory and everyday experience. An event in my file notes that I was invited to serve on a distinguished board that met occasionally in a distant city. I looked forward to the first meeting with trepidation. My arrival in the city confronted me with a new airport, a new system of surface transportation, new hotel. My meeting with the new board provided 25 new names, faces, and intellectual/social styles to be absorbed. Following

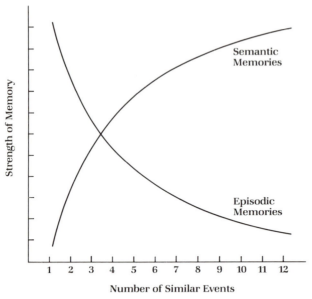

FIGURE 8-1
Number of trials (or experiences) has contrastive effects on episodic and semantic memories. Increased experience with any particular event class increases semantic (or general) knowledge about the event and its context. Increased experience with similar events, however, makes specific episodic knowledge increasingly confusable, and ultimately episodes cannot be distinguished.

this unique, attention-compelling experience this trip would be readily recalled as a discrete episode. It was long anticipated and well encoded, and the specific configuration was easily distinguished from other memory compounds. Emphasizing semantic rather than episodic memory would produce a different result (although not one documented in my study). What do I know about the airport layout? How do the ground transportation systems operate and interact? What are the board members' names? What are their relationships with each other? These questions would be vaguely and inadequately answered after only a single contact. I might know (immediately after the trip) that I was on a United flight and caught a Yellow Cab at the airport. I might recall the names of several individuals who had particularly struck me, and might remember some provocative conversational topics but I have poor understanding and poor recall of the complex interrelations among these fragments.

   Some years later, after many meetings, I have lost my capacity to reliably pinpoint particular board meetings and I could not describe proceedings of most meetings—except perhaps the first, and (if it were recent) the last. But if required I could map the airport terminal; evaluate the airport to city transportation systems; confidently introduce committee members, and reliably predict board members' interaction styles.

By what mechanism do events or episodes become confusable with repetition? It seems plausible that a fairly small number of general schemes provide the basic framework for storing episodic information. These schemes organize the event in terms of actors, action, location, and the like. These elements that comprise the building blocks of *episodic* memories are themselves information from our semantic store. Furthermore, as with all semantic knowledge, some is well and some is less well learned. A specific event is an unique *configuration* of these elements. As our experience with a particular event type increases, we seem at first to make finer discriminations among related events; we may subdivide elements (for example, by characterizing people, actions, or locations more precisely) and identify more complex configurations of these elements. At some point, however, this expansion of elements and configuration ends. The elements, remember, already comprise part of our semantic knowledge. As similar events are repeated, the specific configurations—the patterns that link familiar elements to form unique episodes—themselves become a well-established potentially confusable part of semantic knowledge. This lack of discriminability may be plausibly attributed to encoding or to memorial difficulties: perhaps discriminations with the required resolution are not routinely made among real-world events, or perhaps desultory memory is capable of handling only relatively short descriptive chains.

The issue of memory transformations is reflected in a number of problems I encountered as I wrote events and in the successful and unsuccessful reinstatement of events in my dating exercises. I turn now to these problems.

Problems from the Study

1. **Writing items.** When I designed my study I had intended to include in my event pool each day's most salient experiences. As the preceding discussion suggests, it was relatively simple to characterize the "first event" in some on-going life sequence. A large number of cues suffice: "I go to New York for the first time." "I meet with the Carnegie Foundation for the first time." "I meet Clark Kerr for the first time." In fact, "X, for the first time" has unparalleled effectiveness as a cue. (My event writing strategy permitted any particular first item to sometimes include and sometimes omit this unique specification.) As any series of similar or related events in my life became long, the length

of the descriptions required to uniquely characterize particular events also increased. Indeed, many events could not be adequately characterized in the space permitted. Thus my file—whose contents are shaped by the requirements of brevity and uniqueness—is silent on whole sets of activities that comprise the warp and woof of my existence. One could scarcely know that I teach, or spend many hours each day in academic activities. A perusal of the file hints only faintly of my passion for racquet sports, my enjoyment of good food, or my pleasure in interacting with loved ones. I simply cannot adequately characterize the year's two-hundredth hour in the classroom, my three-hundredth racquet match, or the one-hundredth dinner with friends. But some items do enter: I teach a new class or perform a novel demonstration; I find a new racquet partner, or we find half a boysenberry pie on the court surface; a new restaurant opens, or a special friend makes a rare visit to town. These minor variations (a la Von Restorff) permit a few such items to gleam distinctively among their blurred and coalesced brethren.

2. Forgetting, failing to discriminate, and related processes. My major experimental task was to order and date items. If I could not recall an item from my description, the task ranged from difficult to nonsensical; consequently I eliminated all "forgotten" items from the event pool. Deciding what was forgotten was more complex than I had anticipated. Early in the study I began to distinguish two kinds of recall failure: (a) the "failure to distinguish" an item from others in memory at test time, and (b) simple "failure to recall" the event. Although it is unremarkable in retrospect, I was surprised to identify loss of item distinctiveness as a major source of "forgetting." I hadn't forgotten items in the sense I had anticipated—instead my written descriptions cued a number of plausible events in memory, or sometimes only a generalized memory; in particular, descriptions that discriminated perfectly among early memories in event sequences did not adequately specify happenings as the sequences lengthened.

Thus, part of my forgetting depended on the episodic to semantic transition I've described. Moreover, the study grossly underestimated transitions as a source of memory loss because items most susceptible to these changes were never written. (Recall that I included only items for which I could formulate descriptions that distinguished them from any other remembered events.) One item from the file poignantly captures the difficulty of creating items impervious to memory changes produced by the occurrence of unanticipated events. In 1972 I wrote an item approximately as follows: "I xerox the final draft of the statistics book and mail it to Brooks/Cole." Some years later after the *third* "final draft" had been submitted this item was singularly nondiscriminating.

Which event did I mean? Was the item written when I naively believed that the first draft would be the "final draft"? after the second submission when it was clear that the *final* draft had now been submitted? or was this allusion to the third submission, which historically became the "final draft"? Sometimes, of course, it was possible to guess from the language employed where an event occurred in a sequence. For example, it is most likely that an unqualified statement about "final drafts" refers to the first event in a sequence.

In short, I failed to distinguish events that contained familiar elements and configurations. These configurations pointed not to a single memorial event, but to two or more happenings. Items that I "did not recall" differed somewhat from those that I could "not distinguish." The former items often had lower salience and were more likely to be described in vague terms; in addition, the elements and configurations were sometimes relatively unfamiliar. Such items referred to plausible events that were simply not accessible in memory. Yet another kind of forgetting began to occur late in the study. During the fourth and subsequent years I began to encounter a few old items that simply did not "make sense." Often whole phrases were uninterpretable. Were these items badly written? Successful tests without comprehension problems in earlier years argue against this possibility. Thus, items that I could interpret meaningfully shortly after they were written did not, at the time of the crucial test, permit me to reconstruct a sensible whole. That these nonsense items comprised scraps and fragments from my life made this experience particularly uncomfortable. I could hear my voice describe fragments from my own life that were somehow completely meaningless. Presumably successful event descriptions reinstate general memory (semantic) frameworks that permit items to be interpreted and understood. When this cuing fails— when the semantic framework is not reinstated—I cannot reintegrate the event, and the item seems not to make sense. Total recall failure occurs after much longer delays (after four to six years) than do the other kinds of forgetting (observed as early as the first year) presumably because general semantic frameworks are more robust than specific episodic or semantic information.

3. A forgetting function. I originally expected a rapid loss of to-be-forgotten events that would produce a function resembling Ebbinghaus' classic negatively accelerated forgetting curve. Forgetting in my study should, of course, require longer than the days or weeks characteristic of Ebbinghaus' study because: (a) I employed easily encoded, meaningful, and memorable items, and (b) the study's cued-recall task allowed greater accessibility of memories than did Ebbinghaus' free-recall tasks.

These considerations, however, nowhere suggest that the shape of the present more durable curve would not be negatively accelerated. I was surprised, therefore, when several analyses suggested that items were lost from my event memory at a linear rate. Remember that although dating accuracy was my major dependent variable, if items were forgotten I removed them from my file. Thus, forgetting was a second, almost inadvertant, dependent variable. I began by considering all items written in any particular year (for example, 1,345 items describe events from 1972) and computed the number of items forgotten during each subsequent year as a percentage of the total number of items written in that target year. Cumulative forgetting curves* for each year of the study were similar and a composite function (Figure 8-2: Number forgotten/Number written) shows average forgetting for all years of the study. Fewer than 1 percent of the items were forgotten

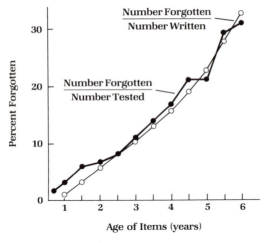

Age of Items (years)

FIGURE 8-2
Percent of items forgotten during six years as a function of number of items written or number of items tested. "Number forgotten/Number written" is a cumulative function; "Number forgotten/Number tested" is a noncumulative function. Both are *composites* over the appropriate years.

---

*[That is, curves that show what proportion of the items originating in a given target year T had been tested, found to be forgotten, and removed from the pool by the end of a specified test year T + k; they are "cumulative" because they include not only items tested and found to be forgotten in year T + k itself but also in all earlier years T, T + 1, T + 2, ... There is a different cumulative curve for each target year (those for the later years of the study having fewer points because there were fewer subsequent test years); corresponding points on these curves were averaged to form the composite "Number forgotten / Number written" function plotted in Figure 8-2.]

during the calendar year in which they were written (to consider 1972 again, ten items were written and forgotten in that year). After the first year, however, items were forgotten at the relatively even rate of 5–6 percent each year. Thus, while Ebbinghaus found rapid forgetting followed by slow forgetting, the present function indicates almost linear forgetting after an early period of almost perfect retention.

Two factors make it likely that this function actually underestimates forgetting rate. First, as items are successively tested, forgotten, and dropped from the pool, the remaining events are increasingly salient and memorable. Second, only a small subset of items of any target age is tested at any time (this is especially significant in the first year when many nonmemorable items have never been tested); hence, to consider forgetting against the baseline of all items originally written probably yields an underestimate of forgetting. These considerations suggested that a second function relating the number forgotten to the *number tested* at a specified test time* (rather than the total number of items written) might provide a more accurate estimate of forgetting rate.[†] A comparison of the resulting, approximately linear, function (Figure 8-2: Number forgotten / Number tested) with the earlier curve shows that not only have 30 percent of the items been forgotten in six years, but that in the sixth year forgetting is apparent in 30 percent of the items tested from the restricted population that remains. The first (cumulative) and the second (noncumulative) functions differ most in the first year and a half with the latter providing a higher estimate of forgetting in this period than does the earlier one.

"Failure to recall" and "failure to distinguish" contribute unequally to the total forgetting described. Because items are complex, some features of a single item may be forgotten while others are confused—thus both kinds of failure may contribute to an item's being forgotten. While the two kinds of forgetting can be discriminated, the general pattern appears to be that for young items, both failures occur about equally often. After the end of the second year, simple recall failures become increasingly frequent until they occur almost twice as often as confusions.

---

*[As noted earlier, about 150 items were tested monthly, 1,800 annually. In 1972, the first year of the study, all tests were necessarily of 1972 items, so the tested subset of those items was very large. (It did not exhaust the pool, however; chance determines which items are selected for test, and many are tested repeatedly.) In later years the tested subsets for various ages became appreciably smaller.]

†[Suppose that m_T items from target year T were selected for test in year T + k, and f_T of them turned out to be forgotten. The m_T tested items are a sample of the M_T items from year T that were still in the pool at that time, so the ratio f_T/m_T estimates the fraction of those remaining items that were no longer in a memorable state. This ratio is called "Number forgotten/Number tested" in Figure 8-2, where it has been averaged over target years and plotted as a function of event age.]

Thus, real-world episodic memories not only were found to be considerably more durable than laboratory induced memories, but over the six-year study the course of forgetting appeared to be almost linear. There are two ways that this linear forgetting of episodic memories may be viewed. If one assumes that the memories themselves are being lost, it would be plausible to hypothesize that the forgetting curve would become negatively accelerated within a few additional years (if the present rate of forgetting—about 5–6 percent a year—continued, in only a dozen more years all items in the pool would be forgotten). An alternative assumption is that even a real-world study of autobiographical memory is more "contrived" than one would guess. I expect memories to be long-lasting because, like everyone else, I can access a large number of very old memories, some of them from two or three decades past. The memories are "real" but the cues with which I dealt in this study were "real" in that sense only at the time that I wrote them. With the passage of every year the cues become more "contrived" and removed from both my contemporaneous memory organization and from cues that I would spontaneously employ to elicit these memories. If this latter notion were correct, it would be possible for most, if not all, existing cue cards to become inadequate over time; that is, these cues would not elicit personal memories which might, however, remain moderately accessible to cues more suited to my contemporary memory. This decreased accessibility of memories to my cues may be responsible for the differences in kind of forgetting. Confusions may occur when the matches between cues and memories are beginning to break down while simple forgetting and total recall failure would reflect more extreme mismatches between cues and memory organization.

Summary

Some recall difficulties in everyday memory result from episodic to semantic transformations associated with repetitions of the same or similar occurrences in our lives. In representations of personal events a number of basic semantic elements are repeatedly used and eventually configurations of these basic elements are themselves repeated, making it difficult to provide unique event descriptions. Although less significant than simple forgetting, for the present set of everyday materials decreased distinctiveness is responsible for a major memory loss. Somewhat remarkably, overall forgetting for these autobiographical items is almost linear (about 5 percent a year).

In this section I have tried to illustrate difficulties associated with describing events and some of the complexities associated with forgetting them. In the following section I make a tentative effort to describe problems in understanding the relationship between emotionality and recall.

EMOTIONALITY AND RECALL

For more than 75 years psychologists have wrestled with the relationship between materials' emotionality and recall. Although Freud cautioned that negative memories may be forgotten through repression, our common experience is that important emotional events are often easily recalled even after many years. Such a prolonged and frustrating inquiry suggests a complex relationship between emotionality and recall. My experiment, which permitted me to examine changes in recall over many years' time with complex and salient life-related materials, seemed an ideal context in which to examine these variables. In the following I suggest some memorial and other factors that complicate this relationship.

Throughout the study I provided emotionality and importance ratings (among others) for each event item, both at the time it was written and each time its recall was tested. Although analyses of these data are not complete, the correlations between initial salience ratings and the recall measures will almost certainly remain small and unimpressive. (The relationship between current salience ratings and recall is stronger but this correlation cannot be easily interpreted.) What are some of the reasons that initial emotionality ratings are not useful in predicting event recall? A number of variables complicate efforts to deal with emotionality over time. First, the ratings of a single event may change over time. Second, superficially similar events do not receive similar ratings over time. Third, the emotionality of ongoing pieces of life, or of memories is inherently difficult to judge.

Emotionality: Habituation, Contrast, and Reinterpretation

Why do emotionality ratings of events change? Repetition of events is an important factor in predicting changed emotionality for similar events; most commonly, the emotionality of events appears to habituate. Even event classes that originally produce high levels of emotionality are likely to be judged less emotional with repetition. Thus, (a) repeated events late in a series of similar events are less emotional—at time of occurrence—than early events in the series, and (b) retrospective judgments of an event's emotionality decrease when other similar events follow.

Emotionality of events may also be affected by *changes* in the cognitive surround. The first of these effects may be referred to as *contrast*. Level of expectation may be raised by a single highly emotional event (Brickman, Coates, and Janoff-Bulman, 1978), or by a number of moderately important or emotional events. After the "enrichment" of the emotional environment, any particular event may look less emotional or important than it did before the change.

But other changes remotely or closely associated with the target item may affect the rated emotionality or importance of the target. Just as historians must interpret and rewrite history as time passes, so we all rewrite our own personal histories. Few of us are wise enough to be able to predict at the time of their occurrence how significant events will prove to be. A person inconspicuously enters our life. He later becomes a friend, a lover, or an antagonist. Others appear with grand flourish and then simply vanish. Thus, our salience judgments are erroneous for many events. We are offered a job. If we accept a new job that involves permanent changes in our life; for example, if it is accompanied by a move, and increased responsibility and status, the events surrounding the job offer are likely to continue to be perceived as important and emotional. If exactly the same job is turned down, salience ratings are likely to decrease over time. In general, events that initially are perceived as important and highly emotional may be perceived as less emotional or important later as the result of changes in the real world. Events may similarly increase in importance or emotionality as our perspectives on them are modified. If they come to be less important than anticipated we may simply delete them from memory. If they become more important we link them to the later crucial events—we rewrite this chapter in our lives.

Under some circumstances, the emotions currently associated with past events may be at variance with our memories of the emotions associated with the events at the time. It is often difficult to recall the intensity of past emotion—indeed, to examine a highly emotional event two, five, or ten years later is an informative experience. Sometimes the memory for the emotion is only remotely present (I may wonder *why* I experienced a strong emotion if it is obvious that I did or I may *remember* having had the emotion but be completely removed from it in the present). This discrepancy between memory of the emotion and the presently experienced emotion creates considerable problems when I attempted to rate items years later. What is the proper rating? The emotion I remember having felt when the event occurred, the emotion that is aroused now, and how do I discern the difference? Sometimes, of course, years later events may elicit clear strong emotions congruent with, continuous with, or clearly identifiable as a part of the feeling present when the event occurred.

Finally, aside from issues of instability of ratings, emotions and events are inherently complex. Events may be conceptualized across small or large units of activity, their structure may be simple or complex, and they may come from many thousands of domains. To show the difficulty of making such judgments, let us attempt to answer the question: Which is more important? What is more emotional?—the love of our significant other, or a promotion? Most people probably value ongoing emotional support more than occupational advancement but any specific comparison is likely to be complicated. In most of my ratings important, unique events receive the highest ratings. Thus, receiving an important promotion would be rated higher than, for example, such repetitive events as a loved one's embrace, or a single dinner with my women's group. Part of the ambiguity results from the difficulty in knowing precisely what it is that is being evaluated, that is, the size of the memorial unit. A kiss against a promotion is hardly a fair comparison. A promotion implies a whole range of future activities—and only that kiss similarly filled with meaning should be rated as high. Furthermore, ratings are anomalous precisely because the importance of the love relationship does not inhere in the single embrace, nor the import of having good friends depend upon a single evening spent with them. On the contrary, for many individuals (although surely not all) the feelings of warmth and closeness and the significance of the relationship increase even as the specific details of the interaction begin to be lost in routine. Thus, some aspects of important events may receive relatively low ratings—and indeed these specific subevents may be forgotten relatively rapidly. But while we may forget a birthday or an embrace we are not likely to forget—ever during our lifetimes—a sustained emotional relationship. The subelements lack significance but the totality of these memories, laid down— as some artists paint—layer upon layer, create a fabric of such extraordinary durability and richness that it is never forgotten.

What features, then, characterize the emotional events that will endure in memory? For which events will emotionality remain relatively strong? Events whose emotionality will endure in memory are likely to have the following features:

1. The event must be salient and be perceived as strongly emotional at the time it occurs (or it must be "rewritten" shortly thereafter).

2. Your life's subsequent course must make the target event focal in recall; the event may be seen as a turning point, the beginning of a sequence, or as instrumental in other later activities.

3. The event must remain relatively unique. Its image must not be blurred by subsequent occurrences of similar events.

A PROPOSED NEW EXPERIMENT

This paper describes some memory phenomena I encountered during the course of my long-term memory study. Because of the restricted dependent variables and the fixed mode (several brief descriptive sentences) of cuing, it is difficult to analytically examine the course of memory in this study. For that reason I have designed a study that employs flexible cuing and far more flexible responses than did the previous study. With this procedure I hope to be able to answer the elusive question "What is an event?" What critical constellation of features is necessary to uniquely redintegrate the memory of a specific past event and how do these critical features change over time? The most provocative aspect of this technique is that it may help illuminate not only the nature of cuing, but also how episodes gradually merge into semantic memories. I record, independently, a set of descriptors, including who, what happened, where, when, why, how. Descriptive elements vary from specific to quite general. Given a pool of features that characterize a unique event, at time of test I can build item descriptions by adding cue upon cue (incremental strategy) or by omitting specific cues from more complete descriptions (deletion strategy) to determine what set of elements are most successful in reinstating a particular memory. That is, I can determine "what an event is," at least in the sense of identifying the minimum set (or sets) of cues necessary to reliably reinstate the target memory.

Before I provide a clarifying example, let me make explicit another advantage of this procedure: this study provides tremendously flexible cuing possibilities, but similarly permits a wide variety of potential responses. Any piece of information that is not *itself a cue* (at the same or a more specific level) may be requested as a response.

Let us imagine the experiment: I have drawn a random cue "John." (For simplicity let us suppose that this is a unique and well-known "John.") In a free response mode I might simply be free to summarize everything I know about John—an acquaintanceship of 25 years to be summarized in a few hundred words. Such free recall would provide me information about my semantic knowledge base. Or in a *required* response mode I might be asked to give "where?". Without further indication of specificity I might merely list cities: San Diego, Riverside. If pressed for greater specificity I could give more detailed locations within these cities. The queries might progressively provide me "who and where"; for example, "John–Sacramento." What additional information leading to a specific episode is available to me as a result of this dual cue? Again in the free response mode I would unload everything I knew about this compound cue. Or I might be queried more specifically "when?". In my memory John and Sacramento have one overlap, the (April) 1975 Western Psychological Association Convention. But the program might continue "John–Sacramento–dinner?". Of course, where had that fantastic dinner been? Specific questions that are still legitimate are now becoming restricted, but the program might still request where–specific? (What was the name/or location of the restaurant?) who? (Who were the other 12 people at dinner?) when? (exact date?) what? (the menu?) why? (What was the specific occasion?)

In short, a small set of general cues should produce broad gauge general memories, semantic memories, and perhaps even some specific favorite episodic memories. The more numerous and specific the discrete cues become, the more precisely memories should be specified. But there is no necessary requirement that any particular level of event description be the correct one. Salience ratings, either of emotionality or importance, will undoubtedly be higher for some cue combinations than others. As the integrity of events are lost over time, these effects on salience should be more pronouned. Repeated queries (spaced by years) of the same events should tell me which features of events are lost (forgotten) and how soon. Perhaps I shall learn which elements on the average are crucial for defining an event, and what happens as similar events in my personal history are repeated. This study promises a closer examination of episodic/semantic transformations, an opportunity to disentangle the impact of rigid cuing from memory loss as factors in forgetting, and perhaps even a partial answer to my old question: How does one best describe an event?

REFERENCES

Brickman, P., Coates, D., and Janoff-Bulman, R. Lottery winners and accident victims: Is happiness relative? *Journal of Personality and Social Psychology*, 1978, *36*, 917–927.

Linton, M. Memory for real-world events. In D. A. Norman and D. E. Rumelhart (eds.), *Explorations in Cognition*. San Francisco: W. H. Freeman and Company, 1975.

Linton, M. Real-world memory after six years: An in vivo study of very long-term memory. In M. M. Gruneberg, P. E. Morris, and R. N. Sykes (eds.), *Practical Aspects of Memory*. London: Academic Press, 1978.

Part III
Testifying

In which the testimony of legal witnesses is shown to be deplorably unreliable. Courts should not rely on such testimony except when it is absolutely necessary, which it usually is. But even a witness with fairly poor memory for individual episodes, like John Dean, may still manage to tell the truth about what matters.

9 Realistic Experiments

William Stern

*There have been many experimental demonstrations
of the unreliability of testimony; this paper was
among the earliest. The author, William Stern, was a
notable German developmental psychologist. (It was
he who suggested that a child's "mental age," as
established by Binet-type intelligence tests, could be
divided by chronological age to obtain a fixed
quotient, the IQ.) Around the turn of the century,
Stern became convinced that psychological research
on memory had important implications for legal
procedure. He founded a journal,* Contributions to
the Psychology of Testimony, *devoted entirely to this
possibility. The present study is from Volume 2 of that
journal. By modern standards, Stern's analysis of the
data leaves much to be desired. There are no tests of
null hypotheses, and the percentages of error on
which he lays so much stress are rather arbitrary;
they depend on the specific questions asked and on
the method of scoring. We can be equally critical of
some of his interpretations, which he delivers with the
assertiveness characteristic of professors in 1904.
Still, his basic claims about the unreliability of
testimony have stood the test of time.*

Two principal procedures have been developed for the psychological
study of testimony: the picture method and the realistic method. In
the former case the testimony deals with a pictorial representation,

From W. Stern, Wirklichkeitsversuche, *Beitrage zur Psychologie der Aussage,*
1904, 2 (1), 1–31. Translation by Ulric Neisser.

while in the latter it is some object or event of real life. In previously published research I have used pictures; here I report two experiments based on the "realistic" procedure. The first deals with testimony about a real place, the other with an actual event. In both cases I hoped to study impressions that had been formed under conditions of less than maximal attention. Almost all previous research has been based on cases of sharply focused attention; it seemed appropriate to raise the practically significant question of the quality and quantity of reports of less attentively observed experiences.

The experiments were conducted during seminars in psychology; the subjects were students and teachers in training. Analysis of the data and discussion of the results were also carried out, in part, in a psychology course.

. . .

[Stern's account of his first experiment is omitted here. In that experiment, 24 students were asked various questions about a classroom where they had heard a lecture eight days before: how many windows there were, if there was a second exit, the details of the (architecturally interesting) ceiling, etc. After the subjects had written their replies, they were asked to underline those which they would be willing to swear to in court. About 20 percent of the answers were incorrect; even the "sworn" answers were wrong 7 percent of the time. (It is hard to know what to make of these percentages, given the varied nature of the questions.) Some people were much more accurate than others. Students who had been in the lecture room repeatedly were more accurate than those who had been only once, but even they were not perfect. Law students were less accurate than those of other colleges, but Stern does not think this result should be too hastily generalized!]

. . .

EXPERIMENT II

The friendly help of Mr. Lipmann (a graduate student) made it possible to stage a small "event" at the first meeting of my psychology course in the winter term 1903–1904. This experiment, like the preceding one, was intended to elicit testimony about facts that had not been closely attended to. For this reason we selected a rather banal event; one that was not noteworthy in its own right but only because it created a small interruption of an ongoing seminar. Lipmann (the target person, designated *T*) entered, asked to speak to me, handed me a large envelope, asked for permission to examine the books in the bookcase, perused one for about five minutes, and took it with him; as he was leaving, I asked him to wait outside for me until the end of the seminar. A detailed scenario of the event appears in Table 9-1. Every action and every word had been carefully rehearsed, and the words I was to speak were written out on a small card, placed where the students could not see it. The entire event took place exactly according to plan, at least as far as we (*T* and myself) were able to judge.

Figure 9-1 illustrates the situation. My position is marked "Stern"; the positions of the students are indicated by letters of the alphabet, the women with an asterisk. It can be seen that there were six women (mostly teachers) and nine graduate students. [*Throughout the paper, Stern distinguishes between the "students"—males, candidates for the Ph.D.—and the "teachers"—all women—in his seminar. He uses the term "listeners" for the full set, which indicates something of the ambience of a turn-of-the-century German seminar.*]

T entered the room as I was in the middle of a lecture, which I interrupted only long enough to accept the manuscript. I continued to lecture during his presence. As he left, I interrupted myself to say,

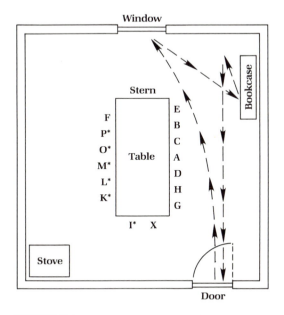

FIGURE 9-1
Sketch of the situation. Letters denote the students in the seminar; females are marked with an asterisk (*). T's route is indicated by → → →.

"Please wait for me outside; I have something to tell you." Thus, the participants in the seminar were given no reason to attend to the detailed course of the event; at most they may have experienced the slight interruption as a nuisance. None suspected that the event had been staged. When I opened the second meeting of the seminar (eight days later) by asking the participants to report the entire event as best they could, the reaction was one of complete astonishment.

As in my earlier experiments with schoolchildren, the required testimony consisted of two parts: a "report" and an "interrogation." The subjects first wrote out an overall report of the event. Then they were asked to "swear" to part or all of their account as follows: "Please underline those parts of your report which you would be willing to swear to, under oath, if you were testifying in court." I then asked them 24 specific questions; each question had to be answered in writing unless the answer had already been included in the report. The questions are listed in Table 9-1 together with the correct answers; 41 specific points altogether. The 24 questions covered all the essential features of the event: questions 1 and 2 dealt with its time and duration, 3–10 concerned the description of T, and 11–24 referred to the course of the event itself.

The analysis of the data proceeded as follows. Each subject's responses were arranged into a protocol like that illustrated in Table 9-1. The subject's initial report was first scanned for information bearing on each question (first column at right); then his responses to the specific questions were added (second column at right). Table 9-1 shows these entries for the subject ($K.$) with the poorest performance. (Responses that the subject was willing to swear to are underlined.) The protocols were scored by marking each correct response $+1$, each false response -1, and each "don't know" with a question mark. Questions 1, 2, and 7 were excluded from this tally since they required a different method of analysis (see below). The protocols were then evaluated in the seminar itself, with each student scoring another student's testimony. Naturally this practice analysis could not be used, and a reanalysis was conducted by a single student, Mr. Zenker. The data presented here are based on my own careful rechecking and partial recalculation of his results.

Results

The numerical results appear in Table 9-2, which gives individual scores as well as means for graduate students, teachers, and the group as a whole. The table shows the absolute numbers of correct, incorrect,

TABLE 9-1

A protocol from the event experiment

Questions on the interrogation Correct answers (points scorable)	Responses of subject *K.,* a teacher Sworn testimony in *italics* (points awarded)	
	Initial Report	Interrogation
I. Time and Duration		
1. When did *T* come in? At 7:30.	*About quarter of eight*	——
2. How long did he stay? 5 minutes.	——	*2 or 3 minutes*
II. Description of *T*		
3. Describe *T's* body build Small (1).	*smaller than average* (+1)	——
4. Color of hair? Brown (1).	——	*Brown* (+1)
5. Had he a beard or moustache? Yes (1).	——	*No* (−1)
6. Describe it Moustache (1) and Pointed beard (1).	——	——
7. His approximate age? 23 years old.	——	*Early twenties*
8. A special indentifying feature? Hair flecked with white (1).	——	*don't know* (?)
9. How was he dressed? Grey jacket, but- toned (3); Brown gloves (2); Soft brown hat (3).	*Brown overcoat* (−2); *Round black hard hat* (−2, +1)	——
10. Describe his voice Soft, slightly hoarse (1); High rather than low (1).	——	*Strong and rather deep voice* (−2)
III. The Sequence of Events		
11. Did *T* have anything in his hand when he came in? Yes (1).	*Yes* (+1)	——
12. What was it? A large envelope (1) and the hat (1).	*His hat (see #9)*	——
13. What did *T* say as he entered? "Excuse me" (1). Could I speak to you for a moment, sir?" (1).	*He begged Stern's par- don for the interruption* (+1, −1).	——

TABLE 9-1 (continued)

Questions on the interrogation Correct answers (points scorable)	Responses of subject K., a teacher Sworn testimony in *italics* (points awarded)	
	Initial Report	Interrogation

III. The Sequence of Events
    (continued)

14. What did Stern reply?
    To *T:* "Please come
    here" (1). To the
    class: "Excuse me a
    moment" (1).

| | —— | don't know (?) |

15. Did Stern get up or
    remain seated?
    He stood up (1).

| | —— | Remained seated (−1) |

16. What did the two of
    them do next?
    Both went over to
    the alcove by the
    window (1); *T* gave
    Stern the envelope
    (1), saying "I just
    wanted to bring you
    the manuscript" (1).

| | —— | Stern did not permit any further interruption (−1). |

17. What did Stern do with
    the envelope *T* had
    given him?
    He tried vainly to
    put it into his jacket
    pocket (1) and then
    laid it on the win-
    dow sill (1).

| | —— | *T* did not give him an enve-lope (−1). |

18. What did *T* do next?
    T asked permission
    to look at a book (1);
    took one from the
    book (1); he then
    stood by the book-
    case (1) reading in
    the book (1).

| | (As soon as he entered *T* went *quickly to the bookcase* (−1, +1); after a *brief search* he took out a book (+1); then *he made his way out just as fast* (−1). | —— |

19. What happend to the
    book?
    T took it with him
    (1).

| | —— | *T* took it with him (+1). |

20. Did *T* have anything in
    his hand as he left?
    The book (1) and his
    hat (1).

| | —— | The book and the hat (+1) |

TABLE 9-1 (continued)

Questions on the interrogation Correct answers (points scorable)	Responses of subject *K.,* a teacher Sworn testimony in *italics* (points awarded)	
	Initial Report	Interrogation
III. The Sequence of Events (continued)		

21. what did *T* say as he left?
   "Thank you sir" (1).
   "I beg your pardon if I've disturbeed you. Goodbye" (1).
	——	Nothing (−1)

22. What did Stern say to *T* say as he was leaving? "Please wait for me outside" (1); "I have something to tell you" (1).	*"Please wait for me outside"* (+1).	——
23. Did *T* wait outside? No (1).	——	I didn't see him (+1).
24. Where did he wait?	——	——
Total possible score: 41	Report: +7, including +4 *sworn;* −7, including −2 *sworn.*	Interrogation: +4, −7, ?2; none *sworn.*

and indeterminate responses for each subject, separately for initial reports and interrogations as well as a combined score. These figures have also been coverted into accuracy percentages: number correct divided by the sum of correct plus incorrect. "Error percentages" may be obtained by subtracting the given entries from 100.

Testimony can be evaluated in terms of two principal criteria: the amount of recall and its accuracy. Table 9-2 shows that the average amount, in terms of the absolute number of correct responses, is far from negligible. The mean of 13.4 per subject is quite substantial, considering the minimal degree of participation and attention that had been devoted to the event, and considering that eight days had elapsed. Accuracy, in contrast, is poor inndeed. On the average a full quarter of the statements in the initial reports are false, and about half of the responses to the interrogation! Overall, about one-third of the subjects' assertions are incorrect.

This level of performance is substantially poorer than was obtained in my picture experiments with schoolchildren, and it is much worse than the outcome of a rather similar experiment with

TABLE 9–2.
Results of the event experiment. Numbers of correct (C), incorrect (I) and indeterminate (?) responses by each subject in both the report and the interrogation. The subset of "sworn" responses is indicated separately.

Subject	Report			Interrogation				Combined Rep. + Interr.			"Sworn" only		
	C	I	%C	C	I	%C	(?)	C	I	%C	C	I	%C
"Students" (male)													
A	7	5	58	4	4	50	(6)	11	9	55	5	2	71
B	11	3	79	3.5	4.5	44	(2)	14.5	7.5	66	11	2	85
C	4	0	100	0.5	2.5	17	(12)	4.5	2.5	64	4	0	100
D	7	0	100	3	3	50	(5)	10	3	77	7	0	100
E	9	2.5	78	5.5	3	65	(3)	14.5	5.5	73	6	0	100
F	13	1.5	90	3	4	43	(5)	16	5.5	74	11	1	92
G	7	1	88	7.5	0	100	(4)	14.5	1	94	7	1	88
H	9	2.5	78	2.5	3	45	(3)	11.5	5.5	68	9	2.5	78
X	14	5	74	5	3	63	(4)	19	8	70	9	0	100
Mean (males)	9	2.3	80	3.8	3	56	(4.9)	12.8	5.3	71	7.7	0.9	90
"Teachers" (females)													
I	12.5	4	76	3	3	50	(5)	15.5	7	69	8	3	73
K	7	7	50	4	7	36	(2)	11	14	44	4	2	67
L	14.5	3	83	0	5	0	(5)	14.5	8	64	10	2	83
M	8	3	73	3.5	2.5	58	(5)	11.5	5.5	68	5	2	71
O	9	1	90	8	4	67	(6)	17	5	77	6	0	100
P	12.5	3	81	3	5	38	(5)	15.5	8	66	9.5	1	90
Mean (females)	10.6	3.5	75	3.6	4.4	45	(4.7)	14.2	7.9	64	7.1	1.7	81
Grand mean	9.6	2.8	77	3.7	3.6	51	(4.8)	13.4	6.3	68	7.4	1.2	86

workers recently reported by Lipmann.[1] That study also dealt with a relatively banal event occurring during an instructional hour, and with an inquiry taking place several days later. The error percentages in Lipmann's experiment—10 percent in the initial report, 19 percent in the interrogation, 16 percent overall—were only half of those reported here. I would regard it as a mistake to conclude that the memories of uneducated subjects are better than those of educated ones. It is clear

---

[1]Lipmann, O. Experimentelle Aussagen uber einen Vorgang und eine Lokalität. *Beitrage zur Psychologie der Aussage*, 1902, *1*, 222–231.

that the witnesses of Lipmann's event paid much closer attention than those in the present study; moreover, his inquiry occurred half a week after the event while ours was eight days later. Finally, Lipmann had no female subjects; those in our experiment lowered the average performance.

Nevertheless, our data lead to a conclusion that it is not unimportant. *The consequence of inadequate attention to an event is not that testimony becomes very brief, but that it becomes very prone to error.* This suggests a general principle: as conditions become more difficult, it is not so much the quantity as the quality of performance that decreases. Similar results have been obtained in experimental studies of fatigue. For a wide range of mental processes, fatigue produces a degradation of performance far in excess of any reduction in the total amount. This is a point at which the psychology of memory has important educational implications. One must struggle against the tendency to maintain a constant amount of poorer and poorer output; the cult of quantity must be replaced by a higher respect for quality.

In agreement with many other studies of testimony, we found a much higher error rate (by a factor of two) in the interrogations than in the initial reports. In the present case there were an equal number of right and wrong answers, so the responses to the interrogation have no credibility at all.

[*Omitted here are two pages of discussion of sex differences in accuracy. We have already seen Stern casually dismiss data that seem to show that law students (in the first experiment) have especially poor memories or that uneducated people are better witnesses than educated ones (in the comparison with Lipmann's experiment, above). Unfortunately, his treatment of data on sex differences shows no such restraint. He notes that his female subjects made more errors than the men even though they were better situated to see most of T's movements; that the most reliable witness was a man and the least reliable a woman; that the single nearsighted male subject D. gave relatively few responses while the nearsighted female subject K. made many errors but used her nearsightedness as an excuse. Stern seems to take considerable satisfaction in this "scientific" demonstration that women are fundamentally unreliable. Of course the data prove no such thing; apart from the different populations involved and the statistical difficulty of concluding anything from such small and variable samples, there are obvious differences in the social situations of men and women both in his seminar and during his interrogation.*]

. . .

The content of the testimony is remarkably varied. For the sake of clarity, we will deal separately with the actual event and with the description of *T*, the target person.

The Event

The event consisted of two main parts: *T*'s delivery of the manuscript to me and his subsequent activity at the bookcase. To show how very differently these stages were understood by the subjects, consider the three following reports (from which descriptions of *T* have been omitted). The first of these is the best report, overall, obtained from any subject; the others are less good.

G., a Ph.D. candidate, reported:

It happened on Monday, November 9, while Dr. Stern was having a seminar with his group in the Psychology Seminar Room, Schmiedebrucke 35. A young man unexpectedly entered the room, went up to Dr. Stern, and asked whether he might look something up in one of the volumes in the bookcase. Dr. Stern naturally granted this request. The man (whom I believe I have never seen before, by the way) left the room again after staying for a total of about three minutes. Dr. Stern called after him just as he was leaving, asking him to wait in the anteroom until the end of the seminar. I would estimate that it was around 7:00 or 7:15 in the evening as he left the room.

In the interrogation G. added the following:

Stern stood up.... *T* handed Stern a letter ... stood for a little while, reading in the book he had taken from the bookcase.... He took the book with him.... He thanked Stern for allowing him to look at the book.

C., a doctor of political science, reported:

On Monday, November 9, during Dr. Stern's class, a gentleman entered the Psychology Seminar Room and wished to speak with Dr. Stern. Dr. Stern, although reluctant to interrupt the seminar, did get up and went briefly over to the window with the man who had come in. Then he told him to wait outside. The time was roughly between 7:30 and 7:45.

During his interrogation, C. added these statements:

The whole event took one minute.... When Lipmann expressed his wish to speak with Stern, the latter said something to indicate that he regretted the interruption.

L., a teacher, reported:

A gentleman appeared during the lecture, apologizing to Dr. Stern for the interruption that his entrance had created. In addition, he asked whether he might take a book from the library and look something up.

Dr. Stern replied, "Please do, and wait outside for me; I have something else to tell you." The man then took one or two volumes from the bookcase and looked into them as he stood there. Then he took his leave and went out of the room. He was in the room for about seven minutes; it was during the second half of the lecture.

During the interrogation, she added that:

Stern remained seated.

When one compares the last two reports, it is hard to believe that they refer to one and the same objective event. All they have in common is that a gentleman entered and exchanged a few words with me, and that I asked him to wait outside for me afterwards. In all other respects they are totally discrepant. According to C., the core of the event was a conversation that T and I held by the window; in L.'s account everything revolves around his taking out and reading a book, for which I gave him permission without getting up. C. reports that I was reluctant to be interrupted and said so explicitly; L. noticed nothing of this. The event lasted one minute for C., seven minutes for L. C. knows nothing about the book, L. knows nothing about the conversation by the window. Finally L. is confused about the chronological sequence of events, in that she places my request (that T wait outside) near the beginning of the conversation instead of at the end.

C. was the only subject who knew nothing of T's activity at the bookcase. Everyone else mentioned this part of the episode, even in their original reports. The results with respect to the earlier part of the episode are quite different, however. A majority of the initial reports (11 of 15) suggest that T asked and received permission to go to the bookcase as soon as he came in; three reports mention that T and I held a brief conversation between his first entrance and his taking out the book; only one witness (J., a teacher) mentioned that he gave me a manuscript. The interrogation helped several subjects to recall additional material. G., for example, had failed to mention the envelope affair in his report (see above); the question "What took place between the two of them?" reminded him of it and he corrected his previous testimony. Four of the other male subjects did not recall this episode until question 17, which explicitly mentions the envelope and asks what became of it. Among the women, oddly enough, the interrogation never rectified the omission of this episode in their original reports. One female subject even insisted, in her response to question 17, that "T gave no envelope." Thus, the women perform badly in this important respect. Five out of six (83 percent) know nothing of the envelope episode, as compared with four out of nine male subjects (44 percent). Here also we see an effect of lack of attention (or of attention directed elsewhere) whose importance is often underestimated. It is an effect

I have pointed out before, one "through which other impressions, although fully present to the senses, can slide by without making the slightest impression on consciousness."

It is important to realize that of the few subjects who knew anything at all about the envelope, three (two men and one woman) maintained that I had put it into my pocket; two other men said I had placed it on the windowsill. Moreover, a third of the males and two-thirds of the females believe I remained seated throughout the entire episode! In short, the testimony about the first phase of the event constituted such a chaotic array of conflicting accounts that it would have been quite impossible for an investigator who had to rely on it to establish the actual facts.

In the second phase of the event, *T* took a book from the bookcase and looked into it. With the exception of a single subject, the witnesses' accounts of these activities were rather consistent. However, their agreement did not extend to his next action, when he left the room and took the book with him. We had deliberately incorporated this action in the scenario in order to present the witnesses with a bit of questionable behavior. Every student is familiar with the strict rule against removing books from the seminar-room shelves, and a notice to that effect is posted on the bookcase itself. Only one subject spontaneously mentioned this "criminal" act in his report, and in his version *T* had asked my permission first! In response to question 19 of the interrogation ("What happened to the book?"), three of the remaining witnesses said they did not know and seven indicated that *T* had put it back in the bookcase. Only four subjects (including one woman) said he had taken it with him.

These results are similar to those obtained by Lipmann in the study mentioned earlier. His experiment also included the unauthorized removal of a book. The question "What happened to the book?" [*Actually, the question was "Did she take anything from the lectern?"*] produced two "don't knows," three wrong answers, and no correct reports. [*There were five subjects.*]

In the present experiment, then, seven accounts indicated that *T* had put the book back in the bookcase—an event that never occurred at all. Indeed, no trace of such a thing had happened; *T* did not even begin to replace the book. These confident answers were given only because the return of the book was taken for granted; it *must* have happened.

We had intended to convey a similarly effective suggestion in the last part of the event, but our procedure was too crude to be very effective. All the subjects heard and reported my parting comment to *T*, asking him to wait outside for me. Only subject *X.*, however, testified that *T* had actually waited. The others said that they didn't know or hadn't noticed, that *T* would have had to wait for this or that amount of time, etc. Even *X.*, who did say that he had waited, was unable to say where. Nevertheless even this single case shows how "He was supposed to wait," "He probably waited," and "He did wait" can become interchangeable under certain circumstances.

The Description of *T*

The typical difference between the sexes, which had appeared in testimony about the event, was not apparent in the descriptions of the target person.

T's height was usually reported correctly as "average." His body build was occasionally described as "slender" although he is in fact somewhat stocky. Similarly, estimates of his age were fairly accurate. Since these data were not included in the overall totals, we present them here. The overall mean of the estimates was 25.4 years; he was actually 23. The men's estimates were further off than the women's: 25.7 versus 24.8. Three estimates were correct; there was only one underestimate (21); the highest estimate, which occurred twice, was 30.

With respect to all other features of *T*'s appearance, the inaccuracy of the testimony is frightening. The greatest number of mistakes occurred in reports of color. His brown hair was described three times as "black," once as "dark blond," and once as "blond" (mostly by men). His gray jacket was called "blue" twice and "brown" four times; his brown hat was termed "black" by one man and three women. These errors take on added significance because the *true* colors of his suit and hat were never mentioned by anyone. The six incorrect reports of the jacket's color are counterbalanced only by five reports that it was "dark." These were counted as correct, but they provide information only about the achromatic lightness of the jacket and not about its actual hue. The hat was always called "black" whenever its appearance was mentioned at all. It must not be supposed that the hat (which *T* carried in his hand) was of a particularly dark brown that might easily be confused with black; on the contrary, it was of a distinct coffee color.

Accounts of *T*'s face and voice also exhibited numerous errors. In fact, he had a moustache and a small pointed beard. Nevertheless, three descriptions credit him with a full beard and two others with a moustache alone, while two female subjects described him as clean-shaven. His voice is soft, slightly muffled, and relatively high in pitch. The five-and-a-half correct descriptions of it contrast with five-and-a-half others that were wrong. According to the incorrect reports his voice was deep and relatively loud; a pleasant baritone.

Finally, several isolated oddities are worth mentioning. One male and one female subject described *T* as wearing spectacles, although he does not do so and never has. Both of them mentioned the spectacles in their spontaneous reports, and the female subject was willing to swear to their existence. In addition, one subject mentioned a nonexistent cap, and another a brown overcoat.

These points are enough to show how remarkably inaccurate and uncritical the memory of a person's appearance can be. Sometimes the errors of testimony cumulate into a complete confabulation. The description given by subject *K*. (see Table 9–1) is one example of this. For another, consider this description give by *X*.: "round black hat; dark or black shoes; reversed collar." In fact the hat was brown, the shoes red, and the collar completely concealed by the closed jacket.

Descriptions of individuals play an extremely important part in the testimony of witnesses. With respect to such testimony, the outcome of the present experiment leads to a clear conclusion. *Retrospective accounts of people's appearance, especially about hair color, beardedness, and color of clothing, should be given no credit whatsoever unless special attention was directed to these features during observation itself.*

10 Reconstruction of Automobile Destruction

Elizabeth F. Loftus and John C. Palmer

Elizabeth Loftus is well known for her extensive work on witness memory. The study reprinted here demonstrates the prejudicial effect of leading questions, or—to put it another way—illustrates the human tendency to combine information from all available sources in reconstructing the past. The elegance of Loftus and Palmer's experiment contrasts sharply with the primitive methods available to Stern seventy years earlier (Selection 9); the difference reflects the methodological progress of psychology since 1904.

How accurately do we remember the details of a complex event, like a traffic accident, that has happened in our presence? More specifically, how well do we do when asked to estimate some numerical quantity such as how long the accident took, how fast the cars were traveling, or how much time elapsed between the sounding of a horn and the moment of collision?

It is well documented that most people are markedly inaccurate in reporting such numerical details as time, speed, and distance (Bird,

From E. F. Loftus and J. C. Palmer, Reconstruction of automobile destruction: An example of the interaction between language and memory, *Journal of Verbal Learning and Verbal Behavior*, 1974, 13, 585–589. Reprinted by permission.

1927; Whipple, 1909). For example, most people have difficulty estimating the duration of an event, with some research indicating that the tendency is to overestimate the duration of events which are complex (Block, 1974; Marshall, 1969; Ornstein, 1969). The judgment of speed is especially difficult, and practically every automobile accident results in huge variations from one witness to another as to how fast a vehicle was actually traveling (Gardner, 1933). In one test administered to Air Force personnel who knew in advance that they would be questioned about the speed of a moving automobile, estimates ranged from 10 to 50 mph. The car they watched was actually going only 12 mph (Marshall, 1969, p. 23).

Given the inaccuracies in estimates of speed, it seems likely that there are variables which are potentially powerful in terms of influencing these estimates. The present research was conducted to investigate one such variable, namely, the phrasing of the question used to elicit the speed judgment. Some questions are clearly more suggestive than others. This fact of life has resulted in the legal concept of a leading question and in legal rules indicating when leading questions are allowed (*Supreme Court Reporter*, 1973). A leading question is simply one that, either by its form or content, suggests to the witness what answer is desired or leads him to the desired answer.

In the present study, subjects were shown films of traffic accidents and then they answered questions about the accident. The subjects were interrogated about the speed of the vehicles in one of several ways. For example, some subjects were asked, "About how fast were the cars going when they hit each other?" while others were asked, "About how fast were the cars going when they smashed into each other?" As Fillmore (1971) and Bransford and McCarrell (1974) have noted, *hit* and *smashed* may involve specification of differential rates of movement. Furthermore, the two verbs may also involve differential specification of the likely consequences of the events to which they are referring. The impact of the accident is apparently gentler for *hit* than for *smashed*.

EXPERIMENT I

Method

Forty-five students participated in groups of various sizes. Seven films were shown, each depicting a traffic accident. These films were segments from longer driver's education films borrowed from the Evergreen Safety Council and the Seattle Police Department. The length of the film segments ranged from 5 to 30 seconds. Following each film, the subjects received a questionnaire asking them first to "give an account of the accident you have just seen," and then to answer a series of specific questions about the accident. The critical question was the one that interrogated the subject about the speed of the vehicles involved in the collision. Nine subjects were asked, "About how fast were the cars going when they hit each other?" Equal numbers of the remaining subjects were interrogated with the verbs *smashed*, *collided*, *bumped*, and *contacted* in place of *hit*. The entire experiment lasted about an hour and a half. A different ordering of the films was presented to each group of subjects.

Results

Table 10-1 presents the mean speed estimates for the various verbs. Following the procedures outlined by Clark (1973), an analysis of variance was performed with verbs as a fixed effect, and subjects and films as random effects, yielding a significant quasi-F ratio, $F'(5,55) = 4.65$, $p < .005$.

Some information about the accuracy of subjects' estimates can be obtained from our data. Four of the seven films were staged crashes; the original purpose of these films was to illustrate what can happen to human beings when cars collide at various speeds. One collision took place at 20 mph, one at 30, and two at 40. The mean estimates of speed for these four films were: 37.7, 36.2, 39.7, and 36.1 mph, respectively. In agreement with previous work, people are not very good at judging how fast a vehicle was actually traveling.

Discussion

The results of this experiment indicate that the form of a question (in this case, changes in a single word) can markedly and systematically

TABLE 10-1
Speed estimates for the verbs used in Experiment I

Verb	Mean speed estimate
Smashed	40.8
Collided	39.3
Bumped	38.1
Hit	34.0
Contacted	31.8

affect a witness's answer to that question. The actual speed of the vehicles controlled little variance in subject reporting, while the phrasing of the question controlled considerable variance.

Two interpretations of this finding are possible. First, it is possible that the differential speed estimates result merely from response-bias factors. A subject is uncertain whether to say 30 mph or 40 mph, for example, and the verb *smashed* biases his response towards the higher estimate. A second interpretation is that the question form causes a change in the subject's memory representation of the accident. The verb *smashed* may change a subject's memory such that he "sees" the accident as being more severe than it actually was. If this is the case, we might expect subjects to "remember" other details that did not actually occur, but are commensurate with an accident occurring at higher speeds. The second experiment was designed to provide additional insights into the origin of the differential speed estimates.

EXPERIMENT II

Method

One-hundred-fifty students participated in this experiment, in groups of various sizes. A film depicting a multiple car accident was shown, followed by a questionnaire. The film lasted less than 1 minute; the accident in the film lasted 4 seconds. At the end of the film, the subjects received a questionnaire asking them first to describe the accident in their own words, and then to answer a series of questions about the accident. The critical question was the one that interrogated the subject about the speed of the vehicles. Fifty subjects were asked, "About how fast were the cars going when they smashed into each other?" Fifty subjects were asked, "About how fast were the cars going when they hit each other?" Fifty subjects were not interrogated about vehicular speed.

One week later, the subjects returned and without viewing the film again they answered a series of questions about the accident. The critical question here was, "Did you see any broken glass?" which the subjects answered by checking "yes" or "no." This question was embedded in a list totalling ten questions, and it appeared in a random position in the list. There was no broken glass in the accident, but, since broken glass is commensurate with accidents occurring at high speed, we expected that the subjects who had been asked the *smashed* question might more often say "yes" to this critical question.

Results

The mean estimate of speed for subjects interrogated with *smashed* was 10.46 mph; with *hit* the estimate was 8.00 mph. These means are significantly different, t (98) $= 2.00, p < .05$.

Table 10-2 presents the distribution of "yes" and "no" responses for the *smashed, hit,* and control subjects. An independence chi-square test on these responses was significant beyond the .025 level, $\chi^2(2) = 7.76$. The important result in Table 10-2 is that the probability of saying "yes," $P(Y)$, to the question about broken glass is .32 when the verb *smashed* is used, and .14 with *hit*. Thus, *smashed* leads both to more "yes" responses and to higher speed estimates. It appears to be the case that the effect of the verb is mediated at least in part by the speed estimate. The question now arises: Is *smashed* doing anything else besides increasing the estimate of speed? To answer this, the function relating $P(Y)$ to speed estimate was calculated separately for *smashed* and *hit*. If the speed estimate is the only way in which effect of verb is mediated, then for a given speed estimate, $P(Y)$ should be independent of verb. Table 10-3 shows that this is not the case, $P(Y)$ is lower for *hit* than for *smashed*; the difference between the two verbs ranges from .03 for estimates of 1–5 mph to .18 for estimates of 6–10 mph. The

TABLE 10-2
Distribution of "yes" and "no" responses to the question "Did you see any broken glass?"

	Verb condition		
Response	Smashed	Hit	Control
Yes	16	7	6
No	34	43	44

TABLE 10-3
Probability of saying "yes" to "Did you see any broken glass?" conditionalized on speed estimates

Verb condition	Speed estimate (mph)			
	1–5	6–10	11–15	16–20
Smashed	.09	.27	.41	.62
Hit	.06	.09	.25	.50

average difference between the two curves is about .12. Whereas the unconditional difference of .18 between the *smashed* and *hit* conditions is attenuated, it is by no means eliminated when estimate of speed is controlled for. It thus appears that the verb *smashed* has other effects besides that of simply increasing the estimate of speed. One possibility will be discussed in the next section.

Discussion

To reiterate, we have first of all provided an additional demonstration of something that has been known for some time, namely, that the way a question is asked can enormously influence the answer that is given. In this instance, the question, "About how fast were the cars going when they smashed into each other?" led to higher estimates of speed than the same question asked with the verb *smashed* replaced by *hit*. Furthermore, this seemingly small change had consequences for how questions are answered a week after the original event occurred.

As a framework for discussing these results, we would like to propose that two kinds of information go into one's memory for some complex occurrence. The first is information gleaned during the perception of the original event; the second is external information supplied after the fact. Over time, information from these two sources may be integrated in such a way that we are unable to tell from which source some specific detail is recalled. All we have is one "memory."

Discussing the present experiments in these terms, we propose that the subject first forms some representation of the accident he has witnessed. The experimenter then, while asking, "About how fast were the cars going when they smashed into each other?" supplies a piece of external information, namely, that the cars did indeed smash into each other. When these two pieces of information are integrated, the subject has a memory of an accident that was more severe than in fact it was. Since broken glass is commensurate with a severe accident, the subject is more likely to think that broken glass was present. There is some connection between the present work and earlier work on the influence of verbal labels on memory for visually presented form stimuli. A classic study in psychology showed that when subjects are asked to reproduce a visually presented form, their drawings tend to err in the direction of a more familiar object suggested by a verbal label initially associated with the to-be-remembered form (Carmichael, Hogan, and Walter, 1932). More recently, Daniel (1972) showed that recognition memory, as well as reproductive memory, was similarly affected by verbal labels, and he concluded that the verbal label causes a shift in the memory strength of forms which are better representatives of the label.

When the experimenter asks the subject, "About how fast were the cars going when they smashed into each other?" he is effectively labeling the accident a smash. Extrapolating the conclusions of Daniel to this situation, it is natural to conclude that the label *smash* causes a shift in the memory representation of the accident in the direction of being more similar to a representation suggested by the verbal label.

REFERENCES

Bird, C. The influence of the press upon the accuracy of report. *Journal of Abnormal and Social Psychology*, 1927, 22, 123–129.

Block, R. A. Memory and the experience of duration in retrospect. *Memory and Cognition*, 1974, 2, 153–160

Bransford, J. D., and McCarrell, N. S. A sketch of a cognitive approach to comprehension: Some thoughts about understanding what it means to comprehend. In W. B. Weimer and D. S. Palermo (eds.), *Cognition and the Symbolic Processes*. Hillsdale, N.J.: Erlbaum, 1974.

Carmichael, L. Hogan, H. P., and Walter, A. A. An experimental study of the effect of language on the reproduction of visually perceived form. *Journal of Experimental Psychology*, 1932, *15*, 73–86.

Clark, H. H. The language-as-fixed-effect fallacy: A critique of language statistics in psychological research. *Journal of Verbal Learning and Verbal Behavior*, 1973, *12*, 335–359.

Daniel, T. C. Nature of the effect of verbal labels on recognition memory for form. *Journal of Experimental Psychology*, 1972, *96*, 152–157.

Fillmore, C. J. Types of lexical information. In D. D. Steinberg and L. A. Jakobovits (eds.), *Semantics: An Interdisciplinary Reader in Philosophy, Linguistics, and Psychology*. Cambridge: Cambridge University Press, 1971.

Gardner, D. S. The perception and memory of witnesses. *Cornell Law Quarterly*, 1933, *8*, 391–409.

Marshall, J. *Law and Psychology in Conflict*. New York: Anchor Books, 1969.

Ornstein, R. E. *On the Experience of Time*. Harmondsworth, Middlesex, England: Penguin Books, 1969.

Whipple, G. M. The observer as reporter: A survey of the psychology of testimony. *Psychological Bulletin*, 1909, *6*, 153–170.

Supreme Court Reporter, 1973, *3*. Rules of evidence for United States courts and magistrates.

11   Eyewitness Testimony

Robert Buckhout

This selection is a more general survey of the difficulties of eyewitness identification.

The woman in the witness box stares at the defendant, points an accusing finger and says, loudly and firmly, "That's the man! That's him! I could never forget his face!" It is impressive testimony. The only eyewitness to a murder has identified the murderer. Or has she?

Perhaps she has, but she may be wrong. Eyewitness testimony is unreliable. Research and courtroom experience provide ample evidence that an eyewitness to a crime is being asked to be something and do something that a normal human being was not created to be or do. Human perception is sloppy and uneven, albeit remarkably effective in serving our need to create structure out of experience. In an investigation or in court, however, a witness is often asked to play the role of a kind of tape recorder on whose tape the events of the crime have left an impression. The prosecution probes for stored facts and scenes and tries to establish that the witness's recording equipment was and still is in perfect running order. The defense cross-examines the witness to show that there are defects in the recorder and gaps in the tape. Both sides, and usually the witness too, succumb to the fallacy that everything was recorded and can be played back later through questioning.

Those of us who have done research in eyewitness identification reject that fallacy. It reflects a nineteenth-century view of man as perceiver, which asserted a parallel between the mechanisms of the physical world and those of the brain. Human perception is a more complex information-processing mechanism. So is memory. The person who

From *Scientific American*, 1974, *231* (6), 23–31. Copyright © 1974 by Scientific American, Inc. All rights reserved.

sees an accident or witnesses a crime and is then asked to describe what he saw cannot call up an "instant replay." He must depend on his memory, with all its limitations. The limitations may be unimportant in ordinary daily activities. If someone is a little unreliable, if he trims the truth a bit in describing what he has seen, it ordinarily does not matter too much. When he is a witness, the inaccuracy escalates in importance.

Human perception and memory function effectively by being selective and constructive. As Ulric Neisser of Cornell University has pointed out, "Neither perception nor memory is a copying process." Perception and memory are decision-making processes affected by the totality of a person's abilities, background, attitudes, motives and beliefs, by the environment and by the way his recollection is eventually tested. The observer is an active rather than a passive perceiver and recorder; he reaches conclusions on what he has seen by evaluating fragments of information and reconstructing them. He is motivated by a desire to be accurate as he imposes meaning on the over-abundance of information that impinges on his senses, but also by a desire to live up to the expectations of other people and to stay in their good graces. The eye, the ear, and other sense organs are therefore social organs as well as physical ones.

Psychologists studying the capabilities of the sense organs speak of an "ideal observer," one who would respond to lights or tones with unbiased eyes and ears, but we know that the ideal observer does not exist. We speak of an "ideal physical environment," free of distractions and distortions, but we know that such an environment can only be approached, and then only in the laboratory. My colleagues and I at the Brooklyn College of the City University of New York distinguish a number of factors that we believe inherently limit a person's ability to give a complete account of events he once saw or to identify with complete accuracy the people who were involved.

The first sources of unreliability are implicit in the original situation. One is the insignificance—at the time and to the witness—of the events that were observed. In placing someone at or near the scene of a crime, for example, witnesses are often being asked to recall seeing the accused at a time when they were not attaching importance to the event, which was observed in passing, as a part of the normal routine of an ordinary day. As long ago as 1895, J. McKeen Cattell wrote about an experiment in which he asked students to describe the people, places, and events they had encountered walking to school over familiar paths. The reports were incomplete and unreliable; some individuals were very sure of details that had no basis in fact. Insignificant events do not motivate a person to bring fully into play the selective process of attention.

The length of the period of observation obviously limits the number of features a person can attend to. When the tachistoscope, a projector with a variable-speed shutter that controls the length of an image's appearance on a screen, is used in controlled research to test recall, the shorter times produce less reliable identification and recall. Yet fleeting glimpses are common in eyewitness accounts, particularly in fast-moving, threatening situations. In the Sacco–Vanzetti case in the 1920s a witness gave a detailed description of one defendant on the basis of a fraction-of-a-second glance. The description must have been a fabrication.

Less than ideal observation conditions usually apply; crimes seldom occur in a well-controlled laboratory. Often distance, poor lighting, fast movement or the presence of a crowd interferes with the efficient working of the attention process. Well-established thresholds for the eye and the other senses have been established by research, and as those limits are approached eyewitness accounts become quite unreliable. In one case in my experience a police officer testified that he saw the defendant, a black man, shoot a victim as both stood in a doorway 120 feet away. Checking for the defense, we found the scene so poorly lit that we could hardly see a person's silhouette, let alone a face; instrument measurements revealed that the light falling on the eye amounted to less than a fifth of the light from a candle. The defense presented photographs and light readings to demonstrate that a positive identification was not very probable. The members of the jury went to the scene of the crime, had the one black juror stand in the doorway, found they could not identify his features and acquitted the defendant.

The witness himself is a major source of unreliability. To begin with, he may have been observing under stress. When a person's life or well-being is threatened, there is a response that includes an increased heart rate, breathing rate, and blood pressure and a dramatic increase in the flow of adrenalin and of available energy, making the person capable of running fast, fighting, lifting enormous weight—taking the steps necessary to ensure his safety or survival. The point is, however, that a person under extreme stress is also a less than normally reliable witness. In experimental situations an observer is less capable of remembering details, less accurate in reading dials, and less accurate in detecting signals when under stress; he is quite naturally paying more attention to his own well-being and safety than to nonessential elements in the environment. Research I have done with Air Force flight-crew members confirms that even highly trained people become poorer observers under stress. The actual threat that brought on the stress response, having been highly significant at the time, can be remembered; but memory for other details such as clothing and colors is not as clear; time estimates are particularly exaggerated.

The observer's physical condition is often a factor. A person may be too old or too sick or too tired to perceive clearly, or he may simply lack the necessary faculty. In one case I learned that a witness who had testified about shades of red had admitted to the grand jury that he was color-blind. I testified at the trial that he was apparently dichromatic, or red-green color-blind, and that his testimony was probably fabricated on the basis of information other than visual evidence. The prosecution brought on his ophthalmologist, presumably as a rebuttal witness; but the ophthalmologist testified that the witness was actually monochromatic, which meant he could perceive no colors at all. Clearly the witness was "filling in" his testimony. That, after all, is how color-blind people function in daily life, by making inferences about colors they cannot distinguish.

. . .

The tendency to see what we want or need to see has been demonstrated by numerous experiments in which people report seeing things that in fact are not present. R. Levine, Isador Chein, and Gardner Murphy had volunteers go without food for 24 hours and report what they "saw" in a series of blurred slides presented on a screen. The longer they were deprived of food the more frequently they reported seeing "food" in the blurred pictures. An analysis of the motives of the eyewitness at the time of a crime can be very valuable in determining whether or not the witness is reporting what he wanted to see. In one study I conducted at Washington University, a student dressed in a black bag that covered him completely visited a number of classes. Later the students in those classes were asked to describe the nature of the person in the bag. Most of their reports went far beyond the meager evidence: the bag-covered figure was said to be a black man, "a nut," a symbol of alienation, and so on. Further tests showed that the descriptions were related to the needs and motives of the individual witness.

Journalists and psychologists have noted a tendency for people to maintain they were present when a significant historical event took place near where they live even though they were not there at all; such people want to sound interesting, to be a small part of history. A journalist once fabricated a . . . story about a naked woman stuck to a newly painted toilet seat in a small town and got it distributed by newspaper wire services. He visited the town and interviewed citizens who claimed to have witnessed and even to have played a part in the totally fictitious event. In criminal cases with publicity and a controversial defendant, it is not uncommon for volunteer witnesses to come forward with spurious testimony.

Unreliability stemming from the original situation and from the observer's fallibility is redoubled by the circumstances attending the eventual attempt at information retrieval. First of all there is the obvious fact, supported by a considerable amount of research, that people forget verbal and pictorial information with the passage of time. They are simply too busy coping with daily life to keep paying attention to what they heard or saw; perfect recall of information is basically unnecessary and is rarely if ever displayed. The testing of recognition in a police "lineup" or a set of identification photographs is consequently less reliable the longer the time from the event to the test.

. . .

In analyses of eyewitness reports in criminal cases we have seen the reports get more accurate, more complete, and less ambiguous as the witness moves from the initial police report through grand-jury questioning to testimony at the trial. The process of filling in is an efficient way to remember but it can lead to unreliable recognition testing: the witness may adjust his memory to fit the available suspects or pictures. The witness need not be lying; he may be unaware he is distorting or reconstructing his memory. In his very effort to be conscientious he may fabricate parts of his recall to make a chaotic memory seem more plausible to the people asking questions. The questions themselves may encourage such fabrication. Elizabeth Loftus of the University of Washington has demonstrated how altering the semantic value of the words in questions about a filmed auto accident causes witnesses to distort their reports. When witnesses were asked a question using the word "smashed" as opposed to "hit" they gave higher estimates of speed and were more likely to report having seen broken glass—although there was no broken glass.

Unfair test construction often encourages error. The lineup or the array of photographs for testing the eyewitness's ability to identify a suspect can be analyzed as fair or unfair on the basis of criteria most psychologists can agree on. A fair test is designed carefully so that all faces have an equal chance of being selected by someone who did not see the suspect; the faces are similar enough to one another and to the original description of the suspect to be confusing to a person who is merely guessing; the test is conducted without leading questions or suggestions. All too frequently lineups or photograph arrays are carelessly assembled or even rigged. If, for example, there are five pictures, the chance should be only one in five that any one picture will be chosen on the basis of guessing.

Frequently, however, one picture—the picture of the suspect—may stand out. In the case of the black activist Angela Davis, one set of nine photographs used to check identification included three pictures of the defendant taken at an outdoor rally, two police "mug shots" of other women with their names displayed, a picture of a 55-year-old woman and so on. It was so easy for a witness to rule out five of the pictures as ridiculous choices that the test was reduced to four photographs, including three of Miss Davis. The probability was therefore 75 percent that a witness would pick out her picture whether he had seen her or not. Such a "test" is meaningless to a psychologist and is probably tainted as evidence in court.

Research on memory has also shown that if one item in the array of photographs is uniquely different—say in dress, race, height, sex, or photographic quality—it is more likely to be picked out. Such an array is simply not confusing enough for it to be called a test. A teacher who makes up a multiple-choice test includes several answers that sound or look alike to make it difficult for a person who does not know the right answer to succeed. Police lineups and picture layouts are multiple-choice tests; if the rules for designing test are ignored, the tests are unreliable.

No test, with photographs or a lineup, can be completely free of suggestion. When a witness is brought in by the police to attempt an identification, he can safely assume that there is some reason: that the authorities have a suspect in mind or even in custody. He is therefore under pressure to pick someone even if the officer showing the photographs is properly careful not to force the issue. The basic books on eyewitness identification all recommend that no suggestions, hints or pressure be transmitted to the witness, but my experience with criminal investigation reveals frequent abuse by zealous police officers. Such abuses include making remarks about which pictures to skip, saying, "Are you sure?" when the witness makes an error, giving hints, showing enthusiasm when the "right" picture is picked, and so on. There is one version of the lineup in which five police officers in civilian clothes stand in the line, glancing obviously at the real suspect. Suggestion can be subtler. In some experiments the test giver was merely instructed to smile and be very approving when a certain kind of photograph or statement was picked; such social approval led to an increase in the choosing of just those photographs even though there was no "correct" answer. A test that measures a need for social approval has shown that people who are high in that need (particularly those who enthusiastically volunteer information) are particularly strongly influenced by suggestion and approval coming from the test giver.

Conformity is another troublesome influence. One might expect that two eyewitnesses—or 10 or 100—who agree are better than one. Similarity of judgment is a two-edged sword, however: people can agree in error as easily as in truth. A large body of research results demonstrates that an observer can be persuaded to conform to the majority opinion even when the majority is completely wrong. In one celebrated experiment, first performed in the 1950s by Solomon E. Asch at Swarthmore College, seven observers are shown two lines and asked to say which is the shorter. Six of the people are in the pay of the experimenter; they all say that the objectively longer line is the shorter one. After hearing six people say this, the naive subject is on the spot. Astonishingly, the majority of the naive subjects say that the long line is short—in the face of reality and in spite of the fact that alone they would have no trouble giving the correct answer.

To test the effect of conformity a group of my students at Brooklyn College, led by Andrea Alper, staged a "crime" in a classroom, asked for individual descriptions, and then put the witnesses into groups so as to produce composite descriptions of the suspect. The group descriptions were more complete than the individual reports but gave rise to significantly more errors of commission: an assortment of incorrect and stereotyped details. For example, the groups (but not the individuals) reported incorrectly that the suspect was wearing the standard student attire, blue jeans.

The effects of suggestion increase when figures in obvious authority do the testing. In laboratory research we find more suggestibility and changing of attitudes when the tester is older or of apparently higher status, better dressed or wearing a uniform or a white coat—or is a pretty woman. In court I have noticed that witnesses who work together under a supervisor are hard put to disagree with their boss in testifying or in picking a photograph. The process of filling in details can be exaggerated when the boss and his employee compare their information and the employee feels obligated to back up his boss to remain in his good graces. Legal history is not lacking in anecdotes about convict witnesses who were rewarded by the authorities for their cooperation in making an identification.

In criminal investigations, as in scientific investigations, a theory can be a powerful tool for clarifying confusion, but it can also lead to distortion and unreliability if people attempt, perhaps unconsciously, to make fact fit theory and close their minds to the real meanings of facts. The eyewitness who feels pressed to say something may shape his memory to fit a theory, particularly a highly publicized and seemingly reasonable one. Robert Rosenthal of Harvard studied this effect.

He devised a test in which people were supposed to pick out a "successful" face from a set of photographs. There was actually no correct answer, but the experimenter dropped hints to his assistants as to what he thought the results should be. When they subsequently administered the test the assistants unconsciously signaled the subjects as to which photograph to pick, thus producing results that supported their boss's theory. Any test is a social interaction as well as a test.

There is a nagging gap between data on basic perceptual processes in controlled research settings and important questions about perception in the less well-controlled real world. Inspired by the new approach to perception research exemplified in the work of Neisser and of Ralph Norman Haber of the University of Rochester, my colleagues and I have felt that this gap can only be bridged by conducting empirical research on eyewitness identification in a somewhat real world. In one such experiment we staged an assault on the campus of the California State University at Hayward: a student "attacked" a professor in front of 141 witnesses; another outsider of the same age was on the scene as a bystander. We recorded the entire incident on videotape so that we could compare the true event with the eyewitness reports. After the attack we took sworn statements from each witness, asking them to describe the suspect, his clothes, and whatever they could remember about the incident. We also asked each witness to rate his own confidence in the accuracy of his description.

As we expected, the descriptions were quite inaccurate, as is usually the case in such situations. The passage of time was overestimated by a factor of almost two-and-a-half to one. The average weight estimate for the attacker was 14 percent too high, and his age was underestimated by more than two years. The total accuracy score, with points given for those judgments and for others on appearance and dress, was only 25 percent of the maximum possible score. (Only the height estimate was close. This may be because the suspect was of average height; people often cite known facts about the "average" man when they are uncertain.)

We then waited seven weeks and presented a set of six photographs to each witness individually under four different experimental conditions. There were two kinds of instructions: low-bias, in which witnesses were asked only if they recognized anybody in the photographs, and high-bias, in which witnesses were reminded of the attack incident, told that we had an idea who the suspect was, and asked to find the attacker in one of two arrangements of photographs, all well-lit frontal views of young men including the attacker and the bystander. In the unbiased picture spread, all six portraits were neatly set out with about the same expression on all the faces and with similar clothing. In the biased spread the attacker was shown with a distinctive expression and his portrait was positioned at an angle.

Only 40 percent of the witnesses identified the suspect correctly; 25 percent of them identified the innocent bystander instead; even the professor who was attacked picked out the innocent man. The highest proportion of correct identifications, 61 percent, was achieved with a combination of a biased set of photographs and biased instructions. The degree of confidence in picking suspect No. 5, the attacker, was also significantly higher in that condition. We have subsequently tested the same picture spreads with groups that never saw the original incident. We describe the assault and ask people to pick the most likely perpetrator. Under the biased conditions they too pick No. 5.

In another study undertaken at Brooklyn college, a student team, led by Miriam Slomovits, stages a live purse-snatching incident in a classroom. We gave the witnesses the usual questionnaire and got the usual bad scores. This time, however, we were concerned with a specific dilemma: Why is recognition so much better than recall? In private most lawyers and judges agree that the recall of a crime by a witness is very bad, but they still believe people can successfully identify a suspect. What we had to do was to break away from our demonstrations of how bad witnesses are at recalling details and search for what makes a witness good a recognizing a face. To do so we took the witnesses who had predictably given poor recall data and gave them a difficult recognition test. Our witnesses got not only a lineup with the acutal purse-snatcher in the group but also a second lineup that included only a person who looked like the purse-snatcher. The question was: Would the witnesses pick only the real culprit and avoid making a mistaken identification of the person who looked like him?

We videotaped two lineups of five persons each and showed them in counterbalanced order to 52 witnesses of the purse-snatching. Very few witnesses were completely sucessful in making a positive identification without ambiguity. An equal number of witnesses impeached themselves by picking the man who resembled the culprit after having correctly picked the culprit. Most people simply made a mistaken identification. Our best witnesses had also been among the best performers in the recall test; that is, they had made significantly fewer errors of commission (adding incorrect details). They had not given particularly complete reports, but at least they had not filled in. The good witnesses also expressed less confidence than witnesses who impeached themselves. Finally, when we referred to the earlier written descriptions of the suspect we found our successful witnesses had given significantly higher, and hence more accurate, estimates of weight. People guessing someone's weight often invoke a mental chart of ideal weight for height and err substantially if the person is fat. Our purse-snatcher was unusually heavy, something the successful witnesses managed to observe in spite of his loose-fitting clothing. The others were guessing.

Once again we noted that witnesses tend not to say, "I don't know." Eighty percent of our witnesses tried to pick the suspect even though most of them were mistaken. The social influence of the lineup itself seems to encourage a "yes" response.

. . .

Psychological research on human perception has advanced from the nineteenth century recording machine analogy to a more complex understanding of selective decision-making processes that are more human and hence more useful. My colleagues and I feel that psychologists can make a needed contribution to the judicial system by directing contemporary research methods to real-world problems and by speaking out in court.

. . .

It is discouraging to note that the essential findings on the unreliability of eyewitness testimony were made by Hugo Munsterberg nearly 80 years ago, and yet the practice of basing a case on eyewitness testimony and trying to persuade a jury that such testimony is superior to circumstantial evidence continues to this day. The fact is that both types of evidence involve areas of doubt. Circumstantial evidence is tied together with a theory, which is subject to questioning. Eyewitness testimony is also based on a theory, constructed by a human being (often with help from others), about what reality was like in the past; since that theory can be adjusted or changed in accordance with personality, with the situation or with social pressure, it is unwise to accept such testimony without question. It is up to a jury to determine if the doubts about an eyewitness's testimony are reasonable enough for the testimony to be rejected as untrue. Jurors should be reminded that there can be doubt about eyewitness testimony, just as there is about any other kind of evidence.

12 Photographs and Personal Identification: A Legal View

United States Supreme Court

Psychologists only have to show that their effects are statistically significant, but judges must decide individual cases. In this excerpt from a 1968 decision, the Supreme Court tries to reconcile its awareness of the fallibility of eyewitness identification with its responsibility to maintain reasonable legal procedures. The particular issue is this: In the course of the investigation of a bank robbery, witnesses were shown photographs of potential suspects. At trial the same witnesses identified one of those suspects as the robber, and he was convicted. But the experience of viewing photographs may well bias a subsequent identification; at the very least, it means that witnesses will recognize the accused as someone they have seen before. Should such witnesses be automatically disqualified? No, says the Court: Each case must be considered in the light of its individual circumstances.

A federally insured savings and loan association (hereafter "the bank") was robbed by two unmasked men. Five bank employees witnessed the robbery, and on the day it occurred gave the FBI written statements. Petitioners Simmons and Garrett, and another (Andrews) were subsequently indicted for the crime. In the afternoon of the day of the rob-

From *Simmons et al.* v. *United States*, 390 U.S. 377; argued January 15, 1968, decided March 18, 1968. Mr. Justice Harlan delivered the opinion of the Court.

bery, FBI agents made a warrantless search of Andrews' mother's house and found two suitcases in the basement, one of which contained incriminating items. The next morning FBI agents obtained and (without indicating the progress of the investigation or suggesting who the suspects were) showed separately to each of the five bank employee witnesses some snapshots containing mostly group pictures of Andrews, Simmons, and others. Each witness identified pictures of Simmons as one of the robbers. None identified Andrews. Later some of these witnesses viewed indeterminate numbers of pictures and all identified Simmons. Three of the employees identified Garrett as the second robber from other photographs. . . .

The facts as to the identification claim are these. As has been noted previously, FBI agents on the day following the robbery obtained from Andrews' sister a number of snapshots of Andrews and Simmons. There seem to have been at least six of these pictures, consisting mostly of group photographs of Andrews, Simmons, and others. Later the same day, these were shown to the five bank employees who had witnessed the robbery at their place of work, the photographs being exhibited to each employee separately. Each of the five employees identified Simmons from the photographs. At later dates, some of these witnesses were again interviewed by the FBI and shown indeterminate numbers of pictures. Again, all identified Simmons. At trial, the Government did not introduce any of the photographs, but relied upon in-court identification by the five eyewitnesses, each of whom swore that Simmons was one of the robbers.

In support of his argument, Simmons looks to last Term's "lineup" decisions—*United States* v. *Wade*, 388 U.S. 218, and *Gilbert* v. *California*, 388 U.S. 263—in which this Court first departed from the rule that the manner of an extra-judicial identification affects only the weight, not the admissibility, of identification testimony at trial. The rationale of those cases was that an accused is entitled to counsel at any "critical stage of the prosecution," and that a post-indictment lineup is such a "critical stage." See 388 U.S., at 236–237. Simmons, however, does not contend that he was entitled to counsel at the time the pictures were shown to the witnesses. Rather, he asserts simply that in the circumstances the identification procedure was so unduly prejudicial as fatally to taint his conviction. This is a claim which must be evaluated in light of the totality of surrounding circumstances. See *Stovall* v. *Denno*, 388 U.S. 293, at 302; *Palmer* v. *Peyton*, 359 F. 2d 199. Viewed in that context, we find the claim untenable.

It must be recognized that improper employment of photographs by police may sometimes cause witnesses to err in identifying criminals. A witness may have obtained only a brief glimpse of a criminal, or may have seen him under poor conditions. Even if the police subsequently follow the most correct photographic identification procedures and show him the pictures of a number of individuals without indicating whom they suspect, there is some danger that the witness may make an incorrect identification. This danger will be increased if the police display to the witness only the picture of a single individual who generally resembles the person he saw, or if they show him the pictures of several persons among which the photograph of a single such individual recurs or is in some way emphasized. The chance of misidentification is also heightened if the police indicate to the witness that they have other evidence that one of the persons pictured committed the crime. Regardless of how the initial misidentification comes about, the witness thereafter is apt to retain in his memory the image of the photograph rather than of the person actually seen, reducing the trustworthiness of subsequent lineup or courtroom identification.

Despite the hazards of initial identification by photograph, this procedure has been used widely and effectively in criminal law enforcement, from the standpoint both of apprehending offenders and of sparing innocent suspects the ignominy of arrest by allowing eyewitnesses to exonerate them through scrutiny of photographs. The danger that use of the technique may result in convictions based on misidentification may be substantially lessened by a course of cross-examination at trial which exposes to the jury the method's potential for error. We are unwilling to prohibit its employment, either in the exercise of our supervisory power or, still less, as a matter of constitutional requirement. Instead, we hold that each case must be considered on its own facts,and that convictions based on eyewitness identification at trial following a pretrial identification by photograph will be set aside on that ground only if the photographic identification procedure was so impermissibly suggestive as to give rise to a very substantial likelihood of irreparable misidentification. This standard accords with our resolution of a similar issue in *Stovall* v. *Denno*, 388 U.S. 293, 301–302, and with decisions of other courts on the question of identification by photograph.

Applying the standard to this case, we conclude that petitioner Simmons' claim on this score must fail. In the first place, it is not suggested that it was unnecessary for the FBI to resort to photographic identification in this instance. A serious felony had been committed. The perpetrators were still at large. The inconclusive clues which law enforcement officials possessed led to Andrews and Simmons. It was essential for the FBI agents swiftly to determine whether they were on the right track, so that they could properly deploy their forces in Chicago and, if necessary, alert officials in other cities. The justification for this method of procedure was hardly less compelling than that which we found to justify the "one-man lineup" in *Stovall* v. *Denno, supra.*

In the second place, there was in the circumstances of this case little chance that the procedure utilized led to misidentification of Simmons. The robbery took place in the afternoon in a well-lighted bank. The robbers wore no masks. Five bank employees had been able to see the robber later identified as Simmons for periods ranging up to five minutes. Those witnesses were shown the photographs only a day later, while their memories were still fresh. At least six photographs were displayed to each witness. Apparently, these consisted primarily of group photographs, with Simmons and Andrews each appearing several times in the series. Each witness was alone when he or she saw the photographs. There is no evidence to indicate that the witnesses were told anything about the progress of the investigation, or that the FBI agents in any other way suggested which persons in the pictures were under suspicion.

Under these conditions, all five eyewitnesses identified Simmons as one of the robbers. None identified Andrews, who apparently was as prominent in the photographs as Simmons. These initial identifications were confirmed by all five witnesses in subsequent viewings of photographs and at trial, where each witness identified Simmons in person. Notwithstanding cross-examination, none of the witnesses displayed any doubt about their respective identifications of Simmons. Taken together, these circumstances leave little room for doubt that the identification of Simmons was correct, even though the identification procedure employed may have in some respects fallen short of the ideal.[1] We hold that in the factual surroundings of this case the identification procedure used was not such as to deny Simmons due process of law or to call for reversal under our supervisory authority.

---

[1]The reliability of the identification procedure could have been increased by allowing only one or two of the five eyewitnesses to view the pictures of Simmons. If thus identified, Simmons could later have been displayed to the other eyewitnesses in a lineup, thus permitting the photographic identification to be supplemented by a corporeal identification, which is normally more accurate. See P. Wall, Eye-Witness Identification in Criminal Cases 83 (1965); Williams, Identification Parades [1955], *Crim. L. Rev.* 525, 531. Also, it probably would have been preferable for the witnesses to have been shown more than six snapshots, for those snapshots to have pictured a greater number of individuals, and for there to have been proportionally fewer pictures of Simmons. See Wall, *supra*, at 74–82; Williams, *supra*, at 530.

13 Memory for Faces and the Circumstances of Encounter

Evan Brown, Kenneth Deffenbacher,
and William Sturgill

In Simmons et al. *v.* United States *(Selection 12), the Supreme Court suggested that photographs shown to witnesses in the course of an investigation may lead to incorrect identifications later on. In this selection, Brown et al. support that suggestion with experimental evidence.*

Recent research suggests that visual recognition of scenes and faces can be strikingly accurate, at least under optimal conditions. Using self-paced presentations, Shepard's (1967) subjects viewed 612 pictures of "things" and "scenes" in a directed-memory test. Recognition accuracy on an immediate test of 68 "old–new" pairs was about 98 percent. With a one-week delay, accuracy was about 90 percent. In similar tasks but with controlled presentation times, Standing, Conezio, and Haber (1970) and Standing (1973) reported immediate recognition of about 90-percent accuracy on old–new pairs even when several thousand pictures of scenes were presented for only a few seconds each. Accuracy rates for face recognition are somewhat more difficult to compare given procedural variations. However, accuracy here seems generally to be rather good as well, if somewhat below that for scenes. Thus, in a study using procedures similar to Shepard's, Hochberg, and Galper (1967) showed subjects as many as 60 pictures of college-student faces, testing immediate recognition with 15 old–new pairs. Accuracy was about 90 percent.

From the *Journal of Applied Psychology*, 1977, 62, 311–318. Copyright 1977 by the American Psychological Association. Reprinted by permission.

Though these studies suggest that recognition memory for faces or scenes can be quite good, it might be misleading to extrapolate from them to witness identifications of criminal suspects. To be accurate, such witnesses must indeed be able to recognize a previously encountered face; in addition, however, they must be able to recall the circumstances in which that face was encountered, whether in fact at the scene of the crime, whether instead in newspaper or television presentations or police mugshots. The possibility that a witness might be able to recognize a face and at the same time be unable to recall correctly the circumstances of encounter has been addressed by the U.S. Supreme Court (*Simmons et al.* v. *United States*, 1968) [*see Selection 12*]. In that decision, the Court noted the potentially biasing effects of showing a witness a single mugshot or showing mugshots in which a particular suspect is somehow emphasized (e.g., Buckhout, 1974) [*See Selection 11*]. In addition, however, and most relevant to the present question, they noted that even with best procedures, a witness may be biased by a mugshot if he "obtained only a brief glimpse of a criminal, or may have seen him under poor conditions" (p. 383). In such circumstances, they held, "the witness thereafter is apt to retain in his memory the image of the photograph rather than of the person actually seen" (p. 383). On the other hand, in denying Simmons's appeal, the Court noted that he had apparently been visible to witnesses for up to five minutes during a robbery in a well-lit bank.

Experimental evidence regarding this possibility—that recognition might occur with a failure to recall the circumstances of encounter—seems to be lacking. Studies of memory for picture orientation (e.g., Standing, Conezio, and Haber, 1970) do suggest that recall at least for orientation may be poorer and show more marked decline than visual recognition memory. However, the recall task seems too different from that required of a witness to warrant generalization. Similarly, although several studies of witness memory in situations approximating real life have recently appeared (e.g., Buckhout, 1974; Laughery, Alexander, and Lane, 1971; Loftus, 1975), potential differences between visual recognition memory and memory for the circumstances of encounter have not been to our knowledge among the variables investigated. The present experiments were designed to deal with this question.

EXPERIMENT 1

Experiment 1 was designed to compare the highly accurate recognition memory shown by subjects for pictures of faces in directed memory

tasks such as those of Hochberg and Galper (1967) with the same subjects' ability to recall the circumstances in which those faces were
encountered.

Method

Subjects. Subjects were 14 introductory psychology students, 13
women (12 white, 1 black) and 1 (white) man, who volunteered in order
to receive a minor amount of extra course credit.

Stimulus materials and situations. One hundred 7.62 × 12.70 cm
black-and-white photographs of male and female white children ranging in age from 8 to 10 years comprised the stimulus materials. These
photographs were from a single suburban school and were originally
collected to provide an unselected pool of pictures for facial attrac-
tiveness research. The three rooms used for the experiment differed
markedly in size and general appearance.

Procedure. Subjects, tested individually, were presented 25 photographs of faces in one room, and 2 hours later, in another room, were
presented 25 more such photographs. Two days later, in yet a third
room, they were shown 100 pictures of faces in pairs, with one in each
pair having been previously presented and the other a new one. The
subjects were asked to indicate for each pair the picture previously
presented and the room in which it had been presented. In an effort
to maximize memory performance, subjects had been warned in
advance of the original presentation that they would be asked both
these questions and had been given 20 seconds for the study of each
picture. Final presentation was self-paced, with no subject taking more
than 20 seconds.

Results and Discussion

Recognition accuracy was as previous directed memory studies (e.g.,
Hochberg and Galper, 1967) would lead one to expect. Across subjects,
the mean proportion of photographs correctly identified as old versus
new was .96, a proportion far above chance, $z = 24.41$, $p < .01$. Recall
of the circumstances of encounter for correctly recognized photographs was much less impressive, however, with a mean proportion
of only .58, $z = 5.44$, $p < .01$. Examination of the data from individual
subjects showed a similar pattern. Recognition scores ranged from .84
to 1.00, with all scores reliably above chance ($ps < .01$); whereas recall
scores ranged from .44 to .68, with only five of the 14 able to recall the

circumstances of encounter in a statistically reliable fashion ($ps < .01$). Though picture set and room were confounded in the design of this experiment, no systematic bias toward either combination was observed. For purposes of comparison with later experiments, signal detectability analyses were also performed, yielding group d's of 2.48 (obtained from a table for two-alternative, forced-choice experiments in Elliott, 1959) and .40 (hit proportion $= .58$; false alarms $= .42$) for recognition and recall, respectively. Gourevitch and Galanter's (1967) test of significance between two d's indicated that subjects discriminated among faces better than they discriminated among circumstances of encounter ($p = .01$).

These results clearly support the notion that persons are better able to recognize faces than they are able to remember where they saw them. Further, these results suggest that witnesses in real-life situations, might, if sufficiently confused as to whether a suspect's face was seen in mugshots or at the scene of the crime, indict a suspect on the basis of face recognition alone. Given this possibility, Experiment 2 was designed to simulate more closely one possible situation for an actual witness, one somewhat like the *Simmons et al.* v. *United States* (1968) case, in which a witness knows that a crime is taking place and attempts to remember the participants. As compared to Experiment 1, Experiment 2 differs primarily in using actual persons rather than pictures of them (where appropriate) and in using a smaller and probably more realistic number of such persons. In addition, Experiment 2 does not separate recognition responses from recall. Rather, it models the usual criminal identification procedure with its mugshots and line-ups so as to document better any confusions or biases introduced by them.

Experiment 3 was designed instead to simulate less optimal viewing conditions, a situation in which witnesses interact with criminals but do not suspect that a crime is occurring and lack any obvious motivation to remember the criminals, or even to look at them closely. Such a situation is somewhat analogous to laboratory studies of incidental memory. It differs, however, in that it is not of direct concern here whether a given witness may have difficulty for strictly memorial reasons or because of a failure to note the suspect's facial and other characteristics in the first place. In addition to this differnece, Experiment 3 involves fewer criminals than in Experiment 2, the rationale being that it would be futile to expect accurate identification of a large number of criminals under these circumstances.

[*The authors' account of their Experiment 2 is omitted here. In that experiment, ten "criminals" briefly appeared before a class that had been forewarned to observe them carefully. Afterwards the class was shown pictures—"mugshots"—of some of these "criminals" together* with other mugshots of people they had not seen. A week later, the same class was presented with several "lineups" that included some of the original "criminals" whose mugshots had been shown, some who had not appeared in mugshots, some of the noncriminals whose mugshots had been shown, and some new individuals. Because Experiment 3 (below) was very similar in design and somewhat more realistic in its setting, it seems unnecessary to describe the results of Experiment 2 in detail. The authors' summary of those results follows.]

Though our subjects did much better than chance at distinguishing criminals from noncriminals, these results would still not be overly confidence inspiring were they to hold in real-life situations. There was some tendency to mistake having seen a mugshot for having seen a person, as shown by the significantly greater indictment of mugshot suspects over lineup-only suspects. Although these tendencies not to recall circumstances in which faces were encountered did not appear to be so important here as in Experiment 1, there was still a one-in-five probability that a mugshot-only suspect would be indicted and a one-in-two probability that a criminal without mugshot would escape indictment by a typical witness. Compounding this from a forensic standpoint, there was as previously no significant relation between subject confidence and accuracy, $r(62) = .12$, $p > .05$, whereas there was as before a significant relation between confidence when correct and confidence when incorrect, $r(12) = .70$, $p < .01$.

EXPERIMENT 3

Method

Subjects.   Subjects were 238 male and female students in a large second-semester introductory psychology class, with data from 175 (all white) used for the mugshot phase (35 no shows, 9 knew a criminal, and 19 incomplete protocols) and data from 146 used for the lineup phase (29 additional no shows in this phase). Initially, the witnesses were unaware that they were participating in a research project. However, at the start of the mugshot phase, they were informed of what had occurred and were told that they did not have to participate further unless they so wished. All in attendance agreed to participate.

Stimulus persons and materials.   The stimuli were four persons posing as "criminals" and mugshots of 14 persons, including those of the criminals. The criminals were four of the stimulus persons described in Experiment 2 who ranged in height from 1.70 m to 1.76 m. Each criminal was paid $2.50 for each block of activity in which he participated. Mugshots were 20.32 × 25.40 c nonglossy color photographs of the four criminals and of ten other stimulus persons from Experiment 2. Each suspect was represented by one front- and one right-side view, mounted side by side.

Procedure.   At the first midterm of the class, the witnesses were given their examination materials by persons who unbeknownst to them were the criminals. The classroom used had two entrance corridors, and two criminals were in each corridor; one handed out test questions and the other, IBM answer sheets. Witnesses entering through a given corridor were unable to see the criminals in the other corridor. Thus, approximately half the class encountered one set of criminals, and the other half encountered the other set. The IBM sheets were unobtrusively coded so that it could be determined which set had been encountered by each witness.

In their discussion sections two or three days later, witnesses were shown a matrix of 12 mugshot pairs of suspects on a display board. For a given witness, one mugshot pair was of a criminal encountered at the midterm, one was of a criminal from the other corridor—a person not previously encountered and therefore for that witness an innocent—and ten were innocent fillers. Witnesses were asked for each suspect to indicate whether or not he had given them test materials at the midterm and, if so, which sort of test materials (answer sheet or questions). They were also asked to indicate their confidence in each judgment in the same manner as in Experiment 2.

Finally, at the next meeting of the whole class, four or five days after the mugshot session, the witnesses were shown a lineup of four persons, the four criminals. For any given witness, one person in the lineup was a criminal whose mugshot had also been seen (criminal with mugshot); one a criminal whose mugshot had not been seen (criminal without a mugshot); one an innocent—a person from the other corridor—whose mugshot had been seen (mugshot only); and one an innocent—the other person from the other corridor—whose mugshot had not been seen (lineup only). The witnesses were asked to answer the same questions regarding each suspect as they had earlier been asked of the mugshots. In addition, however, they were asked to indicate for each whether or not his mugshot had been among the 12 shown in the discussion section. As before, they were also asked to indicate their confidence in each judgment, using the scale described in Experiment 2.

Results and Discussion

In the mugshot phase of the experiment, the mean proportion of innocents falsely indicted was .15 ($d' = .46$, $p < .01$). As compared to

Experiment 2, these indictment proportions are lowered in part for procedural reasons having nothing to do with memory performance, namely, the presence of 12 mugshots where witnesses were aware that there were at most two criminals. The d' is unaffected by such considerations of relative frequency, however, and the lowered value presumably reflects differences in instructions regarding subsequent tests of memory together with any effects of the greater retention interval, two or three days in this experiment versus $1\frac{1}{2}$ hours in Experiment 2. As previously, there was no correlation of accuracy and confidence across subjects, $r(173) = .03, p < .05$. There was also, as before, a correlation between confidence when correct and confidence when incorrect, $r(173) = .61, p < .01$.

When witnesses at the lineup were asked whether the suspects had been involved in the crime, that is, had given them test materials, indictment proportions for the criminals with mugshots, criminals without mugshots, mugshots-only, and lineup-only conditions were .45, .24, .29, and .18, respectively, with a mean of .29. Four of the pairwise comparisons of indictment proportions were statistically significant ($ps < .05$), with the two exceptions being the comparisons of the criminals without mugshots with the mugshot-only condition and also with the lineup-only condition. Signal-detection analyses yielding the same pattern of results are given in Table 13-1. Again, there was no significant correlation between accuracy and confidence, $r(144) = .12, p < .05$, but there was a significant relationship between confidence when correct and when incorrect, $r(144) = .60, p < .01$.

These results would scarcely be satisfactory were they to hold for real-life situations involving undirected memory. Despite the fact that only two criminals were encountered by each witness, in contrast to the ten of Experiment 2, accuracy was much reduced in this situation.

TABLE 13-1
Between-conditions d' scores in Experiment 3

Conditions	Score
CMS vs. CNMS	.56**
CMS vs. MS	.40**
CMS vs. LO	.76**
CNMS vs. MS	−.15
CNMS vs. LO	.21
MS vs. LO	.36*

Note: CMS = criminals with mugshots; CNMS = criminals without mugshots; MS = mugshots only; LO = lineup only.
*p < .05, **p < .01

Even the suspects appearing both as criminals and in mugshots were only indicted 2.5 times as often as those not previously encountered at all, and those appearing only in mugshots were at least as likely to be indicted as criminals without mugshots. This latter finding is particularly important from a forensic standpoint. Although mugshots might be useful for investigative purposes, we would tend to distrust indictments in situations such as those where witnesses had previously seen the suspects' mugshots.

Witnesses' responses to a further question were even less accurate. They were asked, for each suspect they placed at the crime, about the suspect's actions, that is, whether the suspect had handed them an answer sheet or a test booklet. Even if the analysis was restricted to witnesses who had been correct in their identifications of a criminal, the responses regarding actions were essentially at the chance level. For correctly indicted criminals with mugshots suspects, the proportion of correctly recalled actions was .43, and for correctly indicted criminals without mugshots suspects the proportion of actions correctly recalled was .46; in both cases chance would have been .50.

GENERAL DISCUSSION

The implications of the present experiments for forensic decision making seem fairly straightforward. For this purpose, Experiment 1 is relevant insofar as it clearly demonstrates that face recognition is much better than recall of circumstances of encounter, raising the possibility that on some occasions witnesses might base their indictments on face recognition alone. The results of the other experiments would seem to bear primarily on two questions, the general question of witness accuracy and the question of biases induced by mugshot encounters. With respect to the general question of witness accuracy, the main results of concern are the lack of correlation between accuracy and confidence and the evidence of considerable confusion both in mugshot identifications and in identifications out of lineups. Though real-life situations might produce different hit and false-alarm rates, the differences, or lack thereof, in indictment rates among suspect conditions documented by the d' analyses should be much more generalizable.

More interesting, however, than the general evidence of witness fallibility are the results that relate to mugshot-induced biases, since they could have considerable bearing on questions of legal procedure and admissibility of evidence. Thus, although one cannot abandon the use of witnesses simply because their memories are less than perfect, one can restrict admissibility of testimony in situations where procedures, such as use of mugshots, may most bias such testimony. So far as our present experiments are concerned, the U.S. Supreme Court's strictures would appear to apply to Experiment 3, as involving a brief glimpse under poor conditions; in Experiment 3 the witnesses did appear "to retain ... the image of the photograph rather than of the person ... ," since they were at least as likely to indict a suspect on the basis of a single mugshot encounter as compared to a single live encounter. Experiment 2, in contrast, seems somewhat similar to the Simmons case itself in that they both involved more nearly optimal original viewing conditions. The difference in viewing time is probably not terribly critical, given the finding that observers still show about 90-percent recognition accuracy even with as little as 1 second original viewing time (Standing et al., 1970). Certainly, there would be some greater likelihood of confusion induced by mugshot encounters in a case like Experiment 2 because of the greater number of suspects involved. In any event, we are pleased to report empirical support for the Court's distinctions.

REFERENCES

Buckhout, R. Eyewitness testimony. *Scientific American,* 1974, *231* (6), 23–31.

Elliott, P. B. Tables of *d'.* In J. A. Swets (ed.), *Signal Detection and Recognition by Human Observers.* New York: Wiley, 1964.

Gourevitch, V., and Galanter, E. A significance test for one-parameter isosensitivity functions. *Psychometrika,* 1967, *32,* 25–33.

Hochberg, J., and Galper, R. Recognition of faces: I. An exploratory study. *Psychonomic Science,* 1967, *9,* 619–620.

Laughery, K., Alexander, J., and Lane, A. Recognition of human faces: Effects of target exposure time, target position, pose position, and type of photograph. *Journal of Applied Psychology,* 1971, *55,* 477–483.

Loftus, E. Leading questions and the eyewitness report. *Cognitive Psychology,* 1975, *7,* 560–572.

Shepard, R. Recognition memory for words, sentences, and pictures. *Journal of Verbal Learning and Verbal Behavior,* 1967, *6,* 156–163.

Simmons et al. v. *United States.* 390 U.S. 377 (1968)

Standing, L. Learning 10,000 pictures. *Quarterly Journal of Experimental Psychology,* 1973, *25,* 207–222.

Standing, L., Conezio, J., and Haber, R. Perception and memory for pictures: Single trial learning of 2500 visual stimuli. *Psychonomic Science,* 1970, *19,* 73–74.

14 John Dean's Memory: A Case Study

Ulric Neisser

Witnesses are fallible, but they are not always wrong. If the psychology of memory is to do more than write CAUTION on judicial medicine labels, it must seek to understand the successes of testimony as well as the failures. J. J. Gibson insisted that the study of perception should begin with veridical seeing rather than illusion and error; maybe the study of memory can benefit from a similar approach. It was partly with this possibility in mind that I undertook the study of John Dean's testimony. What could psychology learn from a case where the witness was right?

What I learned, at least, is that being "right" is not a simple notion. Even when Dean was entirely wrong about the course of a particular conversation, he could be giving an essentially true account of the facts lying behind that conversation—of long-run, invariant states of affairs that had manifested themselves in many individual episodes. Combining information from several points in time may indeed lead to error (Selections 10, 13), and it is not what witnesses are supposed to do. Nevertheless, it is often a good way to establish the real facts of the matter—the ones that are worth remembering.

"Have you always had a facility for recalling the details of conversations which took place many months ago?" Senator Inouye of Hawaii asked this question of John Dean with more than a trace of disbelief. Dean,

From *Cognition*, 1981, 9, 1–22. Reprinted by permission.

the former counsel to President Richard M. Nixon, was testifying before the "Watergate" Committee of the United States Senate in June 1973. His testimony had opened with a 245-page statement, in which he described literally dozens of meetings that he had attended over a period of several years. The meetings were with John Mitchell, Robert Haldeman, Charles Colson, Gordon Liddy, and others whose names became American household words as the Watergate scandal brought down the Nixon Administration. Some were with Nixon himself. Dean's testimony seemed to confirm what many already suspected: that these high officials were engaged in a "cover-up" of White House involvement in the original Watergate burglary. But was he telling the truth? How much did he really remember?

In a psychological experiment, it is relatively easy to determine whether what the subject says is true. The experimenter knows what really happened because she staged it in the first place, or because she kept a record with which the subject's report can be compared. Because life does not keep such records, legal testimony is usually evaluated in more indirect ways: corroborative witnesses, cross-examination, circumstantial evidence. For some of Dean's testimony, however, it is now possible to compare what he said with a factual record— the *Presidential Transcripts*. This comparison will enable us to assess the accuracy of his memory rather precisely. In addition, it may clarify our theoretical conceptions of memory itself.

When Dean first testified, his "facility for recalling details" seemed so impressive that some writers called him "the human tape recorder." Ironically, a very real tape recorder had been tuned in to some of the same "details." Not long after its interrogation of Dean, the Senate Committee discovered that all conversations in Nixon's Oval Office were routinely (but secretly) recorded. The result of this discovery was a sharp legal struggle for possession of the tapes. When the President realized that he would not be able to keep the tapes out of the hands of the prosecutors indefinitely, he decided to transcribe some of them and release the transcripts himself. Although he did this reluctantly, he also thought it possible that they might actually help his cause. The published version of the *Presidential Transcripts* (1974) includes a lengthy foreword reiterating Nixon's claim that he knew nothing of the cover-up. (It does admit that there are ". . . possible ambiguities that . . . someone with a motive to discredit the President could take out of context and distort to suit his own purposes" [p. 5]. The foreword explicitly insists that the transcripts discredit Dean's testimony. Dean himself, however, saw them as substantiating *his* side of the story. In his autobiography (Dean, 1976) he describes himself as "ecstatic" (p. 332) to learn of the tapes' existence, because they would prove he had told the truth.

The testimony and the transcripts are now in the public domain. I propose to treat them as data, as if they had resulted from a deliberately conducted memory experiment. The analysis of these data will be somewhat unorthodox, however, because we know its outcome in advance. If Dean had actually perjured himself—if the transcripts had proved him to be fundamentally mistaken or dishonest—the defense lawyers in the subsequent Watergate trials would surely have seized the opportunity to discredit his testimony. Instead, the outcome of those trials has vindicated him: the highest-placed members of the White House staff all went to prison for doing what John Dean said they had done. Nixon, of course, was forced to resign. If history has ever proven anything, it surely proves that Dean remembered those conversations and told the truth about them. I will not quarrel with that assessment here, but we shall see that "truth," "accuracy," and "memory" are not simple notions. Dean's testimony was by no means always accurate. Yet even when he was wrong, there was a sense in which he was telling the truth; even when he was right, it was not necessarily because he remembered a particular conversation well.

These are levels of analysis with which psychology has rarely been concerned. Although there have been many demonstrations of the fallibility of testimony (Stern, 1904 [*Selection 9*]; Buckhout, 1974 [*Selection 11*]), none has dealt with a situation as complex as Dean's: with such significant material, such long spans of time, or such ambiguous motives. We will find it hard to do full justice to John Dean's memory within the conceptual framework of the psychology of memory. Nevertheless, that framework is not irrelevant. It includes a number of valuable ideas: that memory is influenced by mental "scripts" or "schemata" for familiar events (Bartlett, 1932; Bransford and Franks, 1972; Bower, Black, and Turner, 1979); that distortions of memory are often motivated by the needs and character of the individual (Freud, 1956); and that a person's general knowledge ("semantic memory") must be distinguished from his recollection of specific events ("episodic memory," Tulving, 1972). Most obviously, we will have to make a distinction that has been familiar at least since Bartlett: to contrast *verbatim* recall with memory for the *gist* of what was said.

Verbatim recall is word-for-word reproduction. It is not something that we expect of ourselves in everyday life. Dean did not claim to be able to recall conversations verbatim, and indeed he could not. (We shall see that even the few phrases that he seemed to recall exactly may owe their fidelity to frequent repetition.) Memory for gist, on the other hand, occurs when we recall the "sense" of an original text in different words. To remember the gist of a story or a conversation is to be roughly faithful to the argument, the story line, the underlying sequence of ideas. Psychologists have developed a number of methods of evaluating memory for gist. One can divide the text and the recall protocol into so-called "idea units," and count how many of them match. With somewhat more trouble, one can make a structural analysis of the original, perhaps guided by theroretical ideas about "story grammars" and "schemata"; then one can determine how much of the structure reappears in the reproduction (e.g., Mandler and Johnson, 1977). These methods have worked well in the laboratory, where there is nothing to remember except an originally presented text. They are not as easily applied to the recall of actual conversations that take place in a context of real events: The events may be remembered even when the gist of the conversations is not.

Analysis of Dean's testimony does indeed reveal some instances of memory for the gist of what was said on a particular occasion. Elsewhere in his testimony, however, there is surprisingly little correspondence between the course of a conversation and his account of it. Even in those cases, however, there is usually a deeper level at which he is right. He gave an accurate portrayal of the real situation, of the actual characters and commitments of the people he knew, and of the events that lay behind the conversations he was trying to remember. Psychology is unaccustomed to analyzing the truthfulness of memory at this level, because we usually work with laboratory material that has no reference beyond itself. One of my purposes in analyzing John Dean's testimony is to call attention to this level of memory, and perhaps to devise ways in which it can be studied.

DEAN'S OWN ACCOUNT OF HIS MEMORY

It is impossible to survey all of Dean's testimony here; there is far too much of it. Moreover, most of his conversations were not recorded at all (so far as we know); it was only in the President's Oval Office that tape recorderers ran night and day. Not even all of the taped material is fully reproduced in the available transcripts. We will only be able to analyze the two conversations reported in his testimony for which an apparently unedited transcript has been published. The reader should bear in mind that we are dealing with only a small fraction of what Dean said. The present paper is not an effort to assess his overall contribution to the Watergate investigations or to the course of justice; it is a psychological study aimed at clarifying the nature of memory for conversations.

The two conversations we will examine are those of September 15, 1972 and March 21, 1973. These two meetings with the President were crucial for the Senate Committee, which was trying to determine the extent of Nixon's involvement in the Watergate cover-up. Accordingly, Dean was cross-examined about both of them at length. He had already described each conversation in his long opening statement to the Committee: it was that statement which aroused Senator Inouye's incredulity. The interchange between Dean and Inouye is interesting in its own right: it may be the only discussion of mnemonics and metamemory in the Congressional Record.

> *Senator Inouye:* Your 245-page statement is remarkable for the detail with which it recounts events and conversations occurring over a period of many months. It is particularly remarkable in view of the fact that you indicated that it was prepared without benefit of note or daily diary. Would you describe what documents were available to you in addition to those which have been identified as exhibits?
>
> *Mr. Dean:* What I did in preparing this statement, I had kept a newspaper clipping file from roughly June 17 [*June 17, 1972 was the date of the Watergate break-in*], up until about the time these hearings started when I stopped doing any clipping with any regularity. It was by going through every single newspaper article outlining what had happened and then placing myself in what I had done in a given sequence in time, I was aware of all the principal activities I had been involved in, the dealings I had had with others in relationship to those activities. Many times things were in response to press activities or press stories that would result in further activities. I had a good memory of most of the highlights of things that had occurred, and it was through this process, and being extremely careful in my recollection, particularly of the meetings with the President (*Hearings*, pp. 1432–1433).

Note that Dean has spontaneously invented the temporal equivalent of an ancient mnemonic device: the famous "method of loci." In that method, one mentally moves through a familiar series of places in order to recall images that were previously assigned to them. Dean apparently used newspaper clippings in a similar way, to pinpoint moments in time rather than loci in space; then he tried to recall what he had been doing at those moments. Senator Inouye's next questions (I am omitting some additional comments by Dean) indicate that he failed to grasp this point:

> *Senator Inouye:* Are you suggesting that your testimony was primarily based upon press accounts?
>
> *Mr. Dean:* No sir, I am saying that I used the press accounts as one of the means to trigger my recollection of what had occurred during given periods of time.

Inouye still does not understand.

> *Senator Inouye:* Am I to gather from this that you had great faith in the reporting in the press?
>
> *Mr. Dean:* No, I am saying what was happening is that this sequentially—many times White House activities related to a response to a given press activity. I did not have the benefit—in fact, the statement might be

even more detailed, Senator, if I had had the benefit of all the Ziegler briefings where some of these questions came up very specifically in press briefings as to given events at that time, but I didn't have the benefit of those (*Ibid.*).

Senator Inouye: In addition to the press clippings, the logs, what other sources did you use in the process of reconstruction?

Mr. Dean: Well, Senator, I think I have a good memory. I think that anyone who recalls my student years knew that I was very fast at recalling information, retaining information. I was the type of student who didn't have to work very hard in school because I do have a memory that I think is good (*Ibid.*)

A moment later Inouye asks the question I have already quoted, encouraging Dean to say more about his memory:

Senator Inouye: Have you always had a facility for recalling the details of conversations which took place many months ago? (*Ibid.*)

Dean responds with examples of things he would certainly never forget, beginning with conversations in the Oval Office:

Mr. Dean: Well, I would like to start with the President of the United States. It was not a regular activity for me to go in and visit with the President. For most of the members of the White House staff it is not a daily activity. When you meet with the President of the United States it is a very momentous occasion, and you tend to remember what the President of the United States says when you have a conversation with him. [*Dean goes on to mention several other salient events that he remembers well, and concludes*] . . . So I would say that I have an ability to recall not specific words necessarily but certainly the tenor of a conversation and the gist of a conversation (*Ibid.*, pp. 1433–1434).

We shall see later that Dean recalls the "gist" of some conversations and not of others; the determinants of memory are more complicated than he believes them to be. In particular, he did *not* remember what the President said in their first prolonged and "momentous" meeting. But there is no doubt about his confidence in his own testimony: at the end of the exchange with Inouye, he expresses it again:

Mr. Dean: I cannot repeat the very words he [*the President*] used, no, Sir. As I explained to Senator Gurney, my mind is not a tape recorder, but it certainly receives the message that is being given (*Ibid.*).

THE MEETING OF SEPTEMBER 15

On June 17, 1972, five men were arrested in the offices of the Democratic National Committee in the Watergate Office Building. They had planned to tap the Committee's telephones as part of an illegal "political intelligence" operation, mounted on President Nixon's behalf in the 1972 presidential elections. High White House officials then began a major effort to conceal their involvement in the affair, even to the point of paying "hush money" to some of those who had been arrested. John Dean was centrally involved in the cover-up. His chief task was to "contain" the legal investigation of the Watergate break-in, concealing every link between the underlings already caught and the White House. On September 15 this aim seemed achieved, because on that day the Grand Jury handed down indictments against only seven men: the five burglars plus Howard Hunt and Gordon Liddy. Since Hunt and Liddy were "small fish," and the Justice Department said it had no evidence to indict anyone else, Dean felt victorious. When the President summoned him to the Oval Office that afternoon, he expected to be praised.

The transcript indicates that the meeting lasted 50 minutes. It begins with the following interchange among the President (*P*), Dean (*D*), and Robert Haldeman (*H*), Nixon's "Chief of Staff." Note that Dean and Haldeman are both obviously pleased by the events of the day, while the President has little to say about them.

> *P*: Hi, how are you? You had quite a day today, didn't you? You got Watergate on the way, didn't you?
> *D*: We tried.
> *H*: How did it all end up?
> *D*: Ah, I think we can say well, at this point. The press is playing it just as we expected.
> *H*: Whitewash?
> *D*: No, not yet—the story right now—
> *P*: It is a big story.
> *H*: Five indicted plus the WH former guy and all that.
> *D*: Plus two White House fellows.
> *H*: That is good; that takes the edge off whitewash, really. That was the thing Mitchell kept saying, that to people in the country Liddy and Hunt were big men. Maybe that is good.
> *P*: How did MacGregor handle himself?
> *D*: I think very well. He had a good statement, which said that the Grand Jury had met and that it was now time to realize that some apologies may be due.
> *H*: Fat chance.
> *D*: Get the damn (inaudible)
> *H*: We can't do that.
> *P*: Just remember, all the trouble we're taking, we'll have a chance to get back one day. How are you doing on your other investigation? (*Presidential Transcripts*, p. 32)

The next few exchanges are about other details of the Watergate "bugs" (telephone taps), and then about the scope of the investigations being conducted. It all seemed "silly" to them, expecially since they believed that "bugging" was common in politics:

> *P*: Yes (expletive deleted). Goldwater put it in context when he said "(expletive deleted) everybody bugs everybody else. You know that."

D: That was priceless.

P: It happens to be totally true. We were bugged in '68 on the plane and even in '62 running for Governor—(expletive deleted) thing you ever saw.

D: It is a shame that evidence to the fact that that happened in '68 was never around. I understand that only the former director [*J. Edgar Hoover, former head of the FBI*] had that information.

H: No, that is not true.

D: There was evidence of it?

H: There are others who have information (*Ibid.*, p. 34).

This interchange about "bugging" is noteworthy not only because of the light it sheds on the attitudes of the participants, but also because it stuck in Dean's mind. It is one of the few parts of the conversation which will be recognizable in his testimony nine months later.

The conversation continues from this point with more talk about "bugging," plans for action against White House enemies, questions about another pending legal action. It is interrupted briefly when Nixon takes a phone call. As soon as he hangs up, Dean speaks. He wants to point out how well things are going:

D: Three months ago I would have had trouble predicting there would be a day when this would be forgotten, but I think I can say that 54 days from now [*i.e., on election day in November*] nothing is going to come crashing down to our surprise.

P: That what?

D: Nothing is going to come crashing down to our surprise (*Ibid.*, p. 36).

He finally gets a bit of Presidential praise in return:

P: Oh well, this is a can of worms as you know, a lot of this stuff that went on. And the people who worked this way are awfully embarrassed. But the way you have handled all this seems to me has been very skillful, putting your fingers in the leaks that have sprung here and sprung there. The Grand Jury is dismissed now?

D: That is correct... (*Ibid.*).

The conversation goes on to cover many other areas—McGovern's campaign finances, a list of "enemies" that Dean offers to keep, more political strategy. Later on Dean and Haldeman (but not Nixon) seize another opportunity to congratulate each other on the success of the cover-up.

P: You really can't sit and worry about it all the time. The worst may happen but may not. So you just try to button it up as well as you can and hope for the best, and remember basically the damn business is unfortunately trying to cut our losses.

D: Certainly that is right and certainly it has had no effect on you. That's the good thing.

H: No, it has been kept away from the White House and of course completely from the President. The only tie to the White House is the Colson effort they keep trying to pull in.

D: And of course the two White House people of lower level—indicated—

one consultant and one member of the domestic staff. That is not very much of a tie.

H: That's right (*Ibid.*, p. 40).

DEAN'S TESTIMONY ABOUT SEPTEMBER 15

Nine months later, Dean devoted about two pages of his prepared statement to the September 15 meeting. The first paragraph purports to describe the way the meeting began. It is an important bit of testimony because the remarks Dean ascribes to Nixon would indicate full knowledge (and approval) of the cover-up. This is his account:

> On September 15 the Justice Department announced the handing down of the seven indictments by the Federal Grand Jury investigating the Watergate. Late that afternoon I received a call requesting me to come to the President's Oval Office. When I arrived at the Oval Office I found Haldeman and the President. The President asked me to sit down. Both men appeared to be in very good spirits and my reception was very warm and cordial. The President then told me that Bob—referring to Haldeman—had kept him posted on my handling of the Watergate case. The President told me I had done a good job and he appreciated how difficult a task it had been and the President was pleased that the case had stopped with Liddy. I responsed that I could not take credit because others had done much more difficult things than I had done. As the President discussed the present status of the situation I told him that all I had been able to do was to contain the case and assist in keeping it out of the White House. I also told him there was a long way to go before this matter would end and that I certainly could make no assurances that the day would not come when this matter would start to unravel (*Hearings*, p. 957).

Comparison with the transcript shows that hardly a word of Dean's account is true. Nixon did not say *any* of the things attributed to him here: He didn't ask Dean to sit down, he didn't say Haldeman had kept him posted, he didn't say Dean had done a good job (at least not in that part of the conversation), he didn't say anything about Liddy or the indictments. Nor had Dean himself said the things he later describes himself as saying: that he couldn't take credit, that the matter might unravel some day, etc. (Indeed, he said just the opposite later on: "Nothing is going to come crashing down.") His account is plausible, but entirely incorrect. In this early part of the conversation Nixon did not offer him any praise at all, unless "You had quite a day, didn't you" was intended as a compliment. (It is hard to tell from a written transcript.) Dean cannot be said to have reported the "gist" of the opening remarks; no count of idea units or comparison of structure would produce a score much above zero.

Was he simply lying to the Senators? I do not think so. The transcript makes it quite clear that Nixon *is* fully aware of the coverup: Haldeman and Dean discuss it freely in front of him, and while he occasionally asks questions he never seems surprised. Later on he even praises Dean for "putting his fingers in the leaks." Because the real conversation is just as incriminating as the one Dean described, it seems unlikely that he was remembering one thing and saying another. His responses to Senator Baker during cross-examination (see below) also indicate that he was doing his best to be honest. Mary McCarthy's assessment of Dean has stood the test of time: she wrote in 1973 of her overpowering impression "... not so much of a truthful person as of someone resolved to tell the truth about this particular set of events because his intelligence has warned him to do so" (McCarthy, 1975, pp. 40–41).

If Dean was trying to tell the truth, where did his erroneous account of the September 15 meeting come from? Some of it might be explained by the currently popular notion that everyone knows certain "scripts" for common events and that these scripts are used in the course of recall (Bower, Black, and Turner, 1979). Dean's recollection of the very beginning of the meeting may have been constructed on the basis of an "entering-the-room script." People do often ask their guests to sit down, though Nixon apparently did not ask Dean. It is also possible, however, that Dean's recollection of such a request is a case of nonverbal gist recall rather than a script-based construction. Perhaps Nixon *did* ask Dean to sit down, but with a gesture rather than a word—a brief wave of a commanding presidential hand. To recall such a gesture as if it had been a verbal request would not be much of an error. Current theoretical interest in the recall of written texts should not blind us to the nonverbal components of real conversation.

Although familiar scripts and nonverbal cues explain a few of Dean's errors, most of them seem to have deeper roots. They follow, I believe, from Dean's own character and especially from his self-centered assessment of events at the White House. What his testimony really describes is not the September 15 meeting itself but his fantasy of it: the meeting as it should have been, so to speak. In his mind Nixon *should* have been glad that the indictments stopped with Liddy, Haldeman *should* have been telling Nixon what a great job Dean was doing; most of all, praising him *should* have been the first order of business. In addition, Dean *should* have told Nixon that the cover-up might unravel, as it eventually did, instead of telling him it was a great success. By June, this fantasy had become the way Dean remembered the meeting.

Almost. But Dean was not really as confident of his recollection as the tone of his statement suggested; not as sure of himself as he claimed in the exchange with Senator Inouye. This becomes clear in a very sharp interrogation by Senator Baker:

> *Senator Baker*: I am going to try now to focus entirely on the meeting of September 15.
> *Mr. Dean*: Right.
> *Senator Baker*: And I have an ambition to focus sharply on it in order to disclose as much information as possible about the September 15 meeting. What I want to do is to test, once again, not the credibility of your testimony but the quality of the evidence, that is, is it direct evidence.
> *Mr. Dean*: I understand (*Hearings*, p. 1474).

Dean does understand: Baker wants vivid details and exact wording. The next few exchanges show how he struggles to reconcile the vagueness of his actual recollection with Baker's demands for specificity, dodging some questions and eventually committing himself on others. After an uncontroversial account of how he learned that Nixon wanted to see him that evening, Dean begins with his physical entrance into the office:

> *Mr. Dean*: When I entered the office I can recall that—you have been in the office, you know the way there are two chairs at the side of the President's desk.
> *Senator Baker*: You are speaking of the Oval Office?
> *Mr. Dean*: Of the Oval Office. As you face the President, on the left-hand chair Mr. Haldeman was sitting and they had obviously been immersed in a conversation and the President asked me to come in and I stood there for a moment. He said "Sit down," and I sat in a chair on the other side.
> *Senator Baker*: You sat in the right-hand chair?
> *Mr. Dean*: I sat on the right-hand chair.
> *Senator Baker*: That is the one he usually says no to, but go ahead.
> *Mr. Dean*: I was unaware of that. (Laughter)
> *Senator Baker*: Go ahead, Mr. Dean (*Ibid.*, p. 1475).

Now Dean plunges into the conversation, giving almost exactly the same account of it that he had presented in his prepared statement a few days before. Indeed, his opening phrase suggests that he is remembering that statement rather than the meeting itself:

> *Mr. Dean*: As I tried to describe in my statement, the reception was very warm and cordial. There was some preliminary pleasantries, and then the next thing that I recall the President very clearly saying to me is that he had been told by Mr. Haldeman that he had been kept posted or made aware of my handling of the various aspects of the Watergate case and the fact that the case, you know, the indictments had now been handed down, no one in the White House had been indicted, they had stopped at Liddy (*Ibid.*).

Senator Baker is not satisfied with this response; he wants to know how accurate Dean is really claiming to be:

> *Senator Baker*: Stop, stop, stop just for one second. "That no one in the
> White House had been indicted": Is that as near to the exact language—
> I don't know so I am not laying a trap for you, I just want to know (*Ibid.*).

It is now clear that the right answer to Baker's question would have
been "no." Nixon did not use anything remotely like the "exact language" in question; the conversation did not go that way at all. Dean's
answer is cautious:

> *Mr. Dean*: Yes, there was a reference to the fact that the indictments had
> been handed down and it was quite obvious that no one in the White
> House had been indicted on the indictments that had been handed
> down. (*Ibid.*).

Notice that although Dean's answer begins with "Yes," he now avoids
attributing the critical words to Nixon. He hides behind ambiguous
phrases like "There was a reference to the fact that . . . " and "It was
quite obvious . . . " Baker is unsatisfied with these evasions and continues to press for a straight answer:

> *Senator Baker*: Did he say that, though? (*Ibid.*).

Dean decides to be honest about it:

> *Mr. Dean*: Did he say that no one in the White House had been handed
> down? I can't recall it (*Ibid.*).

This is the answer which suggests to me that Dean was being as truthful
as he could. After all, he might easily have answered "yes" instead of
"I can't recall it." But he doesn't want to give up the points he has
already scored, so he repeats them:

> *Mr. Dean* (continuing): I can recall a reference to the fact that the indict-
> ments were now handed down and he was aware of that and the status
> of the indictments and expressed what to me was a pleasure to the fact
> that it had stopped with Mr. Liddy (*Ibid.*).

This paragraph is a nice summary of what Dean remembers from the
conversation, and it is phrased so carefully that everything in it is true.
There *was* reference to the indictments (by Haldeman and Dean); Nixon
was aware of that (though he didn't say so); and somehow he did
express what Dean *interpreted* as pleasure in the outcome. It is fair to
say that Dean here captures the "tenor," though not the gist, of what
went on in the Oval Office that afternoon. But Baker notices that he
still hasn't committed himself to any exact statements by Nixon, and
tries again:

> *Senator Baker*: Tell me what he said.
> *Mr. Dean*: Well, as I say, he told me I had done a good job—
> *Senator Baker*: No, let's talk about the pleasure. He expressed pleasure
> the indictments had stopped at Mr. Liddy. Can you just for the purposes
> of our information tell me the language that he used? (*Ibid.*).

Dean ducks once more:

> *Mr. Dean*: Senator, let me make it very clear: The pleasure that it had
> stopped there is an inference of mine based on, as I told Senator Gurney
> yesterday, the impression I had as a result of the, of his, complimenting
> me (*Ibid.*).

Baker hangs tough:

> *Senator Baker*: Can you give us any information, can you give us any
> further insight into what the President said?
> *Mr. Dean*: Yes, I can recall he told me that he appreciated how difficult
> a job it had been for me.
> *Senator Baker*: Is that close to the exact language?
> *Mr. Dean*: Yes, that is close to the exact language (*Ibid.*, p. 1476).

Finally Dean gives in and puts words into Nixon's mouth. He may just have felt he had no choice: if he didn't claim to remember *any* of Nixon's remarks his whole testimony might be discredited. But also he may have believed it. Nixon's compliment was what he had most yearned for, and his invented version of it may have been the most compelling thing in his memory. Either way, the exchange seems to have hardened his willingness to testify to exact language. He and Baker went at it again a few minutes later when Dean said he had told Nixon "that the matter had been contained." Baker repeatedly asked whether he had used that very word, and Dean repeatedly asserted that he had done so. When Baker questioned him closely about how the President had reacted to "contained," however, Dean said he did not recall. He certainly didn't: the word "contained" appears nowhere in the transcript.

In summary, it is clear that Dean's account of the opening of the September 15 conversation is wrong both as to the words used and their gist. Moreover, cross-examination did not reveal his errors as clearly as one might have hoped. The effect of Baker's hard questioning was mixed. Although it did show up the weakness of Dean's verbatim recall, the overall result may have been to increase his credibility. Dean came across as a man who has a good memory for gist with an occasional literal word stuck in, like a raisin in a pudding. He was not such a man. He remembered how he had felt himself and what he had wanted, together with the general state of affairs; he didn't remember what anyone had actually said. His testimony had much truth in it, but not at the level of "gist." It was true at a deeper level. Nixon was the kind of man Dean described, he had the knowledge Dean attributed to him, there was a cover-up. Dean remembered all of that; he just didn't recall the actual conversation he was testifying about.

So far I have concentrated on the first few minutes of the meeting, covered in a single paragraph of Dean's prepared statement. The next paragraph is interesting because (unlike the first) it refers to a bit of conversation that actually occurred.

> *Mr. Dean*: Early in our conversation the President said to me that former FBI Director Hoover had told him shortly after he assumed office in 1969 that his campaign had been bugged in 1968. The President said that at some point we should get the facts out on this and use this to counter the problems that we were encountering (*Ibid.*, p. 958).

As we have already seen, an exchange about Hoover and bugging in previous campaigns did take place, a little after the beginning of the conversation. But although it was indeed Nixon who raised the subject, it was Dean, not Nixon, who brought Hoover's name into it: "I understand that only the former director had that information." Dean may have forgotten this because Haldeman had put him down so sharply ("No, that is not true"), or he may have preferred to put the words into Nixon's mouth for other reasons. In any case, he isn't quite right.

The remainder of Dean's testimony about the meeting is no better than the parts we have examined. He mentions topics that were indeed discussed, but never reproduces the real gist of anything that was said. Surprisingly, he does *not* remember the President's actual compliment to him ("putting your fingers in the leaks") although it is a fairly striking phrase. At the end of his statement he presents the following summary:

> *Mr. Dean*: I left the meeting with the impression that the President was well aware of what had been going on regarding the success of keeping the White House out of the Watergate scandal, and I also had expressed to him my concern that I was not confident that the cover-up could be maintained indefinitely (*Ibid.*, p. 959).

The first part of this summary is fair enough: Nixon was surely ". . . well aware of what had been going on." The conclusion is less fair; Dean seriously—perhaps deliberately—misrepresents the optimistic predictions he had made. In fact he was *not* wise enough or brave enough to warn Nixon in September, though by June he was smart enough to wish he had done so.

THE MEETING OF MARCH 21

The cover-up was only temporarily successful. Although Nixon was re-elected overwhelmingly in November of 1972, Dean's problems increased steadily. There were more blackmail demands by the indicted Watergate defendants and more investigations moving closer to the White House. Dean met frequently with Nixon, Haldeman, and the others, but their strategems were unsuccessful. Dean began to realize that he and the others were engaging in a crime ("obstruction of justice"), and might eventually go to prison for it. He was not sure whether Nixon understood the gravity of the situaiton. Finally he resolved to ask the President for a private meeting at which he could lay out all the facts. This meeting took place on March 21, 1973.

Dean's autobiography (1976) relates an incident that occurred on the day before the critical meeting. When he was trying to describe the relentlessly increasing complexity of the Watergate affair to Richard Moore, another White House aide, Moore compared it to the growth of a tumor. The metaphor attracted Dean, and he resolved to use it in his report the next day: to tell Nixon that there was a "cancer" growing on the presidency. The transcript of the meeting shows that he did so. After a few minutes of conversation about the day's events, Dean and the President continue as follows:

> D: The reason I thought we ought to talk this morning is because in our conversations I have the impression that you don't know everything I know, and it makes it very difficult for you to make judgments that only you can make on some of these targets, and I thought that—
> P: In other words, I have to know why you feel that we shouldn't unravel something?
> D: Let me give you my overall first.
> P: In other words, your judgment as to where it stands, and where we will go.
> D: I think there is no doubt about the seriousness of the problem we've got. We have a cancer within, close to the presidency, that is growing. It is growing daily. It's compounded, growing geometrically now because it compounds itself. That will be clear if I, you know, explain some of the details of why it is. Basically it is because (1) we are being blackmailed; (2) people are going to start perjuring themselves very quickly that have not had to perjure themselves to protect other people in the line. And there is no assurance—
> P: That that won't bust?
> D: That that won't bust (*Presidential Transcripts*, pp. 98–99).

In this first part of the March 21 meeting, Dean was alone with the President. They remained alone for about an hour, and then Haldeman came in to join the discussion for another 45 minutes or so. Haldeman's entrance proved to be a critical turning point in Dean's later memory of that morning: he forgot the rest of the conversation almost completely. What he said about the first hour, in contrast, was quite accurate. Comparison of the transcript with Dean's subsequent testimony shows clear recall of the gist of what was said. One's admiration for his memory is somewhat diminished, however, by the realization that the March 21 meeting was less a conversation than the delivery of a well-prepared report. Dean did most of the talking, taking 20 minutes to describe the events before the break-in and 40 more for the cover-up. Although Nixon interjected occasional remarks, questions, or expletives, the hour stayed quite close to the script Dean had prepared for it in advance.

The difference between this meeting and that of September 15 is instructive. This one fulfilled Dean's hopes as the earlier one had not: he really did give a personal lecture to the President of the United States, talking while Nixon listened. His testimony, too long to reproduce here, highlights the meeting's didactic quality. Almost every statement begins with "I told him ... ," "I proceeded to tell him ...," "I informed the President ... " or some similar phrase. He was remembering a report that he had rehearsed ahead of time, presented as planned, and probably continued to rehearse afterwards. It became John Dean's own story; March 21 had merely been his first opportunity to tell it.

Dean's testimony includes a fragment of nearly verbatim recall that later achieved some notoriety: he quoted his own remark about the "cancer on the presidency" to the Senate Committee. This, too, was a well-rehearsed passage. We know that he prepared it in advance, and the transcript shows that he used it repeatedly. (He probably used it on other occasions as well; why let such a good phrase go to waste?) His first presentation of the simile, early in the meeting, has been quoted above. Twenty minutes later he refers back to it:

> D. ... When I say this is a growing cancer, I say it for reasons like this ... (*Ibid.*, p. 111).

And still later he brings it in obliquely:

> D. ... we should begin to think ... how to minimize the further growth of this thing ... (*Ibid.*, p. 119).

Interestingly, Dean's self-quotation to the Senators was not faithful to any of these occasions:

> Mr. Dean: I began by telling the President that there was a cancer growing on the presidency and that if the cancer was not removed the President himself would be killed by it. I also told him that it was important that this cancer be removed immediately because it was growing more deadly every day (*Hearings*, p. 998).

A glance back at the excerpt from the transcript shows that Dean is once again giving himself the benefit of hindsight. He did *not* say that the President would be *killed* by the cancer, for example. By June he probably wished he had done so; I don't know whether he altered the wording in his testimony deliberately or whether his memory had already accommodated itself slightly to his self-image.

In Dean's mind, the significance of the March 21 meeting must have lain in the degree to which he dominated it. That may explain why he barely mentioned the second half of the meeting in his Senate testimony; Haldeman's entrance spoiled his private command performance. The rest of the session was by no means uninteresting, however. What actually happened was that Nixon, Haldeman, and Dean considered various options, trying to find the best way to deal with their Watergate dilemma. One of those options was to raise money to meet the blackmail demands of the men who had already been convicted. This possibility seemed to attract Nixon; he returned to it again and again. He had already discussed it in the first hour, when only Dean was with him:

> D: I would say these people are going to cost a million dollars over the next two years.
> P: We could get that. On the money, if you need the money you could get that. You could get a million dollars. You could get it in cash. I know where it could be gotten. It is not easy but it could be done ... (*Presidential Transcripts*, p. 110).

He seemed more enthusiastic about it than Dean himself:

> P: Just looking at the immediate problem, don't you think you have to handle Hunt's financial situation damn soon?
> D: I think that is—I talked with Mitchell about that last night and—
> P: It seems to me we have to keep the cap on the bottle that much or we don't have any options (*Ibid.*, p. 112).

Later he makes it as explicit as he possibly can:

> D: The blackmailers. Right.
> P: Well I wonder if that part of it can't be—I wonder if that doesn't—let me put it frankly: I wonder if that doesn't have to be continued? Let me put it this way: let us suppose you get the million bucks, and you get the proper way to handle it. You could hold that side?
> D: Uh-huh.
> P: It would seem to me that would be worthwhile (*Ibid.*, p. 117).

Remarks like this continue to sprinkle the conversation after Haldeman joins them:

> P: ... First, it is going to require approximately a million dollars to take care of the jackasses who are in jail. That can be arranged ... (*Ibid.*, p. 127).

. . .

> P: Now let me tell you. We could get the money. There is no problem in that ... (Ibid., p. 129).

. . .

P: I just have a feeling on it. Well, it sounds like a lot of money, a million dollars. Let me say that I think we could get that ... (*Ibid.*, p. 130).[1]

These are quite remarkable things for a President to say. They would certainly seem to be memorable, and indeed Dean did not forget them. He just assigned them to a different day! Although he makes no reference to them in his testimony about March 21, his statement includes the following description of a meeting with Nixon on March 13, eight days before:

> *Mr. Dean*: ... It was during this conversation that Haldeman came into the office. After this brief interruption by Haldeman's coming in, but while he was still there, I told the President about the fact that there was no money to pay these individuals to meet their demands. He asked me how much it would cost. I told him that I could only make an estimate that it might be as high as $1 million or more. He told me that that was no problem, and he also looked over at Haldeman and made the same statement ... (*Hearings*, p. 995).

Dean amplifies this account later, during cross-examination:

> *Mr. Dean*: ... We had also had a discussion on March 13 about the money demands that were being made. At the time he discussed the fact that a million dollars is no problem. He repeated it several times. I can very vividly recall that the way he sort of rolled his chair back from his desk and leaned over to Mr. Haldeman and said, "A million dollars is no problem" (*Ibid.*, p. 1423).

It is hardly surprising that Dean remembered these million-dollar statements, especially since Nixon repeated them so often. It *is* a little surprising that he put them into the wrong conversation. (There is a transcript of the March 13 meeting, and it shows no such remarks by the President.) Evidently Dean's improvised method of *temporal loci*, based on newspaper clippings, did not work as well as his exchange with Senator Inouye had suggested. His ego got in the way again. The March 21 meeting had been the occasion for his own personal report to the President; he could not suppose that anything else worth mentioning had happened. Other memories were shifted to another day if they survived at all.

Nixon's eagerness to pay the blackmail money was not the only part of the conversation to suffer this fate. Dean even displaced one of his own jokes; a joke that had drawn a response from Haldeman if not from Nixon. They were discussing various illegal ways of "laundering" the blackmail money so it could not be traced:

---

[1]Nixon never expressed any hesitation about making these payments, or any reluctance to meet the burglars' demands for money. He did, however, agree with Dean that their demands for *executive clemency* should not be met. At one point he said, "No—it is wrong, that's for sure" about the possibility of clemency. The transcript shows no analogous statement about the blackmail payments.

D: And that means you have to go to Vegas with it or a bookmaker in New York City. I have learned all these things after the fact. I will be in great shape for the next time around!
H: (Expletive deleted) (*Presidential Transcripts*, p. 134).

That may not have been the only time Dean used this wisecrack; he probably enjoyed describing himself as increasingly skilled in under-world techniques. Certainly he didn't mind repeating it to the Senators, though his statement assigns it, too, to March 13 rather than March 21:

Mr. Dean: . . . I told him I was learning about things I had never had before, but the next time I would certainly be more knowledgeable. This comment got a laugh out of Haldeman (*Hearings*, p. 996).

It isn't very funny.

IMPLICATIONS FOR THE PSYCHOLOGY OF MEMORY

Are we all like this? Is everyone's memory constructed, staged, self-centered? And do we all have access to certain invariant facts never-theless? Such questions cannot be answered by single case histories. My own guess—and it is only a guess—is that reconstruction played an exaggerated part in Dean's testimony. The circumstances and the man conspired to favor exaggeration. The events *were* important; his testimony *was* critical; its effect *was* historic. Dean was too intelligent not to know what he was doing, and too ambitious and egocentric to remain unaffected by it. His ambition reorganized his recollections: even when he tries to tell the truth, he can't help emphasizing his own role in every event. A different man in the same position might have observed more dispassionately, reflected on his experiences more thoughtfully, and reported them more accurately. Unfortunately, such traits of character are rare.

What have we learned about testimony by comparing "the human tape recorder" with a real one? We are hardly surprised to find that memory is constructive or that confident witnesses may be wrong. William Stern studied the psychology of testimony at the turn of the century and warned us not to trust memory even under oath; Bartlett was doing experiments on "constructive" memory fifty years ago. I believe, however, that John Dean's testimony can do more than remind us of their work. For one thing, his constructed memories were not altogether wrong. On the contrary, there is a sense in which he was altogether right; a level at which he was telling the truth about the Nixon White House. And sometimes—as in his testimony about March

21—he was more specifically right as well. These islands of accuracy deserve special consideration. What kinds of things did he remember?

Dean's task as he testified before the Senate Committee was to recall specific well-defined conversations, "... conversations which took place months ago." This is what witnesses are always instructed to do: stick to the facts, avoid inferences and generalizations. Such recall is what Tulving (1972) called *episodic*; it involves the retrieval of particular autobiographical moments, individual episodes of one's life. Tulving contrasted episodic memory only with what he called *semantic* memory, the individual's accumulated store of facts and word meanings and general knowledge. That concept seems inadequate as a description of data such as these. Dean's recollection of Nixon's remarks about the million dollars was not merely semantic: he talked as if he were recalling one or more specific events. I doubt, however, that any of those events was being recalled uniquely in its own right. A single such episode might not have found its way into Dean's testimony at all. What seems to be specific in his memory actually depends on repeated episodes, rehearsed presentations, or overall impressions. He believes that he is recalling one conversation at a time, that his memory is "episodic" in Tulving's sense, but he is mistaken.

He is not alone in making this mistake. I believe that this aspect of Dean's testimony illustrates a very common process. The single clear memories that we recollect so vividly actually stand for something else; they are "screen memories," a little like those Freud discussed long ago. Often their real basis is a set of repeated experiences, a sequence of related events that the single recollection merely typifies or represents. We are like the subjects of Posner and Keele (1970), who forgot the individual dot patterns of a series but "remembered" the prototypical pattern they had never seen. Such memories might be called *repisodic* rather than episodic: what seems to be an episode actually *re*presents a *re*petition. Dean remembers the million-dollar remark because Nixon made it so often; he recalls the "cancer" metaphor because he first planned it and then repeated it; he remembers his March 21 lecture to the President because he planned it, then presented it, and then no doubt went over it again and again in his own mind. What he says about these "repisodes" is essentially correct, even though it is not literally faithful to any one occasion. He is not remembering the "gist" of a single episode by itself, but the common characteristics of a whole series of events.

This notion may help us to interpret the paradoxical sense in which Dean was accurate throughout his testimony. Give the numerous errors in his reports of conversations, what did he tell the truth about? I think that he extracted the common themes that remained invariant across many conversations and many experiences, and then incorporated those themes in his testimony. His many encounters with Nixon were themselves a kind of "repisode." There were certain consistent and repeated elements in all those meetings; they had a theme that expressed itself in different ways on different occasions. Nixon wanted the cover-up to succeed; he was pleased when it went well; he was troubled when it began to unravel; he was perfectly willing to consider illegal activities if they would extend his power or confound his enemies. John Dean did not misrepresent this theme in his testimony; he just dramatized it. In memory experiments, subjects often recall the gist of a sentence but express it in different words. Dean's consistency was deeper; he recalled the theme of a whole series of conversations and expressed it in different events. Nixon hoped that the transcripts would undermine Dean's testimony by showing that he had been wrong. They did not have this effect because he was wrong only in terms of isolated episodes. Episodes are not the only kinds of facts. Except where the significance of his own role was at stake, Dean was right about what had really been going on in the White House. What he later told the Senators was fairly close to the mark: his mind was not a tape recorder, but it certainly received the message that was being given.

REFERENCES

Bartlett, F. C. *Remembering*. Cambridge: Cambridge University Press, 1932.

Bower, G. H., Black, J. B., and Turner, T. J. Scripts in memory for text. *Cognitive Psychology*, 1979, *11*, 177–220.

Bransford, J. D., and Franks, J. J. The abstraction of linguistic ideas: A review. *Cognition*, 1972, *1*, 211–249.

Buckhout, R. Eyewitness testimony. *Scientific American*, 1974, *231* (6), 23–31.

Dean, J. W. *Blind Ambition*. New York: Simon & Schuster, 1976.

Freud, S. Screen memories. Reprinted in *Collected Papers of Sigmund Freud, Vol. V*. London: Hogarth Press, 1956.

Hearings before the Select Committee on Presidential Campaign Activities of the United States Senate, Ninety-Third Congress, First Session, 1973.

Mandler, J. M., and Johnson, N. Remembrance of things parsed: Story structure and recall. *Cognitive Psychology*, 1977, *9*, 111–151.

McCarthy, M. *The Mask of State: Watergate Portraits*. New York: Harcourt Brace Jovanovich, 1975.

Posner, M. J. and Keele, S. Retention of abstract ideas. *Journal of Experimental Psychology*, 1970, *83*, 304–308.

The Presidential Transcripts. New York: Dell, 1974.

Stern, W. Wirklichkeitsversuche (Reality Experiments). *Beitrage zur Psychologie der Aussage*, 1904, *2*, (1), 1–31.

Tulving, E. Episodic and semantic memory. In E. Tulving and W. Donaldson (eds.), *Organization and Memory*. New York: Academic Press, 1972.

Part IV
Forgetting

In which it appears that people cannot give accurate
reports of coins they handle every day, texts they
have read thousands of times, opinions they
formerly held, or how they raised their children; they
can, however, recognize the names of defunct
television programs. They also cannot remember
their own childhoods; Schachtel's famous discussion
of that amnesia is presented along with a new way of
calibrating its onset, based on memory of the births
of one's siblings. The last selection shows that some
kinds of natural forgetting imitate laboratory results
rather closely.

15 Long-Term Memory for a Common Object

Raymond S. Nickerson and
Marilyn Jager Adams

Do you know what a penny looks like? Probably not;
almost nobody does, according to the research
reported in this selection. Of course, sophisticated
psychologists are free to claim that this finding does
not surprise them. People probably don't attend to
the details on pennies in the first place, and they are
not motivated to rehearse or recode those details
later on. But be honest: Weren't you inclined to
answer "yes" to the question that began this
paragraph? Perhaps you are still so inclined. Why not
turn to the last figure in this selection and try your
luck?

Many things can be recognized on the basis of their visual characteristics. Moreover, laboratory studies have shown that people are quite
adept at discriminating between complex pictures they have seen a
short time before and those they have not, even when given hundreds
(Nickerson, 1965; Shepard, 1967) or thousands (Standing, 1973; Standing, Conezio, and Haber, 1970) of pictures to remember and allowed
to inspect each for only a few seconds. Both of these observations are
consistent with the idea of a visual memory that readily assimilates
and retains an abundance of information about the stimuli to which
it is exposed.

From *Cognitive Psychology*, 1979, 11, 287–307. Reprinted by permission.

In fact, neither introspection nor the results of picture recognition studies tells us how much information regarding any particular visual pattern has been stored. When people demonstrate the ability to recognize something, they may be demonstrating only that they can place that thing in an appropriate conceptual category. And the category may be more or less broadly defined, depending on one's purpose—as when an object is recognized as an automobile, as opposed to being recognized as a Volkswagen, or as the specific Volkswagen that belongs to John Doe. Similarly, when people show that they can distinguish a picture they have seen before from one they are looking at for the first time, they show only that they have retained enough information about the "old" picture to distinguish it from the new one. Given that one typically cannot say how much information *must* be retained in order to permit such categorizations and distinctions, one cannot rule out the possibility that they may be made on the basis of a small portion of the information that the patterns contain.

The experiments reported in this paper are addressed to the question of how accurately and completely the visual details of a common object, a United States penny, are represented in people's memories. We chose to study people's knowledge of a common object rather than of laboratory stimuli because we are interested in the nature of the information that normally accrues in memory. As a stimulus, a penny has the advantage of being complex enough to be interesting but simple enough to be analyzed and manipulated. And it is an object that all of our subjects would have seen frequently.

EXPERIMENT I

The purpose of the first experiment was to see how accurately people could reproduce a penny through unaided recall.

Method

The subjects were 20 adult United States citizens. Each was given a set of empty circles, 2 in. in diameter, and asked to draw from memory what is on each side of a U.S. penny. Subjects were asked to include all the pictorial and alphanumeric detail they could, and they were allowed to draw as many versions of each side as they wanted.

For purposes of scoring the drawings, we focused on the eight features listed in Table 15-1. Each subject's drawing was scored according to: (a) whether each of these eight features was present; (b) whether each was located on the correct side of the coin; and (c) whether it was

TABLE 15-1
Features identified for scoring purposes in Experiment I

Top side
Head
"IN GOD WE TRUST"
"LIBERTY"
Date
Bottom side
Building
"UNITED STATES OF AMERICA"
"E PLURIBUS UNUM"
"ONE CENT"

drawn in the correct position in the circular area. The head was scored as being in the correct position only if it was drawn as an east-facing profile.

Results

In general, performance was remarkably poor. Figure 15-1 shows some examples of the drawings we obtained. Of the eight critical features, the median number recalled and located correctly was three. Not counting the Lincoln head and the Lincoln Memorial, the median number of recalled and correctly located features was one. Only four

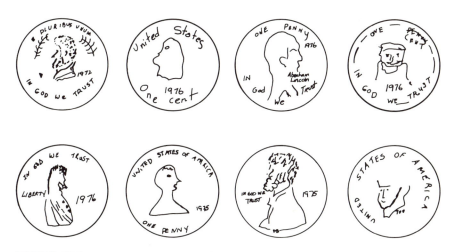

FIGURE 15-1
Examples of drawings obtained from people who tried to reproduce a penny from memory.

of our 20 subjects got as many as half of them. Only one subject (an active penny collector) accurately recalled and located all eight.

Figure 15-2 shows an analysis of the errors with respect to each feature. The overall probability that a feature would be either omitted or mislocated was .61. The probability that a feature would be omitted was .33; excluding the Lincoln head and the Lincoln Memorial, this probability was .43. The only features that all our subjects produced were a head and a date. All but one subject also recalled a building as the central figure on the bottom side. The feature most frequently omitted was LIBERTY: only two of our subjects remembered that this

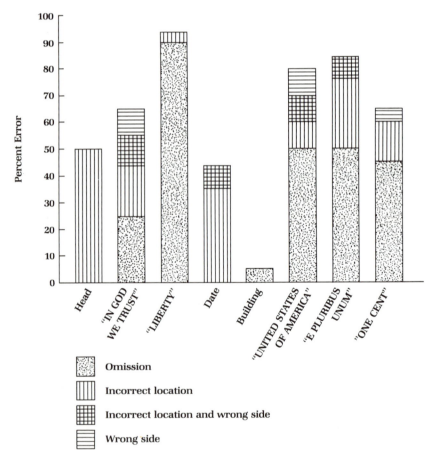

FIGURE 15-2
Types of errors produced when subjects attempted to draw a penny from memory.

is on the coin, and one of them located it on the wrong side. UNITED STATES OF AMERICA, E PLURIBUS UNUM, and ONE CENT were also omitted by about half of our subjects. It is interesting to note that with the exception of Lincoln's head, the Memorial, and ONE CENT, all of these items occur on every current U.S. coin.

Figure 15-2 also shows that subjects were quite poor at locating those features they did recall. The probability of mislocating a correctly recalled feature was .42. The only feature that was consistently located correctly was the building, which would be difficult to position incorrectly if it were recalled at all. Excluding the building, the probability of mislocating a feature was .50. Exactly half of our subjects faced the Lincoln head in the wrong direction.

[*Experiment II omitted.*]

. . .

EXPERIMENT III

The results of Experiments I and II indicate that people cannot accurately recall either the features that appear on a penny or how those features are arranged. We reasoned that these data might not reflect people's lack of knowledge of pennies so much as the inappropriateness of recall tasks for purposes of assessing that knowledge. Perhaps performance would be more impressive on a recognition task. Item recognition is often taken to be a more sensitive test of memory than item production (Anisfield and Knapp, 1968; Kintsch, 1970a, 1970b; Underwood, 1972). Moreover, recognition tasks would seem to be more closely related to what we normally do with pennies. In view of these considerations, Experiment III, IV, and V were done using recognition tasks. Experiment III was designed to assess awareness of the features that are on a penny, independently of awareness of their location or appearance.

Method

Twenty new subjects (adult U.S. citizens) were given a list of 20 features. Their task was to indicate with respect to each feature (a) whether it is on a penny, and (b) their degree of confidence (on a 3–point scale) in their answer. Two answer forms were used, each with ten subjects. The two forms, which are shown in Table 15-2, differed only with respect to the "distractor" items.

TABLE 15-2
The lists of features that were given to subjects in Experiment III

1. The word JUSTICE	1. The words ONE PENNY
2. the words UNITED STATES OF AMERICA	2. The words UNITED STATES OF AMERICA
3. The words LEGAL TENDER	3. The words ONE NATION UNDER GOD
4. The words VERITAS	4. The right side of Washington's face
5. The words ONE CENT	5. The words ONE CENT
6. The date (year) of mint	6. The date (year) of mint
7. The presidential seal	7. The great seal
8. The word COIN	8. The words LINCOLN MEMORIAL
9. The words WASHINGTON, D.C.	9. The number 1 centered
10. The left side of Lincoln's face	10. The full face of Lincoln
11. The right side of Lincoln's face	11. The right side of Lincoln's face
12. The White House	12. A laurel wreath
13. An eagle with spread wings	13. The words MADE IN TAIWAN
14. The Lincoln memorial	14. The Lincoln memorial
15. The words IN GOD WE TRUST	15. the words IN GOD WE TRUST
16. The word LIBERTY	16. The word LIBERTY
17. Sheaves of wheat	17. The words ANNO DOMINI
18. The Roman numeral I	18. The word COPPER
19. The words E PLURIBUS UNUM	19. The words E PLURIBUS UNUM
20. The words MINTED IN USA	20. The Statue of Liberty's torch

Results

Subjects used the highest, intermediate, and lowest confidence levels on about 45, 31, and 24 percent of the test items, respectively. We take this as evidence that the task was not perceived as trivially easy.

The overall probability of a correct response in this task was .85. The relationship between confidence and correctness is shown in Figure 15-3. In general, the higher the subject's confidence in an answer, the more likely was the answer to be correct. The probability that a response would be correct was somewhat higher for negative than for positive responses at all confidence levels, but this could be an artifact of the greater number of negative than of positive items on the answer sheet. Because of this asymmetry, random negative guesses would have been more likely to be correct than random positive guesses.

Figure 15-4 shows the percentages of correct (positive) and incorrect (negative) responses at each confidence level for those features that are in fact on the penny. The bars representing correct responses (left of each pair) are connected, as are those representing incorrect responses (right of each pair). More often than not subjects tended to believe that these eight features were on a penny, but the response distribution was far from bimodal. The only feature that subjects

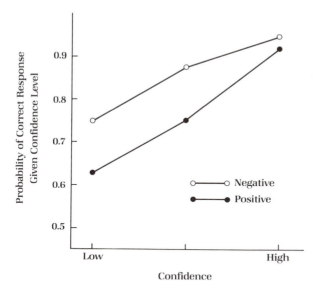

FIGURE 15-3
The relationship between the degree of confidence expressed in a response and the probability that the response was correct.

selected with both consistent accuracy and high confidence was the date. Although several other features were selected by at least 80 percent of the subjects, the degree of confidence in the presence of these items was not uniformly high. Again, LIBERTY proved to be difficult; only two of the 20 subjects were certain that it belonged to the coin. The poor showing with respect to the "right side of Lincoln's face" must be weighed in light of the fact that of the nine subjects who rejected this item, six opted for the "left side of Lincoln's face," one for his full face, and one for the right side of Washington's face.

The distractor features that were judged to be on the penny by at least two subjects were the left side of Lincoln's face (6), a laurel wreath (6), sheaves of wheat (4), the words LINCOLN MEMORIAL (3), the number 1 centered (2), the great seal (2), the Roman numeral I (2), and the words WASHINGTON, D.C. (2). No one voted for MADE IN TAIWAN.

On the whole, the results from Experiment III seem to present a slightly more positive assessment of memory for visual features than did those of Experiments I and II. At least with the particular set of distractor features that was used, subjects were able to distinguish between bona fide features and distractors with fair accuracy. However, this performance measure may be somewhat misleading. It may reflect not only what subjects remember about a penny, but what they can

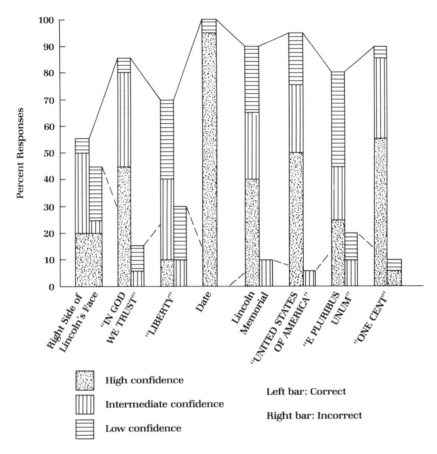

FIGURE 15-4
The percentage of correct (positive) and incorrect (negative) responses, and associated confidence levels, for those features that are on a penny.

infer. Even a subject who had never seen a penny might accept some of the candidate features on the grounds that they ought to be on a U.S. penny (e.g., UNITED STATES OF AMERICA, ONE CENT, a date) and reject others on the grounds that they ought not to be there (e.g., MADE IN TAIWAN). The possibility that our subjects may have done some judicious guessing gets some support from the fact that they often did not report high confidence in their answers even when they were correct.

[*Experiment IV omitted.*]

. . .

EXPERIMENT V

Rather than concluding that we know so little about the appearance of an object that is so very familiar, we again considered the possibility that our tasks had been somwhat inappropriate for tapping that knowledge. We decided to try one more method: each subject was given all 15 of the drawings in Figure 15-5 and asked to select the most plausible from among them. We were sure this task would be quite easy. The subjects would have all 15 versions before them. If the correct version did not just pop out at them, they could compare and contrast the alternatives in any way they pleased.

Method

Each of 36 female students from Lesley College (all U.S. citizens) was given the 15 drawings from Experiment IV, each printed on a separate card. The subjects were told that one of the drawings was correct, whereas each of the others had one or more things wrong with it. The

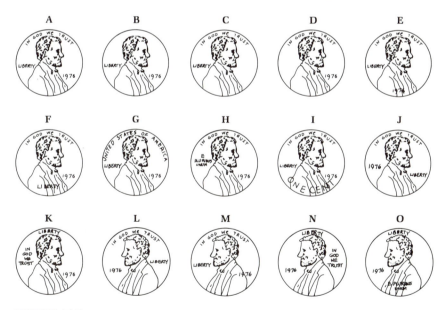

FIGURE 15-5
The fifteen drawings of the top side of a penny that were used in Experiments IV and V. A brief characterization of each drawing is given in Table 15-3.

subject's task was to sort the drawings into the following four categories: (1) the one drawing she thought most likely to be correct; (2) drawings she could easily believe to be correct if the one she had chosen as correct proved not to be; (3) drawings that might possibly be correct; and (4) drawings that she felt sure were incorrect. Suitable labels were provided to faciliate the sorting. Subjects were told that they must assign exactly one drawing to the first category, but that they could have as many or as few drawings in each of the other categories as they wished and that it was not necessary to use all categories. They were given as much time as they wanted and were free to move drawings from one category to another until satisfied with their selections.

Results

The last four columns of Table 15-3 show the distribution of category placements for each of the 15 drawings. Although the correct drawing was more likely to be judged correct than were any of the counterfeits, it was not recognized as the obvious choice by all, or even by a majority, of our subjects. Somewhat less than half (15 of the 36) of our subjects placed it in Category 1. As in Experiment IV, drawing I proved to be relatively plausible, and was selected as the most likely one by seven subjects. Drawings G and M both got four votes, and D, H, J, and L got at least one.

A second general observation that may be made from Table 15-3 is that many of the drawings were considered as possibilities by many of the subjects. In fact, excluding the Category 1 assignments, about one-quarter of the drawings, on the average, were judged as easily believed to be correct, one-quarter were judged conceivably correct, and one-half were judged as certainly incorrect.

Examination of the response distributions shown in Table 15-3 points out one of the dangers involved in making inferences about the contents of memory on the basis of forced-choice recognition tasks. If our subjects had been asked only to select the one drawing they considered most likely to be correct, we might have concluded that recognition memory was rather good, inasmuch as the correct alternative would have been chosen at least twice as frequently as any other. And had the set of distractors been made smaller by exclusion of some of the more plausible alternatives (e.g., versions G, I, M), performance would have been much more impressive. As is apparent from the table, however, although subjects were more likely to choose the correct drawing than any other, they were not, as a rule, able to reject all the

TABLE 15-3

Characterizations of the Drawings Shown in Figure 15-5 and results from Experiments IV and V

| | | Experiment IV | | | Experiment V | | | |
| | | | No. who thought drawing accurate | No. who identified error(s) | Response category | | | |
Drawing	Characterization	No. of Subjects			1	2	3	4
A	Correct	8	4	—	15	12	4	5
B	1 omission	9	0	6(2)	0	0	6	30
C	1 omission	9	0	9(1)	0	1	4	31
D	1 omission	8	2	3(1)	1	3	6	26
E	1 mislocation	9	0	8(0)	0	12	9	15
F	1 mislocation	8	0	5(0)	0	5	17	14
G	1 substitution	9	4	1(0)	4	10	10	12
H	1 substitution	8	0	2(0)	2	6	8	20
I	1 addition	9	6	2(1)	7	5	5	19
J	2 features interchanged	8	2	4(2)	2	18	5	11
K	2 features interchanged	8	3	3(1)	0	5	13	18
L	Mirror image	9	0	4(3)	1	8	4	23
M	Reversed face	8	3	3(1)	4	9	5	17
N	Mirror with 2 features interchanged	9	1	1(1)	0	3	5	28
O	Mirror with 1 omission, 1 mislocation, and 1 addition	8	0	0(0)	0	3	4	29

other possibilities with a high degree of confidence. (Only two subjects classified all but one of the drawings as certainly incorrect, and one of these subjects selected an incorrect drawing—version I—as the one most likely to be correct.)

How does the degree of plausibility of a drawing depend upon the relationship between that drawing and the correct one? On the assumption that, at least in a statistical sense, the correct drawing is more plausible than any of the incorrect ones, we might expect the degree of plausibility of the incorrect drawings to drop off as the degree of their similarity to the correct drawing decreased. Unfortunately, we have no measure of between-drawing similarity. However, one thing seems clear in this regard: If similarity were defined as the number of features with respect to which two drawings differed, the relationship between similarity and plausibility would not be simple. Two of the least plausible drawings (B and C) differed from the correct one with respect to only a single feature; the inscription IN GOD WE TRUST was missing from one and the date from the other.

. . .

CONCLUDING COMMENT

On balance, the results from these experiments demonstrate that irequent exposure to an object and the ability to "recognize" that object for practical purposes do not guarantee that the object is represented accurately in memory in any great detail. To the contrary, they raise the question of whether visual long-term memory is much less rich and elaborate than has often been supposed.

The results also lead us to the following conjecture: Typically, the details of visual stimuli are not retained in memory—or at least they are not available from memory— unless there is some functional reason for them to be. In other words, what one is most likely to remember about the visual properties of objects is what one needs to remember in order to distinguish those objects in everyday life. In general, investigators of human memory have not focused on the question of sufficiency. As one aspect of the study of what is stored in memory, it might be useful to give more thought to the question of what information must be retained in order to permit one to identify common objects or to distinguish them from each other. It may turn out that because of the multiplicity of features with respect to which most objects of interest differ from each other, the constraining effects of the contexts in which objects are typically encountered, and the role of inferential processes, recognition may make much smaller demands on memory than has commonly been believed.

REFERENCES

Anisfeld, M., and Knapp, M. Association, synonymity, and directionality in false recognition. *Journal of Experimental Psychology,* 1968, *77,* 171–179.

Kintsch, W. *Learning, Memory, and Conceptual Process.* New York: Wiley, 1970(a).

Kintsch, W. Models for free recall and recognition. In D. A. Norman (Ed.), *Models of Human Memory.* New York: Academic Press, 1970(b).

Nickerson, R. S. Short-term memory for complex meaningful visual configurations: A demonstration of capacity. *Canadian Journal of Psychology,* 1965, *19,* 155–160.

Shepard, R. N. Recognition memory for words, sentences, and pictures. *Journal of Verbal Learning and Learning Behavior*, 1967, *6*, 156–163.

Standing, L. Learning 10,000 pictures. *Quarterly Journal of Experimental Psychology*, 1973, *25*, 207–222.

Standing, L., Conezio, J., and Harber, R. N. Perception and memory for pictures: Single-trial learning of 2500 visual stimuli. *Psychonomic Science*, 1970, *19*, 73–74.

Underwood, B. J. Are we overloading memory? In A. W. Melton and E. Martin (eds.), *Coding Processes in Human Memory*. Washington, D.C.: Winston, 1972.

16 Professor Sanford's Morning Prayer

Edmund Clarke Sanford

Here is another failure of memory, even more surprising than the prevailing ignorance of pennies that was demonstrated in Selection 15. Perhaps most people don't bother to read what is written on their pennies, but Professor Sanford—a distinguished psychologist of an earlier generation—read his morning prayer aloud day after day. After 5000 trials, he still didn't know it.

The value of distributed repetitions in memory has long been established. It has even been suggested that one repetition a day might show a maximum of economy. This may very well be the case when the repetitions are made with the purpose ... of memorizing, but it is certainly not so when this purpose is absent. A very large number of single repetitions at 24-hour intervals may then have little or no mnemonic result.

It has been my custom for many years to read in my family the form of Morning Prayer provided by the Episcopal Church. The reading has been interrupted at various periods but at a conservative estimate I have read this form of words at least 5,000 times in the last 25 years, usually at 24-hour intervals, often for many weeks in succession, and I am able to read it with a minimum of attention—almost automatically—and yet my memory of it is notably defective, as becomes only

From E. C. Sanford, A letter to Dr. Titchener, in *Studies in Psychology Contributed by Colleagues and Former Students of Edward Bradford Titchener*. Worcester, Mass.: Louis N. Wilson, 1917, 8–10.

too patent when I lose my place in reading or fumble the turning of a page.

In order to obtain a more precise index of my deficiency I have recently made a test of how much I was able to write from memory, starting myself by the sight of a single word and writing as much as I could before being stopped by inability to recall, then uncovering the text until one new word was revealed and again writing as much as I could.

The first of the five prayers composing the group is the Lord's Prayer which I learned as a child, and which I was able to write correctly (71 words) except for the omission of an "and." The group closes with a benediction (25 words) which some years ago I committed to memory intentionally. This I was able to reproduce without error.

The test with the four intermediate prayers gave the following results:

Prayer #1 (124 words) . . . 44 promptings (2.82 words/prompt)

Prayer #2 (73 words)   . . . 20 promptings (3.65 words/prompt)

Prayer #3 (146 words) . . . 38 promptings (3.84 words/prompt)

Prayer #4 (158 words) . . . 27 promptings (5.85 words/prompt)

The increasing size of the groups of words recalled probably indicates increasing adaptation to the method of testing, and introspection confirms this interpretation; but that the material was very far short of complete recall is abundantly witnessed by the fact that even in the most favorable case the average word group was less than six words and that many outright blunders—usually the substitution of words of similar import—were made.

Such a result as this emphasizes two things: First, the dominating importance of the mental set or attitude . . . which is now generally recognized; and second, the probability that repetition under the domination of a particular [set] tends toward the formation of habits which are increasingly specialized. This also is not unknown. As long ago as his original experiments on the learning of nonsense syllables Ebbinghaus noticed that increasing the number of repetitions strengthened the bonds of contiguous syllables relatively more than the bonds of widely separated members of the series. . . .

17 Recalling Previously Held Attitudes

George R. Goethals and
Richard F. Reckman

*This selection illustrates another striking failure of
everyday memory: People often cannot remember
what they used to believe. To be sure, the study itself
is somewhat contrived; the authors present it as a test
of cognitive consistency theories rather than as an
exploration of memory in its natural context. They
began by ascertaining the subjects' attitudes toward
school bussing. Planned group discussions then
changed those attitudes, moving the "pros" toward
"anti" and the "antis" toward "pro." Finally, everyone
was asked what attitude they had indicated at first.
The subjects responded incorrectly: They tended to
report their new attitudes instead of their old ones.*

*We must be cautious in interpreting the results of
such a study. Perhaps the effect only occurs after
artificially induced changes of attitude; perhaps it is
limited to opinions held casually, without conviction;
perhaps it results from the subjects' attempts to
appear consistent rather than from genuine changes
in memory. Nevertheless, I am inclined to believe that
it is a robust and important effect. At Cornell we have
found the same tendency—"recall" that correlates*

From G. R. Goethals and R. F. Reckman, The perception of consistency in
attitudes, *Journal of Experimental Social Psychology*, 1973, 9, 491–501. The
research at Cornell University mentioned in the introductory comments was
conducted by Rosemary S. Phelan as part of her B. A. Honors Thesis, *Memory
for Natural Changes in Opinion.*

better with present opinion than with original opinion—after spontaneously occurring changes of opinion about campus issues. Goethals and Frost (1978) have made a similar finding. In our study, the effect was just as marked for attitudes that had been marked "strongly held" as for those "casually held." However, a different result was obtained by Chris and Woodward (1973). Goethals, Reckman, and Rothman (in another unpublished paper) have shown that the effect is weakened when two experimenters are employed, reducing demands for consistent self-presentation; but it is not eliminated. This finding, too, was confirmed at Cornell.

In everyday life it is often hard to distinguish faulty recall of an earlier opinion from deliberate misrepresentation: Consider what John Dean said he had told Nixon about the cover-up (Selection 14). In any case, the effect cannot be universal or inevitable; all of us remember some opinions we once held and have now abandoned. What makes the difference? Perhaps it is the act of changing our attitudes that we remember rather than the attitudes themselves. Note that the subjects of the experiment described in this selection did not believe that their opinions had been changed.

Sometimes people change their minds. When they do, there is the potential problem that they will perceive themselves as being inconsistent. They may feel that it is inconsistent to hold one belief at one time and the opposite belief at a later time. Even though they may protest to others, and to themselves, that it is legitimate and fair to change one's mind or attitude, there may often be discomfort or embarrassment associated with having changed one's position. In theoretical terms, cognitive dissonance (Festinger, 1957) may be produced by the inconsistency of the cognitions that at a previous time one held a particular belief and that now one hold the opposite. One convenient way of reducing such dissonance would be to overlook, distort, or forget one's original position. If one felt that one's present position was the one he had always or almost always held, he would not be troubled by inconsistency. This suggests that people may be motivated to distort

their original position when they change their attitudes, and to perceive their previous position as being identical to or at least near to the
one they currently are adopting. The present study is designed to
investigate this hypothesis.

A study by Bem and McConnell (1970), though addressed to an
entirely different issue, presents evidence which seems to support the
dissonance theory prediction of distortion of original position in the
service of consistency. Bem and McConnell reported that subjects who
wrote counterattitudinal essays and changed their attitudes in a forced
compliance paradigm recalled their initial attitudes as being "identical
to postmanipulation attitudes" (p. 28). It should be mentioned that
Bem and McConnell viewed their findings as supporting Bem's (1967)
self-perception interpretation of a wide range of dissonance phenomena. It seems, however, that their results can also be interpreted as
support for the new dissonance phenomenon suggested above.

There is evidence, then, supporting the hypothesis that people
distort their recollections of their initial attitudes after attitude change
in order to maintain cognitive consistency. The experiment reported
below was designed to supplement this evidence and demonstrate the
phenomenon in a different setting. Specifically, an attempt was made
to change the attitudes of high school students on the issue of school
bussing to achieve racial balance through discussion with peers and
to investigate the postdiscussion recollection of initial attitudes on this
issue. The experiment attempts to demonstrate that people's errors in
recall or distortions of their initial positions are such as to allow them
to perceive consistency in their attitudes over time.

METHOD

Overview

As part of an alleged assessment of high-school student's attitudes,
small groups of subjects were asked to discuss one of 30 pretested
issues. Each group was composed entirely of subjects in agreement
with the selected issue, bussing, or entirely of subjects opposed to
bussing. An experimental confederate joined each group with the task
of reversing the attitudes of the other group members through discussion. After the discusison, subjects were asked to try to duplicate their
original pretest ratings on eight representative issues including bussing. The discrepancy between each subject's pretest rating and the
attempted duplication was the dependent variable of the study. Subjects in a control condition were simply asked to duplicate their ratings
on the eight issues.

Subjects

The subjects were male and female high-school students who had just completed their junior or senior years at a regional high school in Northwestern Massachusetts. Thirty-three juniors and 41 seniors were pretested at school or in an unrelated study shortly before the beginning of the experiment. Subjects were contacted by telephone and scheduled for participation 4–14 days after the pretest. All subjects were paid $2.00 an hour for their participation in the pretest and the actual experiment. There were two to four subjects in each experimental session.

There were two experimental conditions in the experiment, one composed of probussing subjects (Experimental Pro-condition, three sessions, n = 9) and one composed of antibussing subjects (Experimental Anti-condition, three sessions, n = 9). In addition, there was a control condition (n = 12) composed of six subjects on each side of the issue. Subjects were randomly assigned to one of the three conditions with the constraint that approximately two-thirds of the subjects on either side of the issue be assigned to the appropriate experimental condition while the remaining one-third be used as controls.

Pretest

The pretest attitude survey consisted of 30 statements encompassing a variety of current social and political issues. Subjects were instructed to indicate the extent to which they agreed or disagreed with each statement on a 31-point scale (1 = strongly agree; 31 = strongly disagree). They were also asked to indicate their degree of confidence in each judgment on a 17-point scale (1 = not at all confident; 17 = very confident).

Procedure

At the beginning of each experimental session the experimenter explained to the group composed of the subjects and the confederate that he was trying to obtain more information about the attitudes of high-school students in the area. He said that the attitude survey they had completed earlier had revealed only what percentage of people agreed or disagreed with a particular statement. What he wanted now was to get some idea of the various arguments on both sides of these issues and to find out what beliefs and feelings lay behind the specific opinions they had expressed. In short, he told them, he wanted to know why they held the opinions they did.

The experimenter explained that each group had been randomly assigned to discuss one of the 30 issues. Of course, all groups discussed the same issue which was stated: "Bussing should be widely used to achieve racial balance in the nation's schools." The bussing issue was chosen because it seemed to be an important and salient political issue, although it is not a major issue locally. Our pretest indicated that the pool of subjects was fairly evenly split on this issue, and that most subjects indicated moderately high but not extreme confidence in their bussing opinions.

After announcing the topic, the experimenter explained that the discussion would be taped so that he could later reconstruct the arguments and try to understand better what people were thinking. The taping actually provided a record of the experimental sessions. The experimenter added that he had found it best to ask one individual to start the discussion. He checked the list of subjects and read what he said was the first name on it. In this way the confederate was assured of speaking first, always expressing a position opposed to the one endorsed by all the other group members on the pretest.

The confederate was a senior from the same high school attended by the subjects. He was known and respected by the participants in the experiment. With the aid of the experimenters he had prepared hopefully persuasive arguments on both sides of the issue. The confederate stated the reasons for his position and attempted to undermine expected counterarguments. Throughout the discussion he defended his position and countered opposing statements in a persistent but not belligerent manner. The discussions lasted from six to 20 minutes.

After the discussion, the experimenter passed out a questionnaire explaining that he wished to supplement the results from the survey with the results from the discussion. Further, he said, he wanted to know what they thought were the merits of both methods of assessing attitudes. The first item asked the subjects to write in the statement being discussed and to indicate to what extent they presently agreed or disagreed with the statement. The subjects were offered four choices: definitely agree, tend to agree, tend to disagree, or definitely disagree. Answers on this item were used to determine the success of the attitude change attempt. The questionnaire also asked the subjects about the effects of the discussion, if any, on their opinions and whether the discussion had encouraged them to think more about their position. Finally, they were asked if they preferred the survey or discussion method of assessing attitudes.

After the questionnaire had been completed and collected, a second form was distributed consisting of eight issue statements from the pretest with identical agreement and confidence scales. Included among the eight were the bussing statement and seven others representative of the 30 items surveyed on the pretest (e.g., "All jobs should be open equally to members of both sexes"; "All laws against homosexuality should be repealed"; "Zero population growth is a desirable national goal"). The experimenter explained that one possible weakness of the survey method of attitude assessment was that people may not take them seriously, that they may not fill them out carefully and thoughtfully, that, in fact, people may not even notice exactly what they say. To see if this possible weakness is real, they were being asked to try to remember how they rated these eight issues and to duplicate their original ratings as accurately as they could. The experimenter made it clear that he would be checking on the accuracy of their recall. He added that he certainly hoped that they could recall their original positions; otherwise it would mean that the survey results were not very meaningful or useful. This procedure, like Bem and McConnell's, attempted to place any "experimental demand" on accuracy of recall rather than on consistency of recall with current attitudes. It can be noted that the postdiscussion attitude measure was in quite a different form than the pretest or duplication measures. This difference hopefully separated the postdiscussion measure from the experimenter's subsequent concern with the pretest and duplication of the pretest scores. Further, subjects were prevented from simply duplicating their postdiscussion scores in recalling the pretest.

The completion of this second questionnaire marked the conclusion of the experiment. There followed a final discussion in which the true purpose of the experiment was fully explained.

In the control condition the experimenter simply explained to subjects that he was trying to evaluate the merits of the survey method of assessing attitudes. As in the experimental conditions, he expressed his concern that people did not fill out the surveys carefully and thoughtfully. He continued that he was trying to see whether subjects could duplicate their pretest ratings and he certainly hoped they could. Again it was made clear that accuracy would be checked. Finally, the experimenter explained the true nature of the experiment and the control subjects' role in it.

RESULTS

Pretest Attitudes Toward Bussing

Of the 74 pretest subjects, 42 percent were on the agree side of the neutral point, 53 percent were on the disagree side, and four subjects were exactly on the neutral point (the latter were eliminated from the experiment). The probussing students had a mean score of 12.36 on the 17-point confidence scale and the antibussing students had a mean score of 12.82. Thus, the sample was divided fairly evenly on the bussing question and both sides seemed equally confident of their position. The 30 subjects who returned for the second session were representative of the original sample in terms of their bussing attitudes and confidence scores. The subjects in the three conditions were also comparable in terms of the extremity of their bussing scores.

Manipulation Checks

The experimental manipulations in this study were the attempts to change the attitudes of the subjects on the bussing issue. An attempt was made to change the subjects in the Experimental Pro-condition toward an antibussing position and to change subjects in the Experimental Anti-condition to a probussing position. The success of these attempts was assessed by the scores on the four-point postdiscussion scale (1 = definitely agree; 4 = definitely disagree). These scores can be directly compared with the pretest scores if the 31-point pretest scale is divided into quarters and thus converted to a four-point scale (1–7 = 1; 8–15 = 2; 17–24 = 3; 25–31 = 4). The mean pretest scores on this converted converted scale and the mean postdicussion scores

TABLE 17-1
Pretest and postdiscussion attitude scores

	Pretest		Post discussion
Experimental pro			
$\bar{x}^a$	1.64		3.53
Experimental anti			
$\bar{x}$	3.67		2.44
Source	df	MS	F
Between subjects			
A (pro-anti)	1	.67	7.44
Error	4	.09	
Within subjects			
B (pre–post)	1	.33	1.94
AB	1	7.25	42.64*
Error	4	.17	

$^a\bar{\chi}$ is the mean of the three group means in each condition.
*p < .005.

are presented in Table 17-1.[1] A two-factor repeated-measures analysis of variance ... performed on these data is also summarized in Table 17-1.

The analysis of variance reveals a strong trend ($p < .06$) toward a main effect for conditions reflecting the fact that the confederate was more successful in changing the attitudes of probussing subjects than antibussing subjects.

Most important is the highly significant interaction reflecting that the Experimental Pro-subjects were more opposed to bussing on the post-discussion measure than they were on the pretest ($F(1,4) = 31.41$, $p < .005$) while the Experimental Anti-subjects were more in favor of bussing than the Experimental Pro-subjects ($F(1,7) = 13.54, p < .01$).

Test of Hypothesis

The hypothesis of the study was tested by an examination of the scores subjects gave on the duplication or recall questionnaire. As noted above, subjects were asked to duplicate as accurately as possible their scores on the pretest attitude survey. The mean recall scores as well as the pretest scores for experimental conditions are presented in Table 17-2. A two-factor repeated-measures analysis of variance is also summarized in Table 17-2. The analysis reveals a main effect for treatments reflecting the fact that the recall scores of the Experimental Anti-subjects (like their actual attitude change scores) do not drop toward the probussing position as much as the Experimental Pro-subjects' recall scores change toward the antibussing position. Again, most important is the highly significant interaction. This reflects the fact that the Pro-subjects recall themselves to be more opposed to bussing than they actually were ($F(1,4) = 25.26, p < .01$) while Anti-subjects tend to recall themselves to be more in favor of bussing than they actually were ($F(1,4) = 6.06, p < .08$). The Pro-subjects actually recall themselves to be less in favor of bussing than do the Anti-subjects ($F(1,4 = 12.27 p < .05$).

The subjects' errors in recall can be examined further by assigning each subject an error in recall score based on the discrepancy between his actual pretest score and his recall of that pretest score. This error in recall measure is not designed to be a pure accuracy of memory measure. Rather it is designed to measure the tendency to

---

[1]Since subjects in groups were interacting, the postdiscussion attitude scores of subjects within groups cannot be considered to be independent. Thus, the scores in each experimental group were averaged and the group means were used as the entry for all analyses.

TABLE 17-2
Pretest and recall of pretest scores

	Pretest		Recall of pretest
Experimental pro $\bar{x}$ [a]	8.56		26.08
Experimental anti $\bar{x}$	26.06		17.47
Source	df	MS	F
Between subjects			
A (pro–anti)	1	59.28	31.53**
Error	4	.47	
Within subjects			
B (pre–recall)	1	59.99	3.29
AB	1	511.29	28.03*
Error	4	18.24	

[a] $\bar{x}$ is the mean of the three group means in each condition.
*p < .01. **p < .005.

recall one's initial attitude as being the opposite of what it actually was. Thus, errors in recall toward the end of the scale opposite the subject's original attitude were scored positively; errors toward the end point the subject was originally closer to were socred negatively. This measure of error in recall parallels Bem and McConnell's. The error in recall scores on the bussing issue and on the seven other issues for both experimental and control subject are presented in Table 17-3. The errors that a subject made in recalling the other seven issues were summarized in an overall error in recall score determined by the mean of his error in recall scores on those seven issues.

First, it can be noted that for the experimental subjects the difference between errors in recalling bussing and errors in recalling the other issues is significant ($\bar{d}$ = 9.10; $t(5)$ = 2.60, $p < .05$). This result shows that the experimental subjects recall their bussing attitudes to be in the direction of the opposite position more than they recall their other attitudes to be opposite their actual original positions.

Comparing experimental and control subjects, it can be seen that the errors that experimental subjects make in recalling their bussing attitudes are more in the direction of the opposite end of the scale than are the errors of the controls ($t(16)$ = 2.75, $p < .02$). Thus, the experimental subjects systematically distort their pretest attitudes toward the position opposed to their original attitude more than do control subjects.

In contrast to the results for the experimental subjects, the control subjects' errors in recalling bussing are not significantly different from their errors in recalling the other seven issues. Finally, it can be noted that the control and experimental subjects do not differ in recalling their positions on issues other than bussing.

TABLE 17-3
Error in recall scores

	Bussing issues	Other issues
Experimental subjects $\bar{x}$	+ 13.06	+ 3.96
Control subjects $\bar{x}$	+ 3.25	+ 2.75

In sum, the errors that experimental subjects make in recalling their bussing attitudes are systematically in the direction of recalling their position to be closer to the opposite of what it actually was. Control subjects show this tendency significantly less. Experimental subjects' recall errors on the other seven issues are less in the direction of the opposite end of the scale than are their recall errors on bussing. For control subjects, errors in recall of bussing are no different from their errors on the other issues and these errors are comparable to errors of the experimental subjects on these other issues. The errors which stand out are the errors of the experimental subjects toward bussing.

DISCUSSION

The results seem to offer strong support for the hypothesis of the study. The experimental subjects do recall their pretest attitudes as consistent with their postdiscussion attitudes. There is a very high correlation between these measures ($r = .86$ for all experimental subjects). This correlation does not in itself demonstrate that pretest attitudes are perceived to be the same as postdiscussion attitudes. However, if the recall scores are converted into a four-point scale, as was done for the pretest scores, and compared directly to the postdiscussion scores, it turns out that all but five of the 18 experimental subjects recall their pretest attitudes to be identical to their postdiscussion attitudes and the remainder recall their initial attitudes to be only one position removed. In conclusion, it seems that subjects do distort their original attitudes in order to make them consistent with new attitudes. This allows them to feel that the position they hold now is the one they have always held. An important implication, noted by Bem and McConnell (1970), is that since people cannot recall their original attitudes after having changed them, they may seldom be aware of the fact that they have changed. They can continue to believe in the consistency of their thinking over time.

A crucial question, which unfortunately cannot be answered conclusively by the present experiment, concerns the process involved in the recall errors or memory distortions. Are the subjects truly unable to recall their initial positions? Observations from the experimental sessions are relevant to this question. Some subjects listened carefully to the course of the discussion and began to nod their heads in agreement with the confederate's arguments. They seemed to come to agree with him without any awareness of their earlier attitude. In the debriefing they gave every indication that the position they adopted after the discussion was the position they had basically always held. Further information on this question comes from the item on the postdiscussion questionnaire asking subjects what effect, if any, the discussion had had on their attitudes. Most commented that the discussion had served to broaden their awareness of the issues involved or had provided support for their original position. No subject reported that the discussion had had any effect in changing or modifying his position.

During debriefing the subjects also denied that anyone in the group had influenced them to change their basic position. Indeed, when it was explained that they had changed their position from the pretest many subjects seemed dubious. A number wanted to see their original pretest ratings and appeared to be genuinely surprised to find that they actually had changed their attitude.

By all appearances, then, subjects were truly unable to recall their initial positions. Of course, there is no way to be sure of this. It does seem, however, that subjects distort their perception of their original attitude so as to maintain the perception that their attitudes have been consistent over time.

. . .

REFERENCES

Bem, D. J. Self-perception: An alternative interpretation of cognitive dissonance phenomena. *Psychological Review*, 1967, *74*, 183–200.

Bem, D. J., and McConnell, H. K. Testing the self-perception explanation of dissonance phenomena: On the salience of premanipulation attitudes. *Journal of Personality and Social Psychology*, 1970, *14*, 23–31.

Festinger, L. *A Theory of Cognitive Dissonance*. Evanston, Ill.: Row, Peterson, 1957.

ADDITIONAL REFERENCES

Chris, S. A., and Woodward, H. D. Self-perception and characteristics of premanipulation attitudes: A test of Bem's theory. *Memory and Cognition*, 1973, *1*, 229–235.

Goethels, G. R., and Frost, M. Value change and the recall of earlier values. *Bulletin of the Psychonomic Society*, 1978, *11*, 73–74.

18 On Memory and Childhood Amnesia

Ernest G. Schachtel

*No one can remember their very early childhood,
although the scope of "very early" varies from one
person to the next. It was Freud who first described
this loss as a kind of "amnesia"—an amnesia broken
only by occasional fragmentary images (Selection 5)
or screen memories (Selection 6). He attributed it to
the force of repression: having resolved the Oedipal
crisis by rejecting our infantile sexual wishes, we
cannot tolerate any associated memory that might
bring them back to consciousness. Schachtel, himself
a psychoanalyst, offers an alternative explanation in
this classic paper. His account is surprisingly
modern: The schemata of adults are no longer
appropriate for the experiences of childhood. But
there is also something archaic in his argument; he
tries to persuade his readers with ideas much older
than those of cognitive psychology. He treats
childhood amnesia as a symptom of lost innocence,
as if it were our own fault—and our greatest
misfortune—that we cannot hope to return to the
Garden of Eden of our infancy.*

*The beginning of the article has been omitted.
Schachtel starts with Greek mythology: Mnemosyne,
the Goddess of Memory, is the mother of muses and
hence of all art. There is a conflict between the
realistic requirements of the present and the delights*

From *Psychiatry*, 1947, *10*, 1–26. Copyright © 1947, 1975 by The William Alanson White Psychiatric Foundation, Inc. Reprinted by special permission of The Foundation.

> *of recollection. Proust, the "poet of memory,"*
> *renounced ordinary life entirely to achieve*
> Remembrance of Things Past. *But Goethe did not*
> *share Proust's fascination with memory; Schachtel*
> *quotes him as saying "I do not recognize memory in*
> *the sense that you mean it. Whatever we encounter*
> *that is great, beautiful, significant need not be*
> *remembered from the outside; need not be hunted*
> *up and laid hold of, as it were. Rather, from the*
> *beginning, it must be woven into the fabric of our*
> *inmost self, must become one with it, create a new*
> *and better self in us. . . . There is no past that one is*
> *allowed to long for. There is only the eternally new,*
> *growing from the enlarged elements of the past. . . ."*
> Schachtel *then turns to Freud's contribution.*

Freud, not unlike Proust, approaches the problem of memory not from wondering what or how well or how much man remembers but how hard it is to remember, how much is forgotten and not to be recovered at all or only with the greatest difficulty, and how the period richest in experience, the period of early childhood, is the one which is usually forgotten entirely save for a few apparently meaningless memory fragments. He finds this surprising since "we are informed that during those years which have left nothing but a few incomprehensible memory fragments, we have vividly reacted to impressions, that we have manifested human pain and pleasure and that we have expressed love, jealousy and other passions as they then affected us."[1] The few incomprehensible memory fragments left over from childhood, he considers as "concealing memories" (Deckerinnerungen), and his painstaking work to decipher their language bears more than a superficial resemblance to Proust's attempt to decipher the hieroglyphic characters of the images of a cloud, a triangle, a belfry, a flower, a pebble—a most difficult undertaking, but the only way to the true memories enclosed in these signs which seemed to be only indifferent material objects or sensations. It was Freud who made the discovery that a conflict, leading to repression, is responsible for the difficulty of this work of deci-

---

[1]Sigmund Freud, Three contributions to the theory of sex. In *The Basic Writings of Sigmund Freud.* New York: Random House, 1938, p. 581.

phering and for the difficulty of remembering the past. His well-known explanation of infantile amnesia is that the forgetting of childhood experiences is due to progressive repression of infantile sexuality, which reaches the peak of its manifestations in the third and fourth years of life. This repression is brought about by the "psychic forces of loathing, shame, and moral and esthetic ideal demands." These forces have the sanction of society, they are the product of society, which moulds the functions of all social activity and of that "uniform" memory in which Proust saw the irreconcilable antagonists of the true remembrance of things past.

It is the purpose of this essay to explore further the dynamics of this conflict in memory which leads to the striking phenomenon of childhood amnesia as well as to the difficulty, encountered by Proust though more hidden to the average eye, of recovering any true picture of past experience. To speak of a conflict in memory is a convenient abbreviation. Formulated more explicitly and accurately, the intention of this presentation is to shed light on some of the factors and conflicts in man and his society which make it difficult if not impossible for him really to remember his past and especially his early childhood.

Obviously, the concept of memory which such an approach presupposes cannot be the impersonal, artificial, isolated, and abstract concept implied by experimentation on the recall of digits, nonsense syllables, and similar material, a concept which seems more appropriate for the testing of the capacity of some mechanical apparatus than for the understanding of the functioning of memory in the living person. Nor is such a concept fundamentally changed when logically meaningful phrases or perceptually organized "Gestalten" are substituted for nonsense syllables and memory is investigated for its capacity to reproduce those, rather than meaningless material. Nobody doubts that it is easier to remember meaningful than meaningless material and that the function of memory has not developed in order to make possible the recall of nonsense. Memory as a function of the living personality can be understood only as a capacity for the organization and reconstruction of past experiences and impressions in the service of present needs, fears, and interests. It goes without saying that, just as there is no such thing as impersonal perception and impersonal experience, there is also no impersonal memory. Man perceives and remembers not as a camera reproduces on the film the objects before its lens; the scope and quality of his perceptions and experiences as well as of their reproduction by memory are determined by his individual fears, and interests. This is the more apparent the more significant an experience has been for the person.

With this concept of memory in mind, the puzzling problem of childhood amnesia seems to become more transparent and accessible to understanding. No greater change in the needs of man occurs than that which takes place between early childhood and adulthood. Into this change have gone all the decisive formative influences of the culture transmitted by the parents, laying the fundament of the transformation into the grown-up, "useful" member of society from the little heathen, who is helpless but as yet sees nothing wrong with following the pleasure principle completely and immediately and who has an insatiable curiosity and capacity for experience. An explanation of childhood amnesia that takes into account these changes leads to the following tentative hypothesis: The categories (or schemata) of adult memory are not suitable receptacles for early childhood experiences and therefore not fit to preserve these experiences and enable their recall. The functional capacity of the conscious, adult memory is usually limited to those types of experience which the adult consciously makes and is capable of making.

. . .

A closer examination and comparison of the content and quality of adult and childhood memories may be helpful for the purpose of such an understanding. Both Freud and Proust speak of the autobiographical memory, and it is only with regard to this memory that the striking phenomenon of childhood amnesia and the less obvious difficulty of recovering any past experience may be observed. There is no specific childhood amnesia as far as the remembrance of words learned and of objects and persons recognized is concerned. This type of material is remembered because, in contrast to the autobiographical past, it is constantly reexperienced and used and because it is essential for the orientation and adaptation of the growing child to his environment. In the recall of this type of material we have to deal with memory serving the immediate, practical use of knowledge and perception (recognition) mainly. The memory of the personal past—of one's past experiences, which also contain the material that has gone into the formation of one's character—is a much less efficient and reliable servant than the memory of learned material, on the whole, seems to be. Yet the separation of the "useful" from the "autobiographical" memory is, of course, an artificial abstraction. Actually this distinction of the content of remembered material is not clear-cut, and the two types of material indicated by it are continuously and everywhere interrelated.

The autobiographical memory shows indeed in most persons, if not in all, the amnesia for their early childhood from birth to approximately the fifth or sixth year. Of course, there are considerable gaps in the memory of many people for later periods of their lives also, probably more so for the period before than after puberty; but these gaps vary individually to a much greater extent than does the ubiquitous early childhood amnesia. Freud's observation of this amnesia has not stimulated others, as far as I can see, to significant investigations of the adult autobiographical memory. Yet it would seem that an awareness of the main differences between the type of material remembered from early childhood and that remembered from later life might help in an understanding of the phenomenon of childhood amnesia. If one believes Proust, life after childhood is not remembered either, save for the elusive flashes of a vision given only to the most sensitive and differentiated mind as the rare grace of a fortunate moment, which then the poet, with passionate devotion and patient labor, may try to transcribe and communicate.

Freud contrasts the presumable riches of childhood experience, the child's great capacity for impressions and experience, with the poverty or total lack of memory of such rich experience. If one looks closely at the average adult's memory of the periods of his life after childhood, such memory, it is true, usually shows no great temporal gaps. It is fairly continuous. But its formal continuity in time is offset by barrenness in content, by an incapacity to reproduce anything that resembles a really rich, full, rounded, and alive experience. Even the most "exciting" events are remembered as milestones rather than as moments filled with the concrete abundance of life. Adult memory reflects life as a road with occasional signposts and milestones rather than as the landscape through which this road has led. The milestones are the measurements of time, the months and years, the empty count of time gone by, so many years spent here, so many years spent there, moving from one place to another, so many birthdays, and so forth. The signposts represent the outstanding events to which they point— entering college, the first job, marriage, birth of children, buying a house, a family celebration, a trip. But it is not the events that are remembered as they really happened and were experienced at the time. What is remembered is usually, more or less, only the fact that such an event took place. The signpost is remembered, not the place, the thing, the situation to which it points. And even these signposts themselves do not usually indicate the really significant moments in a person's life; rather they point to the events that are conventionally supposed to be significant, to the cliches which society has come to consider as the main stations of life. Thus the memories of the majority of people come to resemble increasingly the stereotyped answers to a questionnaire, in which life consists of time and place of birth, religious denomination, residence, educational degrees, job, marriage, number and birthdates of children, income, sickness and death. The average traveler, asked about his trip, will tell you how many miles he has made (how many years he has lived); how fast he went (how successful he was); what places he has visited—usually only the well-known ones, often he visits only those that one "simply must have seen"—(the jobs he has held, the prestige he has gained). He can tell you whether the driving was smooth or rough, or whether somebody bumped his fender, but he will be quite unable to give you any real idea of the country through which he went. So the average traveler through life remembers chiefly what the road map or the guide book says, what he is supposed to remember because it is exactly what everybody else remembers too.

In the course of later childhood, adolescence, and adult life, perception and experience themselves develop increasingly into the rubber stamps of conventional cliches. The capacity to see and feel what is there give way to the tendency to see and feel what one expects to see and feel, which, in turn, is what one is expected to see and feel because everybody else does. Experience increasingly assumes the form of the cliche under which it will be recalled because this cliche is what conventionally is remembered by others. This is not the remembered situation itself, but the words which are customarily used to indicate this situation and the reactions which it is supposed to evoke. While this ubiquitous and powerful tendency toward pseudo-experience in terms of conventional cliches usually takes place unnoticed, it is quite articulate in some people and is used widely in advertising. There are people who experience a party, a visit to the movies, a play, a concert, a trip in the very words in which they are going to tell their friends about it; in fact, quite often, they anticipate such experience in these words. The experience is predigested, as it were, even before they have tasted of it. Like the unfortunate Midas, whose touch turned everything into gold so that he could not eat or drink, these people turn the potential nourishment of the anticipated experience into the sterile currency of the conventional phrase which exhausts their experience because they have seen, heard, felt nothing but this phrase with which later they will report to their friends the "exciting time" they have had. The advertising business seems to be quite aware of this. It does not have to promise a good book, a well-written and well-performed play, an entertaining or amusing movie. It suffices to say that the book, the play, the movie will be the talk of the town, of the next party, of one's friends. To have been there, to be able to say that one has been present at the performance, to have read the book even when one is unable to have the slightest personal reaction to it, is quite sufficient. But while Midas suffered tortures of starvation, the people under whose eyes every experience turns into a barren cliche do not know that they starve. Their starvation manifests itself merely in boredom or in restless activity and incapacity for any real enjoyment.

. . .

How well is the average highly conventionalized adult memory equipped to contain and recall the time and the experiences of early childhood? Very poorly or not at all. This will become more apparent through consideration of the quality of early childhood experience. The adult amnesia for this period prevents direct knowledge. Observation of little children and imagination are the only means of learning something about this subject. It is safe to assume that early childhood is the period of human life which is richest in experience. Everything is new to the newborn child. His gradual grasp of his environment and of the world around him are discoveries which, in experiential scope and quality, go far beyond any discovery that the most adventurous and daring explorer will every make in his adult life. No Columbus, no Marco Polo has ever seen stranger and more fascinating and thoroughly absorbing sights than the child that learns to perceive, to taste, to smell, to touch, to hear and see, and to use his body, his senses, and his mind. No wonder that the child shows an insatiable curiosity. He has the whole world to disover. Education and learning, while on the one hand furthering this process of discovery, on the other hand gradually brake and finally stop it completely. There are relatively few adults who are fortunate enough to have retained something of the child's curiosity, his capacity for questioning and for wondering. The average adult "knows all the answers," which is exactly why he will never know even a single answer.

. . .

The incompatibility of early childhood experience with the categories and the organization of adult memory is to a large extent due to what I call the conventionalization of the adult memory. Conventionalization is a particular form of what one might call schematization of memory. Voluntary memory recalls largely schemata of experience rather than experience. These schemata are mostly built along the lines of words and concepts of the culture. Also the so-called visual or the auditory memory reproduces schemata of visual or auditory impressions rather than the impressions themselves. Obviously the schemata of experience as well as of memory[2] are determined by the

---

[2] The term "memory schemata" is taken from Bartlett, but used in a somewhat different sense. Bartlett rightly emphasizes that remembering is "an affair of reconstruction rather than mere reproduction." According to him, this reconstruction serves as a justification of the present attitude toward past experience. Such reconstructions he calls "schemata," and these are determined by sense differences, appetites, instincts, and interests. In this essay, however, the concept of memory schemata is used only to designate socially and culturally determined patterns of reconstruction of the past, as contrasted to individually determined patterns. Obviously the greater part of all individual memory schemata in Bartlett's sense are culturally determined.

culture which has developed a certain view of the world and of life, a view which furnishes the schemata for all experience and all memory. But the range and differentiation of a culture like that of Greece, India, China, or modern Western civilization is of considerable scope. It offers highly differentiated and subtle as well as very conventional, banal, and commonplace schemata. By conventionalization of the memory (and experience) schemata I understand those memory processes which are subject to the most conventional schematization and which, therefore, are not capable of reproducing individual experience, but can only reproduce what John Doe is supposed to have experienced according to the Joneses' and everybody else's ideas of what people experience. Every fresh and spontaneous experience transcends the capacity of the conventionalized memory schema and, to some degree, of any schema. That part of the experience which transcends the memory schema as preformed by the culture is in danger of being lost because there exists as yet no vessel, as it were, in which to preserve it. Even if the schemata of experience have not prevented the person from becoming aware of or sensing that quality of his experience which transcended these schemata, this quality, if it is to be preserved and to become a productive part of the personality, has to overcome the second handicap of the memory schemata, which tend, as time goes on, to supplant this fresh and new element of experience with some preformed notion and thus to bury it. The process of schematization and conventionalization and its effect on the raw material of experience, especially childhood experience, can be well observed in two of its specific developments which take place as the child learns to make use of his senses and to speak.

Language, in its articulating and its obscuring function, may be considered first since the adult, too, encounters the problem of the incompatability of experience with language and the consequent forgetting of experience or its distortion by the cliche of language. The fact that language is adult language, the language of an adult civilization, and that the infant and small child is moulded only very gradually from its natural existence into a member of the civilzation into which it is born makes the discrepancy between his precivilized, unschematized experience and the categories of civilized, conventional language much greater. Yet between this discrepancy and that existing between the adult's experience and his language, there is a difference of degree rather than of kind. Everyone who has honestly tried to describe some genuine experience exactly, however small and insignificant it may have seemed, knows how difficult if not impossible that is. One might well say that the greatest problem of the writer or the poet is the temptation of language. At every step a word beckons, it seem so convenient, so suitable, one has heard or read it so often in a similar context, it sounds so well, it makes the phrase flow so smoothly. If he follows the temptation of this word, he will perhaps describe something that many people recognize at once, that they aleady know, that follows a familiar pattern; but he will have missed the nuance that distinguishes his experience from others, that makes it his own. If he wants to communicate that elusive nuance which in some way, however small, will be his contribution, a widening or opening of the scope of articulate human experience at some point, he has to fight constantly against the easy flow of words that offer themselves. Like the search for truth, which never reaches its goal yet never can be abandoned, the endeavor to articulate, express, and communicate an experience can never succeed completely. It consists of an approach, step by step, toward that distant vantage point, that bend of the road from which one hopes to see the real experience in its entirety and from where it will become visible to others—a point which is never reached. The lag, the discrepancy between experience and word is a productive force in man as long as he remains aware of it, as long as he knows and feels his experience was in some way more than and different from what his concepts and words articulate. The awareness of this unexplored margin of experience, which may be its essential part, can turn into that productive energy which enables man to go one step closer to understanding and communicating his experience, and thus add to the scope of human insight. It is this awareness and the struggle and the ability to narrow the gap between experience and words which make the writer and the poet. The danger of the schemata of language, and especially of the worn currency of conventional language in vogue at the moment when the attempt is made to understand and describe an experience, is that the person making this attempt will overlook the discrepancy between experience and language cliche or that he will not be persistent enough in his attempt to eliminate this discrepancy. Once the conventional schema has replaced the experience in his mind, the significant quality of the experience is condemned to oblivion.

The discrepancy between concepts, language, and experience can be looked upon as a model and as part of the discrepancy between memory schemata and experience. This close relationship, of course, is not accidental since voluntary recall and communication of recalled experience are essentially dependent on conceptual thought and language. While there is also recall of experience without the vehicle of language, a great deal of what we recall, especially of what we recall voluntarily, is recalled already in terms of language and in concepts formed by language. This has considerable bearing on the problem of childhood amnesia. The infant and small child has to undergo and assimilate the comparatively greatest amount of new experience at a time when his language, his concepts, and his memory schemata are poorest or as yet entirely undeveloped. Only very gradually does he acquire the faculty of language, learn the conceptual schemata of his culture, and develop a memory and memory schemata. The experiences of the infant are inarticulate and complex.

. . .

Early childhood amnesia may be considered a normal amnesia. It shares this quality with most, though not all, of dream amnesia and with the constant forgetting of those parts and aspects of experience which do not fit into the ready patterns of language and culture— transschematic experience. Normal amnesia is both akin to and different from pathological amnesia. Their likeness consists in this causation by a conflict between nature and culture or by intercultural conflict. Their difference consists chiefly in the fact that the conflicts causing normal amnesia are ubiquitous in a culture and their solution is part of the development of the personality in that culture; whereas in pathological amnesia, by and large, the conflict is due to individual traumatic experience which, although caused too by the stresses and conflicts operative in the culture, has become traumatic because of the particular history of the individual person. One might say that the normal amnesia, that which people usually are unable to recall, is an illuminating index to the quality of any given culture and society. It is that which does not serve the purposes of that society and would interfere with the pattern of the culture, that which would be traumatic to the culture because it would break up or transcend the conventions and mores of that culture. Early childhood amnesia is the most striking and dramatic expression merely of a dynamism operative throughout the life of people: the distortion or forgetting of transschematic experience, that is, of experience for which the culture provides no pattern and no schema.

Cultures vary in the degree to which they impose cliches on experience and memory. The more a society develops in the direction of mass conformism, whether such development be achieved by a totalitarian pattern or within a democratic framework by means of the employment market, education, the patterns of social life, advertising, press, radio, movies, best-sellers, and so on, the more stringent becomes the rule of the conventional experience and memory schemata in the lives of the members of that society. In the history of the last hundred years of western civilization the conventional schematization of experience and memory has become increasingly prevalent at an accelerating pace.

Even within a culture the degree to which in different *groups* conventional schemata of experience and memory prevent the recall of actual experience may show marked differences. Such a difference seems to exist, for example, between European men and women. There is some reason to assume that European men usually show a more extensive and pervasive amnesia for their early childhood than women.[3] A plausible hypothesis for the explanation of this difference would have to take into account the marked difference in the social status of the two sexes in Europe and, specifically, the difference in what one might call the social self-ideal of man versus that of woman. This idea of what the grown-up person, the respectable citizen ought to be emphasizes the cleft between childhood and adulthood much more in men than in women. All things pertaining to the rearing of children and to the home are the domain of the women and the average man could consider it beneath his "dignity" to know much about them or to be much concerned with them. Hence, to recall details of early childhood would be consistent with the social self-ideal of women whose interests are supposed to center around children, kitchen, and home. But to a man these things are not supposed to be sufficiently "important" to deserve much attention. To approximate the social self-ideal is important for his self-esteem; and the further removed from, and opposed to, the image of childhood the grown-up man's social self-ideal is the more difficult will it be for him to recall experiences showing that once he was an infant and little boy. In general, more extensive childhood amnesias are to be expected in those groups, cultures, and historical epochs which emphasize the belief that childhood is radically different from adulthood, than one is likely to find where the continuity between childhood and adult life is emphasized.[4]

Mankind's belief in a lost paradise is repeated in the belief, held by most people, in the individual myth of their happy childhood. Like most myths this one contains elements of both truth and illusion, is woven out of wishes, hopes, remembrance and sorrow, and hence has more than one meaning. One finds this belief even in people who have undergone cruel experiences as children and who had, without being

---

[3]Oral communication by Ruth Benedict. In interviewing a number of European men and women Benedict found consistently that the women recalled quite a few details of their lives before they had reached the age of six while the men hardly recalled anything. The people interviewed by her did not constitute a representative sample of the population, yet the consistency of the phenomenon in all the people interviewed seemed indicative of its more general significance.

[4]For the general significant of continuity and discontinuity between childhood and adulthood, see Ruth Benedict, Continuities and discontinuities in cultural conditioning, *Psychiatry*, 1938, *1*, 161–167. [*See also Ulric Neisser, Cultural and cognitive discontinuity. In T. E. Gladwin and W. Sturtevant (eds.)*, Anthropology and Human Behavior. *Washington, D.C.: Anthropological Society of Washington, 1962.*]

or remaining aware of it, a childhood with hardly any love and affection from their parents. No doubt, one reason for the myth of happy childhood is that it bolsters parental authority and maintains a conventional prop of the authority of the family by asserting that one's parents were good and benevolent people who did everything for the good of their children, however much they may have done against it. And disappointed and suffering people, people without hope, want to believe that at least once there was a time in their life when they were happy. But the myth of happy childhood reflects also the truth that, as in the myth of paradise lost, there was a time before animalistic innocence was lost, before pleasure-seeking nature and pleasure-forbidding culture clashed in the battle called education, a battle in which the child always is the loser. At no time is life so exlusively and directly governed by the pleasure principle as it is in early infancy; at no other time is man, especially civilized man, capable of abandoning himself so completely to pleasure and satisfaction. The myth of happy childhood takes the place of the lost memory of the actual riches, spontaneity, freshness of childhood experience, an experience which has been forgotten because there is no place for it in the adult memory schemata.

. . .

19 Memory for a Salient Childhood Event

Karen Sheingold and
Yvette J. Tenney

In this ingenious study, Sheingold and Tenney go beyond the traditional method of asking people to report any early memories they happen to have (Waldvogel, Selection 7). The target of their inquiries is a specific episode that took place at a precisely known age: the birth of a younger sister or brother. Memories of such an episode can shed light on two important questions. First, by testing subjects of different ages who were all four years old when their siblings were born, one can estimate the rate at which early important episodes are forgotten. Surprisingly, the data hint that the rate may be zero; older subjects remembered just as much as younger ones. Second, by testing adults who were of various ages when their siblings were born, one can explore the boundaries of childhood amnesia itself. In these data, people recalled almost nothing about sibling births that took place before they were age three. The sharpness of that boundary may just be a characteristic of this

A preliminary version of this paper was presented at the Society for Research in Child Development, San Francisco, March 1979. The research was supported by a Wellesley College Faculty Award. The study mentioned in the introductory comments was conducted by Nancy Batterman at Cornell University. In that study, the median numbers of questions (maximum = 20) answered by the undergraduate subjects were as follows (subjects are categorized by their ages at the time of their sibling's birth): 5 Ss aged 1–2, M = 3; 4 Ss aged 2–2½, M = 8.25(!); 3 Ss aged 2½–3, M = 4; 5 Ss aged 3–3½, M = 5.5; 5 Ss aged 3½–4, M = 9; 5 Ss aged 4–4½, M = 9; 6 Ss aged 4½–5, M = 10.5; 5 Ss aged 5–6, M = 13.5.

particular sample; we turned up more instances of early memory in an informal replication of the study at Cornell. Larger samples will be needed before these results can be considered definitive.

This study is concerned with how much children remember about a salient event in their life, how much is forgotten over time, and whether age at the time of the event affects how much is remembered. The study of natural memory—memory for what people experience or learn in the course of their life—has just begun (Robinson, 1976; Rubin, 1977 [*Selection 29*], Warrington and Sanders, 1971). Of particular interest are two recent studies (Bahrick, Bahrick, and Wittlinger, 1975; Brown and Kulik, 1977 [*Selection 2*]) which found little or no forgetting for certain autobiographical information over a period of years.

Brown and Kulik (1977) asked adults about events in their lives at the time of the assassination of President Kennedy. Because subjects were able to report precisely what they were doing when they heard the news, the authors suggested that events which are surprising, consequential, and emotionally arousing give rise to pemanent "flashbulb" memories. Bahrick, Bahrick, and Wittlinger (1975) tested recall and recognition of the names and faces of high school classmates, varying the retention interval since graduation from two weeks to 57 years. They found virtually no decrement in recognition of pictures and names of classmates, nor in accurate pairing of names and faces of classmates, up to 35 years after graduation.

These studies represent a shift in paradigm toward more ecologically valid studies of memory (Neisser, 1978 [*Selection 1*]; Gibbs, 1979). They support the view that natural memory is worthy of investigation, since the results differ from those of laboratory studies. Although no parallel studies have yet been done with children, it would seem particularly important to do so, since young children do poorly compared to older children on many memory tasks (Brown, 1975a). Systematically asking them about past events in their lives might shed new light on what children can remember.

At least three methodological issues must be dealt with in order to study children's natural memories. The first problem concerns the event to be recalled. While there are many shared experiences one can ask adults about, such as child-rearing practices (Robbins, 1963 [*Selection 20*]) or newsworthy events (Warrington and Sanders, 1971), it is not obvious what one could ask large numbers of children about. We chose the birth of a sibling as an event which would be both common and salient enough for many children to remember.

Second, it is difficult to assess the accuracy of retrospective reports. In the present study, we assessed accuracy by independently asking mothers and children the same questions. It was assumed that questions relating to a birth would elicit high recall from mothers.

Third, it is difficult to measure children's recall independently of their narrative skills, which improve dramatically with age. Subjects in studies of natural memory typically are asked to indicate everything they remember up to their eighth birthday (Waldfogel, 1948 [*Selection 7*]), or to think of a personal experience which particular words remind them of (Robinson, 1976). Young children, who have difficulty constructing a coherent report of sequential events (Brown, 1975b), would not be expected to answer these questions appropriately. We minimized this problem by asking specific questions which could be answered in a few words (e.g., "Who took care of you while your mother was in the hospital?"). Questions were asked in chronological order.

In the current study four-year-old children were interviewed about a sibling birth which occurred within a year of the interview. Eight-year-olds, twelve-year-olds, and college students were asked about sibling births which had occurred when they were four. Thus, retention could be assessed shortly after the event, and at various intervals up to 16 years. Effect of age when the birth occurred was investigated by asking college students about sibling births which took place when they were from one to 17 years old.

METHOD

Subjects

Children and mothers. Six boys and six girls in each of three age groups (Mean ages: 4–6, 8–3, 12–4), all of whom had had a sibling born when they were 3–6 to 4–11 years old, were interviewed. Mean ages at the time of sibling birth were 3–11, 4–3 and 4–2 for the three age groups, respectively. The youngest group was tested one to 12 months after the event, the average interval being 7 months. The mothers filled out questionnaires about the same events. Our subjects were middle-class families in suburban Boston, and were obtained through newspaper advertisements and information provided by schools and participants.

In advance of the interview, families were told that the study concerned children's memory for some past events in their lives. Of those families asked directly to participate by the researchers, only one refused. Many willing volunteers did not meet the subject-age/sibling-age requirements. Families were paid $3.50 for their participation.

College students. Eight female college students (Mean age 20–4), all of whom had had a sibling born when they were 3–6 to 4–11, were interviewed. Mean age at the time of sibling birth was 4–0. Their mothers were mailed questionnaires to return. Thirty-eight other female college students (Mean age 20–7), all of whom had had at least one sibling born when they were three or older, filled out questionnaires about the same events. All college students were fulfilling a course requirement in introductory psychology and were not paid. In total, the college students provided data on 81 sibling births which occurred when they were 1–3 to 17–5 years old: 22 between the ages of 1 and 3; 34 between 3 and 5; ten between 5 and 7; seven between 7 and 9; and eight at age 9 or older. Data on four additional births were eliminated from consideration because of unusual circumstances, such as home delivery.

Materials

The interview schedule and questionnaire consisted of 37 questions about the events in the child's life just prior to the mother's leaving for the hospital, when the mother was in the hospital, and when the mother and infant returned from the hospital. All subjects were asked the same questions in the same order, with probes following specified questions. For each section of the interview, subjects were asked one introductory question (e.g., "In general, what can you recall about your mother's leaving to go to the hospital?"), followed by specific questions (e.g., "Who told you that she was leaving for the hospital?") which could be adequately answered in a few words. Answers were written down by the interviewer and recorded on a Sony Superscope tape recorder.

Procedure

When children and their mothers arrived at the laboratory, the purpose of the interview was explained, and the names and ages of all children in the family were obtained. Then the child was interviewed in one room, while the mother filled out the questionnaire in another. After the interview, which lasted about 15 minutes, the child played while the interviewer asked the mother about inconsistencies between her report and that of her child and wrote down the mother's answers.

College students who were interviewed followed the same procedure. Students who filled out the questionnaire did so in a classroom in small groups, supervised by a student assistant. They first listed all of their siblings, then indicated whether they remembered a great deal, a little or nothing about the birth of each sibling, then filled out questionnaires for each sibling birth about which they remembered anything. They were asked to indicate on the questionnaire those answers which were guesses or information they were told by someone else. Questionnaires were filled out anonymously.

Scoring

Twenty specific questions were scored to assess the relative amount of information recalled (see Table 19-1). Questions not scored were introductory questions, questions about feelings, and questions about rehearsal.

A set of criteria was devised against which to measure the adequacy of each answer. For example, in response to the question, "What presents did the baby get?" subjects had to say something more specific than simply "toys" or "clothes." Credit was given for answers provided anywhere in the interview or questionnaire, even if not in response to the particular question being scored. No credit was given if an answer was not specific enough, of if no answer was given. Thus,

TABLE 19-1
Interview questions scored for recall

1. Who told you that your mother was leaving to go to the hospital?
2. What were you doing when you were told that she was leaving?
3. What time of day was it when she left to go to the hospital?
4. Who went with her? Did you go?
5. Who took care of you right after your mother left to go to the hospital?
6. What did you do right after your mother left?
7. How did you find out that the baby was a boy or girl?
8. Who took care of you while your mother was in the hospital?
9. What things did you do with that person while your mother was in the hospital?
10. Did you visit your mother while she was in the hospital?
11. Did you talk to your mother on the telephone while she was in the hospital?
12. How long did she stay in the hospital?
13. Who picked your mother and the baby up?
14. What day of the week did they come home?
15. What time of day was it?
16. What did you do when your mother and the baby arrived at home?
17. What was the baby wearing when you first saw it?
18. What presents did the baby get?
19. Did you get any presents at that time?
20. How did you find out that your mother was going to have a baby?

each subject received a total recall score, out of a possible 20, indicating the number of questions answered. In addition, children's answers were compared with their mothers'. Answers which corresponded with those of the mother, or which the mother deemed plausible, were "confirmed," while those which contradicted those of the mother, or which the mother deemed implausible, were "disconfirmed." Because only two of the mothers of the interviewed college students returned their questionnaires, we were unable to assess the accuracy of reports for college students, as originally planned. All protocols were scored by a coder who was blind to the purposes of the study, as well as by one of the researchers. Interrater reliability was .96. Disagreements were resolved by discussion.

RESULTS AND DISCUSSION

Effect of Time Since the Event

Mean total recall scores are shown in Table 19-2 for the three groups of children and their mothers. A two-way analysis of variance with status (mother versus child) and current age of the child as independent variables yielded a significant effect of status, $F (1,66) = 50.835, p < .001$, reflecting the higher recall scores of the mothers. The effect of the current age of the child was only marginally significant, $F (2,66) = 2.860, p = .065$, and there was no interaction between the two variables, indicating a similar pattern for children and mothers of virtually no forgetting for eight years after the event.

TABLE 19-2
Mean memory scores for children, college students, and mothers

Subjects	N	Total recall		Confirmed recall		Disconfirmed recall	
		Mean	(S.D.)	Mean	(S.D.)	Mean	(S.D.)
4-year-olds	12	13.58	(3.65)	9.25	(2.99)	4.33	(1.37)
8-year-olds	12	13.58	(4.48)	9.25	(4.59)	4.33	(1.97)
12-year-olds	12	11.83	(3.10)	9.00	(3.28)	2.83	(1.53)
College students	26	10.58	(5.15)				
Mothers of 4's	12	18.92	(1.24)				
Mothers of 8's	12	18.33	(1.56)				
Mothers of 12's	12	16.83	(2.59)				

Note: Maximum score = 20

The mean total recall score for a comparable group of college students can be seen in Table 19-2. This group included all college students who reported on one birth which occurred when they were 3–6 to 4–11 (mean age at sibling birth, 4–2). Twenty-six college students met this criterion, the eight who were interviewed and eighteen of the subjects who filled out questionnaires. (Since the scores of the two groups did not differ significantly from each other ($p > .10$), the data were combined.) An analysis of variance for unequal ns (Winer, 1971) on scores of this group of college students, in addition to the three groups of children, yielded no significant effect of age on the total amount recalled, F (3,58) < 1, extending the finding of no forgetting over time to 16 years after the event.

The average number of children's responses which were confirmed or disconfirmed by mothers appears in Table 19-2 for the three groups of children. An analysis of variance indicated no effect of age on the children's confirmed scores, F (2,33) < 1. There was a significant effect of age, however, on disconfirmed scores, F (2,33) $= 3.33$, $p < .05$, 12-year-olds having fewer disconfirmed scores than the younger groups. While the results for children's total and confirmed scores suggest that no forgetting occurred over time, there may be other explanations for these results.

The lack of age differences in children's confirmed scores might be explained by the fact that mothers are more likely to agree with reports of their older children. Older children might have remembered less accurately than younger, but have obtained equivalent scores due to the mothers' willingness to deem their answers plausible.

In order to explore this possibility, all confirmed answers were placed in one of three categories. If mother and child independently agreed, the answer was coded as an *agreement*. If mother and child gave different answers which were not mutually exclusive, and the mother later deemed the child's answer correct or plausible, it was coded as a *resolved difference*. (For example, a child reported that when the baby was born he received a red rabbit doll, while the mother reported he received a book, and the mother later confirmed that he also received a red rabbit doll.) If mother and child gave different answers which were mutually exclusive, and the mother later deemed the child's answer correct or plausible, it was coded as a *resolved contradiction*. (For example, a child reported receiving no gifts when the baby was born, while the mother reported she received a piggy bank, and the mother later said it's possible she didn't receive any gifts then.) A greater number of resolved differences and resolved contradictions for older than younger children would support the hypothesis that mothers were more likely to confirm older children's answers.

The mean number of agreements, resolved differences, and resolved contradictions are presented in Table 19-3. For none of the categories was there an effect of age on scores, $F < 1$ in all cases. Thus, it seems unlikely that mothers' confirmation of older children's answers was responsible for the lack of age differences.

Another possible reason for the apparent lack of forgetting was that the accurate memory of the younger subjects was replaced by good guessing for the older subjects. Since subjects did not consistently conform to our instructions to indicate which answers were guesses, we looked for other linguistic indications of guessing and uncertainty. A list of words and phrases was constructed which indicated that a remark was qualified (e.g., "probably," "I'm not sure," "possibly"). Because four-year-olds do not have the linguistic and cognitive skills to use qualified language (Miscione, Marvin, O'Brien, and Greenberg, 1978), we did not expect them to express uncertainty often. We assumed, however, that the eight-year-olds, twelve-year-olds and college students were equivalently well equipped to qualify their answers, and that an increase in guessing from age eight to twenty would constitute some support for the hypothesis.

A coder, blind to our hypotheses about qualified answers, judged which answers, of those which had been given credit, were qualified (interrater reliability, 100 percent). The mean number of qualified answers in the four age groups, from youngest to oldest, was 1.5, 4.42, 5.58, and 3.08 (4.13 for college students who were interviewed, and 2.61 for students who filled out questionnaires). Four-year-olds, as expected, used few qualified remarks. Results for the three older groups are similar, if scores from the interviewed college students are considered.

An analysis of variance for the three younger groups, as well as the interviewed college students, revealed a significant age effect $F (3,40) = 8.20, p < .001$, attributable only to differences between the 4-year-olds and the three older groups (Duncan's new multiple range test, $p < .01$). When college students who filled out questionnaires were included in the analysis, results were again significant, $F(3,58)$

TABLE 19-3
Mean number of children's answers confirmed by agreement, resolved difference, or resolved contradiction with mother at each age

Age	Agreements	Resolved differences	Resolved contradictions	Total confirmed
4	6.92	1.92	.41	9.25
8	6.00	2.42	.83	9.25
12	6.42	2.00	.58	9.00

$= 8.32, p < .001$, but scores for college students were indistinguishable from those of the 4-year-olds, and differed from those of the 8- and 12-year-olds ($p < .01$). It seems that the questionnaire elicited a different style of response than did the interview. In neither case, however, was there an increase in qualified remarks after the age of eight. It would appear, then, that the lack of forgetting between the ages of eight and 20 cannot easily be explained by an increase in guessing. The increase in qualified answers from four to eight is probably better explained by the acquisition of the language and thought of qualification than by an increase in actual guessing.

Effect of Age When Event Occurred

College students' total memory scores were correlated with age (in months) when the birth occurred. The correlation was highly reliable, r (81 pairs) $= .59, p < .001$. To test whether the relationship between age and scores was due to age at the time of the event or elapsed time, the scores of those students who had had siblings born when they were approximately four were correlated with elapsed time. The lack of such a correlation, r (26 pairs) $= .02$, supports the notion that age at the time of the event is the critical variable.

Indeed, the age of three would appear to be the youngest age at which anything can be reported about a sibling birth (see Figure 19-1). Only three of the 22 births reported when college students were younger than three had scores above zero. For two of these, the subjects were in the last quarter of their second year. The third, a student who was 18 months old at the time, indicated that she had been told, rather then remembered, much of the information she reported. By four years old, however, subjects reported a substantial amount about a sibling birth. For only four out of 39 births reported from the ages of four to 17 did students indicate they remembered nothing.

GENERAL DISCUSSION

The results of this study provided answers to the three questions initially posed. First, how much can young children remember about a real-life event? Four-year-olds can remember an impressive amount about the birth of a sibling. They could answer a mean of 13 questions out of 20, nine of which were accurate. For example, eight months after the event, one typical subject was able to report accurately what she was doing when she found out her mother had to leave, who stayed with her, whether she visited or spoke with her mother in the hospital,

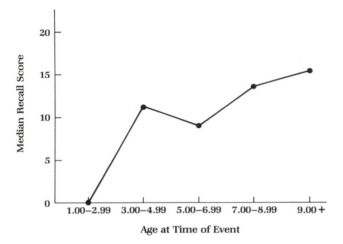

FIGURE 19-1
Median recall scores as a function of age for sibling births reported by college students.

who brought mother home, what time of day they arrived, what the baby was wearing, and what presents she and the baby received. We would suggest, then, that in no absolute sense are four-year-olds poor rememberers. It is important to ask now about other kinds of events and to determine the critical differences between memory in natural situations and in laboratory tasks.

Second, is information about a salient childhood event forgotten? Apparently it is not, for 16 years after the event occurred. This finding, while different from what is generally found in the laboratory, is consistent with the findings of Brown and Kulick (1977) and Bahrick, Bahrick, and Wittlinger (1975) for adults.

The question of why this information is not forgotten is one which deserves further investigation. While rehearsal is the explanation usually put forth to explain long-term memory (Brown and Kulick, 1977; White and Pillemer, 1979), our questions about rehearsal did not produce clear results. Subjects were asked three general questions about rehearsal, and were given credit for rehearsal if they answered any of them positively. The point biserial correlation of reported rehearsal with memory scores was not significant, $r = .22$. We suspect that different results might have been obtained had we asked about rehearsal for each item, rather than about rehearsal in general.

Third, is age at the time of the event related to how much is remembered? The positive association of age and memory scores is consistent with developmental theory. The results of this study support the view that the impact of development is on initial encoding—

that is, on the amount of information initially taken in—rather than on later transformations of the information. The only detectable effect of development after initial encoding was that the disconfirmed answers decreased at age twelve. We assume this reflects the 12-year-olds' increasing knowledge of the world, which permits them to inhibit answers which are unreasonable. For example, while a four-year-old might say that her mother spent a month in the hospital when her sibling was born, a 12-year-old would know that such an answer would be unreasonable.

That virtually no births were reportable by subjects who were younger than three raises an old theoretical question about the meaning of childhood amnesia. Our data point to the period between three and four as being critical for the ability to remember a sibling birth. We suggest that two developments may be necessary for a child to be capable of the type of long-term memory tested here. First, that the child has mastered the language sufficiently to rehearse the event. Second, that the child must have developed schemes or scripts for normal routines against which to contrast the unusual. It may be that in the year from three to four children develop well-organized schemes for their daily routines (Nelson and Gruendel, 1979). Only then do events become memorable.

REFERENCES

Bahrick, H. P., Bahric, P. O., and Wittlinger, R. P. Fifty years of memory for names and faces: A cross-sectional approach. *Journal of Experimental Psychology: General*, 1975, *104*, 54–75.

Brown, A. L. The development of memory: Knowing, knowing about knowing, knowing how to know. In H. W. Reese and L. P. Lipsitt (eds.), *Advances in Child Development and Behavior*, Vol. 10. New York: Academic Press, 1975(a).

Brown, A. L. Recognition, reconstruction, and recall of narrative sequences by preoperational children. *Child Development*, 1975(b), *46*, 156–166.

Brown, R., and Kulick, J. Flashbulb memories. *Cognition*, 1977, *5*, 73–99.

Gibbs, J. C. The meaning of ecologically oriented inquiry in contemporary psychology. *American Psychologist*, 1979, *34*, 127–140.

Miscione, J. L., Marvin, R. S., O'Brien, R. G., and Greenberg, M. T. A developmental study of preschool children's understanding of the words "know" and "guess." *Child Development*, 1978, *49*, 1107–1113.

Neisser, U. Memory: What are the important questions?" In M. M. Gruneberg, P. E. Morris, and R. N. Sykes (eds.), *Practical Aspects of Memory*. London: Academic Press, 1978.

Nelson, K., and Gruendel, J. From personal memories to episodic script: Two dimensions in the development of event knowledge. Paper presented to the Society for Research in Child Development, San Francisco, March 1979.

Robbins, L. C. The accuracy of parental recall of aspects of child development and of child rearing practices. *Journal of Abnormal and Social Psychology*, 1963, *66*, 261–270.

Robinson, J. A. Sampling autobiographical memory. *Cognitive Psychology*, 1976, *8*, 578–595.

Rubin, D. C. Very long-term memory for prose and verse. *Journal of Verbal Learning and Verbal Behavior*, 1977, *16*, 611–621.

Waldfogel, S. The frequency and affective character of childhood memories. *Psychological Monographs*, 1948, *62*, 4, Whole No. 291.

Warrington, E. K., and Sanders, H. I. The fate of old memories. *Quarterly Journal of Experimental Psychology*, 1971, *23*, 432–442.

White, S. H., and Pillemer, D. Childhood amnesia and the development of a socially accessible memory system. In J. Kihlstrom and F. Evans (eds.), *Functional Disorders of Memory*. Hillsdale: Lawrence Erlbaum, 1979.

Winer, B. J. *Statistical Principles in Experimental Design* (2nd ed.). New York: McGraw-Hill, 1971.

20 Parental Recall of Child-Rearing Practices

Lillian Cukier Robbins

One might be tempted to begin the study of memory for early childhood by asking people's parents what really happened in those years. Unfortunately, they may not know. This study suggests that parents may not remember even the most obvious milestones of their baby's development and do not accurately recall their own child-rearing practices. Moreover, their errors are not random. The course of development is recalled as easier and smoother than it really was; remembered methods and procedures have moved closer to expert opinion about what parents should do. Perhaps this is another example of the difficulty of remembering one's own former opinions (Selection 17); parenting is an opinionated business.

The accuracy with which parents can recall and report, after a period of years, details of the early functioning of their children and of their own child-care practices is a significant issue in view of the large number of investigations which have used retrospective parental reports as their primary data. Tests of theories of personality development, and

From L. C. Robbins, The accuracy of parental recall of aspects of child development and of child rearing practices, *Journal of Abnormal and Social Psychology*, 1963, 66, 261–270. Copyright 1963 by the American Psychological Association. Reprinted by permission.

discussions of similarities and differences in the child rearing patterns of varius class and color groups (see, e.g., Davis and Havighurst, 1946; Miller and Swanson, 1958; Sears, Maccoby, and Levin, 1957), have been based on such data, often without sufficient regard for possible factual errors.

. . .

The present study endeavors to examine accuracy of recall by comparing retrospective accounts of child rearing obtained from parents of 3-year-olds with reports they previously gave in the course of a longitudinal study begun with the birth of the child (Thomas and Chess, 1957). It differs from other appraisals of parental accuracy by focusing on objective, nonattitudinal, yet long-term aspects of child development, such as the onset of toilet training and the duration of weaning—items which form the basis for most descriptive and comparative studies of child rearing patterns. Since it is not feasible to have an observer live with families for prolonged periods of time, there can only be assessment of the consistency of parental reports for material of this sort, and not of its validity.

The sample used is particularly favorable for maximizing the accuracy of recall since continued participation in the longitudinal study ensured parents' original awareness of the information sought. In addition, this is a middle-class group, whose practices are predominantly child centered, with the mothers accepting care of the baby as their prime responsibility, so that it can be presumed that maximum attention has been paid to details of the child's functioning.

This report will deal with two aspects of parental recall: the accuracy of retrospective parental reports, and the relationship between errors in retrospective parental reports and recommendations made by authorities in the child rearing field.

METHOD

Subjects

The broader longitudinal study, in progress since March 1956, has been mainly directed at exploring the relationship between initial patterns of reactivity in infants, and subsequent personality development (Chess, Thomas, and Birch, 1959; Chess, Thomas, Birch, and Hertzig, 1960; Thomas, Birch, Chess, and Robbins, 1961; Thomas and Chess, 1957; Thomas, Chess, Birch and Hertzig, 1960). Parents have been seen at frequent intervals and their participation in the study has been extensive. Interviews have been held, usually with both mother and father present, every three months during the child's first year, and at six-month intervals thereafter. Questions were designed to elicit objective and specific description of the child's behavior during the normal routines of daily living, with items of a type which parents can usually answer easily and without defensiveness. Parents were used as the observers since their intimate contact with the child serves to make them the best reporters of consistent patterns and long-range activities. Other procedures have included independent observations of the children in order to check the validity of concurrent parental reports, the Stanford–Binet at three years, and direct observations in nursery school.

When the retrospective interviews were conducted, in the spring of 1959, 49 children of the families under study were approximately 3 years old. Recurrent illness and a recent divorce made scheduling impossible in two cases, so that only 47 families could be interviewed. Six fathers were not seen: four were no longer living with their wives, who had custody of the child; no appointment could be made with another because of the pressures of his business; and one family had moved to the midwest so that only the mother could be interviewed on one of her visits to New York.

In order to make this study more directly comparable to others, the data for three nonwhite families, among them one of the divorced couples, have not been included. As a result, the sample consists of 44 mothers and 39 fathers. All but five of the mothers have attended college, and many have advanced degrees in medicine, law, or psychology. The majority of the men work in a professional or executive capacity, and, with the exception of five, have gone to college. Most hold advanced degrees. The group is predominantly Jewish and is located in the greater New York area. Its socioeconomic status is uniformly high, with the two men who have had no schooling beyond high school at the upper extreme. The median age of the children at the time of interview was 37.0 months, with a range of 29–45 months.

Procedure

Appointments were arranged through the project secretary, who had a long-standing acquaintance with the parents in the study. On the night of the interview, the author and her husband, a psychiatrist, arrived at the parents' home and introduced themselves. Arrangements were made so that interviews could simultaneously be held in two different rooms. This technique made possible the assessment of individual attitudes and recall in a way that joint interviews with both parents could not achieve. At the same time, it eliminated the contamination which might ensue if parents were interviewed one after the other.

. . .

The effect of experts' recommendations on parental recall was evaluated by comparing the kinds of errors made with the advice of authorities. For example, if a mother who had originally described feeding "on schedule" stated in the retrospective interview that she had fed her baby "on demand," this was scored as an error in the direction of the experts' recommendations. Spock (1957) was used as the basis of comparison since all the parents in the present group were more or less familiar with his work. However, his recommendations are so similar to those in other common sources of child rearing advice, such as Infant Care (United States Department of Health, Education, and Welfare, 1955), and women's magazines, that it was felt that parental agreement with experts in general, rather than with Spock alone, was being tested.

RESULTS

Question 1.   How accurate are retrospective parental reports of child rearing practices?

. . .

Table 20–1 . . . demonstrates that parental recall tends to be inaccurate. On four of the 13 quantitative items—those dealing with the age of weaning, beginning of bowel and bladder training, and the stopping of the 2 A.M. feeding—mean retrospective reports by both mothers and fathers differed significantly from the original records. Fathers' reports were also significantly inaccurate on the items dealing with the introduction of cereal, the introduction of the cup, and the child's age when he first stood alone. For two of the six qualitative items—those dealing with feeding on schedule versus demand, and thumbsucking—retrospective reports by both parents differed significantly from the original records.

For certain of the quantitative items, the mean discrepancy scores showed extreme distortion in recall. For instance, with regard to the onset of bowel training, mothers erred by an average of +14.2 weeks and fathers by an average of +22.7 weeks, both recalling the event as occurring later than was originally reported. As for bladder training,

TABLE 20-1
Accuracy of parental recall

Parental recall	N_a	Mothers' mean discrepancy	t	N_a	Fathers' mean discrepancy	t
Quantitative items						
C4b. If breast — how long?	20	+ .4[b]	<1	16	− .4[b]	<1
C5. Cereal — when introduced?	41	− .3	<1	29	+ 7.3	3.09**
D1. Cup — when introduced?	26	+ 7.7	<1	21	+ 12.7	2.48
D2a. Bottle—when stop?	25	− 13.6	3.52**	19	− 18.2	4.7***
Fla. Bowel training— when begun?	44	+ 14.2	3.49**	38	+ 22.7	4.92***
Fla. Bladder training— when begun?	42	+ 22.3	5.23***	36	+ 25.5	4.86***
G5a. 2 a.m. feeding — when stopped?	34	+ 2.8	2.13*	25	+ 5.5	2.15*
G5b. 10 p.m. feeding — when stopped?	28	+ 2.3	<1	16	− 5.9	1.23
Il. When first stood alone?	35	+ 1.9	1.31	31	+ 9.1	3.08**
Ila. When first walked alone?	43	− 1.1	1.36	32	− 1.1	1.08
L2. First injection — when?	27	− 1.6	1.55	22	+ 4.0	<1
L4. Birth weight?	43	+ .02	<1	37	− 1.1 oz	<1
L4a. Birth length?	19	+ .1 in.	1.56	10	+ .2 in.	<1

		% Accurate	Signifi-cance[c]		% Accurate	Signifi-cance[c]
Qualitative items						
C3. Schedule vs. demand?	43	53	.05[d]	38	37	.05[d]
C4. Breast vs. bottle?	44	95	—	39	97	—
D2b. If stop bottle — transition?	23	61	—	19	74	—
D3. Ever suck thumb?	44	84	.01[e]	39	78	.05[e]
D4. Ever suck pacifier?	43	88	—	38	87	—
G5c. How well sleep at 6 months?	42	79	—	38	66	—

[a]Ns vary because of ODM (Original Data Missing), DK (Don't Know), or DNA (Does Not Apply) responses.

[b]In weeks except Items L4 and L4a.

[c]Significance depends upon the direction of errors, rather than the percentage of accurate responses. Thus, seven mothers denied thumbsucking and none erroneously added it in the retrospective reports, so that the responses on original and retrospective interviews significantly differ from one another. For Item G5c, where the percentage accuracy is actually lower, change was not significant since four mothers said the child had slept well when he had slept poorly and three erred in the opposite direction.

[d]Significantly more modified demand and less schedule than had occurred were mentioned in the retrospective interview than in the original reports.

[e]Significantly less thumbsucking than had occurred was reported in the retrospective interview.

*$p \leq .05$. **$p \leq .01$. ***$p \leq .0001$.

the average discrepancies were $+22.3$ and $+25.5$ weeks, respectively. These discrepancies of 3–6 months seem especially large when one considers that they are for behaviors that typically do not begin much before the end of the first year (Thomas et al., 1961), so that they are relative to a maximum time span of approximately two years.

The age of first standing was recalled correctly by a far smaller percentage of parents than the onset of walking. Furthermore, the mean discrepancy scores were opposite in sign, with both mothers and fathers tending to recall standing as having occurred later than it did and walking as having started earlier. The parents considerably shortened the time required for the progression from one stage to the next, with the fathers believing that it took 14.8 weeks on the average and the mothers, 16.8 weeks. The average interval between standing and walking was actually 21.8 weeks.

In the case of weaning, the same tendency to shorten the learning process was found, with the age of introducing the cup recalled as having been later than was really the case, while the age of completion of weaning was placed significantly earlier. The former discrepancy was significant for the fathers only (at the .05 level); the latter for fathers and mothers alike (at the .001 and .01 levels, respectively).

With regard to bowel and bladder functions, the initiation of training was also recalled as significantly later by both sets of parents. Since a majority of the children had not yet been fully trained at the time of the retrospective interviews, information concerning the date of completion was not sought. However, in those families where training was complete, the parents tended to describe its accomplishment as taking place virtually overnight, and to gloss over the lengthy process of acquisition.

. . .

Question 2. Is there any relationship between the recommendations of experts in child rearing and retrospective parental reports of their own practices?

Although no cause and effect relationship can positively be established, the parallelism between experts advice and prevailing direction of distortion is suggestive. . . . Mothers tended to be inaccurate in the direction of the recommendations on every one of the nine items for which suggestions were clearly made in the child-rearing literature. For instance, of the 20 mothers who gave inaccurate responses regarding the mode of infant feeding they employ, 65 percent shifted in the direction of more demand feeding and only 35 percent toward less. This discrepancy suggests that mothers were desirous of appearing to have fed on demand even when they had not actually engaged in the practice. The age of weaning was markedly reduced in the retrospective reports, while the onset of toilet training was recalled as later than was really the case. In both instances, the shifts paralleled the recommendations of Spock (1957; see Table 20–1) regarding the ideal timing of these practices. Finally, with regard to thumbsucking, of which Spock disapproves, and the pacifier, whose use he favors, errors again reflected the recommendations. All seven of the mothers who were inaccurate in their reports of thumbsucking denied that their child had ever sucked his thumb. The original records showed not only that thumbsucking had occurred, in three cases for as long as a year, but also that several of these mothers had expressed concern about it at the time. In contrast, of five mothers who erred in their recall of the use of the pacifier, four stated that their child had used one when, according to the longitudinal records, he had not.

On items for which expert advice was relatively less specific or irrelevant, maternal errors were random in direction. Thus, with respect to the introduction of cereal, 17 mothers recalled the date of onset as later and 18 as earlier, while the birth weight was understated by eight and overstated by six.

... The fathers tended to be less affected by expert advice than the mothers. While they all reported some acquaintance with Spock (1957), the fathers felt they were less thorough in their reading than their wives, and that he influenced them little.

· · ·

REFERENCES

Chess, S., Thomas, A., and Birch, H. G. Characteristics of the individual child's behavioral responses to the environment. *American Journal of Orthopsychiatry*, 1959, *29*, 791–802.

Chess, S., Thomas, A., Birch, H. G., and Hertzig, M. Implications of a longitudinal study of child development for child psychiatry. *American Journal of Psychiatry*, 1960, *117*, 434–441.

Davis, A., and Havighurst, R. J. Social class and color differences in child rearing. *American Social Review*, 1946, *11*, 698–710.

Miller, D. R., and Swanson, G. E. *The Changing American Parent.* New York: Wiley, 1958.

Sears, R. R., Maccoby, E. E., and Levin, H. *Patterns of Child Rearing.* Evanston, Ill.: Row, Peterson, 1957.

Spock, B. *Baby and Child Care (rev. ed.).* New York: Pocket Books, 1957.

Thomas, A., Birch, H. G., Chess, S., and Robbins, L. C. Individuality in responses of children to similar environmental situations. *American Journal of Psychiatry*, 1961, *177*, 798–803.

Thomas, A., and Chess, S. An approach to the study of sources of individual differences in child behavior. *Journal of Clinical and Experimental Psychopathology*, 1957, *18*, 347–357.

Thomas, A., Chess, S., Birch, H. G., and Hertzig, M. A longitudinal study of primary reaction patterns in children. *Comprehensive Psychiatry*, 1960, *1*, 103–112.

United States Department of Health, Education and Welfare, Children's Bureau. *Infant Care*. Washington, D.C.: United States Government Printing Office, 1955 (Children's Bureau Publ. No. 8).

21 An Improved Questionnaire Technique

Larry R. Squire and
Pamela C. Slater

Various methods have been used to assess the course of forgetting in everyday life. Linton's method (Selection 8) may be the best in principle, but so far she is the only person to have used it. Bahrick, Bahrick, and Wittlinger have devised a way to study memory and forgetting of people an individual once knew; it requires access to the individual's own high school yearbook, from which names and pictures are taken for use as test stimuli. Several studies have used questionnaires based on well-known public figures and events that were in the news at specified times; unfortunately, it is hard to equate such items for their original salience. The method described here solves this problem in a most ingenious way. The results suggest that not much forgetting occurs after the first few years, at least for material of the kind tested in these experiments.

Experimental investigations of memory typically involve a learning session and a retention session, separated by a time period that can range from seconds to several days. Because of the practical difficulties of

From L. R. Squire and P. C. Slater, Forgetting in very long-term memory as assessed by an improved questionnaire technique, *Journal of Experimental Psychology: Human Learning and Memory*, 1975, *104*, 50–54. Copyright 1975 by the American Psychological Association. Reprinted by permission.

assessing memory over longer time periods, both experimental studies and clinical examinations of very long-term memory have generally relied on interviews and anecdotal reports. Recently, a questionnaire technique was developed which asked about events and persons that had been in the news during the past four decades (Warrington and Silberstein, 1970). This technique provided an objective means of evaluating remote memory, and it has been usefully applied to problems of aging (Squire, 1974; Warrington and Sanders, 1971) and amnesia (Sanders and Warrington, 1971; Squire, 1975).

This method is limited, however, by the fact that it is difficult to compare the results for one time period with those for another. For any time period it is not possible to know whether the percentage of correct answers reflects the age of the memory or the difficulty of the questions. As a result, forgetting curves obtained by this method are ambiguous, and a variety of other aspects of remote memory cannot be explored (Squire, 1975).

This report describes new remote memory tests, which were designed to overcome this limitation. One test asks the subject to recognize the names of television shows that aired for a single season between 1957 and 1972. A second test asks the subject to recognize the names of American race horses from the same time period. By selecting these names according to rigorous prestated rules, the possibility of sampling bias has been virtually eliminated. The results obtained with these tests provide an objective description of forgetting in remote memory.

METHOD

Test Construction: Television Shows

Microfilm records of the local newspaper *The San Diego Union* were used to compile a list of all weekly television programs airing in San Diego during the first week of October, 1957–1973. Programs were then identified that aired for a single season between 6:00 and 11:00 P.M. This procedure resulted in a list of 237 programs, 9–23 for each of 16 years. Sixteen programs were then eliminated which were also the names of popular movies, songs, comic strips, or plays; eight were eliminated which had titles similar to popular, long-lived television programs.

A list of the remaining 213 shows was distributed to 12 hospital volunteers (mean age = 49 years), with the instruction to "place a check mark beside the TV shows you have heard of." On the basis of their responses, a multiple-choice test was constructed using the five most recognized shows for each year from 1957 to 1972 (a total of 80

TABLE 21-1
Sample questions from the remote memory test

Year	Question
1962	Which of the following was a T.V. show? (a) Bloody Noon, (b) Latest Thing, (c) *Fair Exchange*, (d) Red River Road Which of the following was a famous American race horse? (a) *Sherluck*, (b) Son-in-law, (c) Tracery, (d) Lemberg.
1967	Which of the following was a T.V. show? (a) Bluegrass Country, (b) *Garrisons Gorillas*, (c) Navajo Country, (d) Divorce Lawyer Which of the following was a famous American race horse? (a) *Proud Clarion*, (b) Sir Joseph, (c) Dangerous, (d) Dulcie
1972	Which of the following was a T.V. show? (a) The Cathan Boys, (b) Crime Haters, (c) *Banyon*, (d) Monkey Business Which of the following was a famous American race horse? (a) *BeeBeeBee*, (b) Corfu, (c) Brown Athens, (d) Playing Games

Note: The correct answer to each question is italicized.

programs). Each of the 80 questions was the same: "Which of the following was a TV show?" The correct answer was presented with three incorrect choices, randomly selected from a list of fabricated titles. Sample questions are presented in Table 21-1.

By selecting television programs that aired for a single season, sampling bias has been avoided. In order to compare one time period with another, however, it must also be demonstrated that popular exposure to the programs selected for each time period was relatively similar. Data pertinent to this question was provided by the A. C. Nielsen Co. First, the percentage of time spent watching evening television (5:00–11:00 PM) in the United States has not varied by more than 2 percent for any year since 1965. In those households having a television set,[1] adults aged 18–49 years averaged 15.3–15.6 hours per week of evening viewing over the years 1965–1972. Comparable data were not available for earlier years. Second, individual "Nielsen ratings," which were provided for 81 percent of the 80 programs in the test, indicated that the popularity of the programs selected for each time period was quite similar, $F(7, 57) = 1.0$, $p > .10$. Finally, the number of hours per

[1] In 1965, 94 percent of American households had a television set. By 1972, this figure had increased to 97 percent.

week spent viewing evening television does not markedly vary with age. For example, in the fall of 1973, persons over 50 years old watched about 11 percent more evening television than persons 25–49 years old. In view of these considerations, it seems reasonable to assume that the programs used in this test were exposed to American audiences to approximately the same extent.

Test Construction: Race Horses

A list was compiled of the 39 horses that won the Kentucky Derby, the Preakness, or the Belmont Stakes during the 16-year period 1957–1972. Five horses were eliminated because their names closely resembled the names of other well-known horses. A multiple-choice test of 34 questions was then constructed, which repeated the question: "Which of the following was a famous American race horse?" The three incorrect choices for each question were names of obscure race horses taken from old newspapers. Sample questions appear in Table 21-1.

Procedure

Both tests were administered to volunteers at the Veterans Administration Hospital, San Diego. The television test was given to 17 subjects (77 percent female), aged 26–71 years (M = 54 years). These subjects indicated that they had lived in San Diego since 1957 and that a TV had been in their household throughout this period. The race horse test was given to 42 subjects (52 percent female), aged 26–71 years (M = 51 yr). To determine if opportunities existed to learn about these events after they had occurred, the television test was also administered to a group of high-school students (n = 29, age = 17 yr), and the race horse test was administered to a group of college students (n = 16, age = 21 yr). The students were not old enough to have experienced directly all the events. Another way of determining if the events can be learned about after they have occurred is to test individuals who were relatively isolated from American culture for a period of time. The tests were therefore administered to ten males and two females who resided outside North America during two or more consecutive years between 1957 and 1972. These subjects were aged 28–60 years (M = 45).

To determine to what extent the television test might be useful in other parts of the country, this test was also administered to 39 persons who had lived in San Diego for 1–2 years (M = 3.7 yr) and also to 12 female volunteers at the Veterans Hospital in Denver, Colorado. Finally, to determine how test performance is affected by general intelligence, 32 patients and volunteers at the San Diego Veterans Administration Hospital took both of the remote memory tests as well as the verbal portion of the Wechsler Adult Intelligence Scale (WAIS). All testing was conducted between December 1973 and February 1974.

RESULTS

Remote Memory for Television Shows

The results for the memory test based on television programs are shown in Figure 21-1. For the adult subjects, recognition was best for shows that aired recently and poorest for shows airing many years ago. A one-way analysis of variance with repeated measures on one factor (Winer, 1958) indicated a significant effect of time period on the recognition scores, $F (7, 112) = 10.1, p < .001$. The relationship of time to recognition score was primarily linear, $F (1, 112) = 55.7, p < .001$. The cubic and quadratic components of the variation did not reach significance. The scores of these subjects, who had resided in San Diego for the entire time period covered by the test, were not measurably different from the scores of 39 short-term residents of San Diego, $F (1, 54) = .6, p > .10$, or from the scores of 12 residents of Denver, Colorado, $F (1, 27) = .1, p > .10$. An analysis of main effects indicated, in addition, that none of the comparisons between particular time periods approached significance (average F for 16 comparisons was .4). These results suggest that this test is valid outside the city in which it was constructed.

Figure 21-1 also indicated that high-school students remembered the more recent shows as well or slightly better than adults, but did more poorly than adults in the years 1957–1964, when they were younger than 9 years old. In the years 1957–1960, when the high school students were 1–4 years old, they did not score significantly above chance, $t (15) = .7, p > .10$. Subjects living outside North America between 1957 and 1972 did poorly on questions about television programs that aired while they were away (Table 21-2). Twelve subjects who had been abroad for 2–10 years ($Mdn = 4$ yr), averaged 37 percent correct for programs shown during that time; their expected score for the same time periods was 57 percent, $t (23) = 4.3, p < .01$. In contrast, the same 12 subjects averaged 64 percent correct for programs that aired while they resided in the United States, which was nearly identical to the expected score of 63 percent, $t (23) = .2, p > .10$. Apparently, after these programs have aired, there is only limited opportunity to learn about them.

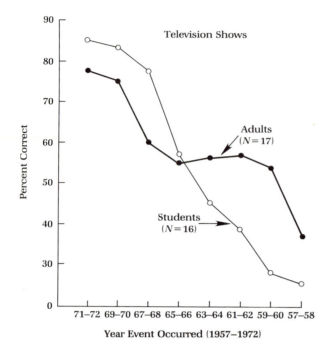

FIGURE 21-1
Recognition of the names of television programs that aired for only one
season between 1957 and 1972. Adult subjects (aged 26–71 yrs, M = 51 yrs)
were compared with 17-year-old high-school students.

TABLE 21-2
Performance on the remote memory tests as affected by living abroad for a
portion of the period 1957–1972

Actual and expected performance	One-season television programs	Race horses
Score on questions pertaining to the time spent abroad (n = 12)	37%[a]	34%
Expected score for the same time period	57%	43%
Score on questions pertaining to the time spent in the U.S. (n = 12)	64%	44%
Expected score for the same time period	63%	46%

[a] Significantly different from corresponding expected score (p < .05).

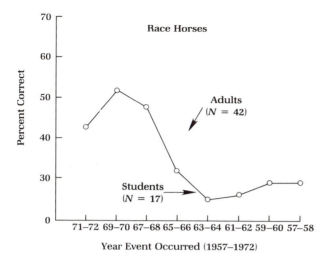

FIGURE 21-2
Recognition of the names of race horses that won the Kentucky Derby, the
Preakness, or the Belmont Stakes during the years 1957–1972. Adult subjects
(aged 26–71 yrs, M = 51 yrs) were compared with 21-year-old college
students.

Remote Memory for Race Horses

The results for the remote memory test based on race horses are shown
in Figure 21-2. There was a significant linear relationship between time
and recognition scores, F (1, 287) = 6.0; p < .01. For the adult subjects
recognition was best for the names of horses that raced from 1969 to
1972, and worst for horses that raced before that time, F (1, 287) = 13.2,
p < .01. The high-school students remembered as well as the adults
the horses that raced in recent years, but they had less recall than the
adults in the years 1957–1966 when they were younger than 14 years
old. For the years 1957–1966, the students' scores did not exceed
chance t (16) < .5, p > .10.

Subjects residing outside of North America between 1957 and
1972 did not score significantly above chance on questions about races
that occurred while they were away, t (11) = 1.7, p > .10. Their score
on these questions was 34 percent, compared with an expected score
of 43 percent, t (23) = 1.8, p < .1 (Table 22–2). In contrast, the same
subjects scored 44 percent on questions about races that occurred
while they resided in the United States, compared with an expected
score of 46 percent, t (23) = .05, p > .10.

No correlation was observed between the scores of 32 adult subjects on the remote memory test for television programs and the verbal

portion of the WAIS, $r = .18$, $t (31) = 1.0$, $p > .10$, or between scores on the race horse test and the verbal portion of the WAIS, $r = .01$, $t (31) = .5$, $p > .10$. Scores on the WAIS ranged from 85 to 129, $M = 108$. Scores on the remote memory tests ranged from 21 percent to 90 percent.

DISCUSSION

A new technique has been described for assessing remote memory for past events. This technique was developed to eliminate sampling bias, a problem that has complicated the interpretation of informal interviews and previously available remote memory tests. The validity of this method was tested in several ways. First, the information covered on the questionnaire was apparently acquired close to the time the events occurred, since (a) students did poorly on questions about events that occurred when they were very young and (b) adults did poorly on questions about events that occurred while they resided outside the United States. Second, questionnaire performance appears to be determined primarily by an individual's experience and knowledge of specific events in the past, and not by his general intellectual ability. Performance was not measurably affected by verbal IQ, over the range of scores investigated.

Taken together, the results indicate that information in very long-term memory can fade gradually for several years. In this respect, the results are consistent with the report that memory for Russian–English word pairs decayed gradually at a decelerating rate for 2 years after learning (Wicklegren, 1972). The present results suggest, in addition, that information stored in remote memory may eventually become resistant to forgetting. With one exception (television programs in 1957–1958), recognition scores were virtually the same for material that had presumably been acquired 8–16 years before the test. Resistance to decay could presumably result from repeated rehearsal, frequent evocation of a memory, or from associations with other well-learned material.

Although a prospective study could provide a more direct method for investigating forgetting in remote memory, very long learning–retention intervals are impractical. In the present case, considerable effort was made to equate the questions from different time periods and thereby to overcome the chief limitation of previous retrospective methods. Tests like the ones described here would seem to be the method of choice for a variety of clinical and experimental investigations of remote memory. For example, it should now be possible to examine critically the phenomenon of prolonged retrograde amnesia and to test the hypothesis that over the years memory becomes gradually invulnerable to disruption (Ribot, 1882).

REFERENCES

Ribot, T. *Diseases of Memory*. New York: Appleton, 1882.

Sanders, H. I., and Warrington, E. K. Memory for remote events in amnesic patients. *Brain*, 1971, *94*, 661–668.

Squire, L. R. Remote memory as affected by aging. *Neuropsychologia*, 1974, *12*, 429–435.

Squire, L. R. A stable impairment in remote memory following electroconvulsive therapy. *Neuropsychologia*, 1975, *13*, 51–58.

Warrington, E. K., and Silberstein, M. S. A questionnaire technique for investigating very long-term memory. *Quarterly Journal of Experimental Psychology*, 1970, *22*, 508–512.

Warrington, E. K., and Sanders, H. I. The fate of old memories. *Quarterly Journal of Experimental Psychology*, 1971, *23*, 432–442.

Wicklegren, W. A. Trace resistance and the decay of long-term memory. *Journal of Mathematical Psychology*, 1972, *9*, 418–454.

Winer, B. J. *Statistical Principles in Experimental Design*. New York: McGraw-Hill, 1962.

ADDITIONAL REFERENCES

Bahrick, H. P., Bahrick, P. O., and Wittlinger, R. P. Fifty years of memory for names and faces: A cross-sectional approach. *Journal of Experimental Psychology: General*, 1975, *104*, 54–75.

Squire, L. R., and Slater, P. C. Anterograde and retrograde memory impairment in chronic amnesia. *Neuropsychologia*, 1978, *16*, 313–322.

22 A Serial Position Effect in Recall of United States Presidents

Henry L. Roediger III
and Robert G. Crowder

In Selection 1, I argued that laboratory research in memory had produced no important generalizations, or at least none that weren't common knowledge already. That may have been an exaggeration, and it seems only fair to present readers of this volume with a possible counterexample. In the study reprinted here, the laboratory strikes back vigorously: Historical knowledge itself is subject to the serial position effect!

A distinction between episodic and semantic memory systems was outlined by Tulving (1972). The crux of the distinction is whether or not temporal factors surrounding the conditions of presentation of to-be-remembered material are stored and retrieved. Recall of the temporal context of the learning situation is considered crucial to successful recall in tasks involving memory for discrete episodes, but relatively unimportant in recall of more or less permanently memorized information involving semantic relations, such as naming the states of the United States. If such a distinction between "autobiographical" and

From the *Bulletin of the Psychonomic Society*, 1976, 8, 275–278. Reprinted by permission.

"permanent" memory systems is accepted, and we think it should be, then it is of interest to ask whether or not the two systems obey the same empirical laws.

In episodic memory experiments, which typically involve an arbitrary list of items to be learned and recalled either with or without regard to the order of presentation, the bow-shaped relation between recall and serial position of the list items was first reported by Ebbinghaus (1902, pp. 624–626) and has since been replicated with overwhelming regularity (see Crowder, 1976, Chapter 12 for a review). The first few and last few elements in a series are best recalled (the primacy and recency effects), while the nadir in performance is slightly after the midpoint in the list, at least with ordered recall. Our experiment was intended, in part, to add to the meager information on serial position effects in the semantic memory system. The most directly relevant previous experiment is a serial position function obtained in latency measures by Koriat and Fischhoff (1974). They simply asked people what day it was and timed the responses. Latencies grew slower from Sunday to Wednesday and then were sharply faster between Wednesday and Friday (no data were collected on Saturday), but there were no such day-to-day changes in latencies to retrieve other facts from semantic memory.

If episodic and semantic memory obey the same laws, a second important issue emerges—whether the same theory should be used in explaining the episodic and semantic memory serial position effects. Hypotheses accounting for the episodic memory serial position effect may be classified according to whether they propose a common explanation for the primacy and recency effects or, instead, propose different explanations for them. Single-factor hypotheses include formulations based on the combined influences of retroactive and proactive inhibition (Foucault, 1928; Hull, 1935), processing order (Feigenbaum and Simon, 1962; Ribback and Underwood, 1950), and distinctiveness of positional stimulus representations (Bower, 1971; Ebenholtz, 1972; Murdock, 1960). Two-factor hypotheses of the serial position effect (especially in free recall) have largely agreed that recency should be attributed to retrieval from some sort of highly accessible, limited capacity, short-term store or primary memory mechanism (Glanzer, 1972; Waugh and Norman, 1965), and that primacy should be attributed to differential processing of early items during learning relative to processing of later items (Bruce and Papay, 1970; Crowder, 1969; Rundus, 1971). If it is assumed that serial position effects in long-term episodic and semantic memory situations are theoretically related, it is obvious that certain of the hypotheses mentioned above are so intimately associated with the circumstances of acquisition that they could never accommodate a serial position effect in semantic memory.

This is because in semantic memory, by definition, the circumstances of acquisition have been dissociated from the remembered knowledge itself.

Subjects in the experiment were asked to recall a well-known series involving a natural serial order, the presidents of the United States, either in any order (free recall) or in their correct ordinal position according to term of office. Our interest was in the relationship of recall to ordinal position in the series.

METHOD

Design and Procedure

Subjects served in two different recall conditions. In both cases, subjects were given 5 minutes to write the names of all the presidents of the United States they could think of on a sheet of lined paper. Subjects in the free recall condition were told to write the names in any order they wished. The other subjects received a "free position recall" instruction. They first numbered their lined response sheets from 1 to 36 (or 1 to 37) and then were instructed that during the 5–minute recall period they were to place each president next to the number corresponding to his term of office. If they remembered the name of a president but not when his term of office occurred, they were instructed to guess or to put his name anywhere on the sheet. Subjects in both instructional conditions were told to distinguish presidents with identical last names by including initials. Free position recall subjects were told that the current president was thirty-sixth or thirty-seventh, depending on when they were tested.

Subjects

The subjects were 159 students from Yale and Purdue Universities. Originally, 31 Yale undergraduates served in the free recall condition and 33 served in the free position recall condition during the Nixon administration. During the Ford administration, 95 graduate and undergraduate students at Purdue were tested under free position recall instructions. Since neither the mean number of items recalled nor the shape of the serial position curve differed from Yale subjects tested under this condition, the results from the two samples were pooled. Thus, altogether, 31 subjects were tested under free recall instructions and 128 were tested under free position recall instructions.

RESULTS

The results of the experiment are presented in Figure 22-1, where the probability of correctly recalling a president is plotted as a function of his ordinal position in office. The open circles joined by dashed lines represent performance of all 159 subjects scored by a free recall criterion, whatever their instructional group. (In the original Yale sample, the two groups did not differ when scored by a free recall scoring criterion, with free recall subjects recalling 23.7 and free position recall subjects recalling 23.4. The shapes of the serial position curves did not differ, either.) The filled circles and solid lines represent performance of the 128 free position recall subjects when scored by a position recall criterion that allowed credit only for correctly placed responses.

The curves of Figure 22-1 resemble quite closely serial position curves from episodic memory experiments. For both curves there is the familiar bowed shape produced by primacy and recency effects. Both curves also show strikingly anomalous performance on Lincoln, who is recalled far more frequently than his unfavorable position would permit us to expect. This performance "spike" is similar to that found when a unique item is embedded in an otherwise homogeneous episodic memory list (the von Restorff effect); our data also show the

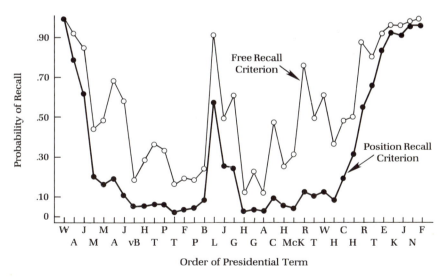

FIGURE 22-1
Recall probability for Presidents of the United States as a function of the order of their terms in office. The free recall criterion requires only that the name appear somewhere in recall, but the position recall criterion requires that each name be placed next to the proper position.

"spread of effect" that is sometimes found in such situations, the elevation in recall of items surrounding the unique item (von Restorff, 1933; Wallace, 1965). A similar tendency appears, in free recall scoring only, on John Adams and Theodore Roosevelt.

Except for performance on Lincoln and his successors, the position recall data are about as "noise free" as one could expect from a carefully counterbalanced episodic memory experiment with randomly selected words. There were more perturbations in free recall, but if one is willing to discount scores from repeated names and repeated terms (note the high scores for J. Q. Adams, Cleveland, and the two Roosevelts), the pattern of data here is also quite acceptable. Free recall was poorest for Hayes and Arthur, located in the notorious point of maximum difficulty just beyond the center of the list. The free recall data of Figure 22-1 were correlated, president by president, with recall from a completely independent group of 90 Purdue undergraduates given free recall instructions and a 3–minute period for recall. The Pearson product-moment correlation coefficient was .95, indicating that the perturbations in Figure 22-1 are probably not experimental error.

Several scoring difficulties should be mentioned. Four names (Adams, Harrison, Johnson, and Roosevelt) belong to more than one president, and thus, in cases where the subject did not include first name initials, it was necessary to decide which of the two was recalled. Often this could be done on the basis of the context; for example, Johnson recalled between Kennedy and Nixon. In cases in which a subject did not include initials and it was not possible to make a decision based on context, half credit was given to both presidents. There were only 19 such cases. Another problem in strict position scoring is presented by Cleveland, who served nonconsecutive terms. The free position recall subjects were given credit for Cleveland if he was recalled in the correct position from the beginning or end. This may result in a slight overestimation. Finally, it should be pointed out that the proportion of subjects recalling Ford is based on 95 observations, that is, only on recall of Purdue subjects.

DISCUSSION

We are strongly inclined to accept the data of Figure 22-1 as evidence for a conventional serial position effect in semantic memory. In order to accept this conclusion, it is necessary to meet two potential criticisms. One is that recall in this task is actually from episodic rather than semantic memory, since many people are required at some point during their years in school to learn the presidents and their terms of office. It seems unlikely that the position effects in Figure 22-1 could be produced by learning a serial list years previously, but nonetheless we asked our original sample of Yale subjects to indicate whether or not they remembered having to learn the presidents in order at any point in their education. Very few did, and the serial position curves for subjects who did and did not remember learning the presidents were quite similar.

A more potent objection is that the serial position effect in Figure 22-1 is simply attributable to differences in degrees of learning the different presidents produced by differing frequencies of exposure. It is, of course, inherently impossible to counterbalance items against serial position when one is studying serial position effects in semantic memory, so this criticism must be seriously considered. Although we cannot now definitely rule out this alternative, there are three reasons we think the data of Figure 22-1 represent a serial effect rather than an effect due to frequency of exposure. First, we are not convinced that the frequency of exposure argument is even true. Is John Adams really a more frequent stimulus than Thomas Jefferson? Or is Coolidge more frequent than Harding? Second, even if frequency of exposure might account for some of the perturbations when a free recall criterion is used in scoring, the serial position effect is even clearer and more regular when strict position scoring is used (the filled circles and lines of Figure 22-1). Since subjects only receive credit for recalling a term in its correct position under this criterion, any simple frequency of exposure argument must be elaborated considerably to account for the serial position effect when recall is scored by the position recall criterion. Finally, even if it were true that frequency of exposure is correlated with recall, this may be simply a manifestation of the same phenomenon. Perhaps it is because the end points in a continuum have a priority in retrieval that the initial and most recent presidents keep emerging. Of course, there is some variation in frequency of exposure, as there is in recall, that is not correlated with term of office. There are actually a number of covariates of recall that might be investigated, including term of office. What we are saying is that, from the looks of Figure 22-1, especially the curve representing recall scored by the position recall criterion, such other factors play a surprisingly small role in determining recall.

Assuming that the data of Figure 22-1 represent a true serial position effect, let us consider the issue of how serial position functions are best explained in light of this new evidence. This result presents no *necessary* implications for theories of longterm episodic memory, because one can adopt a pluralistic theory in which apparently similar serial position functions are produced by different underlying mechanisms in different paradigms. We acknowledge, for example, that there are serial position effects in tachistoscopic experiments (Harcum, 1967) and in auditory immediate memory (Crowder and Morton, 1969) that involve mechanisms distinct from those under discussion here. Our own strong preference is initially to accept the assumption that the long-term episodic and semantic memory serial position functions reflect a common mechanism and then abandon that assumption only as the evidence obliges us to do so. The burden of evidence should fall on those who postulate multiple causality of serial position functions rather than those who postulate common causality. The serial position effect in Figure 22-1 appears quite difficult to reconcile with two-factor theories of the serial position effect (for example, Glanzer, 1972) because of their emphasis on conditions affecting initial acquisition. The single-factor theories based on inhibition (Foucault, 1928; Hull 1935) and processing order (Feigenbaum and Simon, 1962; Ribback and Underwood, 1950) also seem to require extensive modification to account for serial position effects in semantic memory.

The concept of distinctiveness of positional cues (Bower, 1971; Ebenholtz, 1972; Murdock, 1960) is one idea that is general enough to encompass data from both semantic and episodic memory. One elaboration of this idea has recently been applied by Bjork and Whitten (1974) to recency in free recall as a consequence of results that seem to refute the more popular ascription of such recency to primary memory. A related idea comes from Shiffrin (1970), who articulated a search model of retrieval that would apply with equal ease to episodic and semantic memory. He argued that memory search is begun around distinctive locations at the beginning and end of a list and goes on to say that, "If the search explanation of the primacy effect is correct, then the provision of a distinctive cue at some intermediate point in a free recall list should result in a pseudo-primacy effect [a la the 'von Restorff' effect commonly examined in serial learning]" (1970, p. 410). Such a distinctive point occurs in Figure 22-1 in the recall of Lincoln and, as Shiffrin argues, recall of succeeding presidents (Johnson, Grant) is elevated over most other presidents occupying interior serial positions. Primacy, recency, and the von Restorff effect are thus seen as cases of the same retrieval anchor mechanism. This argument is, of course, somewhat circular at the moment, since there is no way to establish distinctive positions (other than the ends of a list) independently from recall level; nonetheless this account appears to better accommodate the generality of serial position effects than do the alternatives.

REFERENCES

Bjork, R. A., and Whitten, W. B. Recency-sensitive retrieval processes in long-term free recall. *Cognitive Psychology*, 1974, 6, 173–189.

Bower, G. H. Adaptation-level coding of stimuli and serial position effects. In M. H. Appley (ed.), *Adaptation Level Theory*. New York: Academic Press, 1971.

Bruce, D., and Papay, J. P. Primacy effects in single trial free recall. *Journal of Verbal Learning and Verbal Behavior*, 1970, *9*, 473–486.

Crowder, R. G. Behavioral strategies in immediate memory. *Journal of Verbal Learning and Verbal Behavior*, 1969, *8*, 524–528.

Crowder, R. G. *Principles of learning and memory*. Hillsdale, N.J.: Lawrence Erlbaum, 1976.

Crowder, R. G., and Morton, J. Precategorical acoustic storage (PAS). *Perception and Psychophysics*, 1969, *5*, 365–373.

Ebbinghaus, E. *Grundzüge der Psychologie.* Leipzig: von Veit, 1902.

Ebenholtz, S. M. Serial learning and dimensional organization. In G. H. Bower (ed.), *The Psychology of Learning and Motivation* (Vol. 5). New York: Academic Press, 1972.

Feigenbaum, E. A., and Simon, H. A. A theory of the serial position effect. *British Journal of Psychology*, 1962, *53*, 307–320.

Foucault, M. Les inhibitions internes de fixation. *Année Psychologique*, 1928, *29*, 92–112.

Glanzer, M. Storage mechanisms in recall. In G. H. Bower (ed.), *The Psychology of Learning and Motivation* (Vol. 5). New York: Academic Press, 1972.

Harcum, E. G. Parallel functions of serial learning and tachistoscopic pattern perception. *Psychological Review*, 1967, *74*, 51–62.

Hull, C. L. The conflicting psychologies of learning—a way out. *Psychological Review*, 1935, *42*, 491–516.

Koriat, A., and Fischhoff, B. What day is today? An inquiry into the process of time orientation. *Memory and Cognition*, 1974, *2*, 201–205.

Murdock, B. B. The distinctiveness of stimuli. *Psychological Review*, 1960, *67*, 16–31.

Ribback, H. and Underwood, B. J. An empirical explanation of the skewness of the bowed serial position curve. *Journal of Experimental Psychology*, 1950, *40*, 329–335.

Rundus, D. Analysis of rehearsal processes in free recall. *Journal of Experimental Psychology*, 1971, *89*, 63–77.

Shiffrin, R. M. Memory search. In D. A. Norman (ed.), *Models of Human Memory.* New York: Academic Press, 1970, 375–447.

Tulving, E. Episodic and semantic memory. In E. Tulving and W. Donaldson (eds.), *Organization of Memory.* New York: Academic Press, 1972, 590–600.

von Restorff, H. Über die Wirkung von Bereichsbildungen im Spurenfeld. In W. Köhler and H. von Restorff, Analyse von Vorgängen in Spurenfeld. I. *Psychologische Forschung*, 1933, *18*, 299–342.

Wallace, W. P. Review of the historical, empirical, and theoretical status of the von Restorff phenomenon. *Psychological Bulletin*, 1965, *63*, 410–424.

Waugh, N. C. and Norman, D. A. Primary memory. *Psychological Review*, 1965, *72*, 89–104.

Part V
Performing

In which a number of noteworthy mnemonic performances are described, some from exotic places and some very close to home. The notion of "rote memory" receives a good deal of attention. Whether memory is "rote" or not turns out to depend on the demands of well-specified public performances as they occur in particular cultural settings.

23 Literacy and Memory

Ulric Neisser

There are astonishing feats of memory in the next few selections. Illiterate bards sing long epic poems in remote Yugoslav taverns; masters of totemic knowledge in New Guinea recall thousands of deeply significant names; oral historians in Liberia remember the histories of whole clans and tribes. Their performances are impressive: How can anyone remember so much?

All these performances take place in traditional societies, and all the performers are illiterate. Does that fact alone give them any special mnemonic advantage? A century ago, that suggestion might have seemed acceptable: Early explorers and missionaries in Africa, for example, told many stories about the wonderful "rote memory" of the "natives." Even today, when that kind of condescension is unacceptable, a related suggestion is often made. Perhaps illiterate people have particularly good memories to compensate for being unable to write things down, just as the blind are popularly believed to have especially keen ears or sensitive fingers.

Such arguments must be rejected. By itself, the absence of something has no causal effects. Illiteracy cannot improve memory any more than my lack of wings improves my speed afoot. And while it would be logically possible to argue that literacy and schooling make memory worse, the fact of the matter is that they don't. On the contrary: cross-cultural studies have generally found a positive relation between schooling and memory. When people who have attended school are compared with those who have not, matching on other relevant variables, the schooled subjects turn out to be much better at list learning, categorized recall, and all forms of rote memory.[1] This is only to be

---

[1] The basic data supporting this claim are from M. Cole, J. Gay, J. Glick, and D. Sharp, *The Cultural Context of Learning and Thinking*, New York, Basic Books, 1971. The theoretical argument is made most clearly in S. Scribner and M. Cole, The cognitive consequences of formal and informal education, *Science*, 1973, *182*, 553–559. More recent work confirms the positive effect of schooling, though other cultural institutions are also important; see, for example, D. A. Wagner, Memories of Morocco: The influence of age, schooling, and environment on memory, *Cognitive Psychology*, 1978, *10*, 1–28.

expected, given the important role that memorization and tests of recall play in school.

What these selections illustrate, then, is not any direct relation between illiteracy and memory. Instead, they show the degree to which particular abilities can be nourished by particular cultural institutions. Skilled performances by oral poets are found only in nonliterate societies because the concept of poetry itself changes when literacy appears. So does the concept of memory, in Lord's view (Selection 24). He suggests that the very idea of "literal" recall is a product of literacy; oral poets are not very clear about what it means to recall a poem "word for word and line for line." Indeed, none of the exotic performances in the next few selections fits the stereotype of "rote memory" at all. The Yugoslav epic poems are reinvented each time they are sung; the totemic names of the Iatmul are produced only when the argument demands them; the Gola historian refers to his knowledge when it becomes relevant to some specific question. In Selection 27, Dube's demonstration that Africans (literate or otherwise) recall stories better than Americans is based on scoring for themes and episodes, not words. The Sherlock Holmes buffs in Selection 28 do not recall their beloved stories literally either; sentences are easy to identify only when they are relevant to the actual development of the plot.

Literal, verbatim memory does exist, nevertheless. It makes its appearance whenever a performance is *defined* by fidelity to a particular text. It isn't "The Star Spangled Banner" unless you sing just those words, so it is the words that you remember (Selection 29). The same principle applies more generally in music (see Selection 43 on Toscanini's memory) and in some religious contexts as well: the feats of the "Shass Pollack" documented in Selection 30 show what can be achieved when sacred texts are committed to memory. Finally, Selection 31 shows that even the utterances of our friends may be worth remembering word for word if they are colorful enough.

24 Oral Poetry
in Yugoslavia

Albert B. Lord

*The songs described in this selection were recorded
in the mountains of Yugoslavia almost fifty years ago.
Albert Lord and Millman Parry, who recorded them,
were classicists; they hoped that a study of
contemporary oral poetry would further their
understanding of the* Iliad *and the* Odyssey. *That
hope was richly rewarded. Although nothing in the
repertoires of the singers they found approached the
two Homeric poems (which total some 27,000 lines),
there were striking structural similarities between the
modern Balkan epics and the ancient Greek epics.
Parry and Lord interpreted this structure as the mark
of oral composition itself.*

*The Yugoslav epics show repetition of units at two
levels of analysis, known as* themes *and* formulas.
*Themes are types of events that occur in many
different songs: a council of war, the arming of a
warrior, the return of the hero in disguise. The
formula, a much smaller unit, is "a group of words
which is regularly employed under the same metrical
conditions to express a given essential idea" (Lord, p.
30). The singer may have a dozen formulaic ways to
describe daybreak: "When dawn put forth its wings,"
"When it was dawn and white day," or "When the sun
had warmed the earth," for example. When he comes
to a part of the action that takes place at dawn, he*

Excerpted by permission of the author and publisher from A. B. Lord, *The
Singer of Tales*. Cambridge, Mass.: Harvard University Press, 1960. Copyright
© 1960 by the President and Fellows of Harvard College. Reprinted by permission.

*uses the one that best fits the meter and his mood.
He knows dozens of themes and thousands of
formulas, not from having memorized them but from
having heard and used them, as we know the words
and phrases of our own language.*

*Experienced singers in this tradition would know at
least thirty songs; some claimed a hundred. Such a
song, often several thousands of lines long, would take
hours to sing. But as this selection emphasizes, the
Yugoslav bards were not "remembering" the songs as
singers do today, faithfully following a fixed and
previously composed text. Instead, they composed
their songs anew on each occasion, and no one
presentation was more "original" than any other. The
two versions of* Marko and Nina *reproduced in the
Appendix to this selection illustrate the range of
variation that might be involved. In the absence of
literacy and technology, it would be difficult indeed to
know whether these two versions—heard days or
years apart—were "the same" or not. That is why the
singers give such apparently contradictory answers
when they are asked if they can sing " ... the same
song, word for word and line for line." They know
little of words or lines; what they know are formulas,
themes, and above all songs. Those they know well.*

Were we to seek to understand why a literary poet wrote what he did
in a particular poem in a particular manner or form, we should not
focus our attention on the moment when he or someone else read or
recited his poem to a particular audience, or even on any moment
when we ourselves read the poem in quiet solitude. We should instead
attempt to reconstruct that moment in time when the poet wrote the
lines. Obviously, the moment of composition is the important one for
such a study. For the oral poet, the moment of composition is the
performance. In the case of a literary poem there is a gap in time
between composition and reading or performance; in the case of the
oral poem this gap does not exist, because composition and performance are two aspects of the same moment. Hence, the question

"When *would* such and such an oral poem be performed?" has no meaning; the question should be "When *was* the oral poem performed?" An oral poem is not composed *for* but *in* performance. The implications of this statement are both broad and deep. For that reason we must turn first in our analysis of oral epic to the performance.

We must grasp fully who, or more correctly what, our performer is. We must eliminate from the word "performer" any notion that he is one who merely reproduces what someone else or even he himself has composed. Our oral poet is a composer. Our singer of tales is a composer of tales. Singer, performer, composer, and poet are one under different aspects *but at the same time*. Singing, performing, composing are facets of the same act.

It is sometimes difficult for us to realize that the man who is sitting before us singing an epic song is not a mere carrier of the tradition but a creative artist making the tradition. The reasons for this difficulty are various. They arise in part simply from the fact that we are not in the habit of thinking of a performer as a composer. Even in the realm of oral literature most of us in the West, at least, are more accustomed to the ballad than to the epic; and our experience has been formed in large part by "folk" ballad singers who are mere performers. The present revival of folk singing on the concert stage and elsewhere has distorted our concept of the essence of oral composition. The majority of such "folk" singers are not oral poets. The collector even in a country such as Yugoslavia, where published collections have been given much attention for over a century, some of which have become almost sacrosanct, must be wary; for he will find singers who have memorized songs from these collections. In spite of authentic manner of presentation, in spite of the fact that the songs themselves are often oral poems, we cannot consider such singers as oral poets. They are *mere* performers. Such experiences have deceived us and have robbed the real oral poet of credit as a creative composer; indeed to some extent they have taken from epic performance an element of vital interest. Our task in this chapter is to restore to performance and performer their true significance.

When we realize that the performance is a moment of creation for the singer, we cannot but be amazed at the circumstances under which he creates. Since these circumstances influence oral form we must consider them. Epic poetry in Yugoslavia is sung on a variety of occasions. It forms, at the present time, or until very recently, the chief entertainment of the adult male population in the villages and small towns. In the country villages, where the houses are often widely separated, a gathering may be held at one of the houses during a period of leisure from the work in the fields. Men from all the families assemble and one of their number may sing epic songs. Because of the distances between the houses some of the guests arrive earlier than others, and of course this means that some leave earlier. Some very likely spend the whole night.... The singer has to contend with an audience that is coming and going, greeting newcomers, saying farewells to early leavers; a newcomer with special news or gossip may interrupt the singing for some time, perhaps even stopping it entirely.

What is true of the home gathering in the country village holds as well for the more compact villages and for towns, where the men gather in the coffee house (*kafana*) or in the tavern rather than in a private home. The taverns are entirely male establishments, whether the district is predominantly Moslem or not. Neither Moslem nor Christian women are ever allowed in these places. This is a man's world. Here the men gather at the end of the day. The farmers of the nearby villages may drop in for a short while to sit and talk, sip coffee or raki, and listen to songs. They come and go. The townspeople join them. There are shopkeepers and caravan drivers who have come in with merchandise from other districts or are stopping on their way through. Frequently the tavern is also an inn, a "han," and here the drivers will spend the night. Many of these men are also singers and the carriers of tradition from one district to another. They are a critical audience.

In market centers such as Bijelo Polje, Stolac, Novi Pazar, and Bihać, market day, the one day in the week when the town is crowded with people from the countryside who have come in to buy and sell, will be the busiest day in the han or in the kafana. Some of the business is done there during the day, and some of the money which has changed hands will be spent in the kafana at night before the men return to their own villages. They may even stay the night there and return the next morning, if they feel so inclined, or if the day has been particularly profitable. This is a good opportunity for the singer because, although his audience may not be stable, it does have money and is willing to reward him for his pains. He is not really a professional, but his audience does buy him drinks, and if he is good they will give him a little money for the entertainment he has given them.

When the singing takes place, as it occasionally does, at a wedding festival, the amount of confusion is increased by the singing of lyric songs and dancing carried on by the young people. The evenings offer the best opportunity for the singer of the old songs, when the older men are not watching the games or gossiping with their neighbors and are content to relax and sit back and listen to the bard.

Among the Moslems in Yugoslavia there is a special festival which has contributed to the fostering of songs of some length. This is the festival of Ramazan, when for a month the men fast from sunrise to sunset and gather in coffee houses all night long to talk and listen to epic. Here is a perfect circumstance for the singing of one song during the entire night. Here also is an encouragement to the semiprofessional singer to attain a repertory of at least thirty songs. It was Parry's experience that such Moslem singers, when asked how many songs they knew, frequently replied that they knew thirty, one for every night of Ramazan. Most Moslem kafanas engage a singer several months in advance to entertain their guests, and if there is more than one such kafana in the town, there may be rivalry in obtaining the services of a well-known and popular singer who is likely to bring considerable business to the establishment.

[*Some sketches of individual singers are omitted.*]

. . .

There seem to be two things that all our singers have in common: illiteracy and the desire to attain proficiency in singing epic poetry. If the second of these sets them apart from their fellows, it is the first, namely their illiteracy, which determines the particular form that their composition takes, and which thus distinguishes them from the literary poet. In societies where writing is unknown, or where it is limited to a professional scribe whose duty is that of writing letters and keeping accounts, or where it is the possession of a small minority, such as clerics or a wealthy ruling class (though often this latter group prefers to have its writing done by a servant),the art of narration flourishes, provided that the culture is in other respects of a sort to foster the singing of tales. If the way of life of a people furnishes subjects for story and affords occasion for the telling, this art will be fostered. On the other hand, when writing is introduced and begins to be used for the same purposes as the oral narrative song, when it is employed for telling stories and is widespread enough to find an audience capable of reading, this audience seeks its entertainment and instruction in books rather than in the living songs of men, and the older art gradually disappears. The songs have died out in the cities not because life in a large community is an unfitting environment for them but because schools were first founded there and writing has been firmly rooted in the way of life of the city dwellers.

[*A section dealing with the early stages of the singers' development is omitted here.*]

. . .

Increase in repertory and growth in competence take place in the third and last stage of the learning process. We can easily define its beginning as the point at which he sings his first song completely through for a critical audience, but it is much more difficult to set the other limit. That is a question of when a singer is an accomplished practitioner of the art, a matter to be considered shortly. Let us look more closely at what goes on in the third stage. First the singer learns to sing other songs all the way through. If he has already learned them in part, he finishes the process. But again this does not involve memorizing a text, but practicing until he can compose it, or recompose it, himself.

Our proper understanding of these procedures is hindered by our lack of a suitable vocabulary for defining the steps of the process. The singers themselves cannot help us in this regard because they do not think in terms of form as we think of it; their descriptions are too vague, at least for academic preciseness. Man without writing thinks in terms of sound groups and not in words, and the two do not necessarily coincide. When asked what a word is, he will reply that he does not know, or he will give a sound group which may vary in length from what we call a word to an entire line of poetry, or even an entire song. The word for "word" means an "utterance." When the singer is pressed then to say what a line is, he, whose chief claim to fame is that he traffics in lines of poetry, will be entirely baffled by the question; or he will say that since he has been dictating and has seen his utterances being written down, he has discovered what a line is, although he did not know it as such before, because he had never gone to school.

While the singer is adding to his repertory of songs, he is also improving the singing of the ones he already knows, since he is now capable of facing an audience that will listen to him, although possibly with a certain amount of patronizing because of his youth. Generally speaking, he is expanding his songs in the way I have indicated, that is, by ornamenting them. This process will be treated in a later chapter, but it will suffice here to say that this is the period in which he learns the rudiments of ornamentation and expansion. The art of expanding the old songs and of learning new ones is carried to the point at which he can entertain his audience for a full evening; that is one of his goals.

Here, then, for the first time the audience begins to play a role in the poet's art. Up to this point the form of his song has depended on his illiteracy and on the need to compose rapidly in the traditional rhythmic pattern. The singers he has heard have given him the necessary traditional material to make it possible for him to sing, but the length of his songs and the degree to which he will ornament and expand them will depend on the demands of the audience. His audience is gradually changing from an attitude of condescension toward the youngster to one of accepting him as a singer.

It is into the world of kafana, informal gatherings, and festival that our young singer steps once he has mastered the singing of a song. Here he learns new songs. The form of his singing is being perfected, and its content is becoming richer and more varied. This audience and this social milieu have had an effect on the length of the songs of his predecessors, and they will have a similar effect on the length of his songs.

We might say that the final period of training comes to an end when the singer's repertory is large enough to furnish entertainment for several nights. Yet it is better to define the end of the period by the freedom with which he moves in his tradition, because that is the mark of the finished poet. When he has a sufficient command of the formula technique to sing any song that he hears, and enough thematic material at hand to lengthen or shorten a song according to his own desires and to create a new song if he sees fit, then he is an accomplished singer and worthy of his art. There are, to be sure, some singers, not few in number, who never go beyond the third stage in learning, who never reach the point of mastery of the tradition, and who are always struggling for competence. Their weakness is that they do not have enough proficiency in formula-making and thematic structure, nor enough talent, to put a song together artistically. Although such singers can show us much about the workings of the practice and of the tradition, it is the finest and longest songs and the most accomplished singers in whom we are interested for comparative purposes in the study of individual singers and individual songs.

The singer never stops in the process of accumulating, recombining, and remodeling formulas and themes, thus perfecting his singing and enriching his art. He proceeds in two directions; he moves toward refining what he already knows and toward learning new songs. The latter process has now become for him one of learning proper names and of knowing what themes make up the new song. The story is all that he needs; so in this stage he can hear a song once and repeat it immediately afterwards—not word for word, of course—but he can tell the same story again in his own words. Sometimes singers prefer to have a day or so to think the song over, to put it in order, and to practice it to themselves. Such singers are either less confident of their ability, or they may be greater perfectionists.

Sulejman Makić, for example, liked to have time to put his song in order. In Parry Text 681, Records 1322-23 (I, pp. 265-266) we can hear his own words:

Nikola: Could you still pick up a song today?
Sulejman: I could.
N: For example, if you heard me sing a song, let's say, could you pick it up right away?
S: Yes, I could sing it for you right away the next day.
N: If you were to hear it just once?
S: Yes, by Allah, if I were to hear it only once to the gusle.
N: Why not until the next day? .. What do you think about in those two days? Isn't it better to sing it right away than later, when you might forget it after so long a time?

S: It has to come to one. One has to think ... how it goes, and then little by little it comes to him, so that he won't leave anything out.... One couldn't sing it like that all the way through right away.
N: Why couldn't you, when it's possible the second or third day afterwards?
S: Anybody who can't write can't do it.
N: All right, but when you've learned my song, would ... you sing it exactly as I do?
S: I would.
N: You wouldn't add anything ... nor leave anything out?
S: I wouldn't ... by Allah I would sing it just as I heard it.... It isn't good to change or to add.

    Đemo Zogić also gave us information on this point (I, pp. 240–241).

N: We have heard—we've been in those places in our country where people sing—and some singers have told us that as soon as they hear a song from another singer, they can sing it immediately, even if they've heard it only once, ... just as it was word for word. Is that possible, Demaill?
Đ: It's possible.... I know from my own experience. When I was together with my brothers and had nothing to worry about, I would hear a singer sing a song to the gusle, and after an hour I would sing his whole song. I can't write. I would give every word and not make a mistake on a single one....
N: So then, last night you sang a song for us. How many times did you hear it before you were able to sing it all the way through exactly as you do now?
Đ: Here's how many times I heard it. One Ramazan I engaged this Suljo Makić who sang for you here today those songs of the Border. I heard him one night in my coffee house. I wasn't busy. I had a waiter and he waited on my guests, and I sat down beside the singer and in one night I picked up that song. I went home, and the next night I sang it myself.... That singer was sick, and I took the gusle and sang the whole song myself, and all the people said: 'We would rather listen to you than to that singer whom you pay.'
N: Was it the same song, word for word, and line for line?
Đ: The same song, word for word, and line for line. I didn't add a single line, and I didn't make a single mistake....
N: Tell me this, if two good singers listen to a third singer who is even better, and they both boast that they can learn a song if they hear it only once, do you think that there would be any difference between the two versions? ...
Đ: There would.... It couldn't be otherwise. I told you before that two singers won't sing the same song alike.
N: Then what are the differences?
Đ: They add, or they make mistakes, and they forget. They don't sing every word, or they add other words. Two singers can't recite a song which they heard from a third singer and have the two songs exactly the same as the third.
N: Does a singer sing a song which he knows well (not with rhymes, but one of these old Border songs), will he sing it twice the same and sing every line?

Đ: That is possible. If I were to live for twenty years, I would sing the song which I sang for you here today just the same twenty years from now, word for word.

In these two conversations we have accomplished singers discussing under guidance the transmission, not of the art of singing, but of songs from one well-trained singer to another. They are also telling us what they do when they sing a song. Here the creative performer speaks. In the case of Đemo Zogić we can test his statements and thus we can learn how to interpret this information that singers can give us about their own art.

Note that both singers express some attitude toward writing. Makić gives the opinion that only a person who can write can reproduce a song immediately; whereas Zogić's boast is that although he can't write he can reproduce a song an hour after he has heard it. In other words, one says that the man with writing is superior; and the other, that he is as good as the man with writing. They reflect the unlettered man's admiration of the lettered, but their statements are inaccurate. Their admiration goes too far, for the man with writing cannot do what they believe he can and what they in actuality can do.

Both singers stress that they would sing the song exactly as they heard it, Zogić even boasting that he would sing the song in the same way twenty years later. Makić indicates that changing and adding are not good, implying that singers do change and add; and Zogić states plainly that two singers won't sing the same song alike. How do we disentangle these contradictions?

Zogić learned from Makić the song under discussion in his conversation, and both versions are published in Volume I of the Parry Collection (Nos. 24–25 and 29). Zogić did not learn it word for word and line for line, and yet the two songs are recognizable versions of the same story. They are not close enough, however, to be considered "exactly alike." Was Zogić lying to us? No, because he was singing the story as he conceived it as being "like" Makić's story, and to him "word for word and line for line" are simply an emphatic way of saying "like." As I have said, singers do not know what words and lines are. What is of importance here is not the fact of exactness or lack of exactness, but the constant emphasis by the singer on his role in the tradition. It is not the creative role that we have stressed for the purpose of clarifying a misunderstanding about oral style, but the role of conserver of the tradition, the role of the defender of the historic truth of what is being sung; for if the singer changes what he has heard in its essence, he falsifies truth. It is not the artist but the historian who speaks at this moment, although the singer's concept of the historian is that of a guardian of legend.

Although Makić's and Zogić's versions of the same song differ considerably, Zogić's version itself changes little in the course of years.

It was my good fortune to record this song from him seventeen years later, and it is remarkably close to the earlier version, though hardly word for word. It even still contains a glaring inconsistency in the story which was not in Makić's version.

But when Zogić is not defending himself as a preserver of the tradition, when he is thus freed to speak of the art of singing as such, in other words when he can talk about someone else's practice, he can be more objective. Then he states that two singers won't sing the same song alike; then he can recognize changes, additions, and mistakes, and give us a clearer picture of what happens in transmission.

And the picture that emerges is not really one of conflict between preserver of tradition and creative artists; it is rather one of the preservation of tradition by the constant re-creation of it. The ideal is a true story well and truly retold.

. . .

[*In the following extract from a later chapter that focuses on the song rather than the singer, Lord returns to the question of "originality."*]

As long as one thought of the oral poet as a singer who carried in his head a song in more or less the exact form in which he had learned it from another singer, as long as one used for investigation ballads and comparatively short epics, the question of what an oral song is could not arise. It was, we assumed, essentially like any other poem; its text was more or less fixed. But when we look more closely at the process of oral composition and come to appreciate more fully the creative role of the individual singer in carrying forward the tradition, we must begin to query our concept of a song.

When the singer of tales, equipped with a store of formulas and themes and a technique of composition, takes his place before an audience and tells his story, he follows the plan which he has learned along with the other elements of his profession. Whereas the singer thinks of his song in terms of a flexible plan of themes, some of which are essential and some of which are not, we think of it as a given text which undergoes change from one singing to another. We are more aware of change than the singer is, because we have a concept of the fixity of a performance or of its recording on wire or tape or plastic or in writing. We think of change in content and in wording; for, to us, at some moment both wording and content have been established. To the singer the song, which cannot be changed (since to change it would, in his mind, be to tell an untrue story or to falsify history), is the essence of the story itself. His idea of stability, to which he is deeply devoted, does not include the wording, which to him has never been fixed, nor the unessential parts of the story. He builds his performance, or song in our sense, on the stable skeleton of narrative, which is the song in his sense.

When one asks a singer what songs he knows, he will begin by saying that he knows the song, for example, about Marko Kraljević when he fought with Musa, or he will identify it by its first lines. In other words, the song is the story of what someone did or what happened to some hero, but it is also the song itself expressed in verse. It is not just a story; it is not merely a tale divorced from its telling. Sulejman Makić said that he could repeat a song that he had heard only once, *provided that he heard it to the gusle* (I, p. 266). This is a most significant clue. The story in the poet-singer's mind is a story in song. Were it not for remarks like that of Makić, we might be led to think that the singer needs only "a story," which he then retells in the language of verse. But now we know that the story itself must have the particular form which it has only when it is told in verse.

Any particular song is different in the mouth of each of its singers. If we consider it in the thought of a single singer during the years in which he sings it, we find that it is different at different stages in his career. Its clearness of outline will depend upon how many times he sings it; whether it is an established part of his repertory or merely a song which he sings occasionally. The length of the song is also important, because a short song will naturally tend to become more stable the more it is sung.

In some respects the larger themes and the song are alike. Their outward form and their specific content are ever changing. Yet there is a basic idea or combination of ideas that is fairly stable. We can say, then, that a song is the story about a given hero, but its expressed forms are multiple, and each of these expressed forms or tellings of the story is itself a separate song, in its own right, authentic and valid as a song unto itself. We must distinguish then two concepts of song in oral poetry. One is the general idea of the story, which we use when we speak in larger terms, for example, of the song of the wedding of Smailagić Meho, which actually includes all singings of it. The other concept of song is that of a particular performance or text, such as Avdo Mededović's song, "The Wedding of Smailagić Meho," dictated during the month of July, 1935.

Our real difficulty arises from the fact that, unlike the oral poet, we are not accustomed to thinking in terms of fluidity. We find it difficult to grasp something that is multiform. It seems to us necessary to construct an ideal text or to seek an original, and we remain dissatisfied with an ever-changing phenomenon. I believe that once we know the facts of oral composition we must cease trying to find an original of any traditional song. From one point of view each performance is an original. From another point of view it is impossible to retrace the work of generations of singers to that moment when some singer first sang a particular song.

We are occasionally fortunate enough to be present at a first singing, and we are then disappointed, because the singer has not perfected the song with much practice and by the test of repeated performance. Even after he has—and it may change much as he works it over—it must be accepted and sung by other singers in order to become a part of the tradition, and in their hands it will go through other changes, and so the process continues from generation to generation. We cannot retrace these steps in any particular song. There was an original, of course, but we must be content with the texts that we have and not endeavor to "correct" or "perfect" them in accordance with a purely arbitrary guess at what the original might have been.

Indeed, we should be fully aware that even had we this "original," let us say, of the wedding of Samilagić Meho, we would not have the original of the basic story, that is, the song of the young man who goes forth into the world to win his spurs. We would have only the application of this story to the hero Meho. Each performance is the specific song, and at the same time it is the generic song. the song we are listening to is "the song"; for each performance is more than a performance; it is a re-creation. Following this line of thinking, we might term a singer's first singing of a song as a creation of the song in his experience. Both synchronically and historically there would be numerous creations and re-creations of the song. This concept of the relationship between "songs" (performances of the same specific or generic song) is closer to the truth than the concepts of an "original" and "variants." In a sense each performance is "an" original, if not "the" original.

The truth of the matter is that our concept of "the original," of "the song," simply makes no sense in oral tradition. To us it seems so basic, so logical, since we are brought up in a society in which writing has fixed the norm of a stable first creation in art, that we feel there must be an "original" for everything. The first singing in oral tradition does not coincide with this concept of the "original." We might as well be prepared to face the fact that we are in a different world of thought, the patterns of which do not always fit our cherished terms. In oral tradition the idea of an original is illogical.

[Lord's frequent use of general terms like "oral tradition" may be misleading. Not all oral poetry is like the Yugoslav epics. More recent studies in Africa and elsewhere show that it can take many forms: some include more nearly verbatim repetition; in others, the poet composes in advance of performance. Different societies prize and develop different abilities. *For more about oral poetry, see R. Finnegan, What is oral literature anyway? In B. A. Stoltz and R. S. Shannon (eds.) Oral Literature and the Formula. Ann Arbor, Michigan: University of Michigan Center for the Coordination of Ancient and Modern Studies, 1976.*]

APPENDIX

[*In an appendix to* The Singer of Tales, *Lord reproduces four different versions of* Marko and Nina *as performed on different occasions by the same poet. These two were sung two days apart.*]

Parry 805	Parry 846
Marko arises early in his tower in Prilip and drinks raki. With him are his mother, his wife, and his sister Andelija (1–6).	Marko arises early in his stone tower. With him are his mother and his wife (1–5).
Marko says that a letter arrived the day before from the sultan calling him to serve in the army for nine years (7–10).	A messenger arrives with a letter for Marko. He reads it and is silent. His mother asks him where the letter is from and why it makes him sad. Marko says the letter is from the sultan calling him serve in the army for nine years and to bring his horse and sword (6–30).
He tells his mother that if Nina of Koštun should come and capture his tower, take away his wife and sister, and tread on his mother, she should write him a letter and send it to him by his falcom (11–22).	If Nina of Koštun hears, he will come to Prilip, tread on Marko's mother, and take away his wife and sister Andelija. If that happens, his mother is to send him a letter by his falcon, who will be able to find him in the army. His mother agrees to do this (31–54).
	Marko prepares to depart. He tells his wife to look for the sun and moon, but never again for him. He goes to Carigrad (55–65).
	When Marko joins the army he greets the sultan, who takes his horse and sword. Marko serves the sultan for nine years (66–77).
Nina and his three brothers capture Marko's tower, take his wife and sister, and tread on his mother (23–30).	Nina and his four brothers hear (in the ninth year) that Marko is in the army, and they go to Prilip. They

capture Marko's tower, take away his wife and sister, and tread on his mother (78–96).

Marko's mother writes a letter telling him what has happened, and sends it by his falcon (31–46).

Marko's mother writes a letter telling him what has happened, and sends it by his falcon (97–122).

The falcon seeks out Marko and delivers the letter (47–51).

The falcon seeks out Marko and delivers the letter (123–127).

Marko reads and is angry. He writes to the sultan, who gives him back his horse and sword, and his choice of twelve warriors. The sultan says to bring back Nina's head (52–71).

Marko reads and is angry. He shows the letter to the sultan, who gives him back his horse and sword, and his choice of twelve warriors with Delibaša Ibro at their head. The sultan says to bring back Nina's head. Marko chooses his men (128–154).

They depart (72–75).

They depart (155–159).

On the mountain they stop to drink. Marko says they will go to a church and ask for monks' clothes, and they do. The monks refuse, and Marko kills them, and he and his companions disguise themselves in monks' clothes. They proceed to Koštun (76–110).

On the mountain they stop to drink. Marko says they will go to a church and ask for monks' clothes. The monks refuse, and Marko kills them, and he and his companions disguise themselves in monks' clothes. They proceed to Koštun (160–194).

When they arrive at a spring near Koštun where Marko's wife and sister are washing clothes, his wife recognizes Šarac, and asks where the monk got Marko's horse. Marko says that he died nine years ago. He has heard that Nina will marry and he has come for that. He sent his wife to tell Nina. Marko tells his men to stay outside. Nina asks where Marko got the horse, and he says Marko gave it to him for burying him. Marko goes into the tower (111–155).

When they arrive at a spring near Koštun where Marko's wife and sister are washing clothes, his wife recognizes Šarac, and asks where the monk got Marko's horse. Marko says that he died nine years ago, and gave him the horse for burying him. He sends his wife to tell Nina that the monk has come to marry the two. He leaves his men outside and rides into the courtyard. Nina asks where he got the horse, and Marko tells him. He also tells him that he has come to marry him. They enter the tower (195–241).

Nina entertains Marko with wine and Marko asks permission to dance a little for the soul of Marko and the

Nina entertains Marko with wine and meat and Marko asks permission to dance and sing a little for the health of Nina. The permission is granted (156–165).

Marko dances, and Nina says he shakes the tower. Marko asks permission to sing, and it is granted. Marko shouts: "For the soul of Nina!", swings his sword and cuts off Nina's head (166–177).

Nina's three brothers flee and Marko and his men pursue them. He kills Šćepan at Šćepan's Cross, Jasenko at Jasena, and Radoje at Radimlja. He gathers their heads. He himself has lost only one man (178–191).

Marko returns with his wife, his sister, and his men to Prilip (192–200).

In Prilip Marko shows Nina's head to his mother, and tells her that he will trouble her no more. Marko eats and drinks (201–212).

Marko goes to the sultan. He gives him the heads and reports that Ibro has been killed. The sultan rewards him and sends him back to Prilip, with greetings to his mother, and the offer of assistance whenever Marko needs help. Marko returns to Prilip (213–234).

soul of Marko and the health of Nina. The permission is granted (242–256).

Marko dances and Koštun shakes. Nina says that to judge by his strength this must be Marko. Marko dances and sings for the soul of Nina and the health of Marko. His sword swings and he kills Nina (257–271).

Nina's brothers flee and Marko and his men pursue them. They kill Šćepan at Šćepan's Cross, Jasenko at Jasena, and Radoje at Radimlja. They erect monuments at each place (272–285).

They return to Koštun. Marko gathers the heads in a bag, and returns to Prilip, having set fire to Koštun. Ibro is missing (286–310).

They go to Marko's tower and eat and drink and rest (311–317).

Marko takes the heads to the sultan, who sends him home to Prilip with the offer of assistance whenever he needs it. Marko returns to Prilip (318–324).

25 Tribal History in Liberia

Warren L. D'Azevedo

We have seen that oral poetry is not a watered-down version of its written counterpart but a unique artistic achievement in its own right. Oral history, too, must be understood on its own terms. Oral historians, sometimes called "griots," play significant roles in many different African societies. This selection is a careful account of the practice of history in one such society, the Gola of the Liberian coast. It is clear that the Gola historians do much more than simply remember facts about the past; they use their knowledge constructively in the present as well.

Knowledge of the past is a highly valued commodity among the Gola of West Africa. "Setting things straight" and "putting a proper form to things" is a major preoccupation of this highly articulate people. There is no man among them worth his salt who is not ready at the slightest provocation to "make new ideas from old ones" (*ke djike dje yun gogo*), or, more literally, to present "new ideas of the old people." But there are many cultural restrictions and formal requirements which must guide the approach to things past. The past is considered to be the repository of all important sacred and secular knowledge, and the act of formal retrospection is the duty of qualified men of wisdom who are

---

From W. L. D'Azevedo, Uses of the past in Gola discourse, *Journal of African History*, 1962, 3, 11–34. Reprinted by permission of Cambridge University Press. Copyright © 1962 Cambridge University Press.

expected to apply their accumulated memories to the solution of problems confronting the living present.

. . .

The Gola are forest agriculturalists, organized into sections whose boundaries conform essentially to the traditional territories of the old chiefdoms (*ma fuwa*) which had been established prior to Liberian colonial occupation in the second decade of the last century. In the present day these sections constitute Paramount Chieftainships, but in the old days they were made up of a multiplicity of petty monarchies with a high degree of local autonomy. The traditional arrangement involved a central village surrounded by satellite hamlets in which the dominant class of the population was a land-owning patrilineage made up of the descendants of the founder. The related sublineages were ranked according to distance from this founding ancestor. A large proportion of the population of these minute societies, however, was contained in numerous attached lineages of nonrelated immigrants—whether Gola or non-Gola—who had been incorporated by patronage or intermarriage, and whose members were granted theoretically tentative rights to the use of the lands. In addition to these, the small households of the various clients, slaves, and other dependents of the wealthier families contributed still further to the social heterogeneity of the chiefdoms.

Much of coastal territory which the Gola now occupy was a dense uninhabited rain forest until as late as the eighteenth century. Their slow westward migration from the interior region of Komgba in the mountains of northeastern Liberia began in the seventeenth century under pressure from the powerful savanna empires of the Western Sudan. Like many of their neighbors, the Gola retreated into the coastal forests where they became widely dispersed through migration, warfare and the slave trade. In the early nineteenth century they had just succeeded in consolidating their new territory when they were faced with the growing power of European and American colonial settlements on the coasts of Sierra Leone and Liberia. For over a century they resisted Liberian government authority, and established themselves as successful entrepreneurs in the trade between the coast and the far interior markets. With the termination of the Kanga War in 1918–1919, their resistance to Liberian domination of the hinterland was broken, and the last of the recalcitrant chiefdoms of the Western Province was broght under effective Liberian control.

With these facts in mind we may turn to an inquiry into the nature of Gola retrospect.

. . .

There are two basic values involved in the Gola concept of the past. First of all, it is believed that no person can know his place in society or appreciate fully the kind of person he is unless he is familiar with the genealogy of his own family. The term *djewe mio* refers to "my line of ancestors," or to "those people from whom I have come." ' Though emphasis is placed on patrilineal descent, one may reckon one's *djewe* through either mother's or father's patrikin, or both, depending upon the advantage that is to be gained by whatever choice is made. Usually, however, an individual has been raised by the kin of either one or the other of his parents so that his knowledge of his ancestors will be limited exclusively to the *djewe* of that side of his family which has trained him.

The advantage of a great family with many well-informed elders lies in the degree to which the record of one's *djewe* is carefully maintained. By means of the amply stocked memories of the elders, one's kinship ties may be asserted at the appropriate time to include a vast number of one's contemporaries. A small family with unimportant and ill-informed elders will be limited in its range of useful alliances, and will lack the prestige and unity of a family that can offer its younger members a sense of pride and security in a clearly defined tradition.

A genealogy involving important ancestors and great deeds is a crucial factor in the individual's self-evaluation. A family whose ancestral record is sketchy is forced to rely on others for this information and is always at a disadvantage in seeking its own interests. A real *dja kwe*—"a free-born person of the country"—knows his own worth because he is able to ramify his line of descent and validate its connexions within the larger society of which he is a part.

A second basic value in the Gola concept of the past is the importance attached to the ancestors as distinct personalities who continue to concern themselves with the affairs of their living descendants. These ancestors guard their own personal interests and that of the family jealously. They are easily angered by an infraction of family laws, or any failure to demonstrate proper respect and concern for their interests. Furthermore, their memory of the issues which confronted them during their own lifetime is great, and they expect their descendants to fulfill whatever pledges they might have made, revenge any wrongs done them, and respect the important decisions they have handed down. In so far as the ancestors resent and envy the living, they are easily provoked. It is within their power to bring sickness,

---

'The *djewe* is any reckoning of lines of descent through either or both parents. But in the specific sense implied by *djewe mio* it refers to the line of descent by which the speaker defines his position within a particular patrilineage—his *ke kpo*.

poverty and death upon any descendants who fail in their duty. For this reason it is considered extremely important that the history of a family be sufficiently complete so that slights to the ancestors can be avoided or—should they occur—the source of the resulting difficulties may be ascertained.

In the event of illness or disaster a well-informed group of elders in any family consult among themselves and arrive at an agreement as to the specific ancestor or ancestors whose wrath may have been incurred. Where such family knowledge is incomplete or lacking it is necessary to employ a specialist whose services are expensive and frequently unsatisfactory. A family that knows its main ancestors and the crucial incidents of their lives is in a position to "settle matters" quickly and successfully. It is said that many problems which might have been resolved simply through knowledge of the family past become extended and costly matters because of the failure of an individual or a family in this regard. Moreover, to know the heroic achievements of one's ancestors is to be able to assert a prestigious tradition with regard to one's own kin group.

With the emphasis upon the *djewe* in the Gola view of the past, it follows that any "history" is family history and is limited in scope by the extent of known kinship ties and generational depth. Accounts of the past are, therefore, not only highly localized but tend to be restricted to the *djewe* of the individual providing the account, touching on broader events and relationships only to the extent which the ancestors' interests and activities warrant it. As this knowledge is considered to be the property of the elders of each family, great care and delicacy must be brought to bear in each account so as not to infringe upon the prerogatives of others. A single elder questioned about the kinship relations or family history of persons not directly related to him will invariably state, "I cannot speak for their part . . . you must go to them."

Occasionally there is, among the elders of a large and well-established town, a very old and greatly respected person who is believed to surpass all the others in knowledge of the past. By virtue of his age and vast experience the other elders will defer to him when any disagreement arises among them as to detail in substance or chronology. Such ancient persons—whether men or women—transcend the boundaries of disparate kindred, for they have become in a real sense the grandparents of all within the community. In that they may speak of all the members of a town and its surrounding villages as "my children" it follows that they alone possess the license to speak freely and generally about the history of a town or *fuwa* (the traditional territory which a ruling family controls). If such an ancient elder happens to be a member of the ruling family as well, his or her knowledge is taken as irrefutable regardless of how distasteful a version of history may be to any particular family of the community.

It is only from these very old persons that one receives anything like a chronologically ordered and dramatically unified view of past events in the sense that "a history" implies in Western thought. They have arrived at a point in age and experience where they can see the whole, and may be allowed to do so without criticism or fear of reprisal. They are considered to be objective, having passed beyond the stage of life in which petty rivalries or self-interest would cause them to distort their judgements. The whole of the known past becomes the special property of such persons, and it is to them that all others repair for information and advice. They are the closest to the *yun fa*—the ancestors—for it is indeed through them who are about to enter the ancestral ranks that the *yun fa* speak to the living. During their lifetime they associated with the living ancestors who are now *yun fa*. They are closer to the beginnings and are the only members of the community who have a right to speak with assurance about the origins of things.[2]

But even the boundaries of knowledge of such remarkable old people are usually limited to the town or *fuwa* of their extended family. They will readily affirm that they know little or nothing of the past of the Gola of other "countries," unless, by chance, one of their parents had been an elder of that *fuwa* and had imparted that knowledge directly. The phrase "We Gola" most often refers to those people within the *fuwa*, or within that complex of adjacent *fuwa* who have had long-standing interrelationship. Nevertheless, it will be affirmed that all people who speak the Gola language are remotely related and that they have a common origin. The idea of an all-Gola past, however, is a vague one and the elders of any one section of the Gola tribal area will admit that they know very little about the Gola of remoter sections or "how those people came to be."

The exception to this general rule is provided by a few renowned individuals in each generation who have attained considerable age after a lifetime of varied experience, travel and responsible position. The fame of such persons extends far beyond their local group, and they may be called upon to preside at councils in distant Gola chiefdoms, or may even be visited by delegations seeking authoritative his-

---

[2]The sacredness of such persons is derived from the hierarchical and gerontocratic values of Gola society. Accumulated experience and great age have made them "holy," a phenomenon of particular significance in a region where life-expectancy is less than forty years. Yet it must be noted that the powers which such very aged persons wield seem to be relegated to the sphere of blessings and sage advice. Their role is that of the revered exemplar and does not intrude upon that of specialists such as diviners, magicians, or curers.

torical data. The late Kpongbo Zu, an elder of the Te-Gola, was honoured by the Liberian Government as a "Tribal Historian" for these reasons, and he was invited to participate as an expert witness in all major proceedings involving the Western Province. His name was known by the elders of the remotest Gola sections, and the author was frequently advised to seek his opinion when questions arose which could not be resolved. Gola tradition refers to such persons in the past as advisors of powerful rulers, or as revered persons sought out to arbitrate tribal or intertribal disputes among chiefdoms.

The sectionalism and kin group orientation of Gola society discourages the maintenance of an all-Gola or regional tradition on the local level. Such comprehensive historical traditions are the special property of specific individuals whose knowledge is solicited only in those instances where validation of this kind is considered appropriate. In the local situation individual family tradition is a rigorously guarded body of information, and detailed knowledge of other families in the same area may be disclaimed despite the fact of generations of intermarriage and close association. Though much of this behaviour is a matter of protocol in the interrelations between kin groups, it represents a profoundly basic value in Gola culture. One does not learn what is not one's business to know—or better still, one does not divulge what one is not supposed to know. For this reason the elders of a given town—comprising the leadership of a group of more or less related families—prefer to discuss the history of their town in council. In this way each elder can rise in turn to present a formal "public" version of the genealogy and important historical events which constitute the tradition of his family. The presentation will require a considerable amount of improvisation and skilful editing in order to bring its form and content into line with the unified product which is the goal of the council. One can expect great variation among accounts of family history depending upon whether the presentation is made in a public or private gathering.

Any meeting called by the elders for the purpose of clarifying a problem which has arisen between families will attract a large crowd. For it is under these conditions that the elders will compete among themselves for stature as historians, orators, and representatives of their own kin groups. They can also be counted on to use the opportunity for admonishing the "hard-headed" youth of the community, and it is said that at such times "one can learn the secrets of the elders without showing respect (giving a gift) for each is trying to make himself great before the others." Much surreptitious humour passes among the younger men at these meetings to the effect that "the old men are wasting their property: they are like a man with a hole in his full sack of rice who does not know why the chickens have come running."

These councils, which begin as informal court proceedings, often turn into history-making debates. A major disagreement arises and each elder stands in order of rank, to give his version of the past which has bearing upon the matter. As the narrations continue they become intricately enmeshed with mutual reference and subtle innuendo. At times, one or more of the old men will interrupt a speaker with an epithet, or turn to the watching crowd to shout a disclaimer. All the techniques of Gola "palaver" are used to dramatize one's own position at the expense of the others, and to convince the listeners of its reasonableness. Councils of this sort may continue for days, or be dropped for long intervals and reconvened at a later date. It is said of some councils that "the palaver has never finished, but hangs upon a hook for ever waiting to be taken down again."

It is customary, however, for councils to remain in session until a consensus is reached. This is often achieved by appealing to the oldest and most revered man among them to "settle this matter properly, or we shall seem as small boys before the people." Upon accepting the assignment, the old man may use any of a number of means to bring about a compromise. He may repeat the version of events he gave earlier in the meeting, he may reconstruct one of the other elder's versions which had been well received, or by astutely adjusting the essential features of all the presentations he may create a compromise version which brings him fame throughout the countryside. Once he has spoken under these conditions, his version of the matter becomes "the true history" produced by that particular council. All members of the community are admonished on the spot to remember it well so that they will know how they "came to be one people." Many elders conclude their speeches in such councils by turning to the assembled crowd and stating, "You are hearing your ancestors speak through us today: do not forget these things or you will be a stupid people!"

Despite these admonitions, each of the elders who has participated in the council will return to his own house, call his oldest sons and his brothers together, and reinstruct them concerning the original and unique family version of the matter. This will include much that he had not revealed in public—"the secrets which make our family strong and which others wish to learn in order to bring us low." The public consensus version is derided as "the proper truth of children and strangers," while the family version is praised as "the truth for grown men that will make them kings in the world."

But should the same elders be confronted with questions as to events prior to the earliest known ancestor or more general regional relations, the attitude and behavior is quite different. Here the responses will take such form as "that was before our old people knew themselves" (before the memory of the ancestors) or "the old people did not see that."

. . .

These considerations provide a clue to still another dimension of the Gola concept of the past. When the Gola elder speaks of his "old people" (*yun fa* or *yun gogo*) he is referring to all of his known ancestors. In the recent past these comprise a host of maternal, paternal and affinal relatives; but in the more distant past the host dwindles to the thin line of patrilineal descent of either the maternal or paternal side— though occasionally both are remembered—terminating in the founder of a town or the first known ancestor to have established himself in the area. In a few cases the route of migration to the area is known and the genealogical depth may be extended a generation or two, but this is rare. Genealogical depth varies slightly from section to section and offers some indication of the relative occurrences in time of the major Gola migrations from the homeland area. But there are many towns which are known to be far older than the earliest ancestor who appears in the genealogy. This ancestor may be thought to be the descendant of founders of the town, but his predecessors have been forgotten. A clear distinction is made between those "real" events which took place during the lives of the known ancestors and those dimly perceived and often mysterious events which may be attributed to the forgotten and unknown people of the far distant past.

Any responsible Gola elder will intersperse his historical account with frequent interjections of such comments as "This is what I have seen myself," or "My old people saw this and told it to me." As long as it is possible to state that a known ancestor reported the information personally to a descendant, and that by this process the information was at least conveyed to the one who is now speaking, the account is considered valid. "Fact" is what one has seen oneself or what has been reported to one by responsible persons who have seen it, or by still others whom they considered to be responsible. Thus "history" is made up of this kind of fact. There is no Gola term equivalent to the word "history" in English. *Ke yun fa* may be used loosely to mean "matters or things pertaining to the ancestors or the dead," but this is more like our phrase "days gone by." The closest approximation would be the word *kabande* which in one of its usages designates a whole class of tales which are meant to convey a moral lesson. "Parables" might be offered as an adequate translation of the term *kabande*. Another meaning of the term is "to put things in order."

Any story which provides directly or indirectly a comment on human behavior and succeeds in making a point from which an evaluative lesson can be extracted would be called *kabande*. This would include the entire repertoire of Gola myth and legend involving animals of the forest, strange creatures, and human beings. These tales are never told in isolation except under the artificial conditions created by the outside investigator. Invariably they are told in order to provide a specially significant comment about an event familiar to all the listeners, or to point up criticism or praise of the human behavior manifested in the event. Though the main body of the tale is seldom altered, slight alterations might be made by the teller in order to stress his message. On the other hand the tale may be told without change while the teller allows the particular situation and time in which it is told to produce the desired effect. This is true *kabande*. All tales, whether told by professional storytellers, spontaneously at informal gatherings, or by older people to children in order to amuse them or put them to sleep, are *kabande* in the sense that intrinsically they provide instruction and examples pertaining to conduct.

The word *kabande* is also used in reference to anecdotes about persons in the past. This is to be distinguished from the mere description of the *djewe*—the account of a genealogy. It is difficult for even the best informed Gola elder to confine himself to a strictly chronological presentation of persons or events either forward or backward in time. If he is prodded into doing so by an overzealous investigator he will soon become bored or annoyed. This is not the way knowledge of the past is normally presented. It is never given all at once, or in a particular chronological sequence. It is episodic, for in actual practice an old man will choose from his vast store of knowledge of the past some event or situation which illustrates a point he wishes to make. Unless it is pertinent to some matter at hand it would not be recalled. Gola history takes the form of *kabande*. These are dramatic episodes from the past which illustrate a point. A council of elders called together to present the "history" of their town will begin with a statement of one of its members about the special greatness of the town, or allude to the secret laws which have protected it. Then one by one the elders will rise and describe the exploits of one or a group of his ancestors in regard to a war, a significant marriage, a feud, or a rise to power—with little regard for orderly sequence in time, but every account adhering closely to the primary theme developed in the initial statement. *Kabande*, therefore, as applied to an historical or any other account is a form of instruction. It has been variously defined for the present writer at different times as "real experiences," as "the facts," as "truth," as "examples," and as "real happenings." It would seem to follow from all evidence that "history" to the Gola means real experiences of real people which can be referred to as a guide in conduct and as an assurance of the continuity of values. A living person may present a *kabande* about his own experience, but if he wishes to be particularly effective he will recount one which was the experience of some remote ancestor and place it in conjunction with his own in order to indicate dramatically the enduring qualities of the advice or comment he had put forward.

A concept of empirical fact is, therefore, closely associated with *kabande* in its role of providing formal structure to the knowledge of the past. "History" is an account of the experiences of known persons whose relationship to one can be clearly defined. Its validation is the degree of respect commanded by the age, intelligence, and record of responsibility of the person who pronounces it. A responsible and convincing person will qualify each individual statement regarding the past with remarks to the effect that "This was told to me by my brother who saw it," or "I did not see this myself, but my grandfather was there and told me," or "Though this happened long before my parents knew life, their old people told this to them and they told it to me." A most effective way of closing an account of historical events is to state, "This is how it was told to me and if I am wrong the old, old people will know how to deal with me!"

. . .

The Gola respect for knowledge of the past is a response both to its instrumental value in solving problems of the present and its quality of sacredness as the thoughts and experiences of the ancestors. The test of validity is not the consistency or "fit" of a given version of past events, but whether or not the ancestors of the spokesman would be in agreement with the version. As the ancestors remain deeply concerned about their private interests, embodied in the prestige and property which they have passed down to their descendants, it follows that they prefer a view of the past which protects these interests. And though the elders of families are the custodians of knowledge of the past in this world, the ancestors are the final arbiters. It is taken for granted that the view of the past put forward by an elder will be the view which is most advantageous to him, his family, and his ancestors. Regardless of what may appear to the outsider as inconsistencies between rival family versions of the pasts, all is taken as the truth until that situation arises in which the past must be entered as evidence in a matter of honor or litigation. Then one's own version is held up as the truth and all others are characterized as incompetent. Should one fail to press one's family's interests in terms of a partisan appeal to the events of the past, the ancestors will take their revenge. Truth, then, is that which brings about the desired results, and no man can be blamed for stating what it is in his interests to state. He can only be blamed for lack of skill and failure to tie his own interests to issues sufficiently broad to attract an effective group in his support.

The ramifications of this approach to what is "true," or "fact," are great. The custodians of the true and the factual are those who posses the power to control the lives and the will of those about them. In the case of knowledge of the past, it is the ancestors and the elders who are the custodians. They have the power to bestow or withhold their blessings. One's parents, one's owner, or one's ruler may be the custodian of truth in other matters. Regardless of one's private opinions, one accepts publicly the authoritative statements of one's superiors. There is a famous and ironic Gola *say* (proverb) which advises, "When you are walking in the rain with the King listen to his words. He may look at the sky and say, 'See how the sun shines and how clear it is.' And you will say, 'Yes, King, the sun shines and the day has never been so clear.' " To correct the king, or to disagree with him, would imply one's equality or superiority. Thus there is a duality to truth: There is the truth which is accepted as such for practical reasons, or for reasons of good form; and there is the truth which one has learned through one's own experience, or which one's own judgment has selected.

Much of Gola humor emerges from a consciousness of this duality of truth based upon a hierarchy of authoritativeness. When the oldest elder has spoken—and should his view of a past event have diverged from that of others in significant detail—no one will contest it. Even in private the response to questioning about it would be "That is what he claims, that is what he knows." If the speaker had been a man of the same age or younger, he might be corrected or even ridiculed.

On one occasion, when the investigator had pressed for an explanation of the discrepancy between the genealogies of two families, an old man shook his head and said:

> You *kwi* (strangers from over the seas) want everything to be one way. We Gola see things in different ways. A country man does not hold himself so high as to think he can know what is true about everything. If someone higher than him says "This is how it was" then he does not question that. What more about it does he know? If his grandfather and his King tell him two different things, *you* would say they are two different things, and *you* would want to make palaver (dispute) to find which one was above the other. But how can one know whether a grandfather or a King is greater? A country man does not ask what is true by talking to the words, but he asks "Who is it that said the words," and from that he decides what is right. But if the grandfather and the King say different, then it is not different to a country man. Both are true, but one must wait a while to understand that. No one can know everything at once.

26   Totemic Knowledge in New Guinea

Gregory Bateson

Does each culture have its own characteristic cognitive style? Bateson thought so. He even invented a technical term, "eidos," to refer to the mode of thinking that was typical for a given culture. In this excerpt from his famous account of the Iatmul, a New Guinea tribe, he studies their remarkable mnemonic performances in an effort to understand their "eidos." The analysis does not seem entirely successful, perhaps because cultures do not actually have general cognitive styles in Bateson's sense. Nevertheless, his observations are by no means unimportant; indeed, they are among the most intriguing to be found anywhere in the literature of memory. Among other things, they show again how inappropriate the concept of "rote memory" is for the accomplishments of nonliterate people.

Let us first consider the cultural stimulation of memory.[1] We have already seen that vast and detailed erudition is a quality which is cultivated among the Iatmul. This is most dramatically shown in the debating about names and totems, and I have stated that a learned

---

[1] I have been much influenced in my own thinking about these problems by Professor Bartlett's book *Remembering*, 1932, which I read after my return from New Guinea.

From Gregory Bateson, *Naven*, 2nd edition. Stanford, Calif: Stanford University Press, 1958. Reprinted by permission of the publishers, Stanford University Press. © 1958 by the Board of Trustees of the Leland Stanford Junior University.

man carries in his head between ten and twenty thousand names. This figure was arrived at by very rough estimation from the number of name songs possessed by each clan, the number of names in each song, and the general ability of such men to quote, in considerable detail, from the name-cycles even of clans other than their own. The figure must therefore be accepted with caution, but it is certain that the erudition of these men is enormous.

Further it would seem that rote memory plays a rather small part in the achievement of these feats of memory. The names which are remembered are almost all of them compounds, each containing from four to six syllables, and they refer to details of esoteric mythology, so that each name has at least a leaven of meaning. The names are arranged in pairs, and the names in any one pair generally resemble each other much as the word Tweedledum resembles the word Tweedledee—with the notable difference that the altered syllable or syllables generally have some meaning and are connected together by some simple type of association, e.g. either by contrast or by synonymy. A progressive alteration of meaning may run through a series of pairs.

Thus the series of names contain tags of reference which would make it possible for them to be memorized either by processes of imagery or by word association. I collected a great quantity of these names and noticed again and again that the *order* in which the pairs were given was subject to slight but continual variation. There is a vaguely defined standard order for the recitation of every series of names. But I never heard any criticism of the order in which names were recited. In general, an informant will alter the order of his recitation slightly every time he repeats the series. Occasionally even, the pairing of the names is altered, but changes of this type are definitely regarded as mistakes.

Bartlett[2] has pointed out that one of the most characteristic qualities of rote remembering is the accuracy with which the chronological sequence of events or words can be recalled. So that from the continual alteration of the order in which the names are given we may deduce that the mental process used is not chiefly that of rote memory. Additional evidence for this conclusion may be drawn from the behavior of informants when they are endeavoring to recall an imperfectly remembered series of names. I do not remember ever to have heard an informant go back, like a European child, to the beginning and repeat the series of names already given, in the hope that the "impetus" of rote repetition would produce a few more names. Usually my informants would sit and think and from time to time produce a name (or more

---

[2]*Remembering*, pp. 203, 264–266.

often a pair), often with a query as to whether that name has already been given—as was frequently the case.

Again, when a Iatmul native is asked about some event in the past, he can as a rule give an immediately relevant answer to the question and does not require to describe a whole series of chronologically related events in order to lead up to the event in question. The Iatmul indulge very little in the sort of chronological rigmarole which, as Bartlett has pointed out, is characteristic of those primitive peoples who have specialized in rote remembering.

[*Actually Bartlett did not think that rote remembering and chronological rigmarole were restricted to "primitive peoples"—he noted that a certain amount of "low-level remembering" occurs in all of us. And although he did suggest that some aspects of tribal social organization might encourage "rote recapitulation," that was probably a mistake. No "primitive peoples who have specialized in rote remembering" have ever been found.*]

One detail of the culture is worth mentioning as likely to promote the higher processes rather than rote memory. This concerns the technique of debating. In a typical debate a name or series of names is claimed as totemic property by two conflicting clans. The right to the name can only be demonstrated by knowledge of the esoteric mythology to which the name refers. But if the myth is exposed and becomes publicly known, its value as a means of proving the clan's right to the name will be destroyed. Therefore there ensues a struggle between the two clans, each stating that they themselves know the myth and each trying to find out how much their opponents really know. In this context, the myth is handled by the speakers not as a continuous narrative, but as a series of small details. A speaker will hint at one detail at a time—to prove his own knowledge of the myth—or he will challenge the opposition to produce some one detail. In this way there is, I think, induced a tendency to think of a story, not as a chronological sequence of events, but as a set of details with varying degrees of secrecy surrounding each—an analytic attitude which is almost certainly directly opposed to rote remembering.

But though we may with fair certainty say that rote memory is not the principal process stimulated in Iatmul erudition, it is not possible to say which of the higher processes is chiefly involved. There are, however, several details of the culture which point to visual and kinaesthetic imagery as likely to be of great importance. In debate, objects are continually offered for exhibition. For example, when the totemic ownership of the Sepik River was in dispute, a shell necklace was hung in the center of the ceremonial house to represent the river.

In the debating, clan *A* claimed that the elephant grass which forms a conspicuous and picturesque fringe along the banks of the river was indubitably theirs; and that therefore the river must belong to them. They accordingly produced a beautiful spear decorated with leaves of the grass and pointed to it, saying "Our Iambwiuishi!!"[3] Clan *B* on the other hand claimed that the river was their snake, Kindjin-kamboi, and their protagonist, Mali-kindjin, went off to get brightly colored leaves to ornament a representation of his snake which adorned one of the gongs in the ceremonial house. Again in a debate about the Sun, a number of the participants dressed themselves up to represent characters in a myth of origin of the Sun.

In the technique of debating the speaker uses bundles of leaves, beating on a table with them to mark the points of his speech. These leaves are continually used as visible or tangible emblems of objects and names. A speaker will say, "This leaf is So-and-so, I am not claiming that name," and he will throw the leaf across to the opposition. Or he may say, "This leaf is So-and-so's opinion," and he will throw it onto the ground with contempt; or he will sweep the ground with the leaves, brushing away his opponents' rubbishy statements. Similarly a small empty leaf packet is used as an emblem of some secret, of which the speaker is challenging the opposition to show a knowledge: he will hold it up asking them scornfully if they know what is inside it.

The proneness to visual or kinaesthetic thought is shown too in the continual tendency to diagrammatize social organization. In almost every ceremony, the participants are arranged in groups so that the total pattern is a diagram of the social system. In the ceremonial house the clans and moieties are normally allotted seats according to the totemic system of groupings: but when initiation ceremonies are to be performed this arrangement is discarded and in its place comes another based upon the cross-cutting initiatory moieties and grades.

Lastly we may cite the *naven* ceremonies as a further example of this proneness to visual and kinaesthetic thought. We have seen how the abstract geometrical properties of the kinship system are here symbolized in costume and gesture; and we may note this in passing as a contribution of eidology to our understanding of the ceremonies.

But the connection between the expression of eidos in the contexts which I have described, and the culture as a whole, is still not perfectly clear. I have illustrated the eidos chiefly from the totemic debating, and have shown that very great activity of memory is demanded and promoted in certain individuals by the sport of debating. Further, I have given facts which indicate that rote memory plays only a small part in this activity, while visual and kinaesthetic imagery

---

[3]The totemic name of the grass.

appears to be important. In the special business of memorizing names, I showed that it is possible to suppose that word association plays a part. But these facts might well be isolated in their effects. On the one hand, the active cultivation of memory might be confined to a few selected specialists and, on the other hand, it might occur only in the special contexts in which names are important. Until these two possibilities have been examined, we cannot step from the facts given to the statement that the active development of memory has affected the culture as a whole and the *naven* ceremonies in particular.

We will first consider how far this activation can be supposed to have affected the whole community, and how far it is confined to a small minority of specialists. On the whole, the remarkable keenness in memorizing names is to be found in the majority of the men. When I was collecting the names, I got my material as far as possible from specialists, but it was noticeable that, even when I was talking about other matters with informants who would never have dared to pose as erudite in public debate, they would continually bring the talk round to matters connected with the totemic system and would attempt to give me lists of names. This was true, for example, of the informant . . . whom I have described . . . as conspicuously enthusiastic and inaccurate. He inisted upon discussing esoterica and giving lists of names belonging to his clan, full of blunders and contradictions. In the younger men, however, this passion for showing off even weakly developed erudition is almost completely checked by the feeling that erudition is only appropriate in senior men. I had three very intelligent youths who consistently avoided giving me names, and who referred me to their seniors when I pressed them. But I was told by other people in their absence that two of these youths were already well on the way towards erudition, and would be great debaters when they were older. Thus the reticence of the younger men on the subject of names does not imply that they are not, like their seniors, keen on this form of mental virtuosity.

But a more complete answer to the question of how the stimulation of a small number of specialists can react on the culture as a whole is provided by the fact that these specialists constantly set themselves up as unofficial masters of ceremonies, criticizing and instructing the men who are carrying out the intricacies of the culture. Their voice is heard not only in the debates which concern totemic names, but also in those on every subject from initiation to land tenure. Thus the culture is to a great extent in the custody of men trained in erudition and dialectic and is continually set forth by them for the instruction of the majority. From this we may be fairly certain that the individuals most affected by the stimulation of memory actually contribute very much more than their fellows to the elaboration and maintenance of the culture.

27 Literacy, Cultural Familiarity, and "Intelligence" as Determinants of Story Recall

Ernest Frederick Dube

Although Bateson did pause to wonder whether the abilities he described might be "confined to a small minority of specialists," his aim was to describe the cognitive style of the Iatmul as a whole. Ethnologists rarely stress individual differences. Nevertheless, there is no reason to believe that people in distant lands are any more homogeneous than we are. In the thesis from which this selection is taken, Dube showed that illiterate villagers in Botswana have notions of "intelligence," "shrewdness," and other dimensions of human variation that are just as differentiated as our own. As the present experiment shows, they also vary a great deal in their ability to remember stories. Moreover, their "intelligence"— which Dube assessed by a method as remarkable as it is direct—accurately predicted how much they would remember, just as grade-point average predicted analogous performances by schoolchildren elsewhere in Botswana and in upstate New York.

Dube studied memory for stories—both African and European in origin—that were too long for any

From E. F. Dube, *A Cross-Cultural Study of the Relationship Between "Intelligence" Level and Story Recall*. Doctoral Dissertation, Cornell University, 1977. Reprinted by permission.

attempt at verbatim recall. His goal was to clarify the relation, if any, between memory and literacy. Do schooling and memorizing make memory worse, as some have suggested, or better, as most experiments using list-learning procedures have found? Where story memory is concerned, Dube's results cast doubt on both alternatives. When one averages across individual differences, schooled and unschooled Africans did about equally well. (There was a wider range among the unschooled villagers, however. The "high intelligence" nonliterates recalled more and forgot less than any other subgroup in the study, while the "average" and "low intelligence" nonliterates were substantially below their schooled counterparts.) On the other hand, there was a striking difference between continents: Both African groups remembered much more than the American subjects did. Indeed, the best American subgroup was about on a par with the poorest African subgroups from either village or school.

This result is not difficult to explain. Although Dube himself sometimes speaks of a general "literacy/ technology hypothesis" and sometimes of familiarity with specific skills, it seems to me that the latter factor is the important one. Members of a culture tend to excel in the skills which that culture encourages, at least if they have the talent to do so. (Incidentally, this principle explains why Westerners usually outperform people from traditional societies on IQ tests and similar academic tasks.) Many African cultures encourage story-telling; older children are often expected to tell stories to their younger siblings. In America, story-telling is rare. Stories may be read aloud or watched on television, but they are hardly ever told. This specific difference in cultural practices turned out to affect performance more than schooling itself; it was also more powerful than familiarity with particular types of stories (African or Western), which had a small effect as well.

Botswana is a land-locked African nation about the size of Texas. About 80 percent of its three-quarters

*of a million people are illiterate. Most of them reside
in traditional villages and live by raising cattle and
farming, though many men do migrant labor in South
African mines. The people call themselves "Batswana"
and claim kinship with other Tswana groups in Africa.
Their language is called "Setswana." E. F. Dube,
himself a Zulu who was born in South Africa, spoke a
dialect of Setswana called "Sesotho" and was familiar
with the Tswana people.*

*Dube's account of his first study is omitted here,
but some grasp of his method is necessary to
understand how the "intelligence" of the nonliterate
subjects in the memory experiment was assessed. He
visited many rural Botswana villages, interviewing
small groups of nonliterate adult informants. He
asked each group to discuss the meanings of thirteen
previously selected Setswana words. All the words had
some relation to intellectual ability or cognitive skill,
but they differed from one another much as "wise,"
"cunning," "intelligent," and "clever" differ in English.
The Batswana entered animatedly into these
discussions, suggesting many examples to illustrate
the meanings of the words. The upshot was that two
Setswana words, "Botlhale" and "Lethalefi," represent
notions rather similar to our "intelligence."*
*"Botlhale" was the word used in the rating procedure,
described below, by which the "intelligence" of the
nonliterate subjects was assessed. The present
selection begins with the method section of Dube's
second study, which deals with memory for stories.*

In this study we planned on using three groups of subjects; nonliterate
Africans, African junior high school adolescents, and America junior
high school adolescents. Since the African groups came from a rural
community, their American counterparts were also sought from what
may be a rural town: Albion, in upstate New York. While the two African
groups shared the same cultural background and were part of a non-

technologically developed society, the American group came from a technologically developed society. However, the American group also had something in common with the African junior high school group: They were both literate. Thus on this score they are both different from the nonliterate African group. These similarities and differences were used to tease out the effects of literacy and cultural background.

1. "INTELLIGENCE"

The term "intelligence" in this study will be used to mean an individual's ability to perform well on a cognitive task. This ability is assumed to vary between individuals, regardless of culture or education. Since individual differences in the ability to perform well on cognitive tasks occur everywhere, judgments of "intelligence" in this sense must also occur everywhere. We assume, then, that adults who have been in a position to observe an individual in different situations that demand competence, over a long period, would be able to judge his "intelligence." The accuracy of such judgments is assumed to be comparable in validity to the grades a literate individual might receive in school.

In accordance with the above assumption a group of four or five adults, who had served as informants in our investigation of the Botswana concept of "intelligence," were asked to rate a group of subjects who had been brought before them.

The subjects to be rated came from the same villages as the adults who were to rate them. The subjects were made to stand in a row while the raters viewed them through a window some ten to fifteen yards away. The raters, who were all nonliterate, were asked to use their concept of *Botlhale* to rate the subjects into three groups, namely: High "intelligent," Average "intelligent," and Low "intelligent." To make certain that each rater knew which subject was being rated at every occasion, the experimenter's assistant at a signal would point at the subject to be rated. The subjects themselves did not know why they were being pointed out, or what the adults were doing inside the office. They were beyond earshot.

After the raters had seen the subjects, they were asked individually how they rated that particular individual. There were few problems in deciding which subjects were obviously High and which were obviously Low. The problem arose when the Average group was being rated. Some raters would rate a subject up instead of in the middle, and another down, also instead of in the middle. To resolve such differences in opinions, each rater was asked to state his/her reason for thinking that a certain subject should not fall under Average group but with the High or Low group, as the case might be. A short discussion was allowed so that other raters might advance their differences with a particular speaker they differed with on the reasons to rate High or Low. Usually a quick decision was reached. In most cases one rater might have used one criterion for his/her rating when others might have used more than one. The main criterion used in backing up one's argument was usually a situation or a number of them when the rated subject had failed to show or had shown that he had ability or did not have the ability to be rated High or Low. There were a few occasions when unanimity failed altogether. In such cases a majority principle was employed, unless it was in the opinion of the experimenter that the minority view was sound, in which case longer discussion was allowed to make it possible for a unanimous decision to be reached. Where it was felt necessary, the experimenter asked probing questions to assist in the discussion.

. . .

In the case of literate subjects, who were all adolescents enrolled in school, current year grade averages were used to categorize them into the three "intelligence" groups. In Botswana the grades were obtained from the principal of the school, while in America they were obtained from the student advisor's office. The ratings in these groups were based on the subject's grade average for the current year. Subjects were obtained through an announcement during morning assembly. Those who wished to participate in the experiment were asked to enlist through the principal (or the student advisor's office in the case of American subjects). This resulted in a somewhat biased sample: the volunteers came from among those students with relatively high grade averages. For example, in the American group only students above 70 came forth as volunteers, and among the Botswana group only those above 50. This fact caused a difference in the criteria for assignment to the subgroups. Thus, whereas in America the Low group was composed of subjects whose grade averages were between 70 and 79, with the Botswana group this group was made up of subjects whose grades were 50 to 65. The other grades' breakdowns were, for the American subjects, 80 to 85 for the middle "intelligence" group, and 86 upwards for the high group; while in Botswana the breakdown was 66 to 79 and 80 upwards, respectively.

In both school settings, additional steps were necessary to fill up each intelligence level to balance the groups. The procedure was to ask the principal or the students' advisor to approach some students who had not volunteered originally. In this way we were able to balance the groups.

. . .

2. SUBJECTS

As already indicated above, there were three groups of subjects: non-literate Africans, Africans attending junior high school, and Americans also attending junior high school. Fifteen of the 36 nonliterate African subjects were male, the rest female. The ages of the nonliterates were mostly estimated by making use of an event that occurred during or at about the time of the subject's date of birth. For example, one subject said he was born soon after the mine strike in the Republic (South Africa). There have not been many strikes in South Africa by miners, so it was fairly easy to pinpoint this to the 1946 mine strike. This subject's age was then estimated to be 29 years. Thirty of these subjects had estimated ages between 14 and 20 years; the other six were older.

There were also 36 junior high school African subjects. Of this group 20 were male and 16 were female. Their ages ranged between 14 and 19 years. The American junior high school group consisted of 24 subjects, 12 male and 12 female. Their ages ranged between 14 and 18 years.

3. EXPERIMENTAL DESIGN

The experimental design for this study was a 3 × 3 × 3 × 2 design. . . . There were three main groups: one nonliterate African group, one literate African group, and one literate American group. . . . There were three subgroups within each main group . . . High "intelligent," Average "intelligent," and Low "intelligent." There were also three recall periods: immediate recall, that is a recall taken soon after the presentation; one recall taken a week after the first recall; and one taken five weeks after the first recall. Finally, there were two types of stories: two from African folk tales and two from European fairy tales.

. . .

4. STIMULI

. . . For inclusion a story had to meet certain basic requirements: It had to be complex, that is, it had to be long and consist of at least three characters and a number of episodes. It had to be understandable and internally consistent, unlike the "War of the Ghosts" used by Bartlett, which was in some parts ambiguous and disjointed. It had to be easily translatable from the language of its origin to the language used by each group of subjects as mother tongue. It had to be . . . unfamiliar to any of the groups used as subjects in this experiment. Two of the stories had to have a Western background and two an African background.

The stories used in this study [*were*] . . . *Maakga and Inkanyamba, Lintswe and Mapule, The Hunter, His Wife and the Gazelle,* and *Jorinda and Joringel.* [*The text of* Maakga and Inkanyamba *appears in the Appendix to this section.*]

Each story was translated from its original language to the language of the other group of subjects by two bilingual translators (English and Setswana). One translator translated from English into Setswana, and the other from Setswana to English. This means each story was translated twice, once away from its own language and then back to its own language. This form of translation is called "backtracking," and its purpose is to ensure that the translation was as correct as is possible. . . .

After all translations had been done and checked for consistency, the stories were then recorded into tapes for use as stimuli. For the English version a native English-speaking American male recorded the stories for use in America, and for the Setswana version a Setswana native male recorded the stories for use among Botswana subjects. Thus, each group of subjects listened to the stories spoken in their own mother tongue, and spoken by a native male voice. The stories were presented at a normal speaking pace and voice, neither loud nor too soft.

5. SCORING

In this work we [*used the*] . . . method of breaking down the story into idea units. Our method . . . takes into account inferred ideas and does not consider these as intrusions. Our scoring method differentiates between *Themes* and *Episodes*, but . . . we do not expect that [*either type of unit*] . . . will be remembered verbatim. The words as they are, are not considered to be as important as the sense they deliver when recalled.

The following was our scoring procedure:

a. Themes.   A Theme is here defined as a combination of words that convey a single idea. The number of words used to convey that single idea is not of any importance. At times it does happen that two ideas become so interlinked that their separation becomes difficult. This happens when one of the two ideas that are linked would be rendered awkward, or become clumsily formulated by a separation. In such a case the two ideas are left interlinked as though they actually were a single idea for scoring purposes. The following is an example of this level of scoring:

Maakga was a likeable boy,/jovial and full of jokes./

He loved hunting,/ and he was very good at it./

Each . . . group of words constitutes a Theme by our definition.

. . .

b. Episodes.   Episodes were the most important units of analysis in our scoring procedure. An episode is a combination of Themes that describe an occurrence of an event. An occurrence of an event is usually preceded by an introduction which sets the stage for an event, and it usually ends with a consequence which is a result of that happening. . . . The following is an example of an Episode [*from* Jorinda and Joringel]:

> One day they walked until the sun was about to set and they suddenly realized that they were lost! At the same time they found that they were unable to speak nor to move! They were filled with fear.

As it can be observed from the example above, an Episode begins with a setting of the stage or the scene which is then followed by an actual event or happening which is the heart of an Episode,and it then ends with a consequence that is traceable to that happening. A consequence, then, usually heralds the end of an Episode. Episodes are scored similarly as Themes. There are two points for a correctly remembered Episode, and one point for a partially remembered one, regardless of the degree of its completeness. Remembering does not have to be verbatim to be considered correct.

We have already indicated that Episodes were considered more important units of analysis in this study. The main reason for this is that Episodes more than Themes are an approximation of how information is usually found in the real world. Information is not found in bits but in something more complete, such as an event, with a beginning and a meaningful end. On the other hand, a Theme can begin but end somewhere in the air. For example, consider Theme 20 in the story of *The Hunter*. "Go back" is a complete idea, but the real meaning of *go back* where and for what can only be understood fully by either referring to what went on before or what follows thereafter, but never when it is by itself.

Scoring was done by one person, an undergraduate student who had been taught by the experimenter in the use of his scoring system. To check whether the scorer had a full understanding of this scoring method and also whether the method was consistent between two scorers, a third person was brought in, a graduate student who was also taught by the experimenter for this purpose. When the two scorers were compared it was found that their scores were identical in four out of five papers scored, while the remaining one differed by one point.

Since the experimenter himself was involved in this checking and his scores had been similar to those of the main scorer, it was concluded that not only is the stystem working, but that the scorer was also competent.

6. PRESENTATION

Each subject was presented with the stories and tested individually. A subject was brought into the experimental room (a small office provided for our use by a chief) by the experimenter's assistant. The subject was then given a seat (chair) which had been placed in front of a small table on which stood a Sony portable cassette tape recorder. A subject was allowed some time to calm down before the experiment began. Some subjects took longer than others to calm down, and the experimenter then became obliged to provide some distraction that would help to settle a subject. These distractions took the form of jokes and teasing. As soon as the experimenter was satisfied that the subject was sufficiently at ease, the following instructions were given:

> You are going to be presented with two stories which we hope you will find as interesting as we find them to be. They are very long stories, so please listen to them very carefully because they will be presented to you only once, and their recall will be asked from you. They will be presented to you at the rate of one story at a time, and then its recall will be taken followed by the second story and then its recall also. The stories will come to you through this tape recorder in front of you. Because the stories are very long you may not remember every word in them, but still do try to remember as much of each as you can. Your recalls will be taped to conserve time. Is everything clear? Do you have any questions before we begin? Now please get ready, here is the first story.

The tape recorder was turned on as soon as the subject indicated that he/she was ready for presentation. . . . After each presentation tape recorders were changed, one used for presentation only and the other used for recording only. After the recall had been taken for the first story there was a short break to allow the resetting of the second story. . . . Before presenting the second story the subject was again warned to get ready, and then the recorder was turned on, and later its recall taken as well. At the end of the two story presentations and recalls, subjects were thanked but not warned about the subsequent requests for recalls that would be made a week and a month later.

RESULTS

The results of [*the episode analysis are presented in Table 27-1 and Figure 27-1]. . . . All the results were analyzed with the BMD revised computer program with a four-way ANOVA. . . . Where necessary a Bonferroni t* test was used for further breakdown.

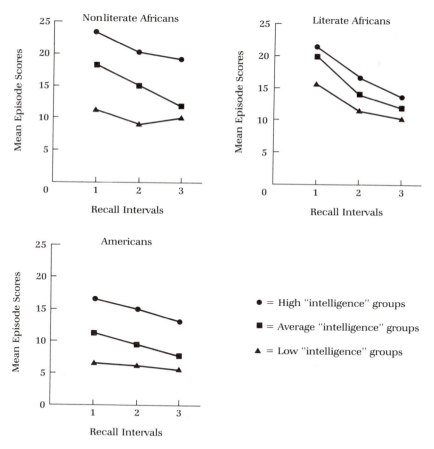

FIGURE 27-1
Mean recall episodes by three main groups (nonliterate Africans, literate Africans, and Americans).

TABLE 27-1

Mean episode scores for recall from two European and two African stories by different "intelligence" and cultural groups. (Each perfectly recalled episode counts 2 points.)

Nonliterate Africans (12 Ss per cell)

"Intelligence":	High			Average			Low			Total Mean
Type of story:	African	European	Mean	African	European	Mean	African	European	Mean	
Immediate Recall	24.25	23.08	23.67	18.00	17.25	17.63	12.25	12.08	12.17	17.82
After 1 Week	22.25	21.25	21.75	15.25	14.92	15.09	10.83	11.08	10.96	15.93
After 1 Month	21.17	19.92	20.55	13.58	13.08	13.33	10.00	10.08	10.04	14.64
Mean	22.56	21.42	21.99	15.61	15.08	15.35	11.03	11.08	11.06	16.13
Dif. bet. 1 & 3 R.	3.08	3.16	3.12	4.42	4.17	4.30	2.25	2.00	2.13	3.18
1st & 3rd % dif.	12.70	13.69	13.18	24.56	24.17	24.39	18.37	16.56	17.50	17.85

Literate Africans (12 Ss per cell)

"Intelligence":	High			Average			Low			Total Mean
Type of story:	African	European	Mean	African	European	Mean	African	European	Mean	
Immediate recall	23.08	21.83	22.46	21.17	20.42	20.80	17.33	16.33	16.83	20.03
After 1 Week	17.83	16.25	17.04	17.00	14.33	15.67	14.25	11.33	12.79	15.17
After 1 Month	16.03	14.67	15.38	15.41	13.67	14.54	13.58	11.50	12.54	14.15
Mean	18.98	17.58	18.29	17.86	16.14	17.00	15.05	13.05	14.05	16.45
Dif. bet. 1 & 3 R.	7.05	7.16	7.08	5.76	6.75	6.26	3.75	4.83	4.29	5.88
1st & 3rd % dif.	30.55	32.80	31.52	27.21	33.06	30.10	21.64	29.58	25.49	29.36

TABLE 27-1 (continued)

Americans (8 Ss per cell)

"Intelligence":	High			Average			Low			Total Mean
Type of story:	African	European	Mean	African	European	Mean	African	European	Mean	
Immediate recall	15.88	15.63	15.76	11.13	11.38	11.26	7.25	7.75	7.50	11.50
After 1 Week	11.50	11.75	11.63	8.00	8.37	8.19	5.25	6.88	6.07	8.63
After 1 Month	11.50	11.38	11.44	7.00	6.63	6.83	5.13	6.63	5.88	8.05
Mean	12.96	12.92	12.94	8.71	8.79	8.75	5.88	7.09	6.48	9.39
Dif. bet. 1 & 3 R.	4.38	4.25	4.32	4.13	4.75	4.43	2.12	1.12	1.62	3.45
1st & 3rd % dif.	27.58	27.19	27.41	37.11	41.74	39.34	29.24	14.45	21.60	30.00

All Groups

"Intelligence":	High			Average			Low			Total Mean
Type of story:	African	European	Mean	African	European	Mean	African	European	Mean	
Overall means	18.17	17.30	17.74	14.06	13.34	13.70	10.65	10.41	10.53	13.99

Note: Difference between 1 & 3 R. = Difference between immediate recall and recall after one month.

1st & 3rd % dif. = Percentage difference between immediate recall and recall after one month.

[285]

An inspection of [*Table 27-1 and Figure 27-1*] reveals the following information:

a. That African subjects as a whole show better recalls as compared to the American group. The BMD analysis of variance reveals that there was a significant difference between the two cultural groups (African and American groups) ($F = 63.31$, $p < .001$). A Bonferroni t test also confirms this by revealing that there was no significant difference between the two African groups ($t = 0.21$), but there was a significant difference between nonliterate African subjects and American subjects ($t = 4.01, p < .01$), and between literate Africans and Americans ($t = 4.20, p < .01$).

b. . . . That "intelligence" had a substantial effect on performance. The High-intelligence subjects, taken across cultural groups, had a mean score of 17.74 while the Average subjects had a mean score of 13.70, and the Low groups had a mean score of 10.57. This reveals a significant difference of ($F = 59.38, p < .001$) on the BMD program. A Bonferroni t test shows that the three groups were significantly different from each other (high vs. average, $t = 4.59, p < .01$).

c. . . . That the High "intelligent" group among the nonliterate outperforms every other group in this experiment. And also that this group, while remembering more than all other groups, also forgets the least, thus showing the importance of considering both culture and "intelligence" in studies of this kind. The interaction between culture and "intelligence" level was significant on the BMD program ($F = 5.78, p < .001$).

d. . . . That nonliterate African High subgroup and the nonliterate Low group, together with the American Low group, forget less than the other groups. However, it can be argued that the two Low groups had started on a lower baseline as compared to the other groups, and they therefore had less to remember from the very beginning. This argument, while it is correct in the case of the two Low groups mentioned here, would not be true in the case of the nonliterate High group because they started on a higher baseline than any of the groups in this experiment.

e. the BMD F test reveals that when all groups are averaged across, there was significant forgetting over recall intervals ($F = 236.43, p < .001$). An inspection of Table 27–1 shows that this forgetting occurred greatly between the first and second recall intervals. Between the second and the third there was little forgetting in relative terms.

f. The BMD program reveals that there was an interaction between recalls and cultural group ($F = 14.37$, $p < .000$.) In absolute terms the American group and nonliterate group showed about an equal amount of forgetting (3.45 and 3.18 respectively in Episode scores), as compared to 5.88 for the literate African group. In percentage terms, however, the non-literate African group show much less forgetting as compared to either of the two literate groups (13.18, 24.39, and 17.50 for the three intelligence levels, as compared to 31.52, 30.10, and 25.49 for the literate African group, and 27.41, 39.34, and 21.60 for the American group). To be sure, both the Average and Low nonliterate African groups began at a lower baseline than corresponding literate African groups. The nonliterate High-intelligence level group, however, started at a higher baseline and showed less forgetting as compared to all other groups in this study. As a group, nonliterate subjects tend to show less forgetting than literate subjects ($M = 17.85$ percent as compared to 29.36 percent for literate African and 30.00 percent for the American group).

. . . There was a tendency in all three main groups to forget less in stories taken from cultures that are similar to their own than in culturally dissimilar stories. This tends to support Bartlett's theory of the cultural biasing of memory. However, the trend is a weak one.

g. There was also a significant interaction between recalls and intelligence levels ($F = 7.27$, $p < .001$). In absolute terms, the Low–intelligence level subjects tended to forget the least (Mean for Low groups $= 3.69$, while that of the Average group was 5.00, and for the High groups it was 4.85). This was also true in percentage terms (21.53, 31.28, and 24.04 respectively). These results are at a glance surprising, but when you look at Table 27-1 you realize that the Low groups began at a low baseline, meaning they had little information to remember, and therefore, they had also little information to forget.

h. The analysis of variance reveals another marginal significant interaction between type of story and cultural group ($F = 4.40$, $p < .015$). The direction here again is in favor of the Bartlett theory, even though weak as previously shown.

. . .

[*The results of Dube's analysis of what he called* themes, *"smaller" idea units than* episodes, *are omitted here. They closely parallel the* episode *data.*]

CONCLUSION

The results of this study support the hypothesis that there are wide differences *within* cultural and educational groups in the ability to recall stories, and that these differences can be predicted on the basis of the subject's rated "intelligence"—thus validating the rating procedure. The more "intelligent" subjects, as determined by ratings or grade averages, performed better than the others. Formal education did not prove to be the main determining factor in performance of the task set for this study.

There was a weak support for Bartlett's theory in that subjects did tend to remember better those stories which were related to their cultures. The fact that the American group did not perform better or even equal to the African subjects on the European type of stories does weaken the Bartlett theory. However, the literacy/technology hypothesis was more strongly supported by this study. Both African groups performed higher than the American group even on those stories which are Western in origin. As pointed out under "Background," Botswana, from which the two groups of African subjects came, is still largely a traditional society and therefore less technologically developed as compared to the American culture and society.

The above results support a hypothesis that familiarity with doing something, rather than its mere presence in a culture, leads to better performance. Although the American subjects performed poorly in this task as compared to the African subjects, there is no reason to believe that this had anything to do with their intelligence. Rather, it probably had something to do with their not being practiced in the skills required for story recalls. The interactions among culture, intelligence, and familiarity that were shown in this study seem to suggest that . . . explanations that consider one factor as an explanation for high or poor performance may be oversimplifying the causal relationships. . . .

APPENDIX: The Story of Maakga and Inkanyamba

[*Note: The 99 themes are indicated by numbers; the 18 episodes are indicated by spacing.*]

Story Introduction

1. Maakga was a son of a warlike king.
2. He was to become his father's successor to the throne.
3. From childhood,
4. he was assigned a group of boys of his own age,
5. to be his attendants.
6. Maakga was a likeable boy,
7. jovial and full of jokes.
8. He loved hunting.
9. and he was very good at it.
10. His choice and love of dangerous spots
11. were always a source of anxiety to his mother,
12. and yet she knew that he had to show bravery
13. if he was to be respected as his father's son.

Episodes Begin

14. One day he called on his companions,
15. and asked them to go for a hunt with him
16. on the following day.
17. Asking was a mere formality,
18. they could not say no to their future king.
19. So they all said yes.

20. That evening the boys began to make preparations for the following day's hunt.
21. Early on the following day,
22. they began their long journey.

23. They walked for miles through thick forests and plains
24. without spotting any game to kill.
25. At last, they saw a large herd of game,
26. and they began to kill as many as they thought they could carry.

27. They had traveled far,
28. and they were now tired and hungry.

29. They carried their meat,
30. and searched for wood to roast their meat.
31. They could see no wood near by,
32. except a small little bush further on.
33. They dragged themselves to it,
34. sat and kindled a fire.
35. There, they roasted their meat and ate.

36. After eating, they felt even more thirsty.
37. The meat, the sun, and the walk had all contributed to their thirst.
38. They needed water,
39. but they could not remember passing a stream near by.
40. As though they were bewitched,
41. their thirst became unbearable.
42. They took what was remaining of their meat and walked.
43. Ultimately, they saw a stream.

44. They joyfully ran to the stream,
45. but did not forget the ways of their fathers.
46. The sons of high officials drank first,
47. just to test if the water was safe for their Prince.
48. It was safe.

49. Maakga then knelt to drink,
50. but no sooner than he knelt,
51. the stream dried up.
52. To no other member of the group did this happen.

53. They pondered for a while,
54. and then one of them remembered a story told to him by his grandmother,
55. some years ago.
56. The story was about Inkanyamba the king of streams.

57. Maakga had no choice,
58. to drink, he had to make a promise to Inkanyamba.
59. The promise was that he would give to Inkanymba the first thing he will see when he gets back home.

60. He made the promise.

61. To his greatest sorrow,
62. the first thing he met was his youngest sister,
63. the thing he loved the most.
64. He became very sad.

65. the little girl who had come running to meet her brother
66. was surprised to find her brother sad.
67. She demanded to know the reason for his sadness.
68. He then told her the whole dreadful story.
69. On hearing the story, she said,
70. "Do not worry, I am still too young,
71. the snake will not come to take me."

72. Days ran into months and months to years without a sign of a snake.
73. But on the day she was to be declared a woman, it appeared.
74. It could be seen from afar uprooting trees
75. and flattening houses on its path.
76. It was coming in a form of a storm.

77. Maakga, realizing what all this meant,
78. he ran to his uncle to tell him of the dreadful story.

79. On hearing the story,
80. his uncle summoned the household and began to give quick instructions.
81. the girl was to take a bath,
82. She was to keep calm, alone in her hut.
83. Her whole body was medicated,
84. in addition, she was given some medicine to conceal in her hand.
85. This she was told to pass over the snake's nostrils.

86. On reaching the yard, the storm ceased
87. and the snake appeared for everyone to see.
88. It immediately declared, "I have come for my wife."
89. It then headed for the girl's hut.

90. The girl unafraid, invited the snake in.
91. It crawled to her, resting its ugly head on her lap.
92. The little girl did as she had been told,
93. she caressed his head, while passing the concealed medicine over his nostrils.

94. The snake went limp,
95. and he began to snore.

96. The girl then ran to her uncle who came in running.
97. He and Maakga chopped the snake's head first,
98. and then its body.
99. They kindled a fire and burned the snake to ash.

28 A Sherlockian Experiment

Ulric Neisser and
John A. Hupcey

We turn now from the oral tradition to the written,
from people who hear stories and tell them to people
who read stories and talk about them. The memory
materials here are not folk tales but well-known
works of literature. Nevertheless, the method is still
naturalistic—the Sherlock Holmes fans who served as
subjects were just doing what they had often done
before. The experiment described here has little in
common with other current research on "story
memory"—research that invariably uses short,
artificial stimulus materials and standard laboratory
procedures. That research has produced some
interesting theoretical concepts, including the notion
of a "grammar" to which stories must conform if they
are to be remembered well. It remains to be seen,
however, whether those concepts will help us
understand how genuine works of fiction are
remembered by their readers. The present
experiment, undertaken as much for fun as for
science, does not address so serious a question, but
its results are interesting. Relevance to plot made for
more effective cueing than concreteness of
description, and verbatim recall of the text almost
never occurred.

From *Cognition*, 1974, 3, 307–311. Reprinted by permission.

"It would be superfluous to drive us mad, my dear Watson," said he. "A candid observer would certainly declare that we were so already before we embarked upon so wild an experiment." (*Devil's Foot*)

In most studies of memory, the subject encounters or learns the material during the course of the experiment itself. We know very little about memory for materials which subjects have mastered on their own time and for their own reasons. Moreover, despite a certain amount of research on memory for stories (e.g., Bartlett, 1932), we also know little about how genuine works of literature are remembered. With such material will "concrete" items serve as better cues than "abstract" ones? Will the relevance of the item to the theme of the story make a difference? Are names and descriptions of persons effective as cues? The present experiment is offered as a first step toward filling those gaps.

Conan Doyle's sixty stories about Sherlock Holmes and Dr. Watson have a powerful and continuing fascination for many readers. It is not unusual for Holmes' fans to form small societies, which meet regularly for Sherlockian purposes. At such meetings the members may read or discuss some of the famous "analyses" or "exposés" of Holmes' life and loves, argue about his methods, or compare favorite stories. A frequent pastime at these convocations takes the form of a test of memory. One member opens a volume of the stories at random and reads a sentence; the others must name the adventure from which it comes or even (ideally) go with the text from memory. More complicated questions may also be asked. In what stories does Holmes' brother Mycroft appear? Which ones involve animals? How many does Dr. Watson *not* narrate? The present study became possible because the junior author was a member of such a group, the Baker Street Underground of Cornell University.

METHOD

Five types of sentences were selected from the Holmes stories. NAME sentences contained little information but the name of a protagonist: "Mr. Holmes, I am the unhappy John Hector McFarlane" (*Norwood Builder*[1]); "Good evening, Mr. James Windibank" (*Case of Identity*). DESCRIPTION sentences provided personal description of characters: "His tall, gaunt, craggy figure had a suggestion of hunger and rapacity"

---

[1]Redundant phrases in story titles, such as "The Adventure of the . . .", have been omitted.

(*Thor Bridge*); "He was an elderly man with a thin projecting nose, a high bald forehead, and a huge grizzled moustache" (*Empty House*). ISOLATED ABSTRACT sentences were comments which did not carry any reference to the story or the setting in which they were made: "To let the brain work without sufficient material is like racing an engine" (*Devil's Foot*); "Deceit, according to him, was an impossibility in the case of one trained to observation and analysis" (*Study in Scarlet*). ISOLATED CONCRETE sentences describe objects or concrete deductions which do not bear on the main theme of the story, as when Holmes is simply impressing Watson with his powers: "My eyes tell me that on the inside of your left shoe, just where the firelight strikes it, the leather has been scored by six almost parallel cuts" (*Scandal in Bohemia*); "Each of these mends, done as you observe with silver bands, must have cost more than the pipe did originally" (*Yellow Face*). RELEVANT CONCRETE sentences are specific observations integrally related to the story or the solution: "The gun was made to conceal" (*Valley of Fear*); "Were it mixed with any ordinary dish, the eater would undoubtedly detect it, and would probably eat no more" (*Silver Blaze*).

Ten sentences of each type were originally selected, and the first two subjects were run with all 50. This proved too burdensome, and the remaining eight subjects were tested with only about 27 sentences each, drawn randomly from those available. Thus, the sentences were not all used equally often; presentation data appear in Table 28-1.

The subjects were asked four questions about each sentence. (1) From what story is it taken? (2) In what context does it occur? (3) What sentence occurs next in the story? (4) Which of these two alternative sentences (shown to the subject) occurs next in the story? The present report is based on the answers to the first two questions alone. The remaining data were discarded because adequate *recall* of the next sentence (question 3) almost never occurred; correct *recognition* of the next sentence (question 4) was often based less on memory than on considerations of logic or of literary style.

The subjects, all members of the Cornell Baker Street Underground, varied in their familiarity with the stories. By their own accounts, they had been interested in Holmes from two to ten years, and had read the entire works from one to twelve times. They were tested individually, and all sessions were tape-recorded.

Each key sentence was read aloud by the experimenter and repeated as often as desired. The subject was asked to name the story from which it came; if he was wrong, he was allowed to make a second guess. He was scored "correct" even without recalling the title itself, if he could convince the experimenter that he knew the story in question (perhaps by giving a brief outline of the plot). If he was unable to do this, he was scored "failed." When a failure occurred, it became important to determine whether the subject had *any* recollection of the story whatsoever. The experimenter began to describe the main plot, carefully avoiding any reference to the incident involving the key sentence. He continued until either the subject began to pick up and continue the story line himself, or both of them became convinced that he didn't know it. In the latter case, data from the sentence was not included in further analyses.

The subject was then asked to report the general context in which the given sentence occurred. He was prompted with such questions as "Who said it?" "Where were they?" and so on. No positive information was contained in the prompts. The experimenter had a check-list of the major points in the context of each sentence, enabling him to prompt and rate subjects consistently. He scored their responses on a four-point scale (3 = excellent; 2 = good; 1 = some partial recall; 0 = nothing), rechecking his rating from the tape later. After his recall of context had been determined, the subject was asked to report the next sentence from the story if he could, and was given a pair of alternative next sentences from which to select. (As noted above, these data will not be presented.) The experimenter then continued with the next randomly chosen sentence, and so on for about an hour. The subject was also asked about his familiarity with the stories and his methods of recall.

RESULTS

The major results of the study appear in Table 28-1. It is clear that different types of sentences produced very different results. In 57 presentations of DESCRIPTION sentences (ten different sentences, presented from two to nine times), the subjects identified the story on only seven occasions, even counting second guesses. In 64 presentations of RELEVANT CONCRETE sentences, however, the story was identified 46 times! Other sentence-types fell between these extremes. Similarly, good to excellent description of the context was achieved in only about a third of the NAME and DESCRIPTION sentences, but in over two-thirds of the RELEVANT CONCRETE. The data suggest that relevance to the story line was the most important variable. RELEVANT CONCRETE sentences produced strikingly more recall of titles and substantially more recall of context then ISOLATED CONCRETE ones. The latter, in turn, were somewhat better then ISOLATED ABSTRACT sentences, but this may be because they do at least fit into a tiny story of their own (often a Holmesian deduction) rather than because they are concrete. DESCRIPTIONS, while extremely concrete in (say) Paivio's (1971) sense, were quite ineffective as cues.

TABLE 28-1

Numbers and percentages of recalls and failures, for various types of sentences. (Each sentence was presented to at least two of the ten subjects; most were presented to six or more.)

Type of sentence	Name	Description	Isolated Abstract	Isolated concrete	Relevant concrete
Number of sentences	10	10	11	10	9
Total presentations	57	54	59	63	64
Title recall					
Correct title or story	11 (19%)	6 (11%)	13 (22%)	17 (27%)	44 (69%)
Correct second guess	2 (4%)	1 (2%)	0 (0%)	2 (3%)	2 (3%)
Failed	44 (77%)	47 (87%)	46 (78%)	44 (70%)	18 (28%)
Context recall					
Excellent or good	20 (35%)	17 (31%)	17 (29%)	35 (56%)	46 (72%)
Some partial recall	6 (11%)	10 (19%)	20 (34%)	6 (10%)	11 (17%)
Failed	31 (54%)	27 (50%)	22 (37%)	22 (35%)	7 (11%)

The sentences within a category differed in their effectiveness. This variation was most striking in the ISOLATED categories, where some sentences led to correct recall by nearly every subject while others never produced a correct answer at all. This held true for recall of context as well as of title, and sentences easy on one task were also easy on the other. Some of the intersentence variation was probably due to the presence of a few particularly famous, often-quoted passages ("He never spoke of the softer passions, save with a gibe and a sneer," *Scandal in Bohemia*).

Subjects who could identify the story almost always remembered at least a little bit of context as well. In 98 cases of correct title or story recall (counting second choices), only a single instance of failed context recall occurred. This observation confirms the existence of a link between context and title mentioned in many of the introspective reports. Given a sentence, most subjects would try to remember an incident in which it might have occurred and work from there to the whole story and its title. As one might expect, the subjects most familiar with the stories remembered most. The Spearman rank correlation between familiarity (the number of times each subject said he had read the stories) and the number of titles recalled was 0.72; that between familiarity and context recall was 0.66.

CONCLUSIONS

It appears that the links between individual sentences and the stories in which they occur are strongest for sentences directly relevant to the main theme. Coherence with the theme is critical. Descriptions of characters are much less effective, despite their concreteness. Further research will be necessary to determine whether these conclusions apply generally or are a peculiarity of Holmes stories and Sherlockians. We will not speculate further at the present time. "It is a capital mistake to theorize before you have all the evidence. It biases the judgment" (*A Study in Scarlet*).

REFERENCES

Bartlett, F. C. *Remembering*. Cambridge: Cambridge University Press, 1932.
Doyle, A. C. *The Complete Sherlock Holmes* (2 vols.). Garden City, N.Y.: Doubleday, 1930.
Paivio, A. *Imagery and Verbal Processes*. New York: Holt, Rinehart and Winston, 1971.

29 Very Long-Term Memory for Prose and Verse

David C. Rubin

Casual generalization from previous selections might suggest that verbatim memory never occurs in ordinary life at all and that it is an unnatural activity found only in psychological laboratories, or not even there. The most recent trend in memory research is to use stories or texts as stimulus materials and to analyze recall in terms of meaning. Subjects nowadays are said to develop schemas or to store propositions or to assimilate their experiences to scripts; no one expects them to recall what Senator Baker (Selection 14) called "exact language." As a reaction against the earlier emphasis on memory for meaningless lists of syllables or words, this is probably a healthy trend. Nevertheless, it leaves out a lot.

There are many instances of literal recall in our own society. This selection presents one kind of example. Such texts as the Preamble to the Constitution, the Twenty-third Psalm, or Hamlet's soliloquy are remembered word-for-word or not at all. Recall of such texts is typically letter-perfect up to some point (usually a natural breathing point) where the subject says he can't remember any more. Memory in terms of gist or meaning is never observed. Why should it be? To recall Hamlet's soliloquy is to give a kind of performance. That much

From *Journal of Verbal Learning and Verbal Behavior*, 1977, *16*, 611–621. Reprinted by permission.

can be said of many other kinds of memory, but here the performance is defined by fidelity to an exact text. It just isn't Hamlet's soliloquy if it is paraphrased, no matter how well the paraphrase may preserve the original meaning. You just wouldn't be reciting the Preamble if you began "We the citizens of the USA" instead of "We the people of the United States." In a literate society, socially important texts are self-defining; no other sequence of words is that text. That is why we strive to memorize such texts word for word, sometimes even without understanding what they mean. That is also why subjects interpret an experimenter's request to write down such a text as a demand for verbatim recall—a demand with which they comply as well as they can.

While memory for discourse has been studied extensively under laboratory conditions, there are few systematic data on retention intervals longer than those convenient for laboratory study (Bahrick, Bahrick, and Wittlinger, 1975; Cofer, 1943; Squire, Chace, and Slater, 1975; Titchener, 1923; Warrington and Sanders, 1971). In an attempt to provide such data, very long-term memory was tested for several prose and poetry passages that subjects were likely to learn in the course of growing up in America. Experiment 1 analyzes the free recall data of college students from three such passages. Experiment 2 uses the recalls of fifth and sixth graders who were more recently exposed to the material in order to obtain a shorter retention interval. Experiments 3 and 4 use various prompts to examine coding in more detail and to try to separate failures in retrieval from failures in retention.

EXPERIMENT 1

Method

Subjects.   Ninety-two undergraduates volunteered.

Procedure.   Covered booklets were used. On the top of each of the first three pages was one of the following titles: "The Preamble to the

Constitution," "The 23rd Psalm: A Psalm of David," or "Hamlet's Soliloquy." The order of the titles was random. The last three pages were
questionnaires which asked for each passage: "Did you have to memorize it?" "If so, when?" and "What experience have you had with it
since?"

The subjects were asked to write down as much of the first titled
passage as they could, and then to proceed through the booklet at
their own pace.

Results

"The Preamble," "The 23rd Psalm," and "Hamlet's Soliloquy" were
reported memorized by 32, 32, and 11 of the 85, 88, and 82 subjects
who could answer the appropriate question. The average duration
since memorizing the three passages was given by these subjects as 8
(SD = 4.2), 10 (SD = 4.4), and 4 (SD = 1.7) years. Twenty-five, 19, and
18 subjects would report the time of their last experience with the
passages. These times averaged 4 (SD = 3.8), 4 (SD = 6.3), and 3 (SD
= 1.9) years ago. Thus, from the subjects' reports it appears that the
recalls are from very long-term memory, and that less than half of the
subjects memorized the passages. Discussions with local educators
support these reports.

The recalls, while not complete, were verbatim: With few exceptions, subjects either recalled portions of the passage correctly in their
original wording or not at all. While Bartlett's (1932) subjects reconstructed "The War of the Ghosts" after the passage of many years, the
subjects of this study did not reconstruct the Constitution, the Bible,
or Shakespeare.

In order to quantify this finding, the recalls were scored on a
word-by-word basis. Words that appeared more than once (for the
most part, function words) had to appear in their proper context. Mis-
spellings were the only change from verbatim recall allowed, and these
only if they did not change the number or tense of the word. As many
versions of "The 23rd Psalm" exist, the scoring of this passage had to
be relaxed: If a word occurred in any of the several versions sampled,
it was scored as correct on the King James version.

Of the 92 subjects tested 52, 53, and 60 were able to remember
something of "The Preamble," "The 23rd Psalm," and Hamlet's Soliloquy. These subjects recalled an average of 14 (SD = 12), 42 (SD = 32),
and 17 (SD = 12) correct words out of a possible 52, 117, and 277 words.
They wrote down an average of 4 (SD = 6), 5 (SD = 7), and 3 (SD = 7)
incorrect words. All remaining errors were errors of omission. Even
using strict verbatim scoring the number of words in error divided by

the total number of words recalled, or the error rate, is only about 15 percent. Thus, the scoring does not force the results, as only 15 percent of the words written do not enter into the analysis as correctly recalled units. To appreciate how different this finding is from laboratory recall of the results, a verbatim scoring of Bartlett's "The War of the Ghosts" story was attempted. For the five initial free recalls for which Bartlett (1932, pp. 66–67) provides data, the average error rate is 69 percent. That is, using the strict verbatim scoring used here. Bartlett's subjects recalled over twice as many incorrect words as correct words, whereas the subjects in the present study recalled less than one-fifth as many incorrect words as correct words.

Besides being accurate, the recalls are regular across subjects. Figures 29-1, 29-2, and 29-3 each display the recall data for 50 individual subjects selected randomly from among those who recalled something from the passage listed. Each of the 50 vertical columns represents one subject: A line indicates that the word was correctly recalled by that subject, and a blank indicates that it was not. Hamlet's rather long soliloquy was stopped where fewer than four of the subjects remembered any of the reamining words. It should be stressed that each of these figures contains data for 50 individual subjects. The only manipulation of the raw scores that has been made is that the subjects are rank ordered by the amount they recalled. The recalls of the subjects who remembered the most are placed farthest to the left.

The data are quite regular. The Guttman Coefficients of Reproducibility for the "The Preamble," "The 23rd Psalm," and "Hamlet's Soliloquy" are .950, .832, and .991. This implies that if the number of words an individual subject remembers is known, exactly what words that subject remembers can, on the average, be predicted with an accuracy of 95, 83, and 99 percent from the number of times each word was remembered by the group as a whole. That is, if a subject recalled 20 words correctly, the prediction that they would be the 20 words most often recalled by the group as a whole would be correct 95, 83, and 99 percent of the time for the three passages. Thus, each individual is representative of the group. While it is apparent from the figures that the data are far from random, an exact statistical by-chance measure is difficult with as many subjects and words as are used here (Kenny and Rubin, 1977). While qualitatively similar findings are present in laboratory studies (Rubin, 1974), considerably less regularity is found.

For "The Preamble" and "Hamlet's Soliloquy," primacy provides a good description of the data. Based on primacy alone an individual subject's data for the three passages, can be predicted with 92.9, 76.1, and 98.8 percent accuracy. Here, as primacy is a prediction that is

TEXT   INDIVIDUAL SUBJECTS' RECALLS

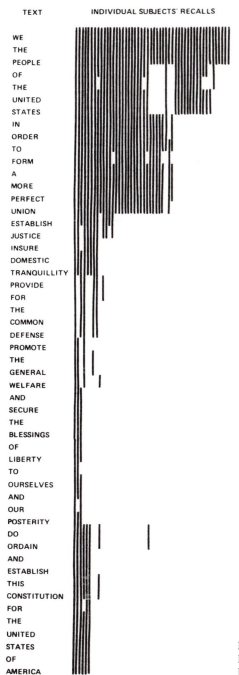

FIGURE 29-1
Free recall data for fifty subjects for "The
Preamble to the Constitution."

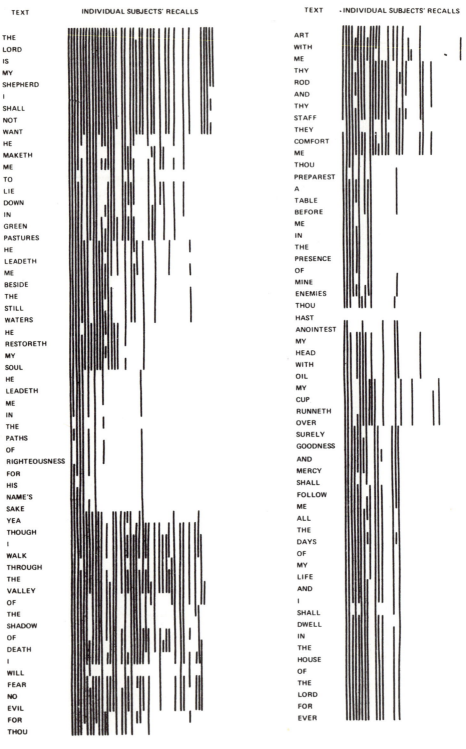

FIGURE 29-2
Free recall data for "The Twenty-Third Psalm."

independent of the data, a binomial by-chance model (Kenny and Rubin, 1977) is appropriate and yields significant differences: 69.4 percent, $t(49) = 11.17$; 69.3 percent, $t(49) = 4.18$; and 88.8 percent, $t(49) = 12.53$; all $p < .001$. Again, it should be stressed that these are predictions of which words individual subjects will recall. These are not predictions of grouped data but, rather, the average of predictions of individual subjects' data. The fact that the primacy effect is not as strong for "The 23rd Psalm," which has a simple rhythmic structure, will be investigated in more detail after examining other passages.

Qualitative examination of Figures 29-1–29-3 shows that subjects tend to begin and end recalling at surface structure boundaries corresponding to what might be breath pause locations (Glanzer, 1976; Suci, 1967). In order to quantify this notion, operational definitions of boundaries in recall and of breath pause locations are needed.

A recall boundary was defined as (1) more than two consecutive

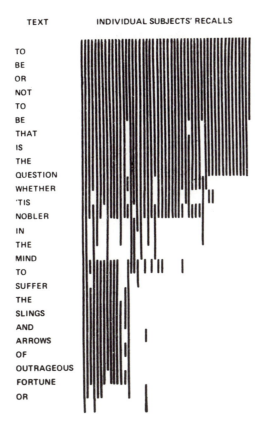

FIGURE 29-3
Free recall data for those words of Hamlet's Soliloquy recalled by four or more subjects.

words correctly recalled followed by more than two consecutive words not correctly recalled: that is, an end of a portion of recall, or (2) more than two consecutive words not correctly recalled followed by more than two consecutive words correctly recalled: that is, a beginning of a portion of recall. One consequence of this definition is that a recall boundary cannot occur in the first or last three words of a passage, so the observation that almost all recalls begin with the first word of the passage is not used to inflate the correspondence of breath pauses and recall boundaries.

Johnson's (1970) technique was followed to quantify breath pauses. Five volunteers enrolled in a Psychology of Language course were asked to "please indicate by means of slashes any location where a pause would be acceptable (i.e., word/word)." Judgments were made on all three passages used here as well as two others used in later experiments. A breath pause was defined as any location that three or more of the five judges marked.

"The Preamble," "The 23rd Psalm," and "Hamlet's Soliloquy" consist of 52, 117, and 277 words, respectively. They therefore have 51, 116, and 276 boundaries between words. Of these, 39, 38, and 43 percent are breath pause locations. Of the 64, 151, and 62 recall boundaries observed for the three passages, 94, 81, and 82 percent fall on the breath pause locations. As some of the subjects provide more than one recall boundary an inferential statistical analysis of this data is difficult. However, if only the first recall boundary provided by each subject is considered, the observations can be assumed to be independent and a χ^2 analysis is appropriate. Of the 45, 46, or 40 first-recall boundaries, 93, 87, and 80 percent fall on breath pause locations: $\chi^2(1) = 53.08$, $\chi^2(1) = 44.97$, and $\chi^2(1) = 21.12$, all $p < .001$. The five, four, and ten subjects whose recalls yielded no recall boundaries were by necessity omitted from this analysis. Thus, the recall boundaries coincide with independently determined surface structure units.

Discussion

Given no control over learning conditions, practice, or retention interval, the recall data produced are among the most regular in cognitive psychology. Not only do all subjects tend to remember the same words, differing only in the amount they recall, but counter to all current thinking about memory for discourse, they also remember in a nonabstractive, nonreconstructive manner. The recall is accurate and organized in terms of surface structure units. In terms of depth of processing approach, there is evidence of only the shallowest process-ing. Thus, in an attempt to extend laboratory findings to the real world, interesting limitations have been encountered.

[*Rubin's next two experiments are omitted here. In Experiment 2, fifth-and sixth-graders who had learned about the Preamble and the Gettys-burg Address—but hadn't been asked to memorize them—produced patterns of recall similar to those of the first experiment. Experiment 3 showed that recall can be increased by providing subjects with cues to the surface structure of the text (e.g., "_____ and _____ _____ _____ our _____ _____ _____ on this _____ ..." for the beginning of the Gettysburg Address).*]

EXPERIMENT 4

Except for "The 23rd Psalm," which has a simple rhythmic structure, the data from previous experiments show a very strong primacy effect. In order to include a second passage of known rhythmic structure and in order to demonstrate that recalls from such passages are remem-bered, in part, by the use of rhythmic structures, subjects were asked to recall "The Star Spangled Banner" either with no music, "The Star Spangled Banner", or "Stars and Stripes Forever" playing. If the sub-jects' recall units were basically ryhthmic, then the proper rhythm should increase the amount recalled and the wrong rhythm should decrease the amount recalled (Glanzer, 1976).

Method

Subjects.   Ninety-five undergraduates volunteered for the experi-ment.

Procedure.   Tape recordings were made of a continuously repeating 1 minute, 10 second instrumental version of "The Star Spangled Ban-ner" and a 2 minute, 45 second instrumental version of "Stars and Stripes Forever." "The Star Spangled Banner" was played to one group of subjects, "Stars and Stripes Forever" was played to a second group, and nothing was played to a third group. All three groups were asked to "please write down the National Anthem, that is, the words to the music that is played at the beginning of sporting events." A question-naire followed.

Results

There were 31, 32, and 32 subjects in the right, wrong, and no music conditions. Twelve, 17, and 10 of these subjects reported having memorized "The Star Spangled Banner" out of the 28, 30, and 28 subjects answering the question. The average duration since last exposure was 12 (SD = 4.0), 11 (SD = 2.5), and 8 (SD = 3.2) years for the 12, 17, and 7 subjects able to answer that question. There were no significant differences between the groups on these questions.

The strongest results cannot be given here in a quantitative fashion. The subjects in the no music condition behaved as most subjects in verbal learning experiments do, with perhaps more of an expression of frustration. The subjects in the wrong music condition appeared to be in slightly more pain, and a few on occasion put their hands over their ears. Most interesting, however, were the subjects in the right music condition. They would write as fast as they could until the music got ahead of them, and then they would switch to the behaviors of the wrong music condition. By the second or third repetition of "The Star Spangled Banner" almost all of the subjects in the right music condition adopted a strategy of waiting until the music came around to where they had stopped writing the previous time, and then writing another burst until the music got ahead of them again. The effect was quite striking and has since provided an effective classroom demonstration of the role of coding in memory.

The subjects in the right, wrong, and no-music conditions remembered an average of 52, 28, and 32 of the 80 words of "The Star Spangled Banner" correctly: $F(2, 92)$ = 12.68, $p < .001$, MS_e = 422. Their recall was quite accurate with an average of only 3.4 (SD = 2.7), 1.6 (SD = 1.8), and 2.5 (SD = 2.2) incorrect words recalled.

As in previous experiments, the data were quite orderly with Guttman Coefficients of Reproducibility of .814, .921, and .892. Under the binomial chance model these figures would be .632, .702, and .658. For the wrong and no-music conditions primacy was again a fairly good predictor of which items would be recalled with coefficients of .836, $t(31)$ = 4.91, $p < .001$, and .852, $t(31)$ = 6.31, $p < .001$. However, for the right-music condition, primacy was essentially equivalent to chance: .624, $t(30)$ = 0.39, n.s. This is not due to a ceiling effect as, even in this condition, subjects recalled only 65 percent of the words correctly.

As "The Star Spangled Banner" consists of 80 words, there are 79 between-word boundaries; of these, 38 percent were acceptable breath pauses. Of the 80, 47, and 35 recall boundaries found in the right, wrong, and no-music conditions, 58, 77, and 71 percent fell on breath pauses. Of the 27, 27, and 23 first-recall boundaries, 59, 78, and 70 percent fell on breath pauses: $\chi^2(1) = 4.33$, $\chi^2(1) = 16.75$, $\chi^2(1) = 8.45$, all $p < .05$.

Discussion

Recalls from college students for five passages have now been presented. Three of these passages ("The Preamble," "Hamlet's Soliloquy," and the "Gettysburg Address") have no simple, repetitive, rhythmic structure to aid in recall. For these three passages, primacy predicts free recall with an accuracy of 93, 99, and 97 percent. Two of the passages, "The 23rd Psalm" and "The Star Spangled Banner," have marked rhythmic structures. For these two passages, primacy predicts free recall with an accuracy of 76 and 85 percent. These results and the raw recall data, such as are shown in Figures 29-1–29-3, are consistent with the following hypothesis. All five passages are remembered by associative chaining of surface structure units. Thus, if one unit is forgotten all remaining units are lost. Where a rhythmic structure is available, subjects can make use of this structure to begin remembering the chain again after a unit is forgotten. While this hypothesis is obviously inadequate for all serial learning (Lashley, 1951; Jones, 1974), it provides a good account of the data collected here. It may be noted that this hypothesis does not make use of the most commonly cited determinant of prose memory: meaning. This is not because meaning has definitely been shown to be irrelevant to the present study, but rather because meaning would greatly increase the complexity of the hypothesis without increasing its ability to account for the data.

REFERENCES

Bahrick, H. P., Bahrick, P. O., and Wittlinger, R. P. Fifty years of memory for names and faces: A cross-sectional approach. *Journal of Experimental Psychology: General*, 1975, *104*, 54–75.

Bartlett, F. C. *Remembering: A Study in Experimental and Social Psychology.* London: Cambridge University Press, 1967. (Originally published, 1932).

Cofer, C. N. Recall of verbal material after a four-year interval. *Journal of General Psychology*, 1943, *29*, 155–156.

Glanzer, M. Intonation grouping and related words in free recall. *Journal of Verbal Learning and Verbal Behavior*, 1976, *15*, 85–92.

Johnson, R. E. Recall of prose as a function of the structural importance of the linguistic units. *Journal of Verbal Learning and Verbal Behavior*, 1970, *9*, 12–20.

Jones, M. R. Cognitive representations of serial patterns. In B. H. Kantowitz (ed.), *Human Information Processing: Tutorials in Performance and Cognition*. Hillsdale, N.J.: Lawrence Erlbaum Associates, 1974.

Kenny, D. A., and Rubin, D. C., Estimating chance reproducibility in Guttman scaling. *Social Science Research*, 1977, 6, 188–196.

Lashley, K. S. The problem of serial order in behavior. In L. A. Jeffress (ed.), *Cerebral Mechanisms in Behavior: The Hixon Symposium*. New York: Wiley, 1951.

Rubin, D. C. *Remembering Prose*. Unpublished doctoral dissertation, Harvard University, 1974.

Squire, L. R., Chace, P. M., and Slater, P. C. Assesment of memory for remote events. *Psychological Reports*, 1975, 37, 223–234

Suci, G. J. The validity of pause as an index of units in language. *Journal of Verbal Learning and Verbal Behavior*, 1967, 6, 26–32.

Titchener, E. B. Relearning after forty-six years. *American Journal of Psychology*, 1923, 34, 468–469.

Warrington, E. K., and Sanders, H. I. The fate of old memories. *Quarterly Journal of Experimental Psychology*, 1971, 23, 432–442.

30 The Mnemonic Feat of the "Shass Pollak"

George M. Stratton

In this selection feats of memory are described that make remembering the Twenty-third Psalm or "The Star Spangled Banner" (Selection 29) seem trivial. Stratton describes Hebrew scholars who have not just memorized the Talmud "literally" (as a sequence of words) but also "typographically," as a set of printed pages. Apparently their definition of the sacred Talmud included the book itself as well as its message. Most of us would accept "Oh say, can you see . . ." as the beginning of "The Star Spangled Banner" no matter how it was printed and—within limits—no matter how it was sung. But if nothing is the Talmud except these volumes, then knowing the Talmud can involve knowing them in every concrete detail.

This selection might well have been included in Part VII (Special People). It appears here instead because it illustrates the same principle as the preceding selection, albeit in extreme form. Culturally defined memory performances differ widely in the kinds of fidelity to the original that they require; individual skills of memory adapt themselves to those definitions.

Some years ago, through the kindness of my friend Professor Hollander, of the Johns Hopkins University, my attention was directed to a special achievement in memorizing which I venture to report; since, so far as

From *Psychological Review*, 1917, 24, 244–247.

I know, it has remained unnoticed by psychologists, and yet should be stored among the data long and still richly gathering for the study of extraordinary feats of memory.

The facts of the case I can hardly do better than to allow the witnesses themselves to state. And first the Reverend Dr. David Philipson, of Cincinnati, to whom I was first referred by Professor Hollander.

"The Babylonian Talmud," he has been good enough to write me, "consist of twelve large folio volumes comprising thousands of pages. All the printed editions of the Talmud have exactly the same number of pages and the same words on each page. This must be borne in mind in order to understand the remarkable feat of memory about to be described. There have been, as there undoubtedly still are, men who know the whole text of the Talmud by heart. Some years ago one of these men, a native of Poland, was in this country. I witnessed his remarkable feats of memory. Thus, one of us would throw open one of the volumes of the Talmud, say the tractate Berakhot, at page ten; a pin would be placed on a word, let us say, the fourth word in line eight; the memory sharp would then be asked what word is in this same spot on page thirty-eight or page fifty or any other page; the pin would be pressed through the volume until it reached page thirty eight or page fifty or any other page designated; the memory sharp would then mention the word and it was found invariably correct. He had visualized in his brain the whole Talmud; in other words, the pages of the Talmud were photographed on his brain. It was one of the most stupendous feats of memory I have ever witnessed and there was no fake about it. In the company gathered about the table were a number of Talmudic experts who would readily have discovered fraud had there been any. The technical name which was used by the Jews of aforetimes to designate these memory experts was *Shass Pollak; Shass* is the abbreviation for the Hebrew terms for the Talmud, and *Pollak* is Pole; nearly all these memory experts came from Poland; a *Shass Pollak* then is a Pole who has memorized the entire contents of the Talmud and is able to give exhibitions of his mnemonic powers like those mentioned above."

And next let me quote from Judge Mayer Sulzberger, of Philadelphia, who in answer to my inquiry, wrote as follows:

"I have met but one 'Shass Pollak' in my life. He was brought into my library one evening by a friend. I conversed with him and experimented upon him.

"After he had been introduced as the expert in question, I expressed some curiosity with perhaps a mien of incredulity. He was eager for the fray.

"You are of course aware that all (or nearly all) modern editions of the Talmud are paged alike and printed alike, each page beginning and ending with the same word in all the editions.

"I went to the case and took out a volume of the *first* edition which has its own paging *not* followed by the other editions. He made an automatic dive for a word in a particular part of the page, and lo! it was not there.

"Confounded by this unexpected event, he thought at first that this was not a Talmud I was showing him; and when convinced finally that it was, seemed to bear it some resentment for its improper behavior.

"I then brought out the corresponding volume of an ordinary edition and he undoubtedly made good.

"He would take a pencil and merely glancing at the page put it down anywhere and without looking told the word on which his pencil had lighted. This he did over and over again. There is no reasonable ground for the suspicion that he saw the words. I watched him closely and am convinced that he did not. He had, I feel sure, a perfect image of the page and the position of every word on it in his 'head.'"

Finally, let me give the testimony of Dr. Schechter, of New York, the late President of the Jewish Theological Seminary of America—testimony the more interesting in that while it depends upon the recollection of an experience many years ago, yet it is an independent account of the same kind of testing which Dr. Philipson reports—namely, by pricking through the pages—and consequently confirms the opinion of Judge Sulzberger that the success of the "Shass Pollak" who was tested merely by pencil was not due to a sly catching of the word by eye.

President Schechter stated to me by letter that once he had come across a "Shass Pollak" but that it was too long a time ago to give an account of him with definiteness. "It is at least forty-five years since the incident occurred," he wrote. "What I remember was that he could tell you the contents of every page of the Talmud by heart. I remember also that the people amused themselves by prying a needle into any volume of the Talmud, and he could tell exactly the word on which the needle touched. But I also recollect distinctly that it was nothing more than a verbal or rather local memory, the students all maintaining that he knew very little about the meaning of the contents, their interpretation and application. I heard afterwards of many similar 'Shass Pollaks,' but it is a fact that none of them ever attained to any prominence in the scholarly world."

This absence of any scholarly grasp of the contents thus memorized, of which President Schechter speaks, also appears in the judgment of Dr. Philipson. "I looked upon his achievement at the time I witnessed it as purely mechanical," he writes. "It is quite likely that he could not interpret the Talmud though he knew its contents by heart." And Judge Sulzberger, when proposing to his "Shass Pollak" that he use his knowledge to some scientific or literary end, was listened to with respect, but nevertheless received the impression that such proposals were deemed by his man to be nonsensical.

All of which confirms the oft-repeated observation, that such extraordinary powers of memory may exist in a kind of intellectual disproportion where there is no corresponding development of other powers—where, indeed, there may be an actual stunting of other powers and interests; as though the mind had "run" to memory, and been enlarged here at the expense of other functions.

As to the more precise amount of matter that was memorized, it should be noted that a page of the Babylonian Talmud consists, as my colleague Dr. Popper has pointed out to me[1], of the text proper, called the *Gemarah*, and printed as a more central portion on the page, and of a commentary printed below and around this text. Upon special inquiry whether the mnemonic feat applied only to the *Gemarah* or included also the Commentary, Dr. Philipson states that the test which he witnessed was upon the *Gemarah* only; and Judge Sulzberger is of the opinion that this was also true in the case that came under his observation. Even so, the task must have been a stupendous one; the amount of reading-matter upon each page is still great, and the number of pages is enormous.

In closing may I express my thanks, in which other students of psychology will certainly unite with me, to the gentlemen who have so generously given the facts above recorded.

---

[1]Professor Popper has also referred me to the articles "Talmud" and "Mnemonics" in *The Jewish Encyclopedia* for evidence that at one period the Talmud was handed down solely by memory. The feat of the Poles here recounted may therefore be regarded perhaps as the survival of a custom among early Jewish students in many and widely separated communities. The work of Brüll, *Die Mnemotechnik des Talmuds*, Vienna, 1864, should also be cited.

31   Pragmatics in Memory: A Study of Natural Conversation

Janice M. Keenan, Brian MacWhinney, and Deborah Mayhew

Reciting a text is an obvious instance of literal recall, but verbatim memory may occur in other situations as well. This selection shows that even casual remarks in everyday settings may be remembered "word for word" if the words themselves are memorable enough. But what makes an expression memorable? The authors have a particular hypothesis on this point. Their study was not intended only as an exploration of memory in its natural context—though that was an acknowledged part of its purpose—but also to illustrate the importance of situational, interpersonal, pragmatic aspects of language.

Laboratory studies of memory for text have found little evidence that specific words and expressions are remembered at all. After delays of a minute or so, subjects typically cannot distinguish sentences they actually heard or read from differently worded sentences that mean the same thing. Keenan et al. attribute these negative results to the constraints of the laboratory situation. There is no "interactional content" in the expressions such subjects are asked to remember. This omission has gone unnoticed, in their opinion, because prevailing theories of language focus on syntax and semantics without sufficiently considering pragmatic factors.

From the *Journal of Verbal Learning and Verbal Behavior*, 1977, 16, 549–560. Reprinted by permission.

315

> My own guess would be that while "interactional
> content" is important, it is not the only aspect of
> language that has often been overlooked and not the
> only thing that can single out a phrase in memory. An
> expression may be memorable for many reasons—its
> uniqueness, its style, its legal implications, or its
> interpersonal significance. We do not remember
> "exact language" very well even when these conditions
> are met; John Dean certainly did not, for example
> (Selection 14). Moreover, the subjects of this study
> were only asked to recognize phrases, not to recall
> them. Even that achievement, however, may have
> important implications for the psychology of memory.

In his recent book, Neisser (1976) argues that "the study of information processing ... has not yet committed itself to any conception of human nature that could apply beyond the confines of the laboratory" (p. 6). With respect to memory, in particular, he states: "Until we know more about memory in the natural contexts where it develops and is normally used, theorizing is premature" (p. 142). However, elsewhere he cautions that "demands for ecological validity are only intelligible if they are specific. They must point to particular aspects of ordinary situations that are ignored by current experimental methods, and there must be good reason to suppose that those aspects are important" (p. 34). The first section of this paper discusses a type of sentential information—pragmatic information—which is rarely involved in laboratory experiments on sentence memory, but which appears to be important when sentences are processed in the context of natural, purposeful communication. This is followed by a series of experiments investigating memory for statements occurring in a natural, conversational setting.

PRAGMATIC INFORMATION IN
NATURALISTIC SENTENCE PROCESSING

A number of the current models of human memory (e.g., Anderson and Bower, 1973; Kintsch, 1974) describe the process of encoding a sentence as drawing upon two types of information: (1) syntax—knowledge of the structure of linguistic expressions, grammatical as well as lexical information; and (2) semantics—knowledge of objects and their relations used to determine the referents of the expression. These models may adequately describe the encoding of linguistic information in the laboratory. But when a sentence is spoken by a real person in a real situation, it appears that additional information is brought to bear in the encoding of that sentence. This additional information concerns knowledge about the context of the linguistic expression, the intentions of the speaker, the speaker's expectations of the hearer, and the formal identity of the speech act. Linguists have utilized such information in determining the conditions governing the well-formedness of sentences and texts (e.g., Stalnaker, 1972). Philosophers have studied the role of such information in determining truth values (e.g., Montague, 1972). Both groups refer to it as the study of pragmatics.

The term *pragmatics* is usually taken to refer to information about the communicative situation, the temporal position of the utterance in the communication, and various types of information about the speaker, e.g., his intentions, beliefs, and knowledge of and attitude toward the listener. Our experiments focus on the latter type of pragmatic information—information about the speaker's intentions, his beliefs, and his relations with the listener. We refer to this information as the interactional content of an utterance. The interactional content of an utterance can be contrasted with its propositional content, since the latter conveys information about objects and events in the world and is essentially independent of personal knowledge of the speaker.

In assessing the role of pragmatics in sentence memory, we examined memory for individual sentences which differed in the amount of interactional content they convey or elicit in interpretation. Typically, the amount of interactional content conveyed by a statement is critically dependent on one's knowledge of the speaker. However, in order to illustrate what is meant by the term interactional content, we present examples of sentences which do not depend on one's knowledge of the speaker, such as (1)–(4) below.

1. *Low interactional content*: Do you always use CRT displays?

2. *High interactional content*: Do you always put your foot in your mouth?

Or, to use an example which does not employ a cliche:

3. *Low interactional content*: I think there are two fundamental tasks in this study.

4. *High interactional content*: I think you've made a fundamental error in this study.

In constructing these examples of high interactional content statements, we simply made the propositional content of the utterance convey interactional information. It should be noted that the difference between high and low interactional content in the actual sentences used in this experiment was quite different from that illustrated by the above pairs. In the experiment, both high and low interactional content statements conveyed similar amounts of propositional content, and, unlike the pairs above, the difference in interactional content could only be detected by someone familiar with the basic sociolinguistic (Ervin-Tripp, 1969) components of the communication, that is, someone who was familiar with the speaker, the topic, the setting, and the purpose of the communication.

In formulating hypotheses for the role of pragmatics in sentence memory, we found but one study which directly addresses this issue (Jarvella and Collas, 1974). These authors examined memory for sentences which can convey either of two intentions of the speaker. An example is:

5. I've never seen you wear that before.

This statement may be either a compliment or an insult, depending on the context. Jarvella and Collas found superior recognition for these statements when the recognition context induced the same interpretation of sentence intention. These results indicate that pragmatic information, such as the speaker's intention, is encoded and stored.

Our experiment on the role of pragmatics in sentence memory goes beyond the Jarvella and Collas study in two respects. First, we tested memory for sentences which occurred spontaneously in a naturalistic conversation, that is, the experimental materials were generated by the subjects themselves, and consequently, were more personally meaningful than Jarvella and Collas' experimenter-constructed sentences presented in a laboratory. Our experiment therefore allows us to examine (a) the generalizability of laboratory experiments on sentence memory to real-world settings and (b) the possible existence of differences in memory for sentences that are personally meaningful versus memory for sentences that are not. Second, we are not simply testing whether pragmatics affects memory, rather we are testing two very specific hypotheses concerning the role of pragmatic information in memory.

First, we hypothesized that the meanings of sentences high in interactional content would be more memorable than those which are low. This hypothesis is based on the belief that subsequent interactions with the speaker often depend upon the contents of earlier interactionally significant events. Second, we hypothesized that memory for the surface structure of high interactional content statements would

exceed memory for the surface forms of low interactional content statements. This hypothesis is based on the fact that frequently the way a
statement is made, the choice of words and the style with which it is
executed, is an integral part of the content of high interactional content
statements. Just consider the difference between (6) and (7):

6. Would everyone please stop talking?

7. Would everyone please shut up?

Here the propositional content of these two sentences may be equivalent in the sense that any situation fulfilling (6) would also fulfill (7).
However, the surface structure of the two sentences reflects marked
differences in interactional content.

Method

Subjects.   Nineteen members of the Psychology Department (faculty
and graduate students) at the University of Denver served as subjects.
They were participating in a research discussion and were unaware
that they would later be given a memory test on the discussion.

Procedure and materials.   The procedural format for a research
luncheon discussion at the University of Denver consists of one participant presenting a set of ideas or experiments and others freely
interrupting to ask questions, expand ideas, give criticism, or make
humorous remarks. The research discussion under study was held in
the usual manner with one exception: it was tape-recorded. Participants were aware of the tape recorder but were not aware of the purpose for taping, nor did anyone inquire as to the purpose. The speaker
for the day was one of the authors. He did not attempt to inject statements particularly suited to the experiment; he simply spoke in his
usual manner.

After the discussion we played the tape, selecting statements for
the recognition test. Two classes of statements were defined: high
interactional content statements and low interactional content statements. High interactional content statements typically conveyed wit,
sarcasm, humor, or personal criticism. We selected, through mutual
decision, 15 such statements for the recognition test. To match these
15 statements, 15 statements which were low in interactional content
were selected from the tape in a random fashion. Eight of the 15 high
interactional content statements were uttered by other participants.
The 15 low interactional content statements were matched with the
high interactional content statements in terms of speakers.

TABLE 31-1
Examples of a high and a low interactional content statement and their distractors[a]

	High interactional content
Target:	Italians, you know what Italians are like, they had a strike, they had a heat wave.
(a)	Everyone knows what happens in Italy, first they had a strike, then they had a heat wave.
(b)	If in Madagascar they're weird enough to put the verb first, you can guess what their eye movements must be like.
(c)	They're so weird in Madagascar they put verbs first; you can imagine what they do with their eyes.

	Low interactional content
Target:	You put a little morpheme that says you're going to choose the object as subject.
(a)	When you get an object topic, you add on another little morpheme.
(b)	What Hungarian does is agree with the object, if the subject isn't salient.
(c)	If the Hungarian subject isn't salient, the object agrees.

[a](a) Paraphrase of target, (b) new content distractor, (c) paraphrase of (b).

Table 31-1 presents one of the high and one of the low interactional content statements. Both were uttered by the same speaker. The statement about Italians is classified as high in interactional content because, for someone who knows the speaker, this statement conveys not only information about Italians but also information about the speaker. It was the speaker's witty way of excusing himself for not having completed running the Italian subjects in his study. The interactional content of this statement might thus be paraphrased as: The speaker is witty and believes that he can convince the listeners it was not his fault that the study was not yet completed. In contrast, the low interactional content statement simply conveys a fact about the world. Notice that in terms of rhythmic pattern and use of the second person, it is just as conversational as the high interactional content statement, but it conveys relatively little information about the speaker or his relation to the listener.

The classification of statements as high or low in interactional content was verified by informally asking three psycholinguists to rate each statement as high or low. These psycholinguists were not from the University of Denver, but were familiar with the main speaker and the topic of the discussion. Their ratings agreed completely with our classification.

For each of the 30 target statements selected, three distractors were constructed. All distractor items preserve the illocutionary force of their targets in the sense that all four items were jokes, sarcastic remarks, descriptive statements, etc. They differ in terms of preservation of propositional content. The three distractor types are: (1) a paraphrase of the target; (2) a statement which differs in propositional content, but whose propositional content was plausible in terms of the discussion; and (3) a paraphrase of (2). This latter distractor is a procedural necessity to make (2) a plausible alternative. Examples of the distractors are also shown in Table 31-1.

The recognition test was thus a 30-item, four-alternative multiple-choice test. Each item identified the speaker, e.g., "Brian said: (a) (b) (c) (d)." Instructions informed the subject that only one of the four statements was actually said. They were told, however, to examine each of the alternatives and to rate each alternative using the following scale:

OLD = I'm sure the statement was said.

GUESS = I cannot remember anything about this statement.

NEW = I'm sure this statement was not said.

This three-point confidence scale was employed, rather than the typical OLD/NEW response categories, in order to separate correct guesses from true hits. It thus provides a clearer interpretation of hits and false alarms. The test was administered by giving each participant in the discussion a booklet and asking him to return it as soon as possible. the interval between research discussion and the recognition test ranged from 27 to 48 hours, with the average at approximately 30 hours.

Results

Table 31-2 presents the overall percentages of OLD responses for each type of test item. The first thing to note is that, even though the subjects were not aware that they would be given a memory test and even though the test was given 30 hours after the discussion, subjects could still discriminate between the meanings of utterances which actually occurred and those which did not occur but were equally plausible. The mean percentage of OLD responses to targets and paraphrases of targets, pooling over high and low interactional content items, was 28 percent contrasted with a mean percentage of 5 percent for statements expressing new content.

TABLE 31-2
Overall percentages of OLD responses to targets, paraphrases of targets, and new content distractors for the conversation experiment

	Target	Paraphrase of target	New content
High interactional content	56	18	2
Low Interactional content	19	18	8

The interactional content of an utterance was an important factor in determining the memorability of its meaning. There were 37 percent OLD responses to high interactional content targets and their paraphrases, and only 18.5 percent OLD responses to low interactional content targets and their paraphrases.

Not only was there better memory for meaning when the interactional content was high, but there was also the predicted finding of better memory for the surface form of the utterance. When the interactional content was high, there were 56 percent OLD responses to targets compared to 18 percent for paraphrases. On the other hand, when the interactional content was low, subjects responded OLD equally often to targets (19 percent) and paraphrases (18 percent).

. . .

[This last finding is the main result of the experiment. The subjects were surprisingly accurate in identifying the exact wording of the statements high in interactional content; they correctly responded OLD to such statements and not to paraphrases of them. The effect of interactional content on recognition of exact wording was significant at the 0.005 level.

In sections omitted here, the authors report three control studies. (1) When all the sentences were included in the stimulus materials of a traditional memory experiment (new subjects listened to 100 sentences and were then given a recognition test) no difference between those with high and low interactional content was found. Thus, it seems that ". . . the high interactional content statements are not intrinsically more memorable than the low interactional content statements." Only the speaker or the situation make them so. (2) New subjects, presented with the original statements and paraphrases, were asked to judge which statement in each pair was more likely to have been uttered in such a meeting. If they had been able to make these judgments accurately, the results of the main study would have been seriously undermined. The implication would have been that the subjects of that study had not chosen the originals on the basis of memory at all; that the paraphrases *were badly-written imitations of natural speech and therefore easy to reject. This did not happen. The actual result was just the opposite: the control subjects were significantly inaccurate in their judgments. That is, they tended to choose the paraphrases rather than the originals! This suggests that Keenan, MacWhinney, and Mayhew (who made up the paraphrases) and their subjects (who preferred them to the originals) have similar but mistaken ideas about what spontaneous speech is really like. (3) In the third control study, subjects who knew the speaker but had not attended the discussion were presented with the sentences and paraphrases. They were unable to guess (for either type of sentence) which ones he had actually uttered.]*

CONCLUSIONS

The central finding of this study is the excellent retention of surface form for statements that have high interactional content within the context of a real-life communication. This finding contrasts sharply with the commonly held belief that memory for sentences involves only memory for their meanings and not for their surface forms (James, 1890; Pillsbury and Meader, 1928; Stern, 1931; Sachs, 1967; Brewer, 1974). The studies which have investigated this issue present a broad range of results. Some experiments (Wanner, 1974) have shown the influence of task demands on memory for surface form, and others (Anderson, 1974; Keenan, 1975) have shown the influence of text structure on memory for surface form. Some experiments have shown that memory for suface form in negligible or, at best, transient (Sachs, 1967; Wanner, 1974); others find that it persists over very long retention intervals (Keenan, 1975, Kolers, 1975). These apparently contradictory findings indicate that the parameters which control the retention of surface form information in laboratory experiments have yet to be worked out. The present experiment demonstrates the importance of a parameter of a quite different nature. This parameter involves the degree to which a statement conveys information about the speaker's intentions, beliefs, and attitudes toward the listener. Our results indicate that the impact of this parameter on memory is more dramatic than that of any of the other parameters which have been examined to date.

REFERENCES

Anderson, J. R. Verbatim and propositional representations of sentences in immediate and long-term memory. *Journal of Verbal Learning and Verbal Behavior*, 1974, 13, 149–162.

Anderson, J. R., and Bower, G. H. *Human Associative Memory*. Washington, D.C.: Winston, 1973.

Brewer, W. F. The problem of meaning and the inter-relations of the higher mental processes. In W. B. Weimer and D. S. Palermo (eds.), *Cognition and the Symbolic Processes*. Hillsdale, N.J.: Lawrence Erlbaum Associates, 1974.

Ervin-Tripp, S. Sociolinguistics. In L. Berkowitz (ed.), *Advances in Experimental Social Psychology*, Vol. 4. New York: Academic Press, 1969.

James, W. *The Principles of Psychology*. London: Macmillan, 1890.

Jarvella, R. J., and Collas, J. G. Memory for the intentions of sentences. *Memory and Cognition*, 1974, 2, 185–188.

Keenan, J. M. *The Role of Episodic Information in the Assessment of Semantic Memory Representations for Sentences*. Doctoral dissertation, Department of Psychology, University of Colorado, 1975.

Kintsch, W. *The Representation of Meaning in Memory*. Hillsdale, N.J.: Lawrence Erlbaum Associates, 1974.

Kintsch, W., and Bates, E. Recognition memory for statements from a classroom lecture. *Journal of Experimental Psychology: Human Learning and Memory*, 1977, 3, 150–159.

Kolers, P. A. Specificity of operations in sentence recognition. *Cognitive Psychology*, 1975, 7, 289–306.

Montague, R. Pragmatics and intensional logic. In D. Davidson and G. Harman (eds.), *Semantics of Natural Language*. Dordrecht, Holland: D. Reidel, 1972.

Neisser, U. *Cognition and Reality*. San Francisco: W. H. Freeman and Company, 1976.

Pillsbury, W. B., and Meader, C. L. *The Psychology of Language*. New York: Appleton, 1928.

Sachs, J. Recognition memory for syntactic and semantic aspects of connected discourse. *Perception and Psychophysics*, 1967, 2, 427–442.

Stalnaker, R. C. Pragmatics. In D. Davidson and G. Harman (eds.), *Semantics of Natural Language*. Dordrecht, Holland: D. Reidel, 1972.

Stern, G. *Meaning and Change of Meaning*. Göteborg: Elanders Böktrycken Aktiebolag, 1931. (Reprinted at Bloomington: Indiana University Press, 1964.)

Wanner, E. *On Remembering, Forgetting and Understanding Sentences*. The Hague: Mouton, 1974.

Part VI
Getting Things
Done

In which the problem is not recalling the past but preparing for the future, or using the past to deal with the present. These are skills that children come to understand only slowly, and psychologists more slowly still.

32 Remembering to Perform Future Actions

John A. Meacham and Burt Leiman

Ordinary language uses the word "remember" in two different senses: We remember what we must do as well as what we have done, our plans for the future as well as events in our past. Meacham and Leiman call these two aspects of memory "prospective remembering" and "retrospective remembering." They offer a valuable conceptual analysis of different kinds of prospective remembering and present a preliminary experiment as well.

In remembering, one engages in various cognitive activities in order to reconstruct information which was known in the past. Not infrequently, such information has implications for actions to be performed in the future, such as stopping at the store on the way home, or keeping an appointment with the dentist. Remembering which involves such implications can be termed "prospective remembering" and can be distinguished from "retrospective remembering," which is concerned solely with the recall of information about the past. For example, in order to deliver a message one must remember not only the message (retrospective) but also to seek out the person for whom the message is intended and to deliver the message (prospective). Although there has been considerable research directed at understanding the processes

A preliminary version of this selection was presented at the meetings of the American Psychological Association, Chicago, September 1975.

which enable us to recall information about the past, there has been little investigation of how it is that we remember to carry out specific actions in the future.

Prospective remembering, because of the emphasis upon performance of actions rather than recall of information, is closely related to at least two other broad areas of behavior. First, prospective remembering is an important feature of those behaviors which we refer to as planned. For example, in order to carry out a plan to leave early in the morning for a fishing trip, one must remember to get gas in the car the previous afternoon, and one must remember to set the alarm clock for four in the morning. Second, the ability to remember such actions ought to bear upon one's self-concept as an efficient, reliable, or well-organized individual. Munsat (1966), for example, suggests that "If a person makes memory claims about what he did in the past, and they are frequently wrong, we say his memory is unreliable. If a person . . . forgets to do things he said he would do and is in general 'forgetful,' it is *he* that we brand as unreliable" (p. 18). Indeed, adults reflecting upon their children's or their own memory lapses often appear more concerned with instances of forgetting to carry out actions than with the forgetting of information about the past.

The context within which prospective remembering occurs must be considered in analyzing the cognitive activities which might facilitate prospective remembering. For example, remembering to carry out an action at a short distance in time from the present may be no different than the problem of maintaining one's vigilance or *attention*—e.g., remembering to transfer clothes from the washer to the dryer. Two major categories of prospective remembering which ought to be distinguished, however, may be termed "habitual" and "episodic." In the case of *habitual remembering*, the activity is one which is routinely engaged in—e.g., remembering to brush one's teeth before going to bed at night. Remembering, or the performance of the activity, may be guided by cues in the immediate environment or by cues from preceding activities (see Atkinson and Birch, 1970). A strategy for facilitating prospective remembering is to integrate the desired activity within the stream of our daily activities—e.g., we plan to take our vitamin pills at breakfast each day, rather than at random times on different days.

Episodic remembering, on the other hand, involves an action which is performed either infrequently or on an irregular basis, so that the performance of the action is dependent upon remembering to carry out the action—e.g., buying bread on the way home from work. Of course, whether a particular activity is said to involve episodic or habitual remembering can depend upon the success of the individual in routinizing the activity. For example, for the growing child the problem of brushing one's teeth at night may be first one of maintaining a set (from the living room, where he is instructed, to the bathroom, where he must carry out the activity), later a problem of episodic remembering (occasional parental prompts may be helpful), and finally a matter of habitual remembering (the last thing to do before going to bed).

What are the means by which episodic remembering might be facilitated? A common strategy is to construct a list of activities to be carried out, and then to routinely examine the list in order to be reminded of what must be done. Such a procedure involves subordinating episodic to habitual remembering—the procedure is useful only if one frequently or regularly examines the list. A second mnemonic strategy is to create an external retrieval cue which can prompt remembering of the activity—e.g., putting the overdue book near the front door, so it will be seen and returned to the library. Note that although habitual remembering can involve integrating an activity (vitamin pills) within the stream of regular activities, episodic remembering can often depend upon a disturbance of the regular stream of activities—e.g., seeing the book by the front door. Third, there may be various cognitive strategies for facilitating prospective remembering, for example, forming elaborated associations between the activity to be remembered and other activities which might be engaged in at a future time—by this means, one might remember to bring the frisbee to the picnic.

To what extent do people use these various strategies in order to facilitate episodic remembering? A preliminary answer is provided by Kreutzer, Leonard, and Flavell (1975), [see Selection 34] who asked children how they could be certain to bring their skates to school in the morning. The majority of the responses involved creating external retrieval cues, such as placing the skates in a particular location or leaving a written note, rather than cognitive processes; the responses of older children were more planful than those of younger children. Thus, not only is prospective remembering important for planned behaviors, as noted above, but planfulness seems a prerequisite for engaging in activities which might facilitate prospective remembering, e.g., making efforts to create external retrieval cues or cognitive associations now in order to better remember to carry out some action in the future. Planfulness has already been implicated in the intentional memorizing strategies which can facilitate retrospective remembering (Flavell, 1970; Meacham, 1972).

The purpose of the present investigation was to assess the effectiveness of external retrieval cues in episodic remembering—do such cues facilitate prospective remembering or not? A traditional external cue for prospective remembering has been to tie a string around one's finger. Such a cue is unusual in that it may remind us of many different things which we ought to do—to buy string, to buy apples, etc. If such an arbitrary cue can facilitate prospective remembering, then other, more efficient cues can later be investigated. Thus, half the subjects were provided with a tag which could be fastened to their key chains in order to assess whether or not such an external cue could facilitate prospective remembering. The task for the subjects was to mail postcards to the experimenter on several specified dates, a task somewhat analogous to returning books to the library. Series length—either four or eight postcards—was varied to determine the effect of this variable and its interaction, if any, with the use of an external retrieval cue. In addition, correlations were sought between prospective and retrospective remembering and with subjects' predictions of their remembering abilities (cf. Flavell, Friedrichs, and Hoyt, 1970).

EXPERIMENT 1

Method

Subjects.   The subjects were 27 students (13 male, 14 female) from the psychology subject pool, randomly assigned to one of four groups: four cards, no tag; four cards, tag; eight cards, no tag; eight cards, tag. The subjects met with the experimenter in one of two group meetings, the first for the no-tag groups, the second for the tag groups.

Materials.   For each subject packets were prepared which contained four or eight stamped postcards marked with identification numbers and addressed to the experimenter. Each packet also contained an instruction sheet indicating appropriate dates on which cards were to be mailed for either the four-card or the eight-card condition. The dates always occurred between Tuesday and Friday, but otherwise were distributed randomly over the 32 days following the group meetings. Subjects in the four-card condition were asked to return cards on the first, third, fifth, and eighth dates in the series for the eight-card condition. The instruction sheet also asked the subjects to write the date and the time on each card as it was mailed. The tags were of colored cardboard with metal rims, of the sort typically used for locker room keys.

Procedure.   The subjects were told that several aspects of memory were being investigated and were asked to complete an eight-item questionnaire on which they evaluated their own ability to recall information and to remember to do things. A retrospective recall test was then administered. The experimenter read aloud eight lists containing five, seven, nine, or eleven common, unrelated words and after each list the subjects were asked to write as many of the words as they could remember in any order.

The packets with the postcards and instructions were then distributed. The instructions asked the subjects to return the postcards on the indicated dates and compared the task to returning library books. The subjects were encouraged to do their best to remember to mail the cards on the appropriate dates and were asked not to discuss the experiment with their classmates. In the tag condition, tags were then distributed and the subjects were asked to attach them to their key chains at that time to help them remember to mail the cards.

After the last cards had been returned, a questionnaire was mailed to the subjects to assess the extent of their cooperation and to ask what was done, if anything, to help them remember to mail the cards.

Results

Cooperation.   Eighty-eight percent of the subjects reported on the questionnaire that they always did their best to carry out the requirements of the experiment; eight percent reported that they often did their best. Ninety-nine percent of the cards were returned, and eighty-six percent were mailed on the appropriate dates. All but one subject in the tag condition reported that they kept the tag on for the entire 32 days. Thus, despite the fact that it was not possible to directly monitor subjects' performance, cooperation was high and effects in the tag condition can be attributed to the presence of the tags on the subjects' key chains.

Remembering.   An evaluation of whether or not the subjects remembered to mail the cards on the specified dates was carried out by considering the date which the subject wrote on the card, the postmark, the time of arrival of the majority of the subjects' cards, and the arrival of a card which the experimenter mailed on the specified date. Many subjects also frankly admitted instances of forgetting. The percentages of cards mailed on the specified dates by subjects in each group are shown in Table 32-1.

A $2 \times 2 \times 2 \times 4$ (Tag vs. No Tag $\times$ Series Length $\times$ Sex $\times$ Dates) analysis of variance with repeated measures on the last factor was carried out for subjects' prospective remembering scores. In the analysis, scores for the first and second, third and fourth, etc. dates in the eight-card condition were averaged in order to provide the number of scores available in the four-card condition. There was a significant

TABLE 32-1
Percentages of cards mailed on specified dates

Group	Date							
	1	2	3	4	5	6	7	8
Experiment 1—Eight cards								
Tag	100	100	100	100	100	100	100	86
No Tag	83	67	100	67	83	83	100	83
Experiment 1—Four cards								
Tag	100		71		86			100
No Tag	86		100		42			57
Experiment 2—Long interval								
Tag	100		100		75			75
No Tag	87		62		62			50
Experiment 2—Short interval								
Tag	100	57	43	57				
No Tag	100	86	57	71				
Experiment 2—Delayed short interval								
Tag					86	86	100	86
No Tag					57	71	71	71

interaction involving tags, series length, and dates, $F (3,57) = 3.68$, $p < .05$. Although the percentage of postcards mailed on the appropriate dates was approximately the same for subjects with tags as without tags (see Table 32-1), this was not the case on later dates in the four-card condition where the percentage was greater for subjects with tags than without tags. In addition, there was a trend for more cards to be mailed on time in the eight-card condition than in the four-card condition, $F (1,19) = 3.71$, $p < .10$, and a trend for more cards to be mailed on time in the tag condition than in the no-tag condition, $F (1,19) = 4.04$, $p < .10$. There were no significant correlations involving prospective remembering, retrospective remembering, or predictions of remembering abilities.

EXPERIMENT 2

Experiment 2 was carried out in part to assess the trend ($p < .10$) for prospective remembering to be facilitated when subjects were provided with an arbitrary external retrieval cue. Further, the significant interaction in Experiment 1 showed that an external retrieval cue was effective on later dates for subjects in the four-card condition. It was not clear, however, whether the tag should be considered an effective cue only (a) for relatively short series of cards to be remembered, or

(b) when the intervals between dates are long since both were the case in the four-card condition relative to the eight-card condition. Thus, in Experiment 2, the series length was four cards for all groups, but the dates and intervals were varied: (a) a long-interval condition was similar to the four-card condition of Experiment 1; (b) a short-interval condition involved intervals similar to those of the eight-card condition of Experiment 1. In addition, we wanted to determine whether the effect of the cue might depend upon the distance of the dates from the initial instructions. Thus, in a third condition, (c) the first date was approximately two weeks after the initial instructions. For each of these three conditions, half the subjects received tags and the other half did not.

Method

The subjects were 44 students (22 males, 22 females) from the psychology subject pool. The procedures were similar to those of Experiment 1, but there was no assessment of remembering abilities and no test of retrospective remembering.

Results

Cooperation.   Fifty-nine percent of the subjects reported on the questionnaire that they always did their best; thirty-four percent often, and seven percent sometimes did their best. Ninety-nine percent of the cards were returned, and 76 percent were mailed on the specified dates. All but three of the subjects in the tag condition kept the tags on throughout the experiment; two of these three gave as a reason the disintegration of the tags in their pockets.

Remembering.   The long-interval, short-interval, and delayed short interval conditions were compared in a $3 \times 2 \times 2 \times 4$ (Conditions $\times$ Tag vs. No tag $\times$ Sex $\times$ Dates) analysis of variance. There were no significant interactions involving conditions and tags. Remembering was greater on earlier dates than on later dates, $F(3,96) = 2.72, p < .05$.

A separate $2 \times 2 \times 4$ (Tag vs. No tag $\times$ Sex $\times$ Dates) analysis of variance[1] for scores in the long-interval condition (similar to the four-card

---

[1]The separate analysis of variance was carried out in order to determine, independently of the data contributed by the two new conditions, whether or not the facilitation by cues in the four-card condition would be replicated in the identical long-interval condition. In addition, the separate analysis was considered more appropriate than the overall analysis, due to a large heterogeneity of variance in Experiment 2, $F_{max}(6,7) = 10.72, p < .01$.

condition in Experiment 1) revealed a significant effect of tags, F (1,12) = 7.68, p < .05. A greater percentage of cards was mailed on time in the tag condition (81 percent) than in the no-tag condition (70 percent), but this effect was not limited to the later dates as in Experiment 1 (see Table 32-1).

The results of the follow-up questionnaire asking what was done to facilitate remembering can be summarized for both experiments. Eighty-eight percent of the subjects were able to report a means of facilitating remembering in addition to the use of the tags. Many of the subjects (32 percent) reported relying upon the calendar to indicate the dates on which the cards were to be mailed; a greater proportion (52 percent) placed the remaining cards in a place that was frequently looked at, such as a bulletin board or dresser top. Only two subjects reported cognitive activities: "I read the list of dates a few times and when the date came I checked to make sure it was one of the dates and mailed the card"; "I made a mental note of what date and day in the next week I had to send another card."

Discussion

These two experiments suggest at a marginally significant level (p < .05) that an aribitrary external retrieval cue such as a tag on a key chain or perhaps a string tied around the finger can facilitate episodic prospective remembering. The reason for the discrepancy between the two experiments—in Experiment 1 the effect held for only the later dates, while in Experiment 2 the effect held for all four dates—is not clear, although it can be noted that it is for only the second date in the four-card condition of Experiment 1 that the data are incongruous (see Table 32-1). Experiment 2 was carried out in part to determine whether the effectiveness of tags was dependent upon either short series of cards or long intervals between dates. The finding of a facilitative effect for tags in the long-interval condition, coupled with the lack of effect in the two short-interval conditions of Experiment 2, suggests that external retrieval cues can be most important when the actions to be remembered do not follow closely upon one another. The effectiveness of such an arbitrary mnemonic as a string around the finger may lie in its ability to remind us from time to time that there is something which we ought to be remembering, and at those times a search is initiated to discover what that something might be. A further possibility, perhaps more reasonable in the present case, is that a specific association is formed between the arbitrary retrieval cue and the action which must be remembered.

The reported reliance on external retrieval cues, such as checking calendars or leaving the cards in an often observed location, rather than strictly cognitive mnemonic activities, is consistent with the interview data obtained by Kreutzer et al. (1975) [see Selection 34]. Indeed, such means were no doubt employed because they were more effective for this particular memory task than was the tag which was provided; this is reflected in the high proportion of cards mailed on time in both the tag and the no-tag conditions. The means that were employed can be interpreted as attempts to convert what was intended to be an episodic remembering task into an habitual remembering task—i.e., the calendar or the bulletin board was to be checked routinely once a day.[2]

The procedures employed were found to be workable and to elicit reasonable cooperation from the subjects. The procedures were chosen so as to have considerable ecological validity, although it should be noted that ordinarily one is faced with the task of having to prospectively remember to engage in many different activities at various times rather than the same activity on different occasions. The procedures may appear unusual in that very little control is exercised over the subjects' behavior and motivation; for example, it is apparant that a subject might remember at the appropriate time to mail the card but simply not care to do so. This problem exists, of course, in studies of retrospective remembering as well (the subject may remember the items in a list but not report them to the experimenter), but in this study the precaution was taken of obtaining reports of efforts to cooperate, and cooperation was found to be high. Anecdotal evidence supports this: one subject wrote on the back of her postcard that she had run from the dormitory at 11:55 P.M. in order to mail the card on the appropriate day. Of course, motivation is assumed to not interact with experimental conditions.

REFERENCES

Atkinson, J. W., and Birch, D. The Dynamics of Action. New York: Wiley, 1970.
Flavell, J. H. Developmental studies of mediated memory. In H. W. Reese and
    L. P. Lipsitt (eds.), Advances in Child Development and Behavior (Vol. 5).
    New York: Academic Press, 1970.

---

[2]Meacham and Dumitru (1976) have found that five-year-olds do not take advantage of external retrieval cues to facilitate their prospective remembering, at least when the task is to remember for seven minutes to obtain an envelope. These children and seven-year-olds were able to choose an appropriate mnemonic cue for future action.

Flavell, J. H., Friedrichs, A. G., and Hoyt, J. D. "Developmental changes in memorization processes. *Cognitive Psychology*, 1970, *1*, 324–340.

Kreutzer, M. A., Leonard, C., and Flavell, J. H. "An interview study of children's knowledge about memory. *Monographs of the Society for Research in Child Development*, 1975, *40*, 1, Serial No. 159.

Meacham, J. A. "The development of memory abilities in the individual and society. *Human Development*, 1972, *15*, 205–228.

Meacham, J. A., and Dumitru, J. Prospective remembering and external retrieval cues. *JSAS Catalog of Selected Documents in Psychology*, 1976, *6*, 65 (ms. No. 1284).

Munsat, S. *The Concept of Memory*. New York: Random House, 1966.

33 External Memory Aids

John E. Harris

*Psychologists are familiar with mnemonic devices—
techniques for improving memory. In this selection
Harris argues that the "internal" devices most often
studied (the famous "method of loci," for example)
see very little use in everyday life. His subjects relied
much more on what he calls "external memory aids":
shopping lists, timers, notebooks, calendars. I do, too;
doesn't everyone?*

*The issues here are subtler than they seem at first.
Future research in this area will have to make finer
distinctions; in particular, to distinguish between
prospective and retrospective memory as they are
defined in Selection 32. All the external aids
mentioned in Harris' questionnaire dealt with
prospective remembering, whereas almost all his
internal aids were retrospective. This confounding is
not inevitable: There are also external aids to
retrospective memory (for example, photographs,
lecture notes) and internal aids to prospective
remembering (for example, mentally rehearsing the
items one intends to buy). Would Harris have
obtained the same results if such "aids" had been
included in his inquiry? I am inclined to think so.
External aids are probably perceived as more
dependable than internal ones; for this reason they
may be preferred in any situation where the need to
avoid forgetting is paramount.*

From M. M. Gruneberg, P. E. Morris, and R. N. Sykes (eds.), *Practical Aspects of Memory*. London: Academic Press, 1978. Copyright by Academic Press Inc. (London) Ltd. Reprinted by permission.

When I recently became interested in methods of aiding memory, I found that most of the psychological investigation was concerned with what may be called *internal aids*. Typical experiments (e.g., Bower and Clark, 1969) compared the performance of two groups of subjects at a memory task, where one group is given a hint as to how to perform the task, for example, "In order to remember these words, make up a story connecting them," while the other group is given no hints as to how to remember the words.

While internal memory aids of this type have attracted most attention from experimental psychologists, it is worth considering just how widely and how often they are used in comparison with such common external aids as diaries, memos, and shopping lists.

This was investigated in a study in which I interviewed 30 students at Southampton University. The interview included questions about which memory aids the students used and how often. Each memory aid I asked about was described in sufficient detail to ensure that the student would recognize any aid he or she might use.

The external aids I asked about were (a) shopping lists, (b) diaries, (c) writing on the hand, (d) alarm clocks, watches and timers—three questions on different uses, (e) writing paper memos to oneself, (f) writing on or marking calendars, year planners, etc., (g) asking someone else to give a reminder, and (h) leaving something in a special place where it will be encountered at the time it needs to be remembered. I also asked whether the students used any other external aids and gave as examples knotted handkerchiefs, changing rings to unfamiliar positions on fingers, and turning wristwatches to underside of wrist.

As far as internal aids were concerned, it was more difficult to know what to include. Some schemes, such as that which leads to clustering in free recall of categorized lists, appear to be widely used, to be effective, and psychologists have studied their results. However, such schemes represent normal memory operations and are not usually referred to as "mnemonics" or "memory aids." they are also automatic in the sense that they are not taught and that in many instances the user is probably not aware of using them. At the other extreme there are the techniques which often have to be consciously learned and used, such as the "peg" and "loci" methods. Indeed it is probably the time and effort involved in learning and employing this type of aid which limits the amount they are used. Unfortunately, there seems to be no clear cut-off point between these internal memory aids and what one might call normal remembering schemes.

Therefore, the way I chose which internal aids to ask about was by including those which I had come across in the memory aid literature as having been investigated, plus some others which were merely mentioned. Those chosen were (a) first letter mnemonics, (b) rhymes,

(c) the method of loci, (d) the story method, (e) mentally retracing a sequence of events or actions, (f) the peg method, (g) turning numbers into letters, (h) face–name association, and (i) searching through the alphabet to find the initial letter of a forgotten name or word. With the exception of (g), these are all described by Morris (1977). In addition the students were asked if they used any other method of committing things to memory or for retrieving them from memory.

The students rated how often they had used these aids, both external and internal, on a seven-point scale which is given in the lower part of Figure 33-1. The points on the scale may appear to be strange choices. However, I needed to use the same scale for all the aids whether they were hardly ever or very frequently used, and an alternative scale I had used in a pilot questionnaire had proved inadequate.

The bar charts in Figure 33-1 show the reported frequencies of use of some of the memory aids. The abcissa represents the level of use of a memory aid, while the ordinate represents the number of students, out of a total of 30 who claimed to use it at a particular level. The top row shows the eight reportedly most used external aids, and the bottom row shows the equivalent internal aids. Both rows have the more frequently used aids on the left, though the categories used and distributions found do not allow perfect ordering.

The most apparent observation is how few of the internal aids are reported to be in frequent use, despite the fact that one might expect students to be among the most frequent users of these mnemonics.

Interestingly, the two internal aids reported to be most used, mental retracing of events or actions and alphabetical searching, are rather different from the rest of the internal aids in the study. They are both pure *retrieval* strategies, in that no special encoding effort needs to have been made in order to use them. The other internal aids I asked about provide schemes for *encoding* or *learning*. It is mainly these which have been investigated and yet they are seldom used.

A comparable though more extreme pattern emerged from a similar study of 30 female members of the Cambridge Applied Psychology Unit subject panel, whose mean age was 46 years, (against a mean of 21 years for the student sample), and consisted mainly of housewives some having part-time jobs. The main difference was far greater reported use of certain external aids by this group, particularly of diaries and writing on calendars/year planners.

Before concluding this section on frequency of use, some additional points should be made. First, investigators of internal mnemonics would not necessarily claim that they are investigating frequently used aids. For example, Morris (1977) admits that even he, with his

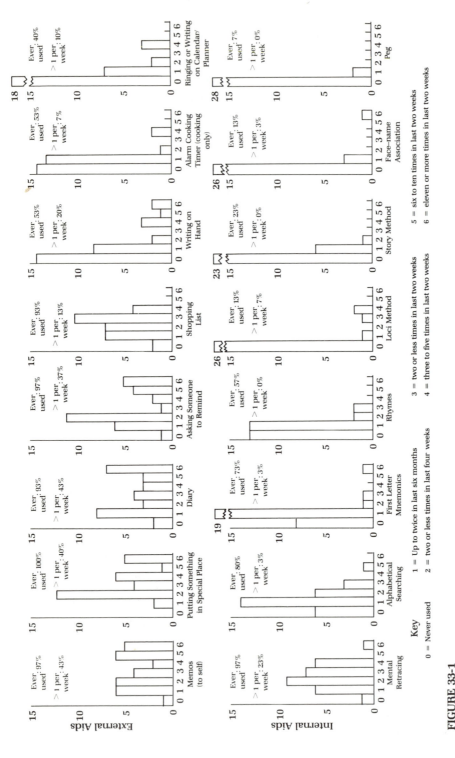

FIGURE 33-1

Reported frequency of use of memory aids by students ($N = 30$). The vertical scale is the number of students in each frequency category.

unusual knowledge of these techniques, makes little use of them in everyday life. There may also be theoretical rather than practical reasons to find out which of them are effective in the laboratory.

Second, some memory aids may be considered important in that they are used on a high proportion of possible occasions, even when the rarity of such possible occasions keeps the absolute frequency of use at a low level.

Third, both the interview studies described in this section were performed with samples from mainly middle-class, high-ability populations. A less-privileged sample might be expected to use less memory aids, both internal and external. Different occupations and living conditions produce varying memory loads as well as different types of memory problems, possibly calling for the use of different aids. While these considerations limit what generalizations can be made from the data presented above to other groups, it is not unreasonable to assume that students' use of internal memory aids is, at least, above average in frequency.

Fourth, mention should be made of the possible divergence between reported frequency of use and actual frequency of use. There does not seem to be much in the memory literature that suggests what this relationship might be. Flavell and Wellman (1977) differentiate four categories of memory phenomena, one of which is *metamemory*. Metamemory refers to an "individual's knowledge of and awareness of memory, or of anything pertinent to information storage and retrieval" (p. 4). From their review it seems that the metamemory literature is developmentally orientated and does not contain a great deal of information about the knowledge of adults about their memories and the way they use them, let alone the aids they use. What information is given appears optimistic, for example, "It seems to us that the adults ... demonstrated an impressive amount of metamemory. They could predict their memory spans accurately; they were sensibly uncertain about their ability to predict them, in view of the novelty of the task situation; they believed that information about peers' performance on a novel memory task might provide a useful clue" (p. 12).

On the other hand Wilkins and Baddeley (1978) have found that when people forgot to push a button, which they had been instructed to push at four specific times each day, they often failed to record this forgetting, though they had been instructed to make a note of it when they realized they had forgotten.

Certainly (from my own questionnaire and interview studies), people appear to have difficulty in *recalling* (without being prompted by examples) what memory aids they use. However, once a particular aid is mentioned, and if necessary described in detail, my interviewees seemed quite ready to tell me how often they had used them, it sometimes being difficult to stop the flow of examples this elicited! The three open-ended questions about any other external and internal aids which they had used, but about which there had been no specific question, produced disappointing results. This is the basis for the above claim that people have difficulty in unprompted recall of the aids they use. This conclusion is dramatically confirmed by data from a later part of the interview (not so far reported here), from which it was apparent that the Cambridge subjects made extensive use of address books, telephone number books, and birthday books. These were rarely mentioned in response to the earlier open-ended questions.

While these were all external aids, there were also indications that there may be internal aids which are more used than those specifically mentioned in the interview. For example, two Cambridge subjects mentioned internal mnemonics used when shopping without a written list. One of these aids was to remember the total number of items to be bought as well as what they are. This ensures that one does not terminate the shopping trip too early leaving some items unbought, and also allows one to make a confident decision to go home when the right number of items has been bought. The second shopping mnemonic is a pure retrieval one. It consists of imagining the contents of the bread-bin, the larder, the fridge, etc. as last seen, in order to remember how empty they were. This can then be used as a basis for what needs buying. It is clearly related to the method of loci, though that involves encoding by imagining things in places where they have never been and so is not a pure retrieval method.

. . .

REFERENCES

Bower, G. H., and Clark, M. C. Narrative stories as mediators for serial learning. *Psychonomic Science*, 1969 *14*, 181–182.

Flavell, J. H., and Wellman, H. M. Metamemory. In R. V. Kail and J. W. Hagen (eds.), *Perspectives on the Development of Memory and Cognition*. Hillsdale, N. J.: Erlbaum, 1977, pp. 3–33.

Morris, P. E., Practical strategies for human learning and remembering. In M. J. A. Howe (ed.), *Human Learning*. London: Wiley, 1977, pp. 125–144.

Wilkins, A. J., and Baddeley, A. D. Remembering to recall in everyday life: An approach to absentmindedness. In M. M. Gruneberg, P. E. Morris, and R. N. Sykes (eds.), *Practical Aspects of Memory*. London: Academic Press, 1978, pp. 27–34.

34 Prospective Remembering in Children

Mary Anne Kreutzer, Sister Catherine Leonard, and John H. Flavell

This selection is from the interview study of children's memory mentioned in Selection 1. Taken as a whole, the study showed that young children already know a good deal about memory—or to put it another way, they already "have" a good deal of "metamemory." In particular, they already know many of the principles taught in psychology courses. This selection shows that they also know something else: how to use external memory aids to improve prospective remembering. Even kindergarteners can generally think of something to help them remember to bring their skates to school, and fifth-graders have a wide variety of mnemonic devices at their disposal.

[*The data presented here were collected as responses to the following interview question: "Suppose you were going ice skating with your friend after school tomorrow and you wanted to be sure to bring your skates. How could you be really certain that you didn't forget to bring your skates along to school in the morning? Can you think of anything else?*

From M. A. Kreutzer, C. Leonard, and J. H. Flavell, An interview study of children's knowledge about memory, *Monographs of the Society for Research in Child Development*, 1975, 40 (1). Copyright © 1975 by the University of Chicago. Reprinted by permission.

How many ways can you think of?" (In the rare cases when S said he didn't skate, E posed a formally equivalent problem involving a different object, e.g., a ball.)]

Unlike the case in most previous items, the child was encouraged here to give multiple answers to a single question ("How many ways could you think of, etc."). If the child failed to produce any relevant, substantive answers at all, he was scored as None. If he produced one or more appropriate answers, each answer was scored according to a three-level hierarchical system consisting of categories, subcategories, and minimally distinguishable responses. Finally, the response protocol as a whole was scored for the presence or absence of something called Preparation.

The three-level scoring system operated as follows. The judge first identified the total number of *responses* that were at least minimally different or barely distinguishable from one another. For example, if a child said he would ask his mother to remind him to bring his skates, and also suggested getting his skating companion to telephone him for the same reason, he was credited with two responses by this criterion of minimal difference. Each response was then assigned to one of four major *categories* (Skates, Note, Self, or Others) and also, except in the case of Others, to one or another *subcategory* of that category. There were four Skates subcategories, three Note subcategories, two Self subcategories, and one Others subcategory (i.e., it was identical to the category itself).

The Skates category referred to any proposed manipulation of the skates themselves that would help ensure their availability at skating time; in many cases this was accomplished by making the skates serve as their own retrieval cue. The subcategories of this category and their total frequencies of occurrence in the sample were: (1) putting the skates in the child's school bag or next to the things he plans to take to school (25 Ss), (2) putting the skates where he is sure to see them the next morning (29 Ss), (3) getting the skates to school or to his friend's house prior to the following morning (two third-graders), (4) attaching the skates to his body (one first-grader and one third-grader).

A Response was categorized as Note if the child suggested using any external retrieval cue other than the skates themselves. The subcategories were: (1) any form of written reminder (32 Ss), (2) tying a string around one's finger (two third-graders and four fifth-graders), (3) the use of a tape recorder (two first-graders).

There were two rather different ways in which the Self was represented as a mnemonic aid: (1) through active, internal efforts to facilitate recall, for example, deliberately thinking about the skates the night before, mentally checking off the next morning everything one is supposed to bring to school (11 Ss); (2) assertions that the excitement and pleasure associated with the prospect of going skating will almost automatically guarantee recall of the skates the next morning (three third-graders).

The category Others was scored whenever the child suggested that one or more other people could be asked to help him remember his skates (19 Ss).

These four categories and their subcategories illustrate the variety of preparation-for-retrieval resources or loci that may be available to an individual in many real-life mnemonic situations: inner-mental-symbolic (Self), outer-mental-symbolic (Others), outer-physical-symbolic (Note), outer-physical-nonsymbolic (Skates).

Some responses seemed more explicitly preparatory, planful, and means-ends-oriented in tone than others. In most such responses, there were at least hints of a conscious separation in time between the act of preparation and its subsequent payoff in good recall. The child might specify that he would put the skates in his bag "that night," for example, rather than simply saying he would put them in his bag. Or he might say that he would put the skates by the door "so that" ("and then," etc.) he would be sure to see them in the morning. Protocols which seemed to contain such putative symptoms of a planful, means-ends orientation were scored as Preparation. Interjudge agreement on presence-absence of Preparation was 85 percent. It was 90 percent in the case of total number of distinguishable responses per protocol, and 100 percent for assignment of responses to subcategories and categories.

Table 34-1 shows the numbers of Ss at each grade level who produced one or more instances of each major category. More Ss gave Skates responses than any other type, with Note strategies constituting a close second. Considerably fewer Ss produced Others responses, and fewer still gave Self answers. Although undoubtedly due in part to the specific nature of this preparation task, it is nonetheless striking to see how frequently Ss of all ages thought of relying on something other than their own internal memory processes (Self) to achieve their mnemonic objective. They seemed to sense that several heads (Other) are better than one and also that properly placed external retrieval cues (Skates, Note) are more certain than internal ones to be available when needed.

There appears to have been no very pronounced age trend in the tendency to think of one versus another of these four categories, either initially (N's in parentheses in Table 34-1) or eventually. There is, however, a developmental increase in the number of protocols showing Preparation (Prep.): combining adjacent age groups $\chi^2(1) = 20.01$,

TABLE 34-1

Preparation: Object (*N* Ss producing one or more responses in each category)

Grade	Category					
	Skates	Note	Others	Self	None	Prep.
K	8 (.58)	4 (.25)	3 (.17)	1 (.00)	8	3
1	7 (.33)	9 (.45)	3 (.17)	3 (.05)	2	7
3	13 (.55)	12 (.35)	5 (.05)	5 (.05)	0	14
5	15 (.40)	11 (.30)	8 (.20)	5 (.10)	0	17
Total ...	43	36	19	14	10	41

Note: N's in parentheses = proportions of *first* responses at each grade level scored under the category in question. (None answers were excluded from consideration.) E.g., of the twelve K Ss who produced one or more substantive responses, seven or 58% of their first responses were scored as Skates.

$p < .001$. Older Ss' strategies thus seem to be more clearly and explicitly planful and means-ends-oriented than younger Ss' strategies. There is also an age increase in the sheer number and variety of Preparation methods described, as Table 34-2 shows. The older children exceeded the younger ones in the numbers of minimally different responses, subcategorically different responses, and categorically different responses they produced. Combining adjacent age groups and using 0–1 versus 2 or more (2 +) answers as the second partition, the χ^2s(1) are 26.72, $p < .001$, for responses; 24.22, $p < .001$, for subcategories; and 19.61, $p < .001$, for categories. The older Ss thus proved to be considerably more knowledgeable and/or inventive than the younger ones in generating effective-looking methods of facilitating the future recall of an object (Table 34-2) even though few of their methods seem to have been wholly inaccessible to the younger groups (Table 34-1). It is more than possible, of course, that the Note category was depressed in the K and perhaps grade 1 groups because of poor or nonexistent writing skills. Instances of it did occur, nonetheless, and were in fact the modal response type at grade 1.

As with most other items, a few of the children performed some very quotable feats of metamemory. For example, E's initial question sufficed to elicit all this from one third-grade girl:

> I could put them in my book bag, or set them on the table. Or I could always write myself a note, and put it up on my bulletin board. Or I could tell my mom to remind me. Or I could take them to school the day before and just leave them there.

TABLE 34-2

Preparation: Object (performance data at the three levels of responses, subcategories, and categories)

Grade	Responses						Subcategories				Categories			
	0	1+	2+	3+	4+	Mean	2+	3+	4+	Mean	2+	3+	4+	Mean
K ··········	8	12	5	0	0	0.85	4	0	0	0.80	4	0	0	0.80
1 ··········	2	18	5	3	1	1.40	4	2	0	1.20	4	0	0	1.10
3 ··········	0	20	15	8	3	2.45	14	6	3	2.15	10	5	0	1.75
5 ··········	0	20	19	13	6	2.95	17	8	2	2.35	4	5	0	†1.95

Note: Col. headings = *N* Ss who produced 1 or more (1 +), 2 or more (2 +), etc. answers at the level of scoring (Responses, Subcategories, Categories) indicated. The 0 and 1+ cols. for Subcategories and Categories would, if shown, be necessarily identical to those for Responses.

This fifth-grade boy seemed to know quite a bit about the frequent interplay between perception, attention, and memory in everyday recall situations:

> Write a note, and stick it in my pocket. Cause usually when I sit down, I don't usually have a piece of paper, then I usually look in my back pockets. And then I'd go to bed, then I'd read the note, then it would be laying right there on my dresser when I got up in the morning. I'd wonder what the piece of paper was, then I'd read it. (Two other, less quotable strategies followed.)

Finally, one kindergartner simply said, "I would forget!" which is also a genuine instance of metamemory.

35 The Development of Voluntary Memory in Children of Preschool Age

Z. M. Istomina

In natural contexts, prospective memory is closely linked to action. There is only a small step from remembering to do something to actually doing it. In young children, there may be no step at all. They have the opposite problem: to distinguish mnemonic activities from the overall rush of their lives, so they can carry out those activities successfully. Istomina's aim in this selection is to understand how memory becomes "voluntary" in that sense—that is, how children gradually come to see it as a separate process in its own right, with its own prospects of success and failure.

The younger subjects of this study are strikingly less sophisticated than the cool kindergarteners of Selection 34. Far from being able to remind themselves of things to be done the next day, they don't even seem to realize that remembering can be a problem. At least, their behavior gives no hint that they do. Istomina's account of the development of that insight between the ages of three and seven is charming as well as convincing. By age seven, "metamemory" seems to be firmly in place. The children know how to memorize as well as how to

From *Soviet Psychology*, 1975, *13* (4). Copyright © 1975 by International Arts and Sciences Press, Inc. Reprinted by permission of M. E. Sharpe, Inc.

> *retrieve, and they execute both processes with*
> *practiced skill. But at all ages, even the most*
> *knowledgeable age, performance on laboratory*
> *memory tests is markedly poorer than in the more*
> *natural kindergarten setting.*

. . .

We have assumed that, initially, in early infancy and during the pre-school age period, memory processes (recall, retention) are not inde-pendent processes, but are integrated into some other activity and are involuntary. Later, specifically during the intermediate school age, these processes are transformed into specific mental acts, i.e., they become cognitive, purposeful, and voluntary.

In other words, we have assumed that the emergence of voluntary memory from earlier forms takes place as a result of the differentiation of a specific type of act, the purpose of which is to remember or recall something from among the child's overall activity. Consequently, this transformation requires, first, that there be mechanisms capable of making such mnemonic goals meaningful. Second, it requires that these goals have some concrete reality, i.e., that remembering be con-scious and intentional and that the operations of remembering and recall themselves be discrete, conscious acts. Third and last, this hypothesis requires that a child have at his disposal some means for carrying out the voluntary acts of retention and recall. These acts do not, of course, suddenly emerge in the child in fully developed form, but are constituted gradually, taking on different forms depending on the specific features of the factors described above.

These, then, are the general postulates constituting the initial hypothesis on which the present study was based. The particular objectives of our study were: (1) to determine the conditions under which a child first is able to differentiate the discrete goals of "remem-bering" and "recalling"; (2) to determine the forms in which the acts of retention and recall first occur and to ascertain the means and techniques (memory operations) by which they are effected.

We worked out a method appropriate to these hypotheses and to the goals of the study. On the assumption that the development of retention and recall as internal, purposeful acts takes place initially as part of a broader, articulated, and meaningful activity (since it is only within the context of such activity that the specific acts of remembering and recall can have any meaning for a child), our first step was to insert these operations of retention and recall into some activity with which the child was intimately familiar; secondly, we tried to organize this activity as far as possible in a way that would enable us to observe and quantitatively assess the processes under study.

Accordingly, in addition to a series of experiments carried out along the customary lines of a laboratory experiment with recall and memorization of meaningful words (these experiments were done as special "tasks" with the children), we also set up a game with roles. This game involved a specific, defined situation that created a motivation for remembering or recall, i.e., it created conditions that enabled the child to set the goals of remembering and recall for himself explicitly. For the main series of experiments we took two simple game themes similar to each other that are often found in the games preschool children customarily play: playing "store" and playing "kindergarten." These two games were combined into a single theme.

For playing "store" we gave the children the following items: a toy cash register and scale, sticks, sand, clay, small representational toys, paper, etc. For playing "kindergarten" we gave them a toy stove, a bowl, a doll, etc. In addition, we also prepared beforehand "admission slips" to the store with a list of "groceries" written on them. The purpose of these will become clear in what follows.

Six children were recruited to play the game at the same time. Three of these were given the roles of store employees (salesclerk, cashier, guard), and three were to play kindergarten (teacher, cook, director). The experimenter and his assistant were obliged to take part in the game. One of them assumed the role of store manager, and the other the role of kindergarten director.

The game was played in two adjoining rooms. One was equipped for playing kindergarten. At the beginning of the game, the experimenter addressed the children with the proposal: "Children, let's play together. Let's have a kindergarten." Then the roles were assigned and explained. The children arranged the dolls and the dolls' things, set up the stove, placed the dishes around, etc. The kindergarten began. The "teacher" organized the children to go for a walk, the "cook" began to prepare lunch, and the "director" did his jobs, i.e., distributed materials, brought firewood in a truck, etc.

At the same time, the other room was set up for playing store. The experimenter's assistant assumed the role of store manager and arranged with the children who was to be the salesclerk, who the cashier, and who the guard. The duties and tasks of each were defined, and the players began to arrange the store. Some goods were put on display in the window, and others were placed on the counter. The scale with its weights, bags, and wrapping paper were placed on the counter. The "cashier" got the receipts and money ready. Finally, all was ready, and the "manager" sent the "guard" into the kindergarten to announce that the store was open.

On hearing this announcement, the kindergarten leader invited one of the children to go on an errand to the store to buy some things for the kindergarten. The errand was always described in the same way: "Here's a permisison slip to go to the store, go and buy . . ." (then the leader would slowly and carefully name several items). The child would then be given the permission slip, money, and basket for the purchases.

In the store, the child showed his permission slip to the guard on request and went over to the manager. The manager took the shopper's permission slip and asked: "What have you been sent to buy?" The manager then listened to what the shopper told her and, at the same time, checked off on the permission slip the items named by the child, numbered them in order, and added any items named by the child but not on the list on the permission slip. If the child forgot any of the items, he was asked: "And what else?" Then the shopper paid his money to the cashier, obtained a receipt, went over to the sales clerk, who handed him his purchase, and returned to the kindergarten. He would then give his permission slip back to the experimenter (director of the kindergarten).

The game continued until all the children playing kindergarten had been in the store. Then the store manager announced that all his merchandise had been sold and the store was closed. This ended the game.

. . .

Simultaneously with the experiments described above, which we carried out in the form of a game, we also did some experiments more along the lines of classical psychology. The experimenter would call a child to him "for a lesson" and would ask him to listen attentively to the words and try to remember them, so that later the child could recount the words that had been read off to him. The words, which were analogous in meaning and difficulty to those presented for memorization in the game experiments, were named at 3-second intervals. After a slight pause (60–90 seconds), the child was asked to recall all the words he could. If he did not name the whole list, the experimenter would ask: "And what else were you to remember: What other words are still missing?" The records of the experiment were kept in the standard way.

These experiments differed sharply from the game experiments in one respect: memorization was motivated in a totally different manner, and the goal of retaining and recalling was set for the child by the experimenter, whereas in the game experiments the child had to set these goals for himself. In all other respects the two types of experiment were similar: in both, the task consisted of voluntary memorization and recall. The material to be remembered was both qualitatively and quantitatively the same (in both, the lists consisted of five items or, in another series, of eight words). In both cases, helping questions were asked; and, finally, in both, time was ordered in the same way (the interval between the words read off, the time elapsed between the naming of the last word on the list and the beginning of recall).

. . .

Our first task was to study the memory efficiency of children in different situations presenting motivations for retention and recall, namely, the direct request of an experimenter versus playing a role in a game. The experiments set up to study this problem constituted the first series in our investigation, and were carried out in accordance with the procedure described above. There were 60 subjects, ranging in age from 3–7 years (15 subjects in each age group: 3–4, 4–5, 5–6, 6–7).

. . .

Retention improved notably with age. For children three to four years old, the average number of words remembered under the standard laboratory conditions was 0.6, i.e., some children did not remember a single word of the five presented, and others remembered only one. This figure increases in the four-to-five-year-old group to 1.5 words, in the five-to-six-year-old group to 2.0 words, and in the six-to-seven-year-olds, 2.3 words.

. . .

What stands out in our results as well as in those of other investigators are the exceedingly low retention indices for the youngest group. We cannot imagine that the word retention of these youngsters can be so poor. Indeed, young children have very good memories; our day-to-day observations and systematic investigations carried out by child specialists give ample evidence of this. It has, in fact, been shown that young children frequently are able to recall very accurately words they have heard after a relatively long period of time has passed, easily remember the details of a situation, and learn long poems by heart, sometimes even without understanding their content. Consequently, there had to be certain special circumstances peculiar to our experiments that were responsible for this poor showing, despite the fact that the task presented to the children was clear and the material to be remembered was within their grasp.

A closer scrutiny of the facts revealed what was at the root of this situation. To anticipate a little, we can say that the extremely low retention scores of three-to-four year-olds were not due to the fact that their mnemonic capacities were, in general, still poorly developed but to the fact that they were as yet unable to memorize and recall deliberately and voluntarily. In other words, the appropriate, purposeful, internal acts—the acts necessary for voluntary memorization and recall—had not yet formed in them. Hence, when a child was given the task of memorizing or recalling something that had no intrinsic relation to what he was doing, to his immediate situation, and to his active desires, he was unable to cope with that task. This seems also to explain the age differences noted in the number of mistakes made of the type in which the child answered with words *that had not been given him*. The number of such words was relatively high in three-year-old children, 11 in all, and thereafter decreased sharply; in four-year-olds there were only 6 such cases, and there were none among five- and six-year-olds. Such mistakes are instructive in that they indicate the nonvoluntary nature of memory.

. . .

The picture becomes clearer if we look at those cases in which we gave the same words or words that were very similar with respect to the psychological difficulty involved in remembering them, but instead of simply asking the child to remember what we would read off to him, we made this task a part of a larger activity meaningful to him, i.e., we "played kindergarten" or "store," as described above.

Our play experiments were run on the same 60 children who participated in the word-recall "assignment," i.e., a standard laboratory memory test.

It was impossible for us not to notice how natural and lively the children were when they took part in the game experiments. We found out that the children would later frequently play the game again among themselves.

[*The quantitative results of both experiments are presented in Table 35-1, adapted from Istomina's Tables 1 and 2.*]

TABLE 35-1
Mean number of words recalled by children of different ages in two
conditions. There are fifteen subjects in each age group.

Age of subjects	Recall in "laboratory" experiment	Recall in play experiment
3–4 years	0.6	1
4–5 years	1.5	3
5–6 years	2.0	3.2
6–7 years	2.3	3.8

Even the most superficial glance at the data in [Table 35-1] reveals
that retention improves much more notably with age in the make-
believe situation than in the pure test situation.

. . .

One striking finding is that, whereas three-year-olds remembered
correctly only one word, on the average, and made the largest number
of mistakes (six), the four-year-olds showed a much better performance: they remembered three words of five, on the average, and made
no mistakes. The older children performed even better.

Comparing the quantitative data obtained in the laboratory test
situation and in the game experiments we find that performance was
much better in the latter case, especially in four-year-olds (almost twice
as good).

. . .

A possible hypothesis is that the poorer performance in the laboratory tests is due to the fact that the external situation was somewhat
unfamiliar to the children, whereas the play situation was more natural. However, this hypothesis is not borne out by the facts. The children, who knew the experimenter well and who like very much to do
things with her, behaved quite freely in the laboratory test situation
and, of course, least of all did they feel that they were test "subjects."
For them, the situation was just like any other in which they had to do
with adults; their incentive to express themselves was no different from
usual, and they had no particular difficulty in coping with the requirements imposed upon them by the task. Psychologically, the really distinctive feature of this test situation was that the task presented to the
child, namely, to memorize words, did not flow intrinsically from the

nature of the situation itself, but was imposed externally, as it were, by the adults. On the other hand, in the game situation, the external conditions were in fact not very favorable for remembering, since they contained many distracting factors. Thus, the difference in memory performances in the two types of experiments must be sought in internal conditions, in the particulars of the child's active involvement rather than in external conditions. This difference also appears when we make a qualitative analysis of the data obtained.

. . .

Let us first look at how our youngest subjects behaved. The most typical feature of their memory behavior in the play situation was that when a child was asked to go to the store, it was by no means always the case that he would immediately see the purpose of remembering and recalling what he had to do there.

This, as the experiments show, is explained by the fact that the youngest children assumed the role of shopper but did not perceive what that role entailed. For them, the role of shopper consisted only of its outward aspects, i.e., to go the store, to carry home groceries, etc. Its internal aspect, which was the meaning of the errand, still escaped their grasp. Hence, they would often run to the store only barely having listened to what they were to do there, and sometimes not even wait for the experimenter to finish explaining it. Let us take some examples.

Valerik S. (three years, five months):
The children are playing boisterously in the "kindergarten."
"Valerik," says the experimenter, "you're our cook. What are you going to prepare for lunch today?"
Valerik answers: "I don't know."
"Well then," say the experimenter, "the children are coming back from a walk and there is nothing to eat. (Valerik smiles and gazes questioningly at the experimenter.) Here is an entry permit to the store. Go and buy . . . " (she then names the items).
Valerik, obviously pleased with the proposition, turns his head immediately toward the store and takes the basket. "O.K.," he says, and runs off without waiting to hear the experimenter's last words.
In the store Valerik inspects all the wares on display with great curiosity. When the store manager (experimenter's assistant) asks him, "What have you been told to buy?" Valerik nods his head toward the toys and then says: "Candy."
"And what else?" asks the manager.
Valerik begins to glance about nervously and frowns. Then the playing children catch his eye.

"Can I be the sales clerk?" he asks. But after being refused, Valerik still doesn't want to return to the kindergarten (Record No. 11).

. . .

Lyuba M. (three years, ten months):
In the game, Lyuba played the role of teacher and put the dolls to sleep.

"Lyuba," says the experimenter, "when the children are asleep you can do an errand and go the store."

Lyuba immediately jumps up and runs up to the experimenter saying: "What should I buy?" She listens to the instructions silently, nodding her head affirmatively. In the store she speaks somewhat confusedly: "Uh, I need, . . . give me . . . uh . . . " she stammers pointing her finger at a plate of tomatoes.

"What?" asks the store manager.

"Berries and chocolate," she says hesitantly.

All the while she has been watching the cashier with interest. "Can I stay here and play?" she asks; but the experimenter reminds her that they are waiting for her and her purchases in the kindergarten and that she therefore has to go back (Record No. 8).

These records show that when a three-year-old takes on a task of going to the store he will not necessarily clearly grasp the goal of remembering the message so that he can pass it on correctly. To use the words of one psychologist, "A child's memory does not yet run on a return ticket." When he listens to something said to him, a child does not note that he may eventually have to have recourse in the future to what has been said. His memory does not yet have a specific direction; it has not yet become an internal activity.

We may ask why the three-year-olds were not yet able to grasp the purpose of remembering, although it was certainly directly a part of the game. This may be explained by the fact that for the youngest children the role in the game as they conceive it does not consist of transmitting a verbal message, but of the outward actions of running to the store, bringing back groceries, etc. Thus, the role as they see it does not contain a reason for remembering or anything that could explain or make the child conscious of its purpose. The purpose remains externally defined and understood, but it is not internalized by the child. Hence, despite all the differences in the remembering situation between the laboratory experiments and the make-believe experiments, they were essentially alike psychologically for children of this age. In both cases, retention and recall have a purpose (different in each case), but for the child these purposes are imposed from without. He does not find them by himself; rather, they are interjected by an adult in the form of an assignment. But to develop the new type of act, the child himself must be able consciously to pose the goal. This necessity for a child to discover the meaning of a task on his own crops up in other developmental studies. We shall have more to say on this later, however.

Our older subjects showed behavior in the game experiments that was different from that just described. If we look at the experimental records for four-year-olds, we are unable at first glance to find any explanation for the sharp increase in their retention scores. The explanations they give and the very process of receiving and transmitting the message are still very similar to the behavior exhibited by three-year-olds. However, if we look more closely at their behavior, we find certain distinctive features that, as a rule, are not found in the younger children.

In the game, these children also grasped the inner content of the role; they actually made an effort to remember and carry out the errand, although for most of them the act of remembering was not initially yet differentiated as a discrete process. Consequently, while they listened to the instructions in a different manner from the youngest children, they still manifested no kind of activity specifically directed toward remembering it, and in transmitting the message they made no attempt to recall what they had forgotten. Here are some extracts from the records of the game with children of this age group.

Igor K. (four years, seven months) prepares the children to go for a walk. "Igor, can you first go to the store?" asks the experimenter.

Igor stops what he is doing with the dolls. He listens to the instructions patiently, attentively looking at the experimenter with an air of importance; he then runs off, forgetting even to take the basket with him. "Give me noodles, a ball, butter, and that's all," he says quickly, giving his permission slip to the manager. "And hurry, because the children are hungry," he says (Record No. 17).

We see from this case that the child enters into the role differently from the way the three-year-olds do. He does not simply go to the store: he goes there to do something, to buy something and take it back to the kindergarten ("The children are hungry"). He acts within an articulated, make-believe situation, with specific, imagined circumstances. Hence, having shopped before, he listens to the message "as if it were real." But he hurries, not to perform the errand (we should recall that the youngest children often didn't even listen to the end), but to get to the store and get said what has to be said as quickly as possible. This characteristic is, moreover, hardly an exception at this age. Many children show a desire to get an errand done in a hurry, and won't be interrupted.

Hence, whereas in the youngest children not hearing the instructions through to the end was characteristic, another type of behavior was typical for this older group, namely, when an attempt was made to stop the child and talk to him on his way to the store, he frequently would not stop and tried to avoid answering questions. Thus, when we introduced the role of the guard, who had the responsibility of checking the entry slips into the store, shoppers of this age group usually tried to slip by him.

Here are some examples of behavior of this type.

Alik (four years, three months) listened to the instructions to the end, nodding his head after each word, and saying: "Uhuh." He recalled correctly two items on the list and when asked "What else do you have to buy?" he answered calmly: "Nothing else; we have everything" (Record No. 19).

Sasha S. (four years, ten months) listened to the errand attentively and seriously. "So we don't need meat," he noted after the list had been read off to him. In the store he recalled three of the items that had been read off to him, and when asked, "What else must you buy?" he called over to the kindergarten director, "K. A., is there anything else we need?" (Record No. 20).

Thus, these subjects also listened attentively to the experimenter to the end. They, too, tried to buy what they had been told, and their behavior in the store was governed by the purpose of the errand. In other words, they were able consciously to define for themselves transmitting the errand as a goal, and were even able to see it as a part of the game. However, does this mean that they also saw remembering as a specific, discrete goal, and that remembering and recall were differentiated for them as discrete acts? There is no evidence that this was so. On the contrary, if we compare the behavior of most of the children of this age with that of children five to six years old, we see that this was definitely not the case. In only a few four-year-olds were we able to observe evidence that specific mnemonic goals had been singled out, in that the behavior of these children always included acts specifically directed toward this end. Here are some cases of active efforts to remember in our four-year-old subjects.

Tima S. (four years, nine months) not only listened to the experimenter to the end but also repeated what had been said, and even asked the experimenter to repeat some of the words. Then in the store, in running down the list, he named three items correctly; and after an unsuccessful attempt to remember ("Let's see: there's something else. What is it?"), he confessed: "That's all. I forgot the rest" (Record No. 28).

Kolya K. (four years, six months) listened to the instructions, nodding his head after each item on the list; but when he repeated it in the store, he named two items correctly and then, shaking his head negatively, asked permission to return to the kindergarten to find out what else he had been told to buy (Record No. 26).

Borya I. (four years, ten months), repeated loudly after the experimenter each word, i.e., he already had a device for remembering (Record No. 21).

In each of these examples, there is no doubt that the objectives of remembering and recall were clear to the children; their behavior shows this quite well. However, such cases are exceptions at this age, and become the rule only in five- and six-year-olds.

Indeed, all our older subjects not only listened to the instructions but also made active attempts to remember them. Sometimes this showed up in the following behavior: they would move their lips, repeating the words to themselves, as they listened to the experimenter. When they transmitted the message, they did not merely blurt it out, but tried to recall what they had forgotten. The active nature of the mnemonic acts of these children is evident from the records.

Alochka A. (five years, two months) was busily engaged in preparing lunch, and several times reminded the experimenter that she needed salt. When it was her turn to go to the store, she asked, with a busy expression on her face: "Z. M., what should I buy? Salt?" The experimenter explained to her that this was not all and named four more items that were needed. Alochka listened attentively, nodding her head. She took the basket, the permission slip, and money and went off, but soon came back. "Z. M., I have to buy salt, milk, and what else?" she asked. "I forgot." The experimenter repeated the items. This time Alochka repeated each word after the experimenter in a whisper and, after saying confidently, "Now I know what I had forgotten," went off. In the store, she went up to the manager and, with a serious expression, correctly named four items, with slight pauses between each. "There is something else, but I forgot," she said (Record No. 31).

Serezha P. (five years, four months) listened attentively to the list and repeated each of the experimenter's words in a whisper. He recalled four items, but could not recall the fifth. He looked confusedly at the experimenter, and repeated the same words one more time. "There's something else I have to buy, but I've forgotten it," he said (Record No. 43).

Slava M. (five years, six months) listened silently as the list was read, looking at the experimenter tensely, and after a slight pause asked him to repeat the list one more time. He did not recall the list immediately, frowning, shrugging his shoulders, and saying: "Wait a minute, I'll get it, hold on . . . " (Record No. 7).

Dima F. (six years, six months) listened to the list, muttering silently, and then repeated it almost as if to himself. He quickly recalled three items, then paused, screwed up his eyes, and said, with concern: "Oh! What else was there? Nope, I can't remember what else I have to buy . . ." (Record No. 47).

These examples show quite clearly that the middle and oldest group of preschool-age children remember and recall for deliberate reasons and objectives, and that these functions are no longer governed by chance factors in the situation; the children use specific techniques to help them remember and recall.

This, then, is the dominant feature in the behavior of these children, i.e., the presence of a specific content and specific processes, which are subordinated to the goal of remembering and recalling the errand. Moreover, the further development of memory involves the expansion of these processes, i.e., the development of techniques for remembering and recall or, in other words, the development of the operations of voluntary memory.

Some of these techniques or operations can be discerned from our records. But first let us examine how memory operations develop.

The simplest memory device available to five-to-six-year-olds is the simple repetition of the message after the experimenter. We have already spoken of this elsewhere. The children themselves become quickly aware of this device, and often mention it when asked how they were able to remember the message. Thus, for example, Dima S. (five years, seven months) gave the following answer: "I repeated the list in a whisper" (Record No. 57).

Another subject answered: "I repeated it to myself and I remembered it" (Record No. 67).

Repetition, as a memory device, has two forms. In the first, the child repeats the message, aloud or to himself, after the experimenter. This form appears earliest. In this case repetition simply accompanies the "reception" of the message. Its function is merely to cement retention of the experimenter's words.

Later, repetition assumes another form and function. The child repeats the message after, not as, it is heard. Objectively, this type of repetition functions as *recollective repetition*. Sometimes it takes on a very distinct external form. For example, Alik K. (five years, eight months) listened to the message to the end and then quickly went off to the store. However, halfway there he turned back. "I can only remember endive. What else was there?" he asked the experimenter (Record No. 38). This indicates that the child tried to repeat the message on the way to the store.

In the intermediate preschool age, we sometimes observe cases in which the subject listens attentively to the message, but does not repeat it aloud or to himself. For example, one of our subjects, Vera D. (five years, three months), showed no outward signs of repeating the message after she heard it. However, when we asked her at the end of the experiment how she had remembered, she answered, "I repeated it to myself" (Record No. 88). Evidently, in such cases repetition is genuinely internal and *mental*. In some cases repetition is done in the two ways at the same time: aloud, in a whisper, or accompanied by noiseless lip movements, and mentally, in internal speech.

This advance to mental repetition is important. After the operation of remembering becomes internal, further possibilities for its development, its further "intellectualization," become possible.

A new type of remembering operation appears toward the end of the preschool-age period. It is first observed in six-to-seven-year-olds, and is characterized by attempts to form logical mental connections between the items to be remembered. The nature of recall is itself evidence that such connections are made. The child rearranges the order of the items named off to him when he recalls them, with the new order based on their meaning: The memory span factor that had been prominent loses some of its importance. This is evidenced by the inaccurate recall we encountered in our older subjects. Most often, these wrong recalls were words with meanings similar to those they replaced. For example, Vova V. (six years, six months) replaced the word "noodles" with the word "macaroni" (Record No. 35): Slava Sh. (five years, nine months) replaced the word "sausage" with the word "meat" (Record No. 41); and Nina M. (six years, nine months) named slippers in place of shoes (Record No. 28).

There are also signs that the formation of meaningful connections to facilitate memorization was done with a recall situation already in mind by these subjects. We shall take up this point in detail further on.

A qualitative analysis of the children's memory behavior in the game experiment does not, of course, exhaustively describe the process taking place. Nevertheless, the data are sufficient to allow us to outline the major types of memory behavior we observed, as we have done in [Table 35-2, adopted from Istomina's Tables 3 and 4].

. . .

TABLE 35-2.
Types of memory behavior and their frequencies in children remembering a make-believe errand (sixty subjects).

	First type of behavior	Second type of behavior	Third type of behavior
Attitude toward the errand	Assumes role of shopper but does not grasp the content of the errand.	Grasps content of errand.	Grasps content of errand.
Characteristics of memorization	Does not listen to the instructions to the end; in transmitting the message, does not try to recall its content.	Attentively listens to the content of the message; tries to carry out errand as quickly as possible.	Repeats message as it is heard and afterward, aloud and to himself; asks experimenter to repeat or remind him of the message.
Principal features of behavior of this type.	The objective of remembering the content of the message is not singled out.	The objective of remembering begins to enter into the picture (mnemonic objectives).	Uses some memory devices (mnemonic operations, external or internal).
Age distribution of cases:			
3–4 years	12	3	–
4–5 years	–	15	–
5–6 years	–	7	8
6–7 years	–	5	10

In observing how the children behaved in committing the message to memory, we of course also noted the way in which they recalled it. Hence, in turning to the chief types of behavior in recall, we may limit ourselves to references to observations already described above.

Initially it never occurred to the children that they would have to recall exactly what they were to buy in the store. They considered their role of "emissary" fulfilled when they entered the store and were ready to turn to something else, for example, to participate in the game going on in the store itself. Even when asked directly by the experimenter's assistant, who played the role of store manager, what they had been sent to buy, the youngest children enumerated the items they saw, or which were suggested to them, or were even ready to take anything that was convenient. (I'll take whatever you give me," said Valya V., three years, two months.)

Older children as a rule exhibited a definite orientation to the task. Entering the store, they first of all transmitted the message. Frequently, they just blurted it out hurriedly: they would utter a few words, and when asked what else they needed, make no attempt to recall, but limit themselves to the comment that they didn't know or that they didn't need anything else ("That's all; nothing else," etc.).

Recall became an articulated process in the majority of cases only in six-year-olds: they tried to remember what they had forgotten. The recall devices that a child made use of in these cases were not always distinctly apparent. Nevertheless, some may be singled out.

Frequently they were external techniques in which the child would repeat loudly the items read off to him, sometimes several times, trying in this way to get the list of items to flow out, as it were, by itself. Sometimes this repetition was done in a whisper, or noiselessly, accompanied only by lip movements. In other cases, the children also

TABLE 35-3.
Types of behavior (and their frequencies) in recalling a play message (sixty subjects).

	First type of behavior	Second type of behavior	Third type of behavior
Attitude toward task of communicating message	The task of transmitting the content of the message does not occur to the child at all.	Tries to transmit message.	Tries to transmit message.
Characteristics of recall	The objective of recalling the content of the message does not emerge.	The objective of recalling the content of the message is present.	Some recall aids are used (external or internal recall operations).
Principal features of behavior of this type.	Instead of recalling the message, the child enumerates objects which he sees or which others suggest to him.	Recall is only immediate; there is no attempt to recall what has been forgotten.	Active attempts to recall what has been forgotten.
Age distribution of cases:			
3–4 years	12	3	–
4–5 years	–	13	2
5–6 years	–	3	12
6–7 years	–	1	14

took their cue from what they had already been able to recall, not by mechanically continuing the sequence, but by repeating only one word, making it a key word, as it were, for recall of the others that had been forgotten. Finally, we should expecially mention those cases, characteristic only of the older children, in which the child recalled what he had forgotten only with long pauses, during which he would try not to look at those around him, i.e., he would direct his gaze downward, to the side, or screw up his eyes. We are inclined to see this as a sign of some kind of internal search, perhaps a return in thought to the memorizing situation. This, of course, is only a hypothesis, since direct self-observation of this mental process, turned toward the past, is very difficult and impossible to demand of preschool-age children.

Thus, the major types of behavior in recall of a play message reduce to the following [*Table 35-3*]; in this table we have taken the remembering paradigm as a model.

The distribution of these types of recall behavior during a make-believe errand by age groups gives a picture almost identical to the age distribution for remembering behavior. This, of course, is not all unexpected: on the contrary, the relationship between these two mnemonic processes suggests that there may even be complete correspondence. That, in any case, is the assumption implicit in the usual use of the term voluntary memory, which refers to both remembering and recall at the same time.

36 Ecological Niche Picking

Michael Cole, Lois Hood,
and Ray McDermott

This may be a good place to take stock of the
naturalistic study of memory; only case studies
remain to be considered after this selection. What
have we learned so far? Most obviously, that some
interesting work has been done. My opening
complaint that "If X is an interesting or socially
significant aspect of memory, then psychologists have
hardly ever studied X" (Selection 1) turns out to have
been a bit unfair. The preceding pages are filled with
counterexamples: childhood amnesia, recall of
particularly salient moments, the reliability of
witnesses, prospective remembering, etc. But
although this work is important, we must be careful
not to exaggerate what has been accomplished. Some
facts have been established, but there has been little
progress at the theoretical level. Few studies have
tried to go beyond commonsense notions of memory;
almost all of them are restricted to deliberate acts of
"remembering" that are understood as such by the
people involved. (Exceptions are the oral poets of
Selection 24 and the young children of Selection 35.)
Is a deeper analysis possible?

It may be possible, but it will not be easy. In the
present selection, Michael Cole and his associates

From M. Cole, L. Hood, and R. McDermott, *Ecological Niche Picking: Ecological Invalidity as an Axiom of Experimental Cognitive Psychology*. New York: Laboratory of Comparative Human Cognition, Rockefeller University, 1978. Reprinted by permission.

*describe their efforts to pinpoint instances of
remembering and other cognitive processes in the
activity at a children's club. The children are not
trying to remember anything for its own sake; they
are just baking cakes or planting seeds. This makes
analysis difficult: Cognitive responsibilities are shared
among the children in confusing patterns,
interpersonal goals are as important as task
achievement, and interruptions of ongoing behavior
occur constantly. The authors believe that the
concepts of experimental cognitive psychology are
fundamentally inadequate for situations of this kind.
Indeed, the greater part of their article (not reprinted
here) is devoted to a discussion of that inadequacy;
they believe that "ecological validity" may be an
impossible goal. For my part, I think it is still too
early to decide such questions. The study of memory
in natural settings may or may not yield further
insights; time will tell. Meanwhile, we must follow the
example of this study by looking at those settings as
carefully as possible.*

In the fall of 1976, we undertook a study with 17 children 8–10 years of age who attended a small, private school in mid-Manhattan, New York City.

Our approach was as direct as it was simple-minded. We video and audio tape-recorded activities of the children in a variety of school settings and in an after-school club modeled loosely on those one would encounter at a community center. We also recorded hour-long testing sessions during which each child individually was presented a variety of laboratory-derived cognitive tasks. We were fully aware that we were sampling a limited set of situations, but we hoped that our observations would allow us to talk about how particular cognitive tasks and performances change as a function of settings.

. . .

The most striking feature of these club sessions was the extreme rarity of identifiable cognitive tasks. If the classroom could be characterized as an environment where cognitive tasks were observable with intervals of "doing nothing" interspersed, the club sessions could be characterized as an environment of chaotic activity with identifiable tasks interspersed at rare intervals. It was certainly *not* the case that the children were sitting quietly, lost in thought. They were active, argumentative, and constantly busy. But classification, inference, and other tasks we had hoped to discover weren't easily detectable, even after several repeated viewings of our video-taped record. We found ourselves in the somewhat absurd situation where activities that clearly required the cognitive processes we were interested in studying *must* have been operating (the recipes got read, the cakes baked, the animals trained), but we could not identify how those goals were accomplished in a way that was directly related to those intellectual tasks that are the backbone of process-oriented cognitive psychology.

. . .

REMEMBERING

The major speculations about remembering in everyday life are that environments for storage and retrieval of information are highly organized (thereby providing individuals with a ready-made structure—a circumstance that has been widely demonstrated to facilitate recall performance) and that everyday life environments are replete with recall cues, both human and physical, to which the individual has recourse. A major implication of reducing memory demands is to permit the individual to devote less of his limited mental resources (Norman and Bobrow, 1976) to the activity of remembering and more to other activities demanded by the tasks at hand.

The fact that many everyday environments (e.g., kitchens) are physically structured in a manner that lessens memory load is so ubiquitous that it is difficult to see. For example, in cooking club, the room was arranged so the utensils were on one set of shelves and ingredients on another. If a child needed to remember where the spatula or measuring spoons were, for example, he or she would have to remember where utensils in general were in order to find the spoons and the spatula. However, when one's expectations concerning the organization of the environment are not met, its facilitating nature becomes apparent.

This can be illustrated by the following excerpt from a cooking club, where the children are making cranberry bread. The recipe calls

for melted shortening, and the children look to the usual place for
ingredients in order to find the shortening.

Example 5

Nadine:	One half a cup melted shortening. Where're we gonna get melted shortening?
Dolores:	Where's the shortening?
Lucy:	(comes over) Where's the melted shortening?
Nadine:	(at other table) Is this shortening? (Dolores stops sifting, watches.)
Rikki:	(going over to shelves) This is shortening (pointing to Crisco can on shelf). But is that where you melt it? (gestures toward stove)
Helene:	(turns from stove to Lucy) Here's the shortening, Lucy (points to measuring cup of melted margarine on stove).
Nadine:	(turning from shelves) Where's shortening?
Helene:	Sitting on the god damn stove (Rikki, Lucy, and Helene go to stove).

Example 6 is an instance of how the memory demands on individuals can be lessened both during storage and in retrieval. This scene is from a club session where the children had cut up some fruits and vegetables, extracted seeds from them, and are about to plant the seeds.

Example 6

Mark:	There's not enough trays.
Mike:	Anybody planted anything yet?
Jackie:	No.
Mark:	Hmmm.
Mike:	O.K. Now, let's wait. What do we got to do?
Jackie:	There's not enough trays.
Mike:	But there *will* be enough trays if we plant i t right.
Carl:	I–I–I–I need another popsicle stick for um, Robert.
Robert:	You're doing tomatoes.
Carl:	Oh! Oh! Oh!
Mike:	What do we . . .
Mike:	Rikki.
Rikki:	Yes.
Mike:	What dif–, how many different kinds of things do we have to plant? What do we got going?
Rikki:	Gourds.
Mike:	The gourd (pause).
Andy:	Tomato.
Jackie:	Green Pepper.

Mike:	Green pepper.
Jackie:	Green PEPPER.
Andy:	Tomato.
?:	Yeah.
Mike:	Tomato.
Jackie:	Tomato.
Rikki:	(inaudible)
Mark:	Apple.
Mike:	Apple.
Mark:	Orange.
Mike:	Orange. And what about ———— (Andy begins to put seed into tray). Wait! Wait! Wait! Andy— nobody can farm like that! What're you gonna take it and just slop it down all over and then how'll we know what's sprouting? O.K.? What does a good farmer do?
Mark:	He makes a hole.
Mike:	He makes little holes and he starts a line.

There are two ways in which the memory load in this memory task is lessened relative to one encountered in the laboratory. First, the items to be remembered are present in the environment: the children have just cut up the fruits and vegetables; their remains are still on the table a few feet away. Second, no one child has to remember all items. Together, the children recalled five of the six items, but no child individually recalled more than two.

. . .

Our description of Example 5 illustrated how everyday environments are physically structured in a way that reduces memory load. What is unspecified in that description are the following features. First, in this case, the structuring is actually misleading. That is, knowing that the shortening is always on the shelves doesn't lead to finding the melted shortening: it actually leads to a detour (the Crisco). The memory that is in the environment interferes (temporarily) with the solution. Second, the utilization of the organized environment gets done not by Nadine, the one who originated the question ("Where're we gonna get melted shortening?") but by another child, Rikki, who points to the Crisco on the shelves. And third, the next step along the route to solution—finding the melted shortening—is done by a third child, Helene. These aspects of this scene nicely illustrate how problem-solving in everyday life can be a social activity, in which interaction provides a multiplicity of well timed stimuli, a feature of our club environments not capturable by the language of the speculations.

The main shortcoming of our description of Example 6, where the children were ready to plant seeds, is that to characterize it as a memory task analogous to a laboratory recall task is misleading. If Mike, the originator of the questioning, had meant it to be such, he would not have settled for five out of six items being recalled, nor would he permit Rikki, the child he questioned, to supply only one of the five items while allowing others to respond. What is left out of our previous description is the multiplicity of activities that are going on, the interactional nature of these activities, and the shifting and negotiable nature of the problem-solving environment. That remembering fruits and vegetables is *not* the goal of the activity is made clear by both the children ("There's not enough trays") and Mike ("There *will* be enough trays if we plant it right").

In fact, it appears that the actual number of items to be planted (remembered) is unimportant at least at this precise moment; that outcome is clearly negotiable. What all the participants agree is necessary is an arrangement permitting seeds to be arranged in trays. This is true in terms of the number of items mentioned (the "answer") and also the planting task itself. When one of the children becomes impatient and puts a seed into the dirt, the activity abruptly changes. The theme and task in general remain the same (how to be a good "farmer") but the specific subtask shifts from how many rows are needed to how the seeds have to be put in the dirt.

. . .

[*We see, then, that:*]

1. Psychologists' speculations about thinking in everyday life, where experimental tasks provide the basis for analogies find some support in observations of children in our clubs: in everyday life settings we can discover examples of cognitive activity that is recognizable as such.

2. There is something underspecified from these examples; not only is the specification of stimuli and responses circular; it is suspect. While a quick reading of any example makes recognizable the basis for one or another speculation, each example seems far too complicated to fit the constraints that the analogue suggests. For each example one feels that we could come up with very different stories for what is happening. The evidence severely underdetermines any of the theoretical speculations.

In our view, uneasiness with our examples is well motivated. It is, in fact, this exact problem which induced us to write this paper.

The central difficulty is captured in that part of our earlier discussion that emphasized the crucial role of closed system analysis to the enterprise that is cognitive psychology. Bruner put the central requirement very succinctly when he said:

> It is the essence in any given experiment that we define in advance what we as experimenters mean by relevant information and do not depend upon the subjects' response to do it for us; otherwise we would be in a complete circle (1951, p. 131).

Given the evidence from our examples, we think that psychologists must take seriously the possibility that defining relevant stimuli in advance is a goal, not an acceptable practice, at least for environments such as those included in our examples from club sessions. In fact, there is nothing more familiar nor more frustrating to the beginning psychologist than the fact that experiments breed more experiments than definitive conclusions. Repeated experimentation around a circumscribed problem is necessary in part because replication and variation operate as the experimentalist's hedge against a false *a priori* definition of the closed system environment under analysis.

In brief, one is advised to think of our examples of everyday cognitive tasks as bearing a relation to closed experimental tasks that is analogous to the relation of a sieve to a bowl. If the bowl is an environment which completely constrains its contents, a sieve is more open space than netting; there is enough metal netting to provide the sieve with the recognizable shape of a bowl. But, like a sieve, and unlike a bowl, our specification of task and behavior in everyday life cannot hold water.

There are a number of reasons why current analyses of cognitive performance in everyday life seem to crumble under close inspection. First, as Neisser (1976) has pointed out, the scenes in which these tasks are embedded are characterized by multiple motives and often strong emotions so that instead of talking about *the* task, or even *these* tasks, we face a situation in which there are several tasks operative at once, some embedded within others, some of which seem to run in parallel, all of which need to be discovered. Second, individuals seem to be able to take advantage of the multiplicity of tasks by selectively responding to one or another at any given moment with the result that response demands for what the psychologist deems to be *the* task are often substantially reduced. We have come to talk of tasks as being "negotiable" by which we mean not only that the requirements for an adequate response to a particular demand characteristic of the environment are flexible, but that individuals use this flexibility to change what the tasks-of-the-moment are.

A third feature of many everyday life settings for thinking which permits (indeed, promotes) people to change the "stimulus conditions" for responding is that other people with variable relations to the multiple tasks at hand are a part of the stimulus environment. In changing the nature of the effective stimulus at different parts of a given cognitive task, the subject is operating on an environment that simultaneously operates on the subject. For example, in deciding who to bake a cake with, figuring out how many trays are required to plant seeds in, etc. the subjects operate on other people, who, in turn, are operating on them in a continuous process of interaction. Consider also the complication that various actors in any setting are engaged in carrying out their own tasks (which may or may not be the same as those of the subject, but are likely to have to be coordinated with those of the subject in some way) and that cognitive activities are engaged in not as an end in themselves, but as a means to some transformation on the environment (getting the cakes baked, seeds sprouted, friendships established) as Vygotsky suggests. The everyday world consists of dynamically organized environments which find no representation in laboratory models of intellectual activity.

It is these ubiquitous features of nonlaboratory tasks which create the conditions permitting some psychologists to suggest that everyday contexts for thinking are relatively simple vis-a-vis the demands of psychological tests and experiments (because individuals divide the labor, the environments are designed to facilitate problem solving, etc.) while others can point to its great difficulty (because so many tasks can, and often must, be dealt with simultaneously).

Difficult or easy, if we are right in claiming that everyday life settings for thinking have some of the characteristics just listed, there are two severe consequences for the experimental, cognitive psychologists concerned with the ecological validity of their observations: (1) everyday life contexts for thinking differ in important ways from the contexts assumed to obtain in laboratory tasks, thereby undermining efforts to say that an individual behaves more or less effectively in one environment than in another and (2) the analytic apparatus we bring to these environments from experimental psychology *does not apply*.

REFERENCES

Bruner, J. Personality dynamics and the process of perceiving. In R. R. Blake and G. Ramsey (eds.) *Perception: An Approach to Personality*. New York: Ronald Press, 1951.

Neisser, U. General, academic, and artificial intelligence. In L. Resnick (ed.), *The Nature of Intelligence*. Hillsdale, N.J.: Erlbaum, 1976.

Norman, D., and Bobrow, D. On the analysis of performance operating characteristics. *Psychological Review* 1976, *83*, 508–510.

Part VII
Special People

In which some unusual mnemonic talents are
reported. They serve to remind us of the range of
phenomena that an adequate theory of memory will
have to explain.

37   Memorists

Ulric Neisser

Webster's dictionary defines a "memorist" as "one having a good memory." I think it will turn out to be a more useful term than "mnemonist," even though the latter appears in the titles of the next two selections. Strictly speaking, a "mnemonist" is a person who uses mnemonic devices. Some of the people described in the following pages do use such aids (usually of their own invention), but others apparently do not. They just have excellent memories.

The literature on memorists/mnemonists documents some very remarkable accomplishments. Almost equally remarkable, however, is the lack of interest in this literature shown by experimental psychologists who specialize in the study of memory. Brown and Deffenbacher (two of the authors of Selection 13) have traced this history of neglect in an intriguing paper called "Forgotten mnemonists".[1] They show that every generation of psychologists since Wundt has had a chance to read about individuals with abilities like those of Luria's *S* or Hunt and Love's *VP* (Selections 38 and 39) and has proceeded to forget them as soon as it was decently possible to do so.

There are many reasons for this neglect. The one on which I wish to focus arises from the prevailing conception of memory itself—a conception that suggests no way in which the study of outstanding individuals could contribute to scientific progress. In this view, each person has a fixed mechanism of memory in the brain that is essentially unmodifiable by experience. One may learn tricks or strategies that allow one to make better use of one's memory, but one cannot change the underlying apparatus or its properties. Moreover, everyone's memory mechanism is fundamentally the same, though the parameters may vary quantitatively from one individual to the next. The primary scientific goal of the study of memory, then, is to understand the

---

[1] Brown, E., and Deffenbacher, K. Forgotten mnemonists. *Journal of the History of the Behavioral Sciences*, 1975, *11*, 342–349.

architecture of that universal system. Anything else—such as the study of how particular individuals happen to use the system—is of less interest.

This is a very well established view. William James was blunt about it in *Principles of Psychology*:

> ... all improvement of the memory lies in the line of *elaborating the associates* of each of the several things to be remembered. No amount of culture would seem capable of modifying a man's *general retentiveness*. This is a physiological quality, given once for all with his organization, and which he can never hope to change. It differs no doubt in disease or health ... ".[2]

Today, our notion of the mechanism involved is slightly more elaborate; it is often expressed by an analogy with computers. In place of "general retentiveness" we have the specific properties of the computer's unalterable "hardware," while the variable strategies used in remembering (e.g., "elaborating the associates") are compared to the different programs ("software") by which the computer can be controlled. Atkinson and Shiffrin made this comparison explicitly some years ago in a paper that established the dominant contemporary theory of memory. They called the paper "Human memory: A proposed system and its control processes."[3] The underlying system in their model consisted of the three separate "memories" that have become the commonplaces of cognitive theory: the sensory register, the short-term store, and the long-term store. Other psychologists have proposed other components (imagery and attention are prominent candidates), but the existence of *some* underlying machinery—identical in everyone and unmodifiable in anyone—is rarely called into question.

It is easy to see how these assumptions lead away from the study of memory in its natural context and into the laboratory instead. If the mechanism we hope to understand is genuinely universal, why not study it in the most convenient and controllable way? Some answers to this rhetorical question were suggested in Selection 1, and there is no need to repeat them here. Consider, however, how the same assumptions tend to discourage the study of people with outstanding memories. There are only two possibilities: Either the memorist has the same underlying machinery as everyone else, or he doesn't. If he does, there is little to be gained by studying him. We would only discover his particular memory strategies and control processes, which

---

[2] James, W. *Principles of Psychology*, Vol. 1, (New York: Holt, 1890; Dover, 1950), 663–664. (Emphasis in original.)

[3] Atkinson, R. C., and Shiffrin, R. M. Human memory: A proposed system and its control processes. In K. W. Spence and J. T. Spence (eds.), *The Psychology of Learning and Motivation*, Vol. 2. New York: Academic Press, 1968.

have no fundamental scientific significance. But if he doesn't, there is still less to be gained by studying him. The results of our work would then have put us into a rather awkward position: The universal underlying mechanism would not be universal after all. We might still claim that it was *nearly* universal—memorists are said to be very rare—but some awkardness would remain. Given these alternatives, the better part of valor may be to ignore the subject entirely.

The widespread use of the term "mnemonist" for people with outstanding memories has probably tended to encourage the belief that nothing fundamental can be learned from them: They are just people who happen to be handy with mnemonics. A recent example of this belief appears in an important paper by Ericsson, Chase, and Faloon.[4] These investigators trained an undergraduate student, *S. F.*, in the digit-span task for about a year and a half. During that time, his span increased from seven to almost 80 digits. *S. F.* accomplished this by developing an elaborate, hierarchically organized retrieval structure for digits. Nevertheless, his underlying memory apparatus (his "short-term memory capacity") had apparently not been altered: His rehearsal groups were still six digits long, his span for letters (as opposed to digits) was no greater than before, etc. The authors compare *S.F.*'s achievements explicitly with those of well-known memorists—with "...*S*, who seemed to remember large amounts of trivial information for years by means of visual imagery, and ... *VP*, who could remember large amounts of material by means of elaborate linguistic associations in several languages" (p. 1182, fn. 2). The implication is that all impressive feats of memory are nothing but the application of special tricks or devices.

From the viewpoint of this book, the first thing to do about memorists is to acknowledge their existence. Whatever the ultimate explanation of their accomplishments, those accomplishments are real. The next thing to do is to establish a rough and preliminary taxonomy. How many kinds of special memory abilities are there? What are their frequencies in the general population? What is the course of development of each type? Are these talents simply the upper extremes of continuous distributions of ability, or are the distributions bimodal? With the answers to questions such as these, we would be in a better position to evaluate the ubiquitous assumption that there is a single, universally shared mechanism of memory. Unfortunately, the answers are not available. Nothing like a normative study of memory abilities— a "memory census"—has ever been undertaken. The battery of tests and questionnaires that such a census would require has not been

---

[4]Ericsson, K. A., Chase, W. G., and Faloon, S. Acquisition of a memory skill. *Science*, 1980, *208*, 1181–1182.

devised. (There is a Wechsler Memory Scale,[5] but it is primarily a clinical instrument for the diagnosis of abnormality.) All we have are case studies.

My own guess—only a guess—is that the abilities described in Selections 38–44 may not be as unusual as is generally believed. To be sure, there have been no other reports of individuals like *S* (Selection 38) or "Elizabeth" (Selection 40).[6] But people with astonishing memory for pictures, musical scores, chess positions, business transactions, dramatic scripts, or faces are by no means unique; judging by the frequency of second-hand reports, they may not even be very rare. Most common of all (if such reports can be credited) is a kind of visual memory that allows one to recall specific pages of books one has read. I have never seen this ability at first hand, but it may not be restricted to the Shass Pollak (Selection 30). At least, I have been told about it by so many different individuals that I am inclined to take it seriously. In almost every lecture audience where I have posed the question, someone has reported possessing this ability at an earlier time in their lives or at least having observed it in others. Typically they report having used it to dazzle their teachers, to pass examinations without studying, etc. Typically, also, they say that they lost it by the end of adolsecence or earlier.

Such reports should not be taken at face value; my respondents may have been no more accurate in characterizing their memories than John Dean was in describing his (Selection 14). In one case, however, I was able to obtain a partial confirmation from an independent source. It was a woman (I will call her *MZ*) whose account was so rich and detailed that I later asked her to answer a series of written questions, eliciting a sort of mnemonic autobiography. *MZ* had maintained her unusual memory abilities until she was 29; they vanished abruptly when she contracted a severe intestinal illness that was followed by a temporary psychotic reaction to the medication she was given. Before that time "... teachers often wrote an outline of a subjects, instructions, etc. on the blackboard, sometimes covering the entire board ... all I had to do was read it and it was memorized." On examinations "... whole paragraphs or sections of what I had read would appear in my mind." Later on "... I could recall the exact date and day of week of future or past events—of almost anything that touched my life ... all personal telephone numbers ... colors of interiors and what people wore ... pieces of music. ... Recalling a picture, as a painting in a

---

[5]Wechsler, D. A standardized memory scale for clinical use. *Journal of Psychology*, 1945, *19*, 87–95. The scale is commercially available from the Psychological Corporation.

[6]Unless you count fiction, like Borges' well-known story *Funes the Memorious*.

museum, was like standing in the museum looking at it again. . . ." Particularly interesting was the way *MZ* had used her memory during two years in her twenties, when she worked as a technician in a zoological laboratory. "I mounted between 100–200 insects a day, mostly ants and bees. Each vial contained anywhere from a few to 30 insects. As I was handed a vial, Dr. *BW* would tell me the number of each type (males, workers, etc.) to be mounted and the arrangement—one to four on a pin . . . As he handed me each vial, he would give verbal instructions for each, and continue until he had given me all the work for the day. I didn't write anything down because I had no trouble remembering what to do with each vial." As it happens, *BW* is an acquaintance of mine. I asked him about *MZ*'s account. He confirmed it in every particular, including the numbers of insects she had to remember on a typical day. She was the best technician who had ever worked for him.

There is no way to tell, now, whether *MZ* was in the same league with *S* or *VP* or "Elizabeth" or "Nancy" or Professor Aitken or even the Reverend Dr. Phelps (all of whom will be introduced in the next few selections). In any case, I have not told her story to increase the number of documented memorists by one. My hope is to stimulate the search for other memorists, so that sometime in the future we can make an informed guess at their numbers. There may be quite a few.

38 The Mind of a Mnemonist

A. R. Luria

Luria's subject S is the exception to many rules. He violates not only the established norms of memory and perception—S almost never forgot anything at all, and his everyday sensory experiences can only be described as mind-boggling–but also my own generalization that psychology doesn't care about memorists. Alexander Luria, the most distinguished Soviet psychologist of his generation, did eloquent justice to S in the book from which these selections are drawn. (Jerome Bruner wrote the introduction to the English translation in 1968.) S just proved to be too sensational to be ignored; his peculiar mental life has earned him a place in almost every subsequent book on cognitive psychology.

Although he certainly deserves his fame, our concentration on S may have fostered some misconceptions about mnemonists and memorists as a group. They do not invariably have bizarre sensory experiences or difficulty with abstractions. The opposite is more nearly the case. S turns out to be an exception even to generalizations about memorists, though he is no less interesting on that account.

From A. R. Luria, *The Mind of a Mnemonist,* translated from the Russian by Lynn Solotaroff. New York: Basic Books; London: Jonathan Cape Ltd., 1968. Reprinted by permission.

. . .

When I began my study of S. it was with much the same degree of curiosity psychologists generally have at the outset of research, hardly with the hope that the experiments would offer anything of particular note. However, the results of the first tests were enough to change my attitude and to leave me, the experimenter, rather than my subject, both embarrassed and perplexed.

I gave S. a series of words, then numbers, then letters, reading them to him slowly or presenting them in written form. He read or listened attentively and then repeated the material exactly as it had been presented. I increased the number of elements in each series, giving him as many as thirty, fifty, or even seventy words or numbers, but this, too, presented no problem for him. He did not need to commit any of the material to memory; if I gave him a series of words or numbers, which I read slowly and distinctly, he would listen attentively, sometimes ask me to stop and enunciate a word more clearly, or, if in doubt whether he had heard a word correctly, would ask me to repeat it. Usually during an experiment he would close his eyes or stare into space, fixing his gaze on one point; when the experiment was over, he would ask that we pause while he went over the material in his mind to see if he had retained it. Thereupon, without another moment's pause, he would reproduce the series that had been read to him.

The experiment indicated that he could reproduce a series in reverse order—from the end to the beginning—just as simply as from start to finish; that he could readily tell me which word followed another in a series, or reproduce the word which happened to precede the one I'd name. He would pause for a minute, as though searching for the word, but immediately after would be able to answer my questions and generally made no mistakes.

It was of no consequence to him whether the series I gave him contained meaningful words or nonsense syllables, numbers or sounds; whether they were presented orally or in writing. All he required was that there be a 3–4 second pause between each element in the series, and he had no difficulty reproducing whatever I gave him.

As the experimenter, I soon found myself in a state verging on utter confusion. An increase in the length of a series led to no noticeable increase in difficulty for S., and I simply had to admit that the capacity of his memory *had no distinct limits*; that I had been unable to perform what one would think was the simplest task a psychologist can do: measure the capacity of an individual's memory. I arranged a second and then a third session with S.; these were followed by a series of sessions, some of them days and weeks apart, others separated by a period of several years.

But these later sessions only further complicated my position as experimenter, for it appeared that there was no limit either to the *capacity* of S.'s memory or to the *durability of the traces he retained.* Experiments indicated that he had no difficulty reproducing any lengthy series of words whatever, even though these had originally been presented to him a week, a month, a year, or even many years earlier. In fact, some of these experiments designed to test his retention were performed (without his being given any warning) 15 or 16 years after the session in which he had originally recalled the words. Yet invariably they were successful. During these test sessions S. would sit with his eyes closed, pause, then comment: "Yes, yes. . . . This was a series you gave me once when we were in your apartment. . . . You were sitting at the table and I in the rocking chair. . . . You were wearing a gray suit and you looked at me like this. . . . Now, then, I can see you saying . . . " And with that he would reel off the series precisely as I had given it to him at the earlier session. If one takes into account that S. had by then become a well-known mnemonist, who had to remember hundreds and thousands of series, the feat seems even more remarkable.

. . .

Our curiosity had been aroused by a small and seemingly unimportant observation. S. had remarked on a number of occasions that if the examiner said something during the experiment—if, for example, he said "yes" to confirm that S. had reproduced the material correctly or "no" to indicate he had made a mistake—a blur would appear on the table and would spread and block off the numbers, so that S. in his mind would be forced to "shift" the table over, away from the blurred section that was covering it. The same thing happened if he heard noise in the auditorium; this was immediately converted into "puffs of steam" or "splashes" which made it more difficult for him to read the table.

This led us to believe that the process by which he retained material did not consist merely of his having preserved spontaneous traces of visual impressions; there were certain additional elements at work. I suggested that S. possessed a marked degree of *synesthesia.* If we can trust S.'s recollections of his early childhood (which we will deal with in a special section later in this account), these synesthetic reactions could be traced back to a very early age. As he described it:

> When I was about two or three years old I was taught the words of a Hebrew prayer. I didn't understand them, and what happened was that

the words settled in my mind as puffs of steam or splashes. ... Even now I *see* these puffs or splashes when I hear certain sounds.

Synesthetic reactions of this type occurred whenever S. was asked to listen to *tones*. The same reactions, though somewhat more complicated, occurred with his perception of *voices* and with speech sounds.

The following is the record of experiments that were carried out with S. in the Laboratory on the Physiology of Hearing at the Neurological Institute, Academy of Medical Sciences.

Presented with a tone pitched at 30 cycles per second and having an amplitude of 100 decibels, S. stated that at first he saw a strip 12–15 cm. in width the color of old, tarnished silver. Gradually this strip narrowed and seemed to recede; then it was converted into an object that glistened like steel. Then the tone gradually took on a color one associates with twilight, the sound continuing to dazzle because of the silvery gleam it shed.

Presented with a tone pitched at 50 cycles per second and an amplitude of 100 decibels, S. saw a brown strip against a dark background that had red, tongue-like edges. The sense of taste he experienced was like that of sweet and sour borscht, a sensation that gripped his entire tongue.

Presented with a tone pitched at 100 cycles per second and having an amplitude of 86 decibels, he saw a wide strip that appeared to have a reddish-orange hue in the center; from the center outwards the brightness faded with light gradations so that the edges of the strip appeared pink.

Presented with a tone pitched at 250 cycles per second and having an amplitude of 64 decibels, S. saw a velvet cord with fibers jutting out on all sides. The cord was tinged with a delicate, pleasant pink-orange hue.

Presented with a tone pitched at 500 cycles per second and having an amplitude of 100 decibels, he saw a streak of lightning splitting the heavens in two. When the intensity of the sound was lowered to 74 decibels, he saw a dense orange color which made him feel as though a needle had been thrust into his spine. Gradually this sensation diminished.

Presented with a tone pitched at 2,000 cycles per second and having an amplitude of 113 decibels, S. said: "It looks something like fireworks tinged with a pink-red hue. The strip of color feels rough and unpleasant, and it has an ugly taste—rather like that of a briny pickle. ... You could hurt your hand on this."

Presented with a tone pitched at 3,000 cycles per second and having an amplitude of 128 decibels, he saw a whisk broom that was of a fiery color, while the rod attached to the whisks seemed to be scattering off into fiery points.

The experiments were repeated during several days and invariably the same stimuli produced identical experiences.

What this meant was that S. was one of a remarkable group of people, among them the composer Scriabin, who have retained in an especially vivid form a "complex" synesthetic type of sensitivity. In S.'s case every sound he heard immediately produced an experience of light and color and, as we shall see later in this account, a sense of taste and touch as well.

S. also experienced synesthetic reactions when he listened to someone's *voice*. "What a crumbly, yellow voice you have," he once told L. S. Vygotsky while conversing with him. At a later date he elaborated on the subject of voices as follows:

> You know there are people who seem to have many voices, whose voices seem to be an entire composition, a bouquet. The late S. M. Eisenstein had just such a voice: Listening to him, it was as though a flame with fibers protruding from it was advancing right toward me. I got so interested in his voice, I couldn't follow what he was saying . . . .
>
> But there are people whose voices change constantly. I frequently have trouble recognizing someone's voice over the phone, and it isn't merely because of a bad connection. It's because the person happens to be someone whose voice changes twenty to thirty times in the course of a day. Other people don't notice this, but I do. (Record of November 1951.)
>
> To this day I can't escape from seeing colors when I hear sounds. What first strikes me is the color of someone's voice. Then it fades off . . . for it does interfere. If, say, a person says something, I see the word; but should another person's voice break in, blurs appear. These creep into the syllables of the words and I can't make out what is being said. (Record of June 1953.)

"Lines," "blurs," and "splashes" would emerge not only when he heard tones, noises, or voices. Every speech sound immediately summoned up for S. a striking visual image, for it had its own distinct form, color, and taste. Vowels appeared to him as simple figures, consonants as splashes, some of them solid configurations, others more scattered—but all of them retained some distinct form.

. . .

When S. read through a long series of words, each word would elicit a graphic image. And since the series was fairly long, he had to find some way of distributing these images of his in a mental row or sequence. Most often (and this habit persisted throughout his life), he would "distribute" them along some roadway or street he visualized in his mind. Sometimes this was a street in his home town, which would also include the yard attached to the house he had lived in as a child and which he recalled vividly. On the other hand, he might also select a street in Moscow. Frequently he would take a mental walk along that street—Gorky Street in Moscow—beginning at Mayakovsky Square, and slowly make his way down, "distributing" his images at houses, gates, and store windows. At times, without realizing how it had happened, he would suddenly find himself back in his home town (Torzhok), where he would wind up his trip in the house he had lived in as a child. The setting he chose for his "mental walks" approximates that of dreams, the difference being that the setting in his walks would immediately vanish once his attention was distracted but would reappear just as suddenly when he was obliged to recall a series he had "recorded" this way.

This technique of converting a series of words into a series of graphic images explains why S. could so readily reproduce a series from start to finish or in reverse order; how he could rapidly name the word that preceded or followed one I'd select from the series. To do this, he would simply begin his walk, either from the beginning or from the end of the street, find the image of the object I had named, and "take a look at" whatever happened to be situated on either side of it. S.'s visual patterns of memory differed from the more commonplace type of figurative memory by virtue of the fact that his images were exceptionally vivid and stable; he was also able to "turn away" from them, as it were, and "return" to them whenever it was necessary.

When S. read a passage from a text, each word produced an image. As he put it: "Other people *think* as they read, but I *see* it all." As soon as he began a phrase, images would appear; as he read further, still more images were evoked, and so on.

As we mentioned earlier, if a passage were read to him quickly, one image would collide with another in his mind; images would begin to crowd in upon one another and would become contorted. How then was he to understand anything in this chaos of images? If a text were read slowly, this, too, presented problems for him. Note the difficulties he experienced:

> ... I was read this phrase: "N. was leaning up against a tree. ... " I saw a slim young man dressed in a dark blue suit (N., you know, is so elegant). He was standing near a big linden tree with grass and woods all around. ... But then the sentence went on: "and was peering into a shop window." Now how do you like that! It means the scene isn't set in the woods, or in a garden, but he's standing on the street. And I have to start the whole sentence over from the beginning .... (Record of March 1937.)

Thus, trying to understand a passage, to grasp the information it contains (which other people accomplish by singling out what is most important), became a tortuous procedure for S., a struggle against images that kept rising to the surface in his mind. Images, then, proved an obstacle as well as an aid to learning in that they prevented S. from concentrating on what was essential. Moreover, since these images tended to jam together, producing still more images, he was carried so far adrift that he was forced to go back and rethink the entire passage. Consequently a simple passage—a phrase, for that matter— would turn out to be a Sisyphean task. These vivid, palpable images were not always helpful to S. in understanding a passage; they could just as easily lead him astray.

And this was only the beginning of the problems S. encountered in reading. As he described it:

> ... It's particularly hard if there are some details in a passage I happen to have read elsewhere. I find then that I start in one place and end up in another—everything gets muddled. Take the time I was reading *The Old World Landowners*. Afanasy Ivanovich went out on the porch. ... Well, of course, it's such a high porch, has such creaking benches. ... But, you know, I'd already come across that same porch before! It's Korobochka's porch, where Chichikov drove up! What's liable to happen with my images is that Afanasy Ivanovich could easily run into Chichikov and Korobochka! ...
>
> ... Or take another example. This one has to do with Chichikov's arrival at the hotel. I see the place, a one-story house. You enter and there's the foyer, downstairs a large reception room with a window near the doorway, to the right a table, and in the center of the room a big Russian stove. ... But I've seen this before. The fat Ivan Nikiforovich lives in this very house, and the thin Ivan Ivanovich is here too—in the garden out in front, with the filthy Gapka running about beside him. And so I've ended up with different people from the characters in the novel. (Record of March 1937.)

Thinking in terms of images was fraught with even greater dangers. Inasmuch as S.'s images were particularly vivid and stable, and recurred thousands of times, they soon became the dominant element in his awareness, uncontrollably coming to the surface whenever he touched upon something that was linked to them even in the most general way.These were images of his childhood: of the little house he had lived in in Rezhitsa; of the yard at Chaim Petukh's, where he could see the horses standing in the shed, where everything smelled of oats and manure. This explains why, once he had begun to read or had started one of his mental walks connected with recall, he would suddenly discover that although he had started out at Mayakovsky Square he invariably ended up at Chaim Petukh's house or in one of the public squares in Rezhitsa.

> Say I began in Warsaw—I end up in Torzhok in Altermann's house. ... Or I'm reading the Bible. There's a passage in which Saul appears at the house of a certain sorceress. When I started reading this, the witch described in "The Night Before Christmas" appeared to me. And when I read further, I saw the little house in which the story takes place—that is, the image I had of it when I was seven years old: the bagel shop and the storage room in the cellar right next to it. ... Yet it was the Bible I had started to read. ... (Record of September 1936.)

> ... The things I see when I read aren't real, they don't fit the context. If I'm reading a description of some palace, for some reason the main rooms always turn out to be those in the apartment I lived in as a child. ... Take the time I was reading *Trilby*. When I came to the part where I had to find an attic room, without fail it turned out to be one of my

neighbor's rooms—in that same house of ours. I noticed it didn't fit the context, but all the same my images led me there automatically. This means I have to spend far more time with a passage if I'm to get some control of things, to reconstruct the images I see. This makes for a tremendous amount of conflict and it becomes difficult for me to read. I'm slowed down, my attention is distracted, and I can't get the important ideas in a passage. Even when I read about circumstances that are entirely new to me, if there happens to be a description, say, of a staircase, it turns out to be one in a house I once lived in. I start to follow it and lose the gist of what I'm reading. What happens is that I just can't read, can't study, for it takes up such an enormous amount of my time. ... (Record of December 1935.)

Given such a tendency, cognitive functions can hardly proceed normally. The very thought which occasions an image is soon replaced by another—to which the image itself has led; a point is thus reached at which images begin to guide one's thinking, rather than thought itself being the dominant element.

39 The Second Mnemonist

Earl Hunt and Tom Love

The second mnemonist to come to the attention of modern American cognitive psychology was VP, a man with whom Hunt and Love had been casually acquainted before they discovered his special abilities. VP's performance on tests of memory seems to be as good as S's, but his mental life is very different. He has hardly any mental imagery at all, let alone any synesthesia; his methods are logical and verbal. Curiously, however, the city of Riga where he grew up is not far from S's birthplace. Is there something special in the Latvian air? VP himself is more inclined to credit his Latvian education, which placed strong emphasis on learning things by heart. Whatever their origin, his memory skills are certainly worthy of note.

In many fields of endeavor we learn by studying the expert. Students of literature read Shakespeare, Henry James, and Mark Twain; students in more prosaic fields study the putting of Arnold Palmer and the serving of John Newcombe. For some reason psychologists have decided to compile statistics on the average and illustrations of the

From a paper presented to the American Psychological Association in Honolulu, September 1972, and distributed by the Department of Psychology of the University of Washington. Reprinted with permission. For more information about *VP*, see E. Hunt and T. Love, How good can memory be? In A. W. Melton and E. Martin (eds.), *Coding Processes in Human Memory*, Washington, D.C.: Winston, 1972.

pathological. We would like to imitate the other disciplines, by describing the performance of a man with a superlative memory. Outstanding mnemonists have been described before, notably by Luria (1968) [*see Selection 38*] and by Stromeyer and Psotka (1970) [*see Selection 40*]. Both these mnemonists relied on their very unusual visual imagery abilities. The man we shall describe is quite different. To continue the analogy with athletic performance, our subject, whom we shall call VP, has combined intense motivation and a good but not superhuman mental endowment to develop his memorizing skills in the same manner as an athlete might sharpen his batting, kicking, and throwing skills. VP is probably the Olympic champion in the memory decathlon.

BIOGRAPHICAL

VP was born in Latvia in 1934 and grew up in the city of Riga, in an intellectually oriented, upper-middle-class family. Due to the unsettled conditions in Latvia during World War II his schooling was interrupted. Eventually his family fled Latvia and spent some time in displaced persons camps in Germany before coming to the United States in 1950. As a result of these experiences and the fact that multilingualism is fairly common in the Baltic states, VP speaks German, Latvian, Russian, Estonian, Spanish, French, Latin, and English. As we shall illustrate, this is of considerable assistance to him in memorizing. He has pointed out to us that as a child he attended schools which placed great stress on rote learning, both for traditional reasons and for the simple fact that very few texts and teaching aids were available. His schools were more authoritarian (and more intellectual) than is currently the fashion in this country. In VP's own remarks, the child who sat in the corner, reading, during recess was encouraged, whereas in this country there would be a parent–teacher conference on social development. VP feels, and we agree, that his early experiences were influential in the development of a style of information acquisition which he uses as an adult.

VP finished college in the United States and has done some graduate work. He has not followed a profession, and is currently employed as a clerk, which is certainly underemployment in a strict economic sense. He has had a lifelong interest in chess, bridge, and other games requiring mental skill. He is an outstanding player and is much involved in the chess subculture. We could describe his current life as being unconventional, but insofar as we know, within the normal range of unconventionality.

VP has a Wechsler–Bellevue Adult Scale IQ of 136. Not surprisingly, he does very well on subtests involving memory. He has taken a number of short tests designed to measure various factors of Guilford's

(1967) structure of intellect model. The general picture obtained from his psychometric profile is of an intelligent individual, but one not beyond the range of bright people normally found at a university. The only psychometric indication of his ability, apart from tests specifically designed to tap memory, is that he has an unusually high score on a test of Guilford's perceptual speed factor, a factor supposedly associated with the ability to notice small details rapidly. Perhaps more revealing were the informal reports made by the psychometric technicians who conducted the tests. They commented that they had seldom seen a more precise subject. VP took exceptional care to make sure that he understood the instructions and how the test was scored. Once he understood what was required, he invented an appropriate strategy.

We shall next describe some experimental results which show that the psychometric observations fail to capture the essence of a truly remarkable mnemonic skill.

TESTS OF GENERAL ABILITY

A classic test of long-term memory is one's ability to recall Bartlett's (1932) information packed Indian folktale, "War of the Ghosts." VP and four university students read the story, completed some distracting tasks, and then reconstructed the story after an hour. Without prior warning, six weeks later, VP and the best of the other memorizers were asked to return and recall the story. A year later, VP reconstructed the story again, also without warning, VP's successive reconstructions are in the Appendix. Table 39-1 presents some summary statistics for each reconstruction. As you can see, VP's memory for this story is little changed from the one hour to the one year interval. This is in contrast

TABLE 39-1
"War of the Ghosts" summary statistics

	Nouns	Verbs
Total count:		
Original story	49	68
Words in original and in:	30 (61%)	39 (57%)
6-week recall		
1-year recall	30 (61%)	39 (57%)
Words in both the 6-week and		
1-year recall:	38 (70%)	39 (70%)
Words in original and in		
both recalls:	27 (55%)	33 (49%)

to the simplifying distortions which Bartlett found to be introduced in recalling the Indian legend.

Recalling "War of the Ghosts" is an exercise in long-term semantic memory use. It deals with recall of a single presentation of meaningful material. We next look at VP's ability to keep track of rapidly changing, meaningless material, using the continuous paired-associates task used by Atkinson and Shiffrin (1968). In this task a small number of arbitrary stimuli are paired and re-paired with one of a large number of responses. On demand, the subject must be able to report the response most recently paired with a given stimulus. A fragment of an experiment is shown in Table 39-2. The major independent variable in this study is the *lag*, or number of trials intervening between a study trial and the test trial on which the subject must recall the appropriate response. Figure 39-1 shows typical data (obtained in our laboratory) relating percentage of response correct to lag. The line at the top is not a border for the top of the figure; it is a graphic record of VP's performance! VP has completed this task four times, with 150 trials in each session. He has missed four items of the 600.

We next tested VP's short-term memory and learning capacity, using Hebb's (1961) repeating sequences procedure. In this procedure digits are presented visually at a one-per-second rate. Immediately after presentation, the subject is to recall the sequence of digits most recently seen. The same sequence of digits is repeated every third trial; consequently, the subject normally displays a longer digit span for repeated than for nonrepeated strings. Typically with 9-digit numbers, subjects correctly report 20 percent of the nonrepeating strings and 60 percent of the repeating strings after eight repetitions. The first time VP did a digit span task his performance was unremarkable. He informed us that he would do better the next time, and he did. In a subsequent session using 25-digit strings he recalled correctly 18 percent of the nonrepeating strings and 63 percent of the repeating strings. That is, he displayed an average digit span of 24.5 for the repeating strings and an average of 21.5 for nonrepeating strings. By contrast, Melton (1963) reports digit spans of less than eight after eighty trials using undergraduate subjects and only nine strings.

TABLE 39-2
Sequence of study-test trials in Atkinson–Shiffrin task.

Study	JUK	23
Test	ROQ	?
Study	ROQ	95
Test	CUH	?
Study	CUH	47
Test	JUK	?

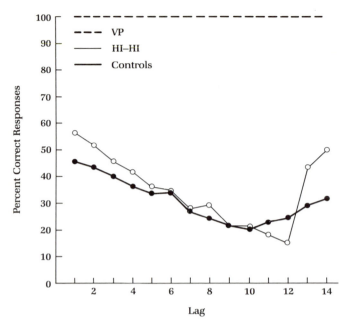

FIGURE 39-1

P (correct) vs. lag, for VP and average subjects, in the continuous-paired-associates task. [*"Controls" are 39 unselected college subjects; "HI—HI" are 12 subjects selected for high scores on both verbal and quantitative aptitude tests.*]

These experiments have convinced us that we were indeed dealing with a man with a superior memory. Note the variety of abilities that these experiments test. VP can hold meaningful material in long-term memory for a very long term, and large amounts of arbitrary information for a short time. Furthermore, he is able to "sort out" current information from recently presented, but no longer current, information as shown by the continuous paired-associates data. We next embarked on a series of studies designed to give us more information about how he did what he did, rather than what he could do.

. . .

[*Hunt and Love's account of several more studies is omitted here.*]

To gain some insight into this process, we asked VP to memorize lists of nonsense syllables, using the "thinking aloud" method of associations developed by Prytulak (1971). In this procedure the subject is presented with a nonsense syllable and asked to generate associates to it. Prytulak noted that most subjects generate these associations by interchanging or dropping letters, or by using some form of acoustic code. VP, on the other hand, very rapidly develops semantic associations. For example, in response to XIB, VP responded "illiterate woman." He later explained that X is the signature of an illiterate person and IB reminded him of LIB, hence Woman's Lib. His first five associations to a list of nonsense syllables were to a Latin proverb, Zygmont Bryzinski (an American political scientist), the Latin word for swan, the Hebrew word for Gentile, and the word half-wit. Throughout the experiment he made frequent associations to words in the various languages which he speaks. In digit-span experiments VP exhibits similar strategies, creating large chunks of numbers by association to dates, arithmetic relationships, distances, and ages. We stress again the rapidity with which he does this. We attempted to train some reasonably bright subjects to use VP's techniques in a digit-span study. The training appeared to have confused them more than it helped.

Given this reliance on semantics, what would happen if semantic information were to be removed, or at least made less obvious? Following a suggestion by Thomas Nelson, we asked VP to learn a list of 20 nonsense syllable–number pairings. Six weeks later he was asked to recall these arbitrary associations. Only four out of 20 associates were recalled, which is quite comparable with data which Nelson has obtained from university undergraduates. Contrast this with his remarkable performance on the meaningful "War of the Ghosts" story.

. . .

Case studies are always interesting reading. Extracting information from them, however, is quite difficult. By their nature, one can suggest but not conclude for cases. Proof of the propositions they suggest will require experimental analysis. We do feel, however, that two general observations are of note.

Previous studies of mnemonists have suggested that they are, in some way, abnormal. In particular, stress has been laid on the use of the mnemonist's unusual visual imagery. VP clearly demonstrates that outstanding visual capabilities are not necessary for outstanding memory. There are three key characteristics of VP's performance to which we would call attention. First, he is very quick at noting the details of a stimulus. This is consistent with his score on the perceptual speed factor, which Guilford reports as emerging in fairly young children. Second, being multilingual and well read, he has a very rich store of information on which to build stimulus codes. Third, from his early childhood, he was rewarded for acquiring and retrieving information. Thus, he has developed both an intense motivation to be a good memorizer and a style of information acquisition which facilitates coding to remember. VP himself has commented on this. He contrasts people who act on the world, such as high powered business executives, and people who observe it, such as himself. We, however, are struck by the active nature of his observations. We have quoted him in detail elsewhere (Hunt and Love, 1972). None of these characteristics make VP an abnormal person, who is controlled by his memory, as was evidently the case for Luria's visual memorizer, S.

Finally, we would like to point out that VP should not be unique. If it is true that he represents a person who has highly developed skills that are latent in many of us, then it should be possible to train other mnemonists of equivalent ability. In fact, there may be many more such individuals. Where can we find them?

APPENDIX I: VP'S REPRODUCTIONS OF A STORY USED BY BARTLETT, "THE WAR OF THE GHOSTS"

Original Story

One night two young men from Egulac went down to the river to hunt seals, and while they were there it became foggy and calm. Then they heard war-cries, and they thought: "Maybe this is a war-party." They escaped to the shore, and hid behind a log. Now canoes came up, and they heard the noise of paddles, and saw one canoe coming up to them. There were five men in the canoe, and they said:

"What do you think? We wish to take you along. We are going up the river to make war on the people."

One of the young men said: "I have no arrows."

"Arrows are in the canoe," they said.

"I will not go along. I might be killed. My relatives do not know where I have gone. But you," he said, turning to the other, "may go with them."

So one of the young men went, but the other returned home.

And the warriors went on up the river to a town on the other side of Kalama. The people came down to the water, and they began to fight, and many were killed. But presently the young man heard one of the warriors say: "Quick, let us go home; that Indian has been hit." Now he thought: "Oh, they are ghosts." He did not feel sick, but they said he had been shot.

So the canoes went back to Egulac, and the young man went ashore to his house, and made a fire. And he told everybody and said: "Behold I accompanied the ghosts, and we went to fight. Many of our fellows were killed, and many of those who attacked us were killed. They said I was hit, and I did not feel sick."

He told it all, and then he became quiet. When the sun rose he fell down. Something black came out of his mouth. His face became contorted. The people jumped up and cried.

He was dead.

APPENDIX II: VP'S REPRODUCTION OF "THE WAR OF THE GHOSTS" (SIX WEEKS AFTER READING THE ORIGINAL)

One night, two young men from Egliac went down to the river to hunt seals. While they were there, it became foggy and calm. Soon they heard the sound of paddles approaching, and they thought: "Maybe it's a war-party." They fled ashore and hid behind a log. Soon, one of the (unspecified number of) canoes came ashore, with five men in it, and one of them said: "What do you think? Let us go up-river and make war against the people."

"I will not go," said one of the young men. "I might be killed. My family does not know where I have gone. But he," said he, turning to the other young man, "will go with you." So one of the young men returned to the village and the other accompanied the party.

The party went up-river to a point beyond Kalama, and when the people saw them approaching, they came down to the river, and they fought. In the heat of the battle, the young man heard somebody say: "Quick, let us go home. That Indian has been wounded."

"They must be ghosts," thought the young man, who felt no pain or injury. However, the party returned, and he walked from the river up to his village, where he lit a fire outside of his hut, and awaited the sunrise.

"We went with a war-party to make war on the people up-river," he told his people who had gathered around, "and many were killed on both sides. I was told that I was injured, but I feel all right. Maybe they were ghosts."

He told it all to the villagers. When the sun came up, a contortion came over his face. Something black came out of his mouth, and he fell over.

He was dead.

APPENDIX III: VP'S RECALL OF "THE WAR OF THE GHOSTS" AFTER ONE YEAR

One day two young men from Egliac went down to the river to hunt seals. While there, it suddenly became very foggy and quiet, and they became scared and rowed ashore and hid behind a log. Soon they heard the sound of paddles in the water and canoes approaching. One of the canoes, with five men in it, paddled ashore and one of the men said: "What do you think? Let us go up-river and make war against the people."

"I cannot go with you," said one of the young men. "My relatives do not know where I have gone. Besides, I might get killed. But he," said he, turning to the other young man, "will go with you." So one of the young men returned to his village, and the other went up-river with the war-party.

They went to a point beyond Kalama, and the people came down to the river to fight them, and they fought. Soon, the young man heard someone say: "This Indian has been wounded."—"Maybe they are ghosts," he thought, because he felt perfectly OK. The war party suggested leaving, and they left, and the young man went back to his village.

There he lit a fire in front of his abode, sat down to await the sunrise, and told his story to the villagers. "I went with a war-party to make war with the people. There was fierce fighting and many were killed, and many were wounded. They said I was wounded, but I did not feel a thing. Maybe they were ghosts."

He had told it all, and when the sun came up, he gave a little cry. Something black came out of his mouth. He fell over. He was dead.

REFERENCES

Atkinson, R. C., and Shiffrin, R. M. Human memory: A proposed system and its control processes. In K. W. Spence and J. T. Spence (eds.), *The Psychology of Learning and Motivation, Vol. 2*. New York: Academic Press, 1968.

Bartlett, F. C. *Remembering*. Cambridge: Cambridge University Press, 1932.

Guilford, J. P. *The Nature of Human Intelligence*. New York: McGraw–Hill, 1967.

Hebb, D. O. Distinctive features of learning in the higher animal. In J. F. Delafresnaye (ed.), *Brain Mechanisms and Learning*. Oxford: Blackwell, 1961.

Hunt, E., and Love, T. How good can memory be? In A. W. Melton and E. Martin (eds.), *Coding Processes in Human Memory*. Washington, D. C.: Winston–Wiley, 1972.

Luria, A. R. *The Mind of a Mnemonist*. New York: Basic Books, 1968.

Melton, A. W. Implications of short-term memory for a general theory of memory. *Journal of Verbal Learning and Verbal Behavior*, 1963, 2, 1–21.

Prytulak, L. S. Natural language mediation. *Cognitive Psychology*, 1971, 2, 1–56.

Stromeyer, C. F., and Psotka, J. The detailed texture of eidetic images. *Nature*, 1970, 225, 346–349.

40　An Adult Eidetiker

Charles F. Stromeyer III

*Stromeyer's "Elizabeth" comes closer to having a
literally "photographic" memory than any other
memorist ever studied. Though Stromeyer reported
few tests of her memory in the conventional sense, he
does describe several astonishing feats of visual
information storage. As reported here, Elizabeth
could combine a stereogram presented to her left eye
with the image of a corresponding stereogram seen
with her right eye the day before; the result was a
figure perceived in depth. "Elizabeth" may be unique.
In the dozen years since the publication of this paper,
no other such eidetiker has been found.*

Elizabeth is a young teacher at Harvard, very intelligent, a skilled artist.
She has a talent that most painters don't have. At will, she can mentally
project an exact image of a picture or scene onto her canvas or onto
another surface. This hallucinated image appears to contain all of the
detailed texture and color of the original. Once the image is formed, it
remains still and Elizabeth can move her eyes about to inspect the
details.

Elizabeth (not her actual name) says that she can project a beard
onto a beardless face, for example, or leaves onto a barren tree—
additions so strong that they can obscure the true image. However,
she never confuses eidetic images with reality, and spontaneous
imagery rarely bothers her.

Her ability to recall and visualize images is not limited to pictures
or scenes. Years after having read a poem in a foreign language, she

can fetch back an image of the printed page and copy the poem from the bottom line to the top line as fast as she can write. She says that she used her eidetic memory for high-school and undergraduate examinations, but found it less useful in graduate school.

[In a section omitted here, Stromeyer describes the accomplishments of other "eidetikers." His list includes S (Selection 38), the Shass Pollak (Selection 30), and eidetic children like those studied by Jaensch, Haber, and others. It seems to me, however, that these cases should be carefully distinguished. Elizabeth's mental life is nothing like S's; she more closely resembles my own informant MZ (described in Selection 37) in the way she has used her talents. The mental life of the Shass Pollak is unknown; Stratton's report only describes what they could accomplish. As for the eidetic children—for whom the term "eidetic" was originally coined— they are not really memorists at all. After inspecting a picture, such a child may report that she can still see it for a minute or so; then it gradually fades from view. Eidetic children are often no more accurate in describing the picture during this period than control children who must describe it from memory alone. Moreover, they cannot retrieve their images once they have faded.*]*

. . . In our experiments with Elizabeth at Harvard . . . we used the computer generated stereograms developed by Bela Julesz of Bell Telephone Laboratories . . . Each stereogram consists of a pair of random-dot patterns. When a person looks at these patterns through a stereoscope, which presents one pattern to the right eye and the other pattern to the left eye, he sees a figure emerge in depth. When he looks at the random-dot patterns without the stereoscope, he can see neither figures nor depth.

Using only her right eye, Elizabeth viewed a 10,000-dot pattern for 1 minute. After a 10-second rest, she looked at the other 10,000-dot pattern with her left eye. We asked her to superimpose the eidetic image for the right-eye pattern on the actual left-eye pattern. Without hesitation she reported that she saw the letter T coming toward her.

Next we showed her both patterns through the stereoscope and she said the T was identical to her eidetic image.

Now we inverted the left- and right-eye patterns. When she projected the eidetic image onto the actual pattern, she saw an inverted T behind the surface. The T oscillated in depth, but had sharp outlines.

---

* *[For a thorough review of the phenomenon of eidetic imagery in children, see Haber, R. N. Twenty years of haunting eidetic images: Where's the ghost?* Behavioral and Brain Sciences, *1979, 2, 583—594, and commentary in the same issue, 594—629.]*

FLOAT

In the next experiment, Elizabeth looked at another random-dot pattern with her right eye. This time she looked at the pattern in 3-minute periods, separated by a minute of rest, until she had looked at it for 12 minutes. Twenty-four hours later she looked at the companion pattern with her left eye and projected the eidetic image of the right-eye pattern onto it. Within 10 seconds she said she saw a square floating above the surface.

These tests provide proof that eidetic imagery exists. Elizabeth had not seen the stereograms before the experiment. It seems impossible that she could memorize the position of 10,000 dots in the brief time we allowed her to look at the patterns. Even if she could, this would not explain the depth she saw. Three-dimensional vision is possible only when each eye sees a different image.

DEPTH

To demonstrate the extremely detailed information contained in the eidetic image, we tested her with a million-dot random pattern. She formed an eidetic image of the pattern and could retain if for up to four hours. We have not yet tested her for longer periods with the million-dot pattern.

Elizabeth could selectively recall any one of a number of images. In one experiment she formed images of four 10,000-dot patterns presented to her right eye. The next day she viewed a single pattern with her left eye and recalled each of the four eidetic images on request. When the images were superimposed on the left-eye pattern, each created a different figure that was seen in depth.

Since she had claimed that an eidetic image could obscure a real object—for example, that a projected beard could hide a chin—we decided to test whether an eidetic image could suppress an actual pattern.

We devised a stereogram that had two patterns, X and Y, for the left eye and one pattern for the right eye. Elizabeth looked at the pattern X with her left eye until she had formed an eidetic image. Then we presented pattern Y to her left eye and the right-eye pattern to her right eye. After she saw the combined figure in depth, we asked her to call up the eidetic image of the left-eye X pattern. The eidetic X image suppressed the Y pattern before her eye, and she reported seeing a new figure in depth.

TILT

These experiments show that the eidetic image is eye-specific and strong enough to obscure a real object. Furthermore, the image does not change its orientation in space as the head is tilted. For example, Elizabeth tilted her head 90 degrees to one side and viewed an upright painting until she formed an eidetic image of it. When she projected the eidetic image, she claimed it always remained upright. She could easily combine the eidetic image with an actual upright pattern and see the resulting figure in depth.

[*An account of another of Elizabeth's feats—combining an image with a presented slide to create colors in an Edwin Land display—is omitted here.*]

. . .

AFTER-IMAGES

We have conducted a number of other perceptual tests to determine the properties of eidetic images. Some early researchers maintained that the eidetic image produces an effect similar to that of an actual visual stimulus. If this were true, then eidetic images should produce after-images and movement after-effects.

To test for after-images, Elizabeth scanned a green-and-black-grating. She reported no after-image while she formed the eidetic image. But later, when she stared at the projected eidetic image she subsequently saw a magenta-and-blue-striped after-image. The after-image appeared identical to one formed by staring at the actual pattern. However, unlike normal after-images, the eidetic after-image remained constant in size when it was projected to different distances, and it did not move when Elizabeth moved her eyes.

SPIRALS

To test motion after-effect one looks at a rotating-contracting spiral for a few minutes and then stares at the center of a stationary spiral. The stationary spiral will seem to expand. If the original spiral rotates in the opposite direction so that the moving spiral appears to expand, the stationary one will seem to contract.

Elizabeth first formed an eidetic image of a stationary black-and-white spiral. She then stared at a rotating-contracting spiral for two minutes. Immediately afterward she shifted her gaze to a black-velvet surface and called up the eidetic image of the stationary spiral. As she stared at its center, the spiral seemed to expand. The after-effect appeared identical to that produced later when she looked at an actual spiral, and the duration of both effects was the same.

SCAN

To form an eidetic image of a complex pattern, Elizabeth prefers to scrutinize the pattern part by part when shutting her eyes to see if she has a good image of that part. She could not form eidetic images without moving her eyes. She had to scan even the simplest shapes to build up the eidetic image.

Simple images can be recalled rapidly, but complicated patterns often do not appear *in toto*; instead, parts may appear successively until the entire image is recalled. For example, it once took Elizabeth about 10 seconds to recall a 10,000/dot eidetic image. We have recorded her eye movements and alpha rhythm while Elizabeth looked at eidetic images. Whether her eyes are open or shut the alpha ryhthm is invariably present when she scans an eidetic image.

BREAKUP

The eidetic images are sharp and finely detailed. Elizabeth formed an image of a fine, high-contrast-stripe grating. Two days later the image was as sharp as the original pattern.

When the eidetic image begins to fade, it does not blur as an after-image does, but dims and breaks apart.

The fact that an eidetic image built up with one eye will combine with a pattern presented to the other eye to form a perception of depth indicates that the eidetic image may be represented quite early in the visual system, before the site of binocular interaction, perhaps beyond the retina in the lateral geniculate nucleus or occipital cortex.

Many intriguing questions remain. Can an eidetiker form an image of a completely imaginary scene? Can eidetic images be altered by removing or introducing new elements? Can one synthesize an image of something not seen before?

MOVIE

Can an eidetic image be formed of a moving scene? Elizabeth claims once to have seen in full detail an eidetic 10-second episode from a Laurel and Hardy movie that she attended the week before.

Obviously, more research is needed. For the past 35 years psychologists have been skeptical about the existence of eidetic imagery. Few modern theories of memory take into account this type of image retention. We have proved that eidetic imagery exists, but we still have much to discover about its nature.

41 An Uncommon Case of Visual Memory

Kent Gummerman and
Cynthia R. Gray

The authors of this selection found their subject,
"Nancy," during an extensive search for individuals
with eidetic imagery. That search was unsuccessful—
Nancy is not an eidetiker, and they found no others.
(No one knows why some investigators find
substantial numbers of eidetic children and others
don't.) But Nancy is no slouch of a memorist; her
descriptions of pictures, given from memory, are
astonishing in their detail.

In recent years considerable interest has centered on the phenomenon known as eidetic imagery. Briefly, eidetic imagery refers to the ability, usually found in children, to retain a very vivid and faithful image of a scene that was viewed for only a number of seconds. The Eidetiker can "project" his image out into space onto a homogeneous surface, move his eyes over it, and describe it in such detail as to suggest that he is "still seeing it."

Here we wish to describe one individual who came to our attention during the course of our work on eidetic imagery. As we will describe fully elsewhere, we have had no success in locating even a single Eidetiker, let alone in learning something new about the phenomenon. This one individual, however, possesses such an unusual ability to recall visually presented material that it is difficult to resist labeling her an Eidetiker. But we must resist, since she fails to meet

From K. Gummerman and C. R. Gray, Recall of visually presented material: An unwonted case and a bibliography for eidetic imagery. *Psychonomic Monograph Supplements*, 1971, 4 (10). Reprinted by permission.

several criteria that have typically been used to identify such persons: (1) She says that her image is "in her head" rather than "out there." (2) She performs equally well with eyes closed, with eyes open and staring upward at the wall or ceiling, with eyes open and fixating a homogeneous surface, and with eyes open and moving about the room. (3) She cannot perform tasks that involve superimposing an image of one picture upon a second picture to produce an unexpected third picture. (4) She cannot perform Stromeyer and Psotka's (1970) [see Selection 40] task of superimposing Julesz patterns. Although Nancy (as we will call her) does not seem to fit the accepted description of an Eidetiker, her memory merits describing, if only for its own sake.

BIOGRAPHICAL DATA

At the time we saw her (March 1971), Nancy was 19 years old and in the second semester of her freshman year in college. She is an only child of parents who have lived in Texas cities throughout Nancy's life; she speaks with a marked "small Texas town" accent.

Her general health has always been good, with the exception of rather severe allergies that were most pronounced when she was a small girl. Once she was hospitalized with suspected double pneumonia, which turned out to be an allergic problem.

Nancy is myopic; she began wearing glasses in the third grade. She now wears contact lenses.

She was a good student in high school (As and Bs) and had a B average through her first year in college. She has had no special art training and has no outstanding artistic talent. She plays the piano but has not kept at it in recent years. She takes great pleasure in listening to music but apparently has no experiences indicating synesthesia while listening.

She says that she dreams frequently (at least five out of seven nights), always in color, and remembers dreams vividly. Her dreams usualy involve her close friends.

Before we met her, she had no idea that her memory was unusual, although she always knew she was rather good at memorizing all types of materials that interested her, including verbal materials. She feels that her memory is poor for uninteresting subjects.

DESCRIPTIONS OF PICTURES

This section presents transcriptions of Nancy's verbal descriptions of four separate pictures. The transcriptions were taken as nearly verbatim as possible from tape recordings of her descriptions. Her speech was typically very rapid, informal, and loosely constructed; the transcriptions reflect this style of speech. Wherever it seemed reasonable to do so, we edited the transcriptions to remove "uh's," false starts of phrases, and the like. Whenever these mannerisms and pauses seemed to indicate confusions or periods of thought, however, they were retained. Words in brackets are from the first writer—they are either editorial comments (when there are no quotation marks in the brackets) or actual participation in the recorded interview (when quotation marks are included). The interviews were conducted informally, with only Nancy and the two writers present.

Immediately prior to each description, Nancy viewed the picture for exactly 30 seconds, after which it was removed from her sight. She had never seen the pictures before.

Nancy indicated that time was not of the essence to her. She could easily delay her description with no loss of accuracy. Nor did she require any period of time between pictures to prevent interference—it was easy for her to keep the memories separate. In fact, she was capable of viewing Picture X, then immediately viewing Picture Y, describing Picture Y, and then describing Picture X with no apparent difficulty.

[Nancy's descriptions of the first three pictures are omitted here.]

. . .

Picture 4[1]

This is a picture of six people—six people—and they're standing in front of a church, and it's a real colorful picture. It's really pretty. On the left-and right-hand sides there's a whole lot of trees, green leaves, and they're really pretty. And they're contrasted, uh, what makes it so pretty is that there's a stained glass window coming up from this church and it's—the stained glass is turquoise and green. And so it really goes, blends, real pretty with those leaves. And on the front of this, uh, window there's, uh, an announcement—I mean it's in white letters, announcing the way they do to tell everyone how the—when the worship services are. And, O.K. now, a lot of letters, a lot of the words, are blocked out because these people are standing in the way. Like the first line is supposed to say "morning worship," but you can't see part of the word "morning" because there's a tall blond-headed

---

[1]From *Psychology Today* (Aug. 1967), p. 44.

boy that is blocking out part of it. But, anyway, it says "morning worship, at 11 A.M." It says something about the nursery. In the middle there is a—it says "Is God on a trip?" All of these people appear to be, uh, I guess you could classify them as hippies or something like that— kind of a bad term, but I guess that's what the everyday person would call them. At the bottom of the picture, it announces—it's telling the name of the preacher, but you can't really exactly tell what his name is because it's blocked out. It's evidently on a radio station, his sermon, KSON, twelve-forty kilocycles. There's a planter in front of the church. It's filled with those little green shrubs. On the left-hand side of the picture, there's a tall blond-headed boy. He has long hair. His hair is parted down the middle. He has a white, little—well, it's not—it's striped, it's a striped shirt, that's the only way I can describe it. It's a striped shirt, it's white with either green or blue little stripes. It's checked, it's kind of checked, but it's not really. He has on levis, but he doesn't have on a belt. He has a cross around his neck, and it's just a simple, brown cross on a chain—I mean not a chain, but it's on the same color—I don't know what material it is, maybe leather—as the cross. To his left, to my right, is a lady, a woman. She's sitting down. She has on her right shoulder, there's some type of a bag. It's turquoise with two different colored stripes in the middle of it. Sitting in her lap is a child. The child has on diapers, and he looks real happy. The mother has long, brownish-blond hair—it's parted down the middle. She's wearing a cross, but this is a different kind of cross. It's not the standard kind, it's—I don't know what they call them, but it's the kind that has the loop at the top and then they go down like that, I don't know what they're called, though. She has on a wedding ring on her left hand. It's silver and it's just a plain band. She's holding the baby in her lap. And then on this—O.K., on this planter to the right of this girl there's a guy, and he has pretty long hair. And it's kind of curly, and it's brown, and you see his profile. He's facing towards the front of the church. He has his right leg up on the planter and the planter's gray brick. He's wearing those—a kind of boots—they're not really boots, but they're—I don't know what they're called. They're just those leather boots. He has on a coat, and I believe a white shirt. He has glasses, and he has one—his right arm is resting on his leg that's up on the planter. And the other arm is on his, you know, on his hip like that [puts hand on hip to demonstrate]. Beside him, to his left, is a girl and you see her full profile. She has on levis. Regular kind of levis. She has on some kind of a striped shirt—it's all different colored stripes, and they're little bitty stripes. And she has on some type of a blouse over—I mean a shirt or something—over this whatever it is underneath too. She has long brown hair. Then behind this guy with the long brown hair that's got his leg up on the planter is another—Oh, wait a minute, the guy that's got his leg up on the planter has on two rings, one on each hand. And they're both real decorative. And they're real—you really take notice of the rings. And then, O.K. behind him there's this other guy. And he has on a gold sweater-type shirt. He has on a cross. The cross—all three of these people have on different kinds of crosses. I mean, I don't know the names of them, but they're all different. None of them are exactly alike. Like this guy that's got on the gold sweater has a real ornate cross. It appears—it's got stones in it, and I think that they look like they're turquoise or something like that, and his is on a chain. And he has on dark sun glasses, he's got dark hair, and he kind of looked like the hoodlum type. I think he—brown slacks I believe. And he's standing, he's leaning up against something. And his right leg is propped up against, I guess, a wall of some type. And on his right leg is his right hand and he's got the peace sign, you know, on his leg. And the other, his left hand's, on his hip. And that's about it. You can see the little roots, I mean the branches of the shrubs in the planter. That's about all. ["Can you see a reflection of anything?"] You see their reflections in the window of the front of the church, it's at the bottom on the right-hand side. And you see, uh, you don't see all of their reflections, you only see [3-second pause] I can only see two or maybe three, but I can see two clearly. ["Which two?"] The guy with his leg up on the planter. And the girl, that girl. Can only see her profile. [5-second pause] And you know that part of the stained window that's up at the top? Well, it's the part that's turquoise, it's—you can see some sort of ornate figure too, it curls around. And then the bottom portion of it's just—it's the white letters and then behind it, it's just stained glass made of little squares. [Time for Picture 4: 9 minutes, 25 seconds.]

PERFORMANCE ON OTHER TASKS

Nancy has shown no outstanding ability to perform the following . . . tasks.

1. Reproduction of complex matrices. The cells of 8 by 8 matrices were filled randomly with 40 items (either dots, the digits 1–5, or five geometric patterns). After viewing each matrix for 30 seconds, Nancy was asked to reproduce the items (by drawing them) in a blank matrix.

2. Reproduction of random shapes. Ten- and 20-angle random shapes were viewed (singly) for 30 seconds. She was then asked to draw each one.

3. Recitation of verbal material. After viewing brief typewritten passages of prose and poetry for 30 seconds, Nancy was asked to recite them.

4. "Span of apprehension." Nancy viewed arrays of nine letters presented in a tachistoscope for 200 msec and was required to either (a) recall the letter that occupied a particular position or (b) decide whether a probe letter shown at a given position was actually the one presented in the nine-element array.

She did very well, but not remarkably well, on the Visual Sequential Memory section of the Illinois Test of Psycholinguistic Ability, which requires reproducing the arrangement of briefly viewed sequences of seven nonsense forms placed side by side.

A final memory task involved viewing and recalling multitem arrays, in which several categories of items (circles, tree, houses, etc.) were represented a number of times in randomly selected locations. Interested in the structure of her memory, we hoped to learn whether the order of her reports was systematically related to position (e.g., reporting by rows or by areas) or to categories (without respect to position). In general, the reports followed *both* schemes simultaneously, as "There are three circles; a red one and yellow one are the first two items in the top row and there's a yellow one in the bottom row. There's an elm tree that's the third item in the top row. a similar tree, but it's red, in the bottom row. And there are two more trees . . . "

CONCLUDING IMPRESSIONS

Nancy's memory, as mentioned earlier, does not seem to be eidetic. Most importantly, it does not have the "externalized" quality that recent researchers (in particular Haber and his associates) have described. She does not "see" and scan an image that is before her in space, even though she does say that she can "see" an image inside her head—both with eyes open and with eyes closed. Furthermore, she cannot perform the superimposition tasks.

In some respects, however, her behavior is very much like that of an Eidetiker. For example, she spontaneously uses the present tense in making her descriptions; she does well in recalling pictorial material, but not in recalling verbal material; she reports that objects are positively colored; and, of course, her reports are extensive and finely detailed.

It is worth noting that Nancy's behavior is not greatly different from that of a typical Eidetiker. Had our interviewing procedures not been as careful and nondirective as they were, it is quite conceivable that we could have unknowingly induced Nancy to report that her image was externalized and perhaps even to move her eyes across the homogeneous background. Then, if we had done no further testing beyond the descriptions of pictures, we could have concluded that Nancy was an Eidetiker.

The image that Nancy can "see in her head" does not seem to differ in quality from that which many people possess: it appears to lie on a continuum with "normal" visual imagery, though it apparently is of greater fidelty and duration. It is not altogether clear, however, that her ability to recall pictorial material is based entirely on this visual image. Her performance may rely on information encoded in other forms as well.

REFERENCE

Stromeyer, C. F., III, and Psotka, J. The detailed texture of eidetic images. *Nature*, 1970, *225*, 346–349.

42 The Talents of the Reverend Dr. Phelps

William Lyon Phelps

The literature of psychology includes quite a few accounts of "calendar calculators"—people who can tell you what day of the week corresponds to any given date in the past. Some of them were strange individuals in more than one respect; the best known case was diagnosed as an "idiot savant". Brett Kahr and I are presently studying a calendar calculator who uses a surprising variety of methods to determine past days of the week. One of those methods, especially relevant here, relies strictly on memory. If the date occurred during his own lifetime, he just remembers what day of the week it was. He also claims to remember what the weather was like every day for the past thirty years or so.

The Reverend Dr. Phelps, described in this brief selection, was apparently a memorist of the same kind. (A more detailed study of a similar case appears in an 1871 paper by Henkle, mentioned in William James' Principles.) Of course, there is no way to know if the Reverend was really right about everything on all those days. I am pretty sure, though, that he was right about the days of the week. We have checked our own subject with a perpetual calendar, and he virtually never makes a mistake.

Inasmuch as, so far as I know, the gift is unique, it may not be an impertinence to record the fact that my brother, the Reverend Doctor

---

From W. L. Phelps, *Memory*. New York: Dutton, 1929.

Dryden William Phelps, can recall some particular thing that has happened on any day during the last sixty years; and he can recall it immediately, on demand, in response to any challenge. First of all, he possesses a talent so unusual that it has, in the case of other persons, been their sole source of income. Visiting on one occasion a dime museum, I found among the performers a man whose task was confined entirely to the following accomplishment. If you told him the date of your birth without mentioning the day he would, by calculations on a blackboard, in five minutes state the proper day of the week. For example: I told him I was born on the second of January, 1865. After some figuring with the chalk on the board, he said confidently "Monday," which is correct. Yet my brother, with no paper, board, or figures, tells you that almost instantly by lightning mental arithmetic.

But his unique gift of memory is this. If you ask "What happened on March sixth, 1879?" or any other date within the last sixty years that you choose, in a few moments he will state the day of the week. Then he will give you the weather for that day, and describe some particular thing that happened. I have seen him tested many times, and have never known him to fail.

43 Toscanini's Memory

George R. Marek

All professional musicians have to know a great deal of music, but sometimes their knowledge is simply astonishing. It is difficult for a nonmusician to evaluate such achievements properly, but it is easy to be impressed by them. Toscanini strikes me as someone special; that is why he appears here in the company of S and VP instead of with the other performers in Part V. Nevertheless, as the author himself points out, there have surely been many other musicians with equally impressive memories.

Of course his memory helped him, and there are no end of instances which attest to its retentiveness.[1] The most famous of these anecdotes has been told in various versions. I believe the one reported by the violinist Augusto Rossi to be correct: it was in St. Louis, just before the start of the concert, that the second bassoonist, Umberto Ventura, came to Toscanini. He was in great agitation. He had just discovered that the key for the lowest note on his instrument was broken; he couldn't use it. What was to be done? Toscanini, shading his eyes, thought for a moment and then said, "It is all right—that note does not occur in tonight's concert."

---

[1] It has been estimated that he knew by heart every note of every instrument of about 250 symphonic works and the words and music of about 100 operas, besides a quantity of chamber music, piano music, cello and violin pieces, and songs.

From G. R. Marek, *Toscanini*. London: Vision Press, 1975. Reprinted by permission.

He thought he would like to have the strings of the NBC play the slow movement of Joachim Raff's Quartet No. 5. The libraries and music stores of New York were searched for a score of the Quartet. None could be found, the piece having fallen out of favor. Toscanini, who had probably not seen the music for decades, let alone played it, wrote the entire movement down, with all the dynamic marks. Much later Bachmann, a collector of musical curiosities, found a copy. They checked it against the Toscanini manuscript: Toscanini had made exactly one error. (Told by Howard Taubman.)

The same Bachmann remembered that once they were playing a game, with Steinberg present. Toscanini said, "Play any excerpt from any of the standard operas or symphonies. Stop when I tell you to stop, but don't take your hands off the piano." Steinberg played. After a few bars Toscanini said, "Stop . . . That is from *Siegfried* Act III, Scene I, bars so and so. The note played by the fifth finger of your left hand is for the bassoon, the second finger clarinet and oboe—" and so on, going through the entire scoring.

I was reading a biography of Rossini and learned that he had composed two endings for his *Otello*, one tragic as in Shakespeare, the other a "happy end," where Othello and Desdemona are reconciled and sing a duet. Rossini's *Otello* is, and surely was at the time, an almost forgotten opera. I happened to mention the curious double ending to Toscanini that night at dinner. He said, "Of course." And he went to the piano and played *both* endings.

In Vienna once Toscanini, in a friendly challenge, wrote out from memory the part the second bassoon plays in the second act of *Die Meistersinger*. He wrote it faultlessly.

Retention of minutiae is an attribute of the interpretive artist; it lies at the base of performance, and it can be trained. Toscanini's astonishing feats were not unique. Bülow's memory was equally precise: he conducted the first performance of *Tristan* entirely without the score and on his first American tour he played 139 concerts without the music on the piano, this at a time when playing from memory had not as yet become the custom. Otto Jahn in his biography of Mozart tells an anecdote now become standard history: Gregorio Allegri's *Miserere* was considered the exclusive property of the Vatican Choir and was so highly prized that no one was allowed to copy it, "on pain of excommunication." Mozart heard it once, went home, wrote the whole thing down from memory, went back, heard it a second time, made a few corrections scribbling secretly in his hat, and performed it later at a gathering at which the papal singer Christofori was present, who confirmed the absolute correctness of Mozart's "theft." (The incident worried Mozart's mother and sister; they thought he had committed a great sin. Wolfgang and Leopold laughed.)

Obviously the ability to remember is no guarantee of performing excellence. *The Oxford Companion to Music* gives the record of a

Mr. Napoleon Bird, barber of Stockport, Cheshire, who in 1894 won the World's Record for what has been called "Pianofortitude" by publicly playing for forty-four hours without repeating a composition; from 11 P.M. to 3 A.M. he played dance music for hundreds of couples, and, during the subsequent forty hours, whenever any vocalist or instrumentalist appeared and asked to be accompanied, the mere statement of the title of the piece and the key required were sufficient.

Phenomenal though Toscanini's memory was, he did not rely on it. He conducted no concert without once again, for the seventieth time, taking the scores of the program and reading through them as carefully as if he were examining them for the first time. He often did this in bed, the night before. At every rehearsal the score was there, just in case he wanted to confirm a point or refer to a letter or number, printed in the score for the convenience of conductor and orchestra. He did not bother to learn these by heart. (Mitropoulos did.)

His memory was strengthened by what I may call the "mind's ear," meaning the ability to hear a composition by reading it. That ability is essential to a conductor, but Toscanini possessed it to an amazing degree. He had but to glance at a page of complex music, his glance seemingly casual, and he heard the page both horizontally and vertically in his imagination. He appeared to be riffling through a new score at top speed and one, two, three could decide whether he liked it and what were its weaknesses. To put it differently, his eyes translated into sound as quickly as those expert translators at the United Nations transpose from one language to another.

There was nothing wrong with what is usually called the sense of hearing. He could hear the slightest false intonation amidst an orchestral turmoil. He could hear subtle differences in the quality of sound, produced by some hidden supporting instrument. Josef Gingold, one of the violinists in the NBC Symphony, recalled:

There was a contemporary piece—I can't remember what—that he programmed, tried once, and took off: he couldn't take it; it was too dissonant for him. He came to that rehearsal knowing the piece by memory; and as we were reading it we came to a terrific discord: it was so dissonant that we actually had to look at the fingerboard to see where our notes were. And he stopped: "Eh, *terzo corno!* Third horn! *Re!* I didn't hear!" The man had had a few bars' rest and had cleaned his horn, and hadn't been able to get it up again in time to come in. Toscanini couldn't see that far, and didn't see that the man wasn't playing, but he heard that the D was missing (B. H. Haggin, *The Toscanini Musicians Knew*).

He could hear the minutest shading not only in what was being played but how it sounded. He would have the orchestra play a chord, stop, think, then tell them to adjust it—a touch more of the first trombone, a shade less of the clarinet—play it again, and it would emerge in clear eloquence and so solidly constructed, so truly a chord, that one could not drive the blade of a knife between the notes.

Gregor Piatigorsky told me of the time when he began to work on Castelnuovo-Tedesco's Cello Concerto. They rehearsed first at the Hotel Astor, where Toscanini then lived. Piatigorsky sat at the far end of the room, Toscanini sat at the piano. The next day they repeated the rehearsal. At a certain passage Toscanini said, "That is better—to use the third finger is better." Piatigorsky was dumbfounded: how could Toscanini possibly know that he had changed the fingering? It was certain he could not see it. Piatigorsky asked, "How do you know I changed the fingering from yesterday?" "I heard it," answered Toscanini.

44 An Exceptional Memory

Ian M. L. Hunter

*I have saved my favorite memorist for last. Aitken
may have been less bizarre than S, less "eidetic" than
Elizabeth, and less famous than Toscanini, but his
talents were still "awesome," as the sportswriters say.
Best of all, he inhabited a particularly "natural
context," at least from my point of view. He was a
professor!*

Professor Alexander Craig Aitken, FRS (1895–1967) was a man of far-outstanding intellect. He was a brilliant mathematician (Whittaker and Bartlett, 1968) who had 'in large measure the kind of mystical insight into problems which characterized, for example, Isaac Newton' (Collar, 1967). He was a uniquely able mental calculator (Aitken, 1954; Hunter, 1962, 1965, 1966, 1968). He was an accomplished violinist. He was also legendary for his memory. The purpose of this paper is to give an account of his exceptional memory.

To say that a man has exceptional memory is like saying he has exceptional athletic or artistic ability: it only roughly delineates his prowess. Thus, exceptional memory can rightly be claimed for the Russian, Shereshevskii (Luria, 1969) [*see Selection 38*], the American, V.P. (Hunt and Love, 1972) [*see Selection 39*], and Aitken; yet each man has a different pattern of memorial talent integral with a different style of mental life. So, in what sense did Aitken have exceptional memory? Briefly, he was unusually erudite with a scholar's disposition to

From the *British Journal of Psychology*, 1977, 68, 155–164. Reprinted by permission.

become absorbed by, and retentive of, things relating to his spheres of erudition. He could readily produce, out of his head, much detailed information and could rapidly learn new information that interested him. His memory was (and this was also his own view) exceptional in degree rather than in kind.

OVERVIEW OF AITKEN'S MEMORY

Aitken could produce a host of recondite facts about numbers, calculative methods, mathematics and mathematicians; play, on the violin, many pieces by heart; recall many musical compositions; securely identify many snatches of music heard or seen in written notation; quote extensively from English literature; and recite tracts of Latin and English verse. He could recall details of many events he had witnessed, so much so that committees often consulted him as an unofficial minute book. In daily affairs, he was conspicuously, but not officiously, precise about names, dates, locations. The following excerpt from his reminiscences about the First World War illustrates his characteristic precision and his recall of details that would elude most people (the platoon mentioned would comprise 39 men). On 14 July 1916, he was in France, lying in a dug-out trying to sleep.

> Sleep proved impossible; each time I closed my eyes I heard again, as though it were in the dug-out itself, the whistle of the falling mortar-bombs, and I saw Hughes, Robertson, Sergeant Bree, Harper, and the line of trees. But gradually, through and across these repercussions, I became aware of a conversation in low tones going on somewhere behind me, apparently between Captain Hargest and Mr Rae, and perhaps occasionally someone else—but I am not sure of this. However that may be, something was missing; a roll-book; the roll-book of Platoon 10, my old Platoon. Urgently required, it seemed; Batallion had rung up, requesting a list of the night's casualties and a full state of the Platoon. Apparently surnames were available, but the book was nowhere to be found. This being suddenly clear, I had no difficulty, having a well-trained memory now brought by stress into a condition almost of hypermnesia, in bringing the lost roll-book before me, almost, as it were, floating; I imagined it either taken away by Mr Johnston or perhaps in the pocket of Sergeant Bree in no-man's-land. Speaking from the matting I offered to dictate the details; full name, regimental number, and the rest; they were taken down, by whom I do not know (Aitken, 1963, pp. 107–108).

Many stories are told about the range, tenacity, rapidity and precision of Aitken's seemingly effortless memory. Two typical, and reliable, stories relate to the early 1920s.

> He taught me Classics at Otago Boys' High School and he used to amuse us at our lessons by demonstrating how he could associate line numbers in our Virgil with the words in the line or conversely could recite the words in any specified line (personal communication from Dr Harold Taylor, sometime Vice-Chancellor of Keele University).

As a young teacher, a single reading of the names and initials of a new class of 35 boys enabled him never to consult the lists again (Hudson, 1967).

His memory, however, had limits. He did not have "total recall" if, by this, is meant some mythical ability to recall absolutely anything he had ever experienced; nor was he always able to recall, on the instant, things he could recall on other occasions. To illustrate, in 1960–1961 he attempted to recall some words and numbers he had learnt, under experimental conditions, in 1932 (see below): he recalled a lot, but by no means all, and made remarks such as 'The others are not recoverable although in an extreme state, such as insomnia, they might come back' and 'I felt this must be wrong, hence I decided to do what I often do, to "wait for illumination," and not to hurry the process.' His knowledge, though great, was not encyclopaedic, e.g., he knew little about sports, and even with regard to music, where he knew a great deal, he remarked that the musical knowledge of Professor Tovey, of Edinburgh University, made him 'feel like a prattling child.' (Examples of Tovey's extraordinary musical memory are given by Grierson, 1952.) Finally, he did have a memory span. Sutherland (1937) reports assessing Aitken's memory span in 1932 by asking him to repeat back sequences of items presented at a rate of two items per second. With auditory presentation of sequences of random letters, the span was 10: with auditory presentation of random digits, 13: and with visual presentation of random digits, 15.

. . .

DISCERNMENT OF MULTIPLE PROPERTIES

Aitken's memory was intimately linked with his ability to discern multiple properties that were interwoven into distinctive patterns. His discernment could work rapidly to produce an unusually rich, densely structured gestalt of properties; and so many things, that would seem chaotic to a bystander, were, to him, embodiments of multiple properties that meshed into an interesting, memorable pattern.

The ease with which he learnt and remembered anything, and indeed whether he learnt and remembered it at all, depended squarely on the meaning and interest it had for him. Thus, whenever something interested him deeply, he was typically able, later, to recall many details of it despite his having had not the slightest conscious intention of committing anything to memory. Again, if he were given material that, for him, had little meaning (say, a random string of digits), he typically pronounced it 'uninteresting' or even 'repellent.' If asked to commit such material to memory, he might oblige if he thought some psychological value might emerge from the exercise, but usually remarked that the exercise was 'unnatural' and 'went against the grain.' (Throughout this paper, all words bounded by single quotation marks are Aitken's, unless otherwise specified.) If he did undertake 'unnatural' memorizing, he adopted a characteristic approach as follows.

When given material that was 'not too repellent' and asked to memorize it, he did not, as might be expected, go tense in concentration. He went noticeably still and relaxed. When asked about this curious behavior, he explained that he was using a subterfuge ("assimilation by interest") on which, he discovered years ago, he could rely. He was relaxing by way of preparing to find interest in the material or 'to let the properties of the material reveal themselves.' He felt best able to secure memorization by refraining from deliberate interpretation and organization; rather, he cleared his mind and relinquished the job to his vast cognitive system, allowing it to work largely autonomously and in whatever way came most naturally. He commented as follows.

> I discovered that the further I proceeded, the more I needed *relaxation*, not concentration as ordinarily understood. One must be relaxed, yet possessed, in order to to this well. Sometimes one enters a bookshop and there, displayed on the stalls, are various interesting books. One selects, dips, reads, becomes intent, until the stage is reached when all surroundings are forgotten. Afterwards, one leaves the shop and enters the street again, blinking at the light and at the people as if one had come out of an anaesthetic. And so it is here. The one requisite is that a live interest in the subject should fix an undeviating attention. ... Interest is the thing. Interest focuses the attention. At first one might have to concentrate, but as soon as possible one should relax. Very few people do that. Unfortunately, it is not taught at school where knowledge is acquired by rote, by learning by heart, sometimes against the grain. The thing to do is to learn by heart, not because one has to, but because one loves the thing and is interested in it. Then one has moved away from concentration to relaxation.

PSYCHOBIOGRAPHY

Aitken's mnemic activities were inextricably part of a larger configuration including all his psychological processes, e.g., his general knowledge, preferred pursuits, emotional and intellectual attitudes to the world and to himself: his memory was nondetachable from his entire psycholphysical make-up, from 'the participation of the whole personality.' Of his personality, it might fairly be said that he was, above all, a reflective man who sought to comprehend events by discerning their inward patterns. With his talents, this mild-mannered man might well have made more of a worldly splash, but it would have 'gone against the grain' to pursue, say, political power or success in business. It was supremely consistent that he found his eventual professional calling in a field of scholarship devoted to uncovering deep mathematical patterns.

"Interest in meaning" was a *leitmotiv* of his psychobiography. Starting in his mid-teens and continuing into his late-twenties, he was enthralled by number, music, poetry and his own intellectual capabilities. These were the years, involving 'a kind of mental Yoga,' in which he became demonstrably exceptional through attempting to penetrate the inwardness of numerical relations, the architecture of poetry and music, the system of his own mental skills, the interconnectedness of phenomena at large. Almost certainly, he was interested, at this time, in testing his mental powers to the limit, e.g., discovering how much Milton he could recite verbatim or how fast he could calculate. Almost certainly, too, he enjoyed demonstrating his prowess to others. But it is equally certain that, in later adult years, he rarely memorized anything merely for the sake of memorizing it. He would deliberately memorize what he thought might be useful to have readily available in his head, e.g., the names of his students. More often, things got memorized as an unintended by-product of his penetrating interest in them.

[*Descriptions of several experiments with Aitken are omitted here. His digit span was about 15. In 1960 he was able—with some effort—to recall all of a 25-word list he had memorized in 1932, and more than half of a list of 16 3-digit numbers from the same year.*]

· · ·

A comparison between Aitken and the "average" adult shows that his accomplishments of memory are, at every turn, stronger than average. He has a longer memory span, a more retentive grip on things he has learnt and, overall, a larger and more finely articulated cognitive system. At the same time, nothing about Aitken violates what we know about the "normal" design features of memory. It is normal, for example, that high-level learning and remembering depends on interest and, crucially, on the process of comprehending material in terms of patterns of multiple properties. Even his subterfuge of "assimilation by interest" is within the experience of many highly intelligent people. For example, when experienced actors deliberately set out to master a new role, they do not focus on the task of memorization as such but, rather, on studying the role with a view to discerning a network of meanings in it: this pursuit of meaning has the effect of securing memorization as a by-product (Smirnov, 1973, chapter 3).

Now, compare the present account of Aitken with Luria's (1969) account of S. V. Shereshevskii (hereafter called "S."). The comparison shows how different is the exceptional memory of a scholar and a mnemonist.

S. was an outstanding professional mnemonist, that is, someone who memorizes haphazard strings of items. He used the classical mnemonist's technique of imagining richly vivid, concrete mental-pictures, which he arranged in a chain of pairs. If given the 25-word list mentioned above, he might take an imaginary walk along a street that has a vivid succession of landmarks. He would represent the first word by a distinctively imaged picture which he would "locate" on the first landmark; the second word would be another mental picture "located" on the second landmark, and so on. During a single, and not too rapid, presentation of the word list, he would progressively devise such a chain of images that was extremely rich in perception-like properties. This would result in accurate, durable memorization. Even years afterwards, he would be able to recapitulate the chain of images, and, so, recall the list of words in either forward or backward sequence. Contrast this procedure with the way Aitken memorized the list, not by a strict chain, but by a kind of overall melody.

The chief similarity between Aitken and S. is that each comprehends materials in terms of a multiplicity of unconventional properties, knits these properties into fairly unconventional patterns, and durably retains these patterns so as to be able to reconstruct the original materials. The chief difference is the *kind* of property involved and the *kind* of pattern woven. Characteristically, S.'s kind of property is perception-like, i.e., particular sensory qualities and particular imaged objects: his kind of pattern is the chain, i.e., short-run links between successively encountered items. Characteristically, Aitken's kind of property is conceptual: his kind of pattern is the panorama or map, i.e., long-run groupings of items into overlapping multilayered configurations.

The following comparison illustrates the different kind of property by which the two men comprehend materials. First, remarks made by S. in 1936. "Even numbers remind me of images. Take the number 1. This is a proud, well-built man; 2 is a high-spirited woman; 3 is a gloomy person (why, I don't know); 6 a man with a swollen foot; 7 a man with a mustache; 8 a very stout woman—a sack within a sack. As for the number 87, what I see is a fat woman and a man twirling his mustache" (Luria, 1969, p. 31). Now, remarks made by Aitken in 1932. Sutherland (1937) showed him a mixed series of written words and numbers, and asked him to report what each item called immediately to mind. Here is the response to "7." 'The line of poetry "They passed the pleiades and the planets seven"—mysteries in the minds of the

ancients—Sabbath or seventh day—religious observance of Sunday—
7 in contrast with 13 and with 3 in superstition—7 as a recurring
decimal ·142857 which, multiplied by 123456, gives the same numbers
in cyclic order—a poem on numbers by Binyon, seen in a review
lately—I could quote from it.'

In broad terms, then, Aitken comprehends materials in terms of
rich conceptual maps; S. in terms of rich perceptual chains. These
contrasting modes of comprehension show in the intellectual profiles
of the two men. S.'s great distinction is in memorizing haphazard
strings of items; Aitken's is in mathematical thinking. In an Olympic
Games for Mental Prowess, S. would win the gold in the section for
mnemonists, while Aitken would scarcely qualify for entry. But S.
would not even be considered for entry to three sections where Aitken
would shine, namely for theoretical mathematicians, mental calculators, and all-rounders.

. . .

REFERENCES

Aitken, A. C. The art of mental calculation: with demonstrations. *Trans. Soc.
Engrs., Lond.,* 1954, *44,* 295–309.

Aitken, A. C. *Gallipoli to the Somme: Recollections of a New Zealand Infantry-
man.* London: Oxford University Press, 1963.

Collar, A. R. Prof. A. C. Aitken. *The Times,* 22 Nov. 1967, p. 12.

Grierson, M. *Donald Francis Tovey: A Biography Based on Letters.* London:
Oxford University Press, 1952.

Hudson, D. 1967, Prof. A. C. Aitken. *The Times,* 7 Nov. 1967, p. 12.

Hunt, E. and Love, T. How good can memory be? In A. W. Melton and E. Martin
(eds.), *Coding Processes in Human Memory.* New York: Wiley, 1972.

Hunter, I. M. L. An exceptional talent for calculative thinking. *Br. J. Psychol.*
1962, *53,* 243–258.

Hunter, I. M. L. *Memory.* Harmondsworth: Penguin, 1964.

Hunter, I. M. L. Strategems for skill. In *Penguin Science Survey,* 1965 *B.* Harmondsworth: Penguin, 1965.

Hunter, I. M. L. "Kopfrechnen und Kopfrechner." *Bild der Wissenschaft,* 1966,
3, 296–303.

Hunter, I. M. L. "Mental calculation." In P. C. Wason and P. N. Johnson-Laird
(eds.), *Thinking and Reasoning.* Harmondsworth: Penguin, 1968.

Luria, A. R. *The Mind of a Mnemonist.* London: Cape, 1969.

Smirnov, A. A. *Problems of the Psychology of Memory.* New York: Plenum, 1973.

Sutherland, J. D. "Phenomenal memory and calculating ability: With illustrations from Dr A. C. Aitken." Unpublished manuscript, 1937.

Whittaker, J. M. and Bartlett, M. S. Alexander Craig Aitken. *Biographical Mem-
oirs of Fellows of the Royal Society,* 1965, *14,* 1–14.

Name Index

Subject Index